Lecture Notes in Computer Scienc

Commenced Publication in 1973
Founding and Former Series Editors:
Gerhard Goos, Juris Hartmanis, and Jan van Leeuwen

T0238162

Editorial Board

Ralf H. Reussner   Judith A. Stafford
Clemens A. Szyperski (Eds.)

Architecting Systems with Trustworthy Components

International Seminar
Dagstuhl Castle, Germany, December 12-17, 2004
Revised Selected Papers

 Springer

Volume Editors

Ralf H. Reussner
Universität Karlsruhe (TH)
Fakultät für Informatik
Am Fasanengarten 5, 76131 Karlsruhe, Germany
E-mail: reussner@ipd.uka.de

Judith A. Stafford
Tufts University
Department of Computer Science
161 College Avenue, Medford, MA 02155, USA
E-mail: jas@cs.tufts.edu

Clemens A. Szyperski
Microsoft
One Microsoft Way, Redmond, WA 98053, USA
E-mail: cszypers@microsoft.com

Library of Congress Control Number: 2006905119

CR Subject Classification (1998): C.2.4, D.1.3, D.2, D.4.5, F.2.1-2, D.3, F.3

LNCS Sublibrary: SL 1 – Theoretical Computer Science and General Issues

ISSN   0302-9743
ISBN-10   3-540-35800-5 Springer Berlin Heidelberg New York
ISBN-13   978-3-540-35800-8 Springer Berlin Heidelberg New York

Springer is a part of Springer Science+Business Media

springer.com

© Springer-Verlag Berlin Heidelberg 2006
Printed in Germany

Typesetting: Camera-ready by author, data conversion by Scientific Publishing Services, Chennai, India
Printed on acid-free paper   SPIN: 11786160   06/3142   5 4 3 2 1 0

Preface

Software components are most generally viewed as a means of software re-use and, as such, much past research has been devoted to the study of problems associated with integrating components into cohesive systems. However, even when a collection of trustworthy components have been successfully assembled the quality of the resultant system is not guaranteed. In December 2004, 41 experts on this topic from around the world, from research as well as industrial organizations, came together at Dagstuhl to discuss pressing issues related to *architecting software systems from trustworthy components*.

During the course of the cold, yet sunny, December days in Dagstuhl, discussion sessions addressed topics such as compositional reasoning on various system-level properties (such as deadlocks, live-locks etc.), compositional prediction models for different quality attributes (such as performance or reliability), blame analysis, interaction protocols, and composition frameworks. Using the liberal form of Dagstuhl Seminars, the days of the seminar were filled mostly with discussion in a variety of settings: in working sessions, around the table at meals, small groups in a corner, and also all together in the main meeting room.

Component software technologies attract much attention for their promise to enable scaling of our software industry to new levels of flexibility, diversity, and cost efficiency. Yet, these hopes collide with the reality that assemblies typically suffer from the proverbial "weakest link" phenomenon. If a component is used in a new compositional variation, then it will likely be stressed in a new way. Asserting useful properties of assemblies based on the used composition schema and theory requires a firm handle on the properties of both the components being composed and the communication mechanisms (connectors) that bind them. For such assertions to hold, these composition elements must meet their advertized properties, even if used under circumstances not explicitly envisaged by their developers. A component or connector that fails to do so becomes a weak link of its hosting assembly and may cause the entire assembly to fail to meet its advertized properties.

In contrast, components that promise to be a strong link in their assemblies can be called 'trustworthy' and ways to get to the construction and proper use of such components was the subject of this seminar. Transitively, the seminar was also concerned with trustworthy assemblies: assemblies that reliably meet their requirements based on trustworthy components and solid composition methods.

The weakest link phenomenon is not a new observation, but the recent trends to move to dynamic and late composition of non-trivial components exasperate the problem. A concrete example promising deep widespread relevance are Web services. The problem space is complex and multi-faceted. Practical solutions will have to draw on combined insights from a diverse range of disciplines, including component software technology, software engineering, software architecture, dependable systems, formal methods, as well as areas such as type systems and proof-carrying code.

A lot of good, and sometimes even groundbreaking, work has been performed in the focus area of this seminar, but many problems remain open. To spark discussions, a small set of core problems was prepared by the organizers:

- Measurement and normalization of extra-functional properties
- Modular reasoning over extra-functional properties
- capture of component requirements in interfaces and protocols
- Interference and synergy of top-down and bottom-up aspects
- Duality of componentization and architecture
- System properties (non-deadlocks, liveness, fairness, etc.)
- Opportunities for correctness by construction/static checking

All of these problems are considered hard today and yet, all of them, if solved appropriately, promise the creation of key stepping stones toward an overall approach yielding trustworthy components as well as trustworthy compositions. It is likely that any such approach supports a multitude of more specialized disciplines and methods, targeting different requirement profiles at the assembly level; for example, those with tight resource management or that rely on real-time characteristics.

Most of the time at Dagstuhl was used for focused discussions in break-out groups; the abstracts of the break-out groups as well as position papers submitted by all participants are available on the seminar Website. In this volume of *Lecture Notes on Computer Science* we present extended papers reflecting work of seminar participants. Among the articles are ten peer-reviewed papers and five invited papers of outstanding researchers whose work is related to the Dagstuhl seminar but were not able to attend. The peer-reviewed papers were submitted by participants after the conclusion of the workshop and were selected based upon the high quality of scholarly work, their timeliness, and their appropriateness to the goals of the seminar, some reflecting ongoing collaboration that grew out of the seminar.

We would like to gratefully acknowledge the friendly and very helpful support of the Dagstuhl administration staff, Alfred Hofmann from Springer for his support during the preparation and publication of the LNCS volume and Klaus Krogmann for preparing the final manuscript for Springer.

Karlsruhe, Medford, and Redmond   Ralf Reussner
February 2006   Judith Stafford
                                                                 Clemens Szyperski

Organization

Architecting Systems with Trustworthy Components

(Dagstuhl Seminar 04511)

Organizers

Ralf Reussner, Universität Karlsruhe (T.H.), Germany
Judith Stafford, Tufts University, USA
Clemens Szyperski, Microsoft Corp., USA

Participants

Uwe Aßmann, TU Dresden, Germany
Colin Atkinson, University of Mannheim, Germany
Steffen Becker, University of Oldenburg, Germany
Jan Bredereck, TZI, Bremen, Germany
Antonia Brogi, Università di Pisa, Italy
Christian Bunse, Fraunhofer IESE, Germany
Ivica Crnkovic, Mälardalen University, Sweden
Viktoria Firus, University of Oldenburg, Germany
Kathi Fisler, Worcester Polytechnic Institute, USA
Felix C. Freiling, RWTH Aachen, Germany
Sabine Glesner, Universität Karlsruhe (T.H.), Germany
Gerhard Goos, Universität Karlsruhe (T.H.), Germany
Ian Gorton, NICTA, Australia
Lars Grunske, The University of Queensland, Australia
Christine Hofmeister , Lehigh Univ. - Bethlehem, USA
Jens-Holger Jahnke, University of Victoria, Canada
Jean-Marc Jézéquel, IRISA (Univ. Rennes & INRIA), France
Bernd Krämer, FernUniversität in Hagen, Germany
Shriram Krishnamurthi, Brown Univ. - Providence, USA
Juliana Küster-Filipe, The University of Birmingham, UK
Stig Larsson, ABB - Västerås, Sweden
Nicole Levy, University of Versailles, France
Raffaela Mirandola, University of Rome TorVergata, Italy
Sven Overhage, Universität Augsburg, Germany
Frantisek Plasil, Charles University, Czech Republic
Iman Poernomo, King's College London, UK
Alexander Romanovsky, University of Newcastle, UK
Christian Salzmann, BMW Car IT, Germany
Thomas Santen, TU Berlin, Germany

Heinz Schmidt, Monash University, Australia
Jürgen Schneider, IBM - Böblingen, Germany
Asuman Sünbül, SAP Research Labs - Palo Alto, USA
Massimo Tivoli, Univ. degli Studi di L'Aquila, Italy
Kurt Wallnau, Software Engineering Institute, USA
Wolfgang Weck, Independent Software Architect, Switzerland
Rob van Ommering, Philips Research - Eindhoven, The Netherlands
Willem-Jan van den Heuvel, Tilburg University, The Netherlands

Invited Contributions

Antonia Bertolino, ISTI CNR Pisa, Italy
Manfred Broy, TU Munich, Germany
Bertrand Meyer, ETH Zurich, Switzerland
Wolfgang Pree, University of Salzburg, Austria
Heike Wehrheim, University of Paderborn, Germany

Publication date: May 2006

Table of Contents

Audition of Web Services for Testing Conformance to Open Specified Protocols*

Antonia Bertolino[1], Lars Frantzen[2], Andrea Polini[1], and Jan Tretmans[2]

[1] Istituto di Scienza e Tecnologie della Informazione "Alessandro Faedo",
Consiglio Nazionale delle Ricerche,
via Moruzzi, 1 – 56124 Pisa, Italy
{antonia.bertolino, andrea.polini}@isti.cnr.it
[2] Institute for Computing and Information Sciences,
Radboud University Nijmegen, The Netherlands
{lf, tretmans}@cs.ru.nl

Abstract. A Web Service (WS) is a type of component specifically conceived for distributed machine-to-machine interaction. Interoperability between WSs involves both data and messages exchanged and protocols of usage, and is pursued via the establishment of standard specifications to which service providers must conform. In previous work we have envisaged a framework for WS testing. Within this framework, this paper focuses on how the intended protocol of access for a standard service could be specified, and especially on how the conformance of a service instance to this specified protocol can then be tested. We propose to augment the WSDL description with a UML2.0 Protocol State Machine (PSM) diagram. The PSM is intended to express how, and under which conditions, the service provided by a component through its ports and interfaces can be accessed by a client. We then propose to translate the PSM to a Symbolic Transition System, to which existing formal testing theory and tools can be readily applied for conformance evaluation. A simple example illustrates the approach and highlights the peculiar challenges raised by WS conformance testing.

1 Introduction

Service Oriented Architecture (SOA) is the emerging paradigm for the realization of heterogeneous, distributed systems, obtained from the dynamic combination of remote applications owned and operated by distinct organizations. Today the Web Service Architecture (WSA) certainly constitutes the most relevant and widely adopted instance of such a paradigm.

A Web Service (WS) is essentially characterized by the capability to "support interoperable machine-to-machine interaction over a network"[5]. This capability is achieved due to the agreement of all major players on the usage of uniform

---

* This work has been supported by the European Project TELCERT (FP6 STREP 507128), by Marie Curie Network TAROT (MRTN-CT-2004-505121), and by the Netherlands Organization for Scientific Research (NWO) under project: STRESS – Systematic Testing of Realtime Embedded Software Systems.

R.H. Reussner et al. (Eds.): Architecting Systems, LNCS 3938, pp. 1–25, 2006.
© Springer-Verlag Berlin Heidelberg 2006

WS interfaces, coded into the standard machine-processable Web Service Definition Language (WSDL) format [9], and of the Simple Object Access Protocol (SOAP) [18] for WS communication. Moreover, WSA interconnects service providers and service requesters via a standard Service Broker called the UDDI (Universal Description and Discovery Integration)[10]. The information in this catalog follows the yellow, green or white pages paradigms open technology, and defines a common mechanism to publish and retrieve information about available Web Services.

From a methodology viewpoint, WSA builds on the extensive framework of the Component-Based Software Development (CBSD) paradigm, of which it can be considered an attractive successor. Where in fact CBSD pursued the development of a composite system by the assembly of pre-existing (black-box) components, WSA chases the dynamic composition of services at client requests. The two paradigms share the underlying philosophy of developing building blocks (either components or services) of a system for external generalized reuse, whose implementation details are hidden behind a published interface.

By building on the extensive results of CBSD, WSs can today rely on a much more mature culture for compositional development, as testified by the emergence of established standard access and communication protocols. On the other hand, by exacerbating the aspects of loose coupling, distribution and dynamism, WSs have also inherited the most challenging issues of the component-based approach, directly descending here from the need of dynamically composing the interactions between services whose internal behavior is unknown. This fact brings several consequences on the trustability and reliability of WSA; in particular, it calls for new approaches to validate the behavior of black-box components whose services are invoked by heterogeneous clients in a variety of unforeseen contexts.

Although similar problems have been encountered and tackled in the area of software components, testing of WSs is even more difficult since the different machines participating in the interaction could be dispersed among different organizations, so even a simple monitoring strategy or the insertion of probes into the middleware is not generally feasible. Moreover, the notion of the WSA establishes rigid limitations on the kind of documentation that can be provided and used for integrating services. In particular, a service must not include information on how it has been implemented. This obviously is desirable to enable the decoupling between requesters and providers of services, but obviously makes integration testing more difficult.

Speaking in general, it is clear that the capability of testing a software artefact is strongly influenced by the information available [3]. In fact, different kinds of testing techniques can be applied depending on the extent and formalization degree of the information available. The technique to be applied will also be different depending on the quality aspects to be evaluated, e.g. functionality, performance, interoperability, etc.

In CBSD, different proposals have been made to increase the information available with software components [24], following what we generally refer to as the metadata-based testing approach [25]. Fortunately, as already said, today the area of WS can rely on a more mature attitude towards the need for standardized documentation, with respect to the situation faced by early component developers, and in fact the interaction among WSs is based on a standardized protocol stack and discovery service. Current practice is that the information shared to develop interacting WSs is stored in WSDL files. However, such documents mainly report signatures (or syntax) for the available services, but no information concerning specific constraints about the usage of the described service can be retrieved. Obviously, this way of documenting a service raises problems regarding the capability of correctly integrating different services. In particular, the technology today relies on the restrictive assumption that a client knows in advance the semantics of the operations provided by a service or other properties of it [1].

To facilitate the definition of the collaborations among different services, various approaches are being proposed to enrich the information that should be provided with a WS. Languages such as the Business Process and Execution Language for Web Services (BPEL4WS) and the Web Service - Choreography Description Languages (WS-CDL) are emerging [1], which permit to express how the cooperation among the services should take place. The formalized description of legal interactions among WSs turned out to be instrumental in verifying interoperability through the application of specific conformance evaluation instruments.

We claim that it would be highly useful to attach this description in the form of an XML Metadata Interchange (XMI [29]) file, since in this form it can be easily reused by UML based technologies. XMI is becoming the de facto standard for enabling interaction between UML tools, and it can be automatically generated from widespread UML editors such as IBM Rational Rose XDE or Poseidon.

It is indeed somewhat surprising how two broad standardization efforts, such as the UML and the WSA, are following almost independent paths within distinct communities. Our motivating goal is the investigation of the possibility to find a common ground for both communities. Hence our proposal is that the WS description (including the WSDL file) will report some additional information documented by the WS developer in UML, and in particular, as we explain below, as a Protocol State Machine, that is a UML behavior diagram newly introduced into the latest version of this language [11]. In this way an XMI file representing the associated PSM could be inserted in the UDDI registry along with the other WS documentation. Moreover, as we show in this paper, the PSM provides a formal description of the legal protocol for WS interaction, and following some translation step it can be used as a reference model for test case derivation, applying well established algorithms from formal testing theory.

The framework for automatic testing of WSs presented in this paper has been specifically defined considering technologies related to the WS domain. It will probably be straightforward to apply a similar approach also in a Component Based (CB) setting when the necessary information is provided as data attached to the component. WSs can be considered as being an extreme consequence of the CB paradigm, in which the developer of a system looses the control, also at run time, of the "assembled" components.

The paper is structured as follows: Section 2 provides an overview of the different flavors of the interoperability notion for WSs, and in particular introduces WS conformance testing; Section 3 presents PSMs and their proposed usage for WS protocol specification; Section 4 synthesizes the general framework we propose for WS testing, and Section 5 outlines related work. In Section 6 a short survey of formal approaches to conformance testing is given, before focusing on the specific formalism which we are going to exploit for WS conformance testing, called Symbolic Transition Systems (STSs). In Section 7 we relate the PSM specification to the presented STS one. Finally, Section 8 summarizes our conclusions and mentions the work remaining to be done.

2   Interoperability of Web Services

Web Services are cooperating pieces of software that are generally developed and distributed among different organizations for machine-to-machine cooperation, and which can act, at different times, as servers, providing a service upon request, or as clients, invoking some others' services. The top most concern in development of WSA is certainly WS interoperability. Actually, WS interoperability is a wide notion, embracing several flavors, all of them important. Without pretending to make a complete classification, for the sake of exposition in our case we distinguish between two main kinds of interoperability issues. A first type of interoperability refers to the format of the information stored in the relevant documents (such as WSDL files, UDDI entry), and to the format of the exchanged SOAP messages. This interoperability flavor is briefly presented below in Section 2.1, in which the approach defined by the WS-I consortium (where the "I" stands for Interoperability) to ensure this kind of interoperability is outlined. A second interoperability issue, discussed in Section 2.2, is instead relative to the correct usage of a WS on the client's side, in terms of the sequencing of invocations of the provided services. Certainly, other kinds of heterogeneity hindering correct interactions of WSs can be identified. For instance, in [16] the authors report about an interesting experience in integrating externally acquired components in a single system. As they highlight, different assumptions made by the different components, such as who has to take the control of the interaction, often prevent real interoperability.

2.1   Data and Messaging Conformance

As said, a first factor influencing the interoperability of WSs is obviously related to the way the information is reported in the different documents (such as SOAP messages, WSDL files, UDDI entries) necessary to enable WS interactions, and to the manner this information is interpreted by cooperating WSs.

This concern is at the heart of the activities carried on by the WS-I consortium, an open industry organization which joins diverse communities of Web Service leaders interested in promoting interoperability. WS-I provides several resources for helping WS developers to create interoperable Web Services and verify that their results are compliant with the WS-I provided guidelines. In particular, WS-I has recently defined several profiles [12] that define specific relations that must hold among the information contained in different documents. In so doing the interactions among two or more WSs are enabled. Besides, WS-I has defined a set of requirements on how specific information reported in these files must be interpreted.

Just to show the kind of interoperability addressed by WS-I we report below without further explanation a couple of examples from the specification of the Basic Profile. Label R1011 identifies a requirement taken from the messaging part of the profile, which states:

R1011 - An ENVELOPE MUST NOT have any element children of soap: Envelope following the soap:Body element.

The second example has been taken from the service description part and describes relations between the WSDL file and the related SOAP action:

R2720 - A wsdl:binding in a DESCRIPTION MUST use the part attribute with a schema type of "NMTOKEN" on all contained soapbind:header and soapbind:headerfault elements.

Alongside the Basic Profile, the WS-I consortium also provides a test suite (that is freely downloadable from the WS-I site) that permits to verify the conformance of a WS implementation with respect to the requirements defined in the profile. In order to be able to verify the conformance of the exchanged messages, part of the test suite acts as a proxy filtering the messages and verifying that the conditions defined in the profile are respected.

The WS-I profile solves many issues related to the representation of data, and to how the same data are represented in different data structures. Another kind of data-related interoperability issue not addressed by the WS-I profile concerns instead the interpretation that different WSs can give for the same data structure. Testing can certainly be the right tool to discover such kind of mismatches. The testing theory presented in Section 6 and its application to the domain of WSs, exerted in Section 7, provides a formal basis for the derivation of test cases that permit to verify that a single implementation of a WS correctly interprets the exchanged data.

2.2   Protocol Conformance

A different interoperability flavor concerns the correct usage of a WS on the client's side, in terms of the sequencing of invocations of the provided services. A correct usage of a WS must generally follow a specified protocol defining the intended sequences of invocations for the provided interface methods, and possibly the pre- and post-conditions that must hold before and after each invocation, respectively.

This is the kind of interoperability we focus on in the remainder of this paper. Generally speaking a protocol describes the rules with which interacting entities must comply in their communication in order to have guarantees on the actual success of the interaction. Such rules are generally defined by organizations that act as (de facto) standard bodies. The aim of companies joining these organizations is to allow different vendors to produce components that can interact with each other. Often the rules released by such organizations are actually established as standards and adopted by all the stakeholders operating in the interested domain.

It is obvious to everybody though that the definition of a standard per se does not guarantee correct interaction. What is needed in addition is a way to assess the conformance of an implementation to the corresponding specification. Different ways can be explored to verify such conformance, among which testing deserves particular attention. Protocol testing is an example of functional testing in which the objective is to verify that components in the protocol correctly respond to invocations made in correspondence to the protocol specification.

Conformance of an implementation to a specification is one of the most studied subjects from a formal and empirical point of view. Several studies have been carried on for assessing conformance when protocol specifications are considered.

Conformance testing is a kind of functional testing in which an implementation of a protocol entity is solely tested with respect to its specification. It is important to note that only the observable behavior of the implementation is tested. No reference is made to the internal structure of the protocol implementation. In [26] the parties are listed which are involved in the conformance testing process. In a SOA paradigm this can be partially revised in the following way:

1. the implementer or supplier of a service that needs to test the implementation before selling it;
2. the user of a service, claiming to be conform, can be interested in retesting the service to be sure that it can actually cooperate with the other entities already in his/her system;
3. organizations that act as service brokers and that would like to assess the conformance of a service before inserting it in the list of the available services;
4. third parties laboratories that can perform conformance testing for any of the previously mentioned parties.

It is worth noting that the standard may provide different levels of conformance, for instance defining optional features that may or may not be implemented by an organization. This has to be taken in to account when it comes to conformance testing.

3   UML and Web Services

As said in the Introduction, an important topic that is not receiving adequate attention in the research agenda of WS developers and researchers is how the Unified Modeling Language (UML) can be fruitfully used to describe a WS specification and interaction scenarios. The basic idea is to increase the documentation of a WS using UML diagrams. The motivation is to find a trade-off between a notation which is widespread and industrially usable on one side, but that is also apt to formal treatment and automated analysis on the other. Therefore, a wealth of existing UML editors and analysis tools could be exploited also for WS development. Moreover, from these diagrams a tester should be able to generate useful test suites that, when run on a specific implementation, would provide a meaningful judgment about conformance with the "standard" specification.

The forthcoming UML 2.0 [23] introduces several new concepts and diagrams, in particular supporting the development of Component-Based software. Among these, Protocol State Machine (PSM) diagrams seem particularly promising for our purposes. The idea underneath PSMs is to provide the software designer with a means to express how, and under which conditions, the service provided by a component through its ports and interfaces can be accessed by a client, for instance regarding the ordering between invocations of the methods within the classifier (port or interface). The PSM diagram directly derives from that of the State Machine but introduces some additional constraints and new features. The UML 2.0 Superstructure Specification [23] provides the following definition for this kind of diagram: *A PSM specifies which operations of the classifier can be called in which state and under which condition, thus specifying the allowed call sequences on the classifier's operations. A PSM presents the possible and permitted transitions on the instances of its context classifier, together with the operations which carry the transitions. In this manner, an instance lifecycle can be created for a classifier, by specifying the order in which the operations can be activated and the states through which an instance progresses during its existence.*

Another interesting feature of these diagrams is that they support the definition of *pre-* and *post-conditions* associated with the methods in the interface. This feature provides an improved semantical characterization of the offered services and at the same time increases the verification capability of testers by permitting the application of the well known Design-by-Contract [22] principles. Using first order logic a contract characterizes a service by specifying the conditions that should hold before the invocation and conditions that will be true after the execution of the service. At the same time a contract can specify invariant conditions that remain true during the whole execution of the service. Contracts have proved to be a useful mechanism in CB development, and in particular for the testing of COTS, as for instance developed in [17], and its usage for WS testing is being explored, e.g. [19].

A pre-condition can contain constraints on the parameters passed to the method, or on the values in any way associated to the current status of the environment. If a pre-condition is fulfilled when the invocation is triggered, the implementation must guarantee the respect of the constraints expressed in the post-conditions. In UML this kind of constraints can be naturally expressed using OCL. When a PSM of a WS is defined also using pre- and post-conditions, the assumption is that a component interacting with this WS needs to know these rules, but no more details than these rules, to correctly interact with the system. In fact, a PSM does not define the detailed behavior elaborated inside a component, since this kind of information stays in the scope of traditional State

Machines (or more precisely, Behavioral State Machine - BSM - as defined in UML 2 Superstructure Specification [23]). Instead a state in a PSM represents the point reached in the foreseen interaction between the client and the server. Obviously the definition of a PSM will also influence the definition of the BSM for the object to which the associated port or interface belongs. In order to have a non conflicting specification, related PSMs and BSMs must in some way be compatible.

In the specification of a PSM it is important that no assumptions about the real implementation of the classifier are made, for instance it is incorrect to refer, within a pre- or post-condition, to an internal (state-)variable of a possible implementation of the classifier. Nonetheless, when dealing with non-trivial specifications, it is somehow inevitable to (abstractly) model the internal state of the system. This is done via (internal) variables of the specification model. These two views on a system, the implementation and specification view, cause sometimes confusion. For instance, there is no semantical correspondence between the variables of the specification model and the implementation model.

Therefore, one central issue when dealing with PSMs is how to make them completely neutral with respect to internal specification variables. Several ways could be found to deal with this issue. The one we will exemplify in this paper is the augmentation of the classifier with side-effect free "get"-methods to increase its observability. These methods can then be used in the corresponding specification PSM instead of internal variables. On the other hand, such specified "get"-methods must then be implemented. This imposes extra work on the implementer for developing these additional methods, but the advantage of this

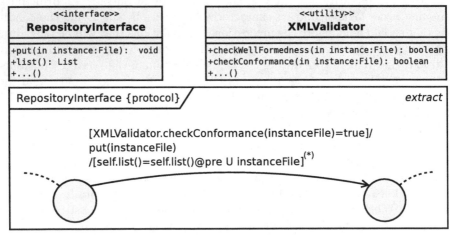

<<interface>>	<<utility>>
RepositoryInterface	**XMLValidator**
+put(in instance:File): void +list(): List +...()	+checkWellFormedness(in instance:File): boolean +checkConformance(in instance:File): boolean +...()

RepositoryInterface {protocol}   *extract*

[XMLValidator.checkConformance(instanceFile)=true]/
put(instanceFile)
/[self.list()=self.list()@pre U instanceFile][*)

(*) To simplify we express with the symbol "U" the union of two
"list" sets so avoiding to expand the definition for the type List

Fig. 1. Introduction of a utility class in a model

practice is the possibility of expressing a more precise definition for the implementation, with corresponding benefits regarding conformance evaluation.

It can also be useful to introduce other elements in the model which ease the specification of pre- and post-conditions in the PSM. For instance, having to handle parameters representing XML files it could be useful to introduce a class with methods that can check the well-formedness or the validity of an instance with respect to a corresponding XML Schema. Again this means extra-burden on the side of the developers, because for checking purposes such a <<utility>> class needs to be instantiated at run-time. Figure 1, for instance, shows an example of a <<utility>> class added in order to facilitate the expression of XML instance conformance within the pre-condition of a generic PSM transaction.

4   A Framework for Web Service Testing

In this section we briefly summarize a framework for testing of WSs, which we have previously introduced in [4]. The framework relies on an increased information model concerning the WS, and is meant for introducing a test phase when WSs ask for being published on a UDDI registry. In this sense we called it the "Audition" framework, as if the WS undergoes a monitored trial before being put "on stage". It is worth noting that from a technical point of view the implementation of the framework does not present major problems, and even from the scientific perspective it does not introduce novel methodologies; on the contrary, one of its targets is to reuse sophisticated software tools (such as test generators) in a new context. The major difficulties we foresee is that a real implementation based on accepted standards requires that slight modifications/extensions are made to such standard specifications as UDDI. This in turn requires wide acceptance from the WS community and the recognition of the importance of conformance testing.

Figure 2 shows the main elements of the framework. The figure provides a logical view, i.e., the arrows do not represent invocations on methods provided by one element, but a logical step in the process; they point to the element that will take the responsibility of carrying on the associated operation.

The process is activated by the request made by the provider of a WS asking for the inclusion of it in the entries of a registry and is structured in eight main steps, which are also annotated in Fig. 2 (numbers in the list below correspond to the numbers in the figure):

1. a Web Service WS1 asks a UDDI registry to be published among the services available to accept invocations;
2. the UDDI service puts WS1 in the associated database, but marking the registration as a pending one, and starts the creation of a specific tester;
3. the WS Testing Client will start to make invocations on WS1, acting as the driver of the test session;
4. during the audition, WS1 will plausibly ask the UDDI service for references to other services;

5. UDDI checks if the service asking for references is in the pending state. If not the reference for the WSDL file and relative binding and access point to the service are provided. In the case that the service is in the pending state the UDDI will generate, using a WS factory, a WS Proxy for the required services;

6. for each inquiry made by WS1 the UDDI service returns a binding reference to a Proxy version of the requested service;

7. WS1 will start to make invocations on the Proxy versions of the required services. As a consequence the Proxy version can check the content and the order of any invocation made by WS1;

8. if the current invocation is conforming, the Proxy service invokes the real implementation of the service and returns the result obtained to the invoking (WS1) service. Then the process continues driven by the invocations made by the testing client.

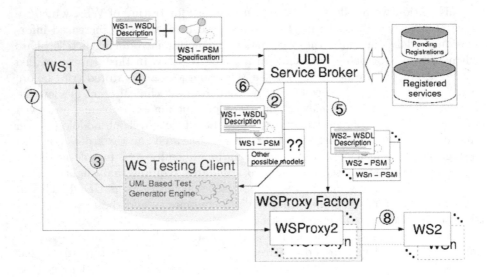

Fig. 2. The Audition Framework

In this framework several testing exigencies and approaches can be identified. Specifically, we address the scenario that a standard body has published some WS specification (adopting the PSM notation) and the conformance to this specification of a developed WS instance must be validated. The conformance theory discussed in the following of this paper is applied to the conformance testing of the interface provided by a single Web service. In Fig. 2 the elements involved in this verification have been shaded. As a future step we want deal with extending the existing results from conformance theory to also consider interactions among services. Before presenting our approach we briefly overview recent related work in the field of WS testing.

5   Related Work in Testing of Web Services

WSs testing is an immature discipline in intense need of further research by academy and industry. Indeed, while on the practitioner's side WSs are evidently considered a key technology, research in the area seems not to draw an adequate attention from the testing community, probably due to the contiguity/overlap with other emerging paradigms, especially with Component-Based Software Engineering (CBSE), or perhaps to the quite technical details that this discipline entails. In this section we give a brief overview of those papers that share some similar views with our work.

The possibility of enhancing the functionality of a UDDI service broker with logic that permits to perform a testing step before registering a service has been firstly proposed in [28] and [27], and subsequently in [20]. This idea is also the basis for the framework introduced in this paper. However, the information we use and the tests we derive are very different from those proposed in the cited papers. In particular while in the cited works testing is used as a means to evaluate the input/output behavior of the WS that is under registration, in the Audition framework we mainly monitor the interactions between the WS under registration with providers of services already registered. In this sense, we are not interested in assessing if a WS provided is bug-free in its logic, but we focus on verifying that a WS can correctly cooperate with other services, by checking that a correct sequence of invocations to the service leads in turn to a correct interaction of the latter with other services providers (and that vice versa an incorrect invocation sequence receives an adequate treatment).

With reference to the information that must be provided with the WS description, the authors of [28] foresee that the WS developer provides precise test suites that can be run by the enhanced UDDI. In [20] instead the authors propose to include Graph Transformation Rules that will enable the automatic derivation of meaningful test cases that can be used to assess the behavior of the WS when running in the "real world". To apply the approach they require that a WS specifically implements interfaces that increase the testability of the WS and that permit to bring the WS in a specific state from which it is possible to apply a specified sequence of tests.

The idea of providing information concerning the right order of the invocations can be found in a different way also in specifications such as BPEL4WS and the Web Service Choreography Interface (WSCI). The use of such information as main input for analysis activities has also been proposed in [15]. However, the objective of the authors in this case is to formally verify that some undesired situations are not allowable given the collaboration rules. To do this the authors, after having translated the BPEL specifications into Promela (a language that can be accepted by the SPIN model checker), apply model checking techniques to verify if specific properties are satisfied. Another approach to model-based analysis of WS composition is proposed in [13]. From the integration and cooperation of WSs the authors synthesize Finite State Machines and then they compare if the obtained result and allowable traces in the model are compatible with that defined by BPEL4WS-based choreography specification.

6   Model-Based Conformance Testing

As said, conformance verification involves both static conformance to an established WSDL interface, and dynamic conformance of exposed behaviors to an established interaction protocol. Clearly the second aspect is the challenging one. In the following we first introduce the basic notion of formal conformance testing and then develop a possible strategy for formal conformance testing of Web Services based on the existing **ioco** implementation relation (see below), and related tools.

We want to test conformance with respect to a protocol specification, given as a PSM. One can see such a PSM as a high-level variant of a simple state machine, such as a Finite State Machine (FSM) or a Labeled Transition System (LTS). Hence we can use classical testing techniques based on these simple models to test for conformance. In this paper we focus on LTS-based testing techniques.

6.1   LTS-Based Testing

Labeled Transition Systems serve as a semantic model for several formal languages and verification- and testing theories, e.g. process algebras and statecharts. They are formally defined as follows:

Definition 1. *A* Labeled Transition System *is a tuple* $\mathcal{L} = \langle S, s_0, \Sigma, \rightarrow \rangle$, *where*

- S *is a (possibly infinite) set of* states.
- $s_0 \in S$ *is the* initial state.
- Σ *is a (possibly infinite) set of* action labels. *The special action label* $\tau \notin \Sigma$ *denotes an* unobservable *action. In contrast, all other actions are* observable. Σ_τ *denotes the set* $\Sigma \cup \{\tau\}$.
- $\rightarrow \subseteq S \times \Sigma_\tau \times S$ *is the* transition relation.

In formal testing the goal is to compare a specification of a system with its implementation by means of testing. The specification is given as a formal model in the formalism at hand, so in our case as an LTS or as an expression in a language with underlying LTS semantics. This formal specification is the basis to test the implementation (System Under Test – SUT). This implementation, however, is not given as a formal model but as a real system about which no internal details are known (hidden in a "black box"), and on which only experiments, or tests, can be performed. This implies that we cannot directly define a formal implementation relation between formal specifications and physical implementations. To define such an implementation relation, expressing which implementations are conforming, and which are not, we need an additional assumption, referred to as the *test hypothesis*. The test hypothesis says that the SUT exhibits a behavior which *could* be expressed in some chosen formalism. Now conformance can be formally defined by an implementation relation between formal specification models and assumed implementation models.

Typically, in LTS testing the formalism assumed for implementations is the LTS formalism itself. So, an implementation is assumed to behave as if it were

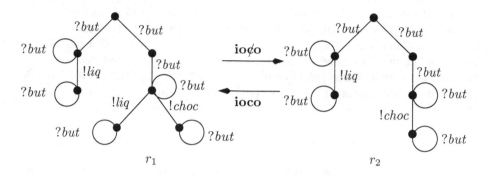

Fig. 3. The **ioco** relation

an LTS. Based on this assumption many different implementation relations on LTSs have been defined in the literature, most of them being preorders or equivalences on LTSs. These relations differ, for example, in the way they treat non-determinism, the extent to which they allow partial specifications, whether they allow "look-ahead" in behaviors, etc. For several of these implementation relations also testing scenarios and test generation algorithms have been published. These testing algorithms are usually proved to be complete in the limit, i.e., the execution of all (usually infinitely many) test cases constitutes a decision procedure for the relation. For an annotated bibliography for testing based on LTSs see [6], for a survey on existing test theory in general see [8].

The ioco Implementation Relation — In this paper we use the **ioco** implementation relation for testing, see [26]. **ioco** is not a preorder relation, but it turns out to be highly suited for testing. Several state-of-the-art testing tools nowadays implement it, e.g. TorX [2] and the TGV-based tools [21].

In the **ioco** setting the specifications are LTSs where the set of action labels is partitioned into input- and output action labels. The test hypothesis is that implementations can be modeled as *input-output transition systems* (IOTS). IOTSs are a subclass of LTSs for which it is assumed that all input actions are enabled in all states (input enabledness). A *trace* is a sequence of observable actions, starting from the initial state. As an example take the LTSs from Fig. 3. We have one input action $?but$, standing for pushing a button on a machine supplying chocolate and liquorice. These are the output actions $!choc$ and $!liq$. Both r_1 and r_2 are input enabled, at all states it is possible to push the button, hence both LTSs are also IOTSs. Some traces of r_1 are $?but \cdot !liq$, $?but \cdot ?but \cdot !choc$, and so on.

A special observation embedded in the **ioco** theory is the observation of *quiescence*, meaning the absence of possible output actions. The machine can not produce output, it remains silent, and only input actions are possible. For instance both r_1 and r_2 are quiescent in the initial state (the upmost state), waiting for the button to be pressed. After applying $?but$ to the systems, both may be quiescent due to nondeterminism (following the right branch). They may also nondeterministically chose the left branch and produce liquorice via the output action !*liq*. Hence, when it comes to test generation, and the tester observes quiescence after pushing the button, it knows that the systems chose the right branch, waiting for the button to be pushed again, and can forget about the left branch of the specification. This waiting for output before generating the next input is the principle of *on-the-fly* testing, which helps in avoiding a state space explosion when computing test cases out of a given specification. The test tool *TorX* implements a test generation algorithm which tests for **ioco**-correctness via such an *on-the-fly* approach, see [2]. The observation of quiescence is embedded in the notion of traces, leading to so called *suspension traces*.

We will not give a formal definition of the **ioco** relation here to keep an introductory flavor. We refer to [26] for a detailed description and give instead an informal intuition of it. Let i be an implementation IOTS and s be an LTS specification of it. Then we have:

> i **ioco**-conforms to s $\Leftrightarrow$
> - if i produces output x after some suspension trace σ, then s can produce x after σ
> - if i cannot produce any output after suspension trace σ, then s can reach a state after σ where it cannot produce any output (quiescence)

The addition of quiescence increases the discriminating power of **ioco**, as illustrated by Fig. 3. Taking r_2 as the specification for r_1, we have that r_1 can produce !*liq* and !*choc* after the suspension trace ?*but* · *quiescence* · ?*but*. The specification though can only produce !*choc* after pressing the button, observing quiescence, and pressing the button again. Hence the **ioco** condition "if i produces output x after suspension trace σ, then s can produce x after σ" is not fulfilled, r_1 is not **ioco**-conform to r_2. On the other hand, r_2 is **ioco**-conform to r_1.

Extensions of ioco — The model of LTSs has the advantage of being simple and highly suited for describing the functional behavior of communicating, reactive systems. But in practice one does not want to specify a system in such a low-level formalism. Instead high-level description languages like statecharts, PSMs, or process algebras with data extensions are the preferred choice. Furthermore, non-functional properties like embedding timing constraints into the model are mandatory means in certain application areas. Recent research activities have produced first promising results in dealing with these extensions, see e.g. [7].

In our setting we are interested in testing based on automata allowing for a symbolic treatment of data, meaning that one can specify using data of different types, guarded transitions, and so on. This makes the specification much more compact and readable. At first sight using such formalisms for **ioco** testing is straightforward, because usually these models have an underlying LTS semantics, meaning that one just has to convert the high-level model into its underlying LTS, and then test as usual based on that. The difficulty here is, that even a small, finite symbolic model has commonly an infinite underlying LTS semantics. This problem is commonly known as *state-space explosion*. To address this problem recent research has focused on testing based directly on a symbolic specification, without mapping it at all to its underlying LTS. The **ioco** relation has been recently lifted to such a symbolic setting based on so called *Symbolic Transition Systems* (STSs), see [14]. Such an STS has many similarities with formalisms like PSMs, and hence serves as a promising choice for testing WSs specified with PSMs.

Symbolic Transition Systems — STSs extend LTSs by incorporating an explicit notion of data and data-dependent control flow (such as guarded transitions), founded on first order logic. The STS model clearly reflects the LTS model, which is done to smoothly transfer LTS-based test theory concepts to an STS-based test theory. The underlying first order structure gives formal means to define both the data part algebraically, and the control flow part logically. This makes STSs a very general and potent model for describing several aspects of reactive systems. We do not give here a formal definition of the syntax and LTS-semantics of STSs due to its extent, and give instead a simple example in Fig. 4 showing all necessary ingredients. For a formal definition we refer to [14].

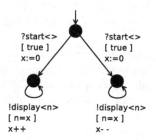

Fig. 4. An STS counter

The shown STS specifies a counter consisting of three so called locations (the black dots). The uppermost one is the initial location, distinguished by the sourceless arrow. Being in this initial location the system is quiescent, it awaits an input called ?start<>, which has no parameters. For instance one can think of it as a button. After this button is pressed, the system nondeterministically chooses the left or right branch (called "switches"), and sets the internal variable x to zero. Both switches are always enabled because both are unconstrained, the guards say **true**. Each switch consists of three parts: first the name of an input- or output action together with its parameters; next a guard talking about the parameters and the internal variables; and finally an update of the internal variables. As commonly done we precede the names of input actions with a question mark, and the names of output actions with an exclamation mark.

If the system chooses the left switch it first performs an output via the action !display<n>. This action has one parameter called n, which is constrained in the guard [n = x], saying that the display has to show the value of the internal variable x (which is zero at first). Next it increments x by one, denoted x++, and loops. The right branch does the same, but decrements x in every loop. Hence think of x and n as being declared as integer in the underlying first order structure. Altogether we have a system which, after a button has been pressed, either displays 0,1,2,..., or 0,-1,-2,... on a display. Another feature not shown is the use of internal so called τ-switches, which become for instance important when composing systems.

In the next section we give a more complex STS, on which we will also exemplify the **ioco** test generation algorithm.

7   Testing Based on PSMs

In this section we want to provide an idea of how WS conformance testing can be based on PSM specifications using the STS testing approach. PSMs serve as formal specifications of WS behavior. These PSMs are transformed into STSs, which, in turn, have an LTS semantics. This allows us to formally root our work in the **ioco**-testing theory as applicable to STSs [14]. The choice of STSs as the formal notation to be used for the derivation of test cases has been mainly influenced by the expressive power of such a formalism which in principle allows to easily embed in an STS diagram all parts of the information that can be found in a PSM diagram.

A practical example can ease the explanation of the approach that we intend to pursue. We first introduce a PSM example in subsection 7.1. Then we present, informally, the transformation of the PSM into an STS in subsection 7.2. Finally, we exemplify the test case generation in subsection 7.3.

7.1   An Example PSM

Fig. 5 shows a PSM for a Web Service dispensing coffee and tea, for simplicity without giving back the possible change. Obviously this is just a toy-example to illustrate our ideas. However, the coffee machine example already exemplifies most of the features of a Web Service specification for which the protocol can be dependent on the data provided by the client. In fact the drinks can be provided only after the specified amount of money has been inserted.

Each invocation of a method will return an object of type **Status** representing all possible output actions which can be observed by the test system. In particular there is a variable **CoffeeButtonLight** expressing the status of the coffee button, a variable **TeaButtonLight** expressing the status of the tea button, a variable **Display** expressing the value reported by the display, and finally a variable **Drink** expressing the possible drink to be dispensed.

Each transition in the PSM is a tuple of the form (actual-state, pre-condition, method invocation, post-condition, final state). The pre-condition expresses under which constraint a transition is admissible from the given source state. For our intended mapping to STSs it is crucial that all method-calls in a pre-condition are query-methods, i.e., they don't affect the internal state of the system (no

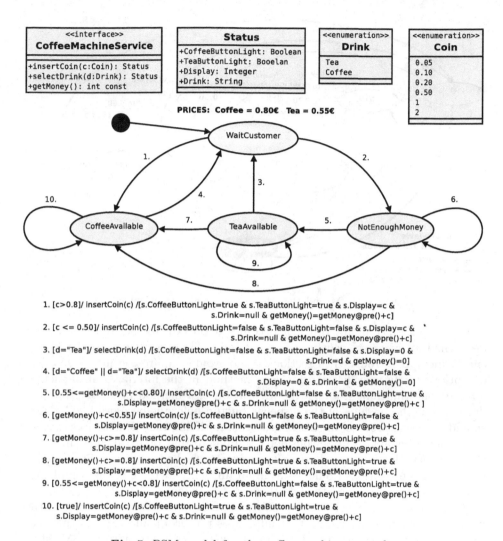

1. [c>0.8]/ insertCoin(c) /[s.CoffeeButtonLight=true & s.TeaButtonLight=true & s.Display=c & s.Drink=null & getMoney()=getMoney@pre()+c]

2. [c <= 0.50]/ insertCoin(c) /[s.CoffeeButtonLight=false & s.TeaButtonLight=false & s.Display=c & s.Drink=null & getMoney()=getMoney@pre()+c]

3. [d="Tea"]/ selectDrink(d) /[s.CoffeeButtonLight=false & s.TeaButtonLight=false & s.Display=0 & s.Drink=d & getMoney()=0]

4. [d="Coffee" || d="Tea"]/ selectDrink(d) /[s.CoffeeButtonLight=false & s.TeaButtonLight=false & s.Display=0 & s.Drink=d & getMoney()=0]

5. [0.55<=getMoney()+c<0.80]/ insertCoin(c) /[s.CoffeeButtonLight=false & s.TeaButtonLight=true & s.Display=getMoney@pre()+c & s.Drink=null & getMoney()=getMoney@pre()+c]

6. [getMoney()+c<0.55]/ insertCoin(c)/ [s.CoffeeButtonLight=false & s.TeaButtonLight=false & s.Display=getMoney@pre()+c & s.Drink=null & getMoney()=getMoney@pre()+c]

7. [getMoney()+c>=0.8]/ insertCoin(c) /[s.CoffeeButtonLight=true & s.TeaButtonLight=true & s.Display=getMoney@pre()+c & s.Drink=null & getMoney()=getMoney@pre()+c]

8. [getMoney()+c>=0.8]/ insertCoin(c) /[s.CoffeeButtonLight=true & s.TeaButtonLight=true & s.Display=getMoney@pre()+c & s.Drink=null & getMoney()=getMoney@pre()+c]

9. [0.55<=getMoney()+c<0.8]/ insertCoin(c) /[s.CoffeeButtonLight=false & s.TeaButtonLight=true & s.Display=getMoney@pre()+c & s.Drink=null & getMoney()=getMoney@pre()+c]

10. [true]/ insertCoin(c) /[s.CoffeeButtonLight=true & s.TeaButtonLight=true & s.Display=getMoney@pre()+c & s.Drink=null & getMoney()=getMoney@pre()+c]

Fig. 5. PSM model for the coffee machine example

side effects). The post-condition expresses the expected results of the corre-sponding method invocation, leading to the given target state. For instance transition 1 declares that entering a coin c greater then 0.80, i.e., 1 or 2 Euro, when being in state WaitCustomer, the result should be the highlighting of the coffee and tea buttons, the visualization of amount "c" in the display, no dis-pense of any drink, and finally an update of the internal state via the invoca-tion of the getMoney() method. The arriving state for the transition will be CoffeeAvailable. A state in a PSM usually corresponds to a quiescent state of the system, i.e., the system waits for an input from its environment.

It is worth noting that the model only specifies the correct sequences of method-invocations. Nevertheless, since a client of a WS can invoke the meth-

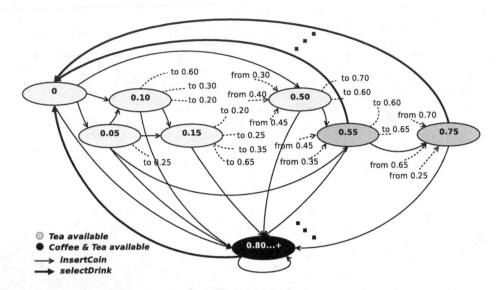

Fig. 6. PSM and the state space explosion problem

ods in the interface in any order, it becomes important to specify the behavior
also when an incorrect sequence is triggered. This corresponds to the input-
enabledness as introduced in section 6, and would require the introduction of
exceptions to the specification for each method in the interface. In particular
for the coffee machine example the invocation of a method in an incorrect order, such as the pushing of the dispense button before it becomes highlighted,
should leave the protocol in the same status, notifying the client with an exception. Such a behavior can be considered similar to that of a real coffee machine
that triggers a beep when a button is incorrectly pushed. However, since the introduction of exceptions would result in an unwieldy increase in the complexity
of the diagram we decided to elide them in the model.

Our simple example shows the influence of the special "get"-method in the
interface, related to state data that influences protocol transitions, in this case
the `getMoney()` method. Fig. 6 shows an extract of the resulting PSM when
no such method is provided (omitting return values). In particular the whole
machine contains 17 states and 70 state transitions, a clear complexity increase
with respect to the machine in Fig. 5. Having the possibility of logically
expressing values through the usage of the `getMoney()` method permits to produce manageable models.

7.2   Mapping from PSM to STS

In Fig. 7 the STS variant of the coffee machine example of Fig. 5 is shown. It
consists of 14 locations and 20 switches. The (linear) increase in the number of
locations and switches is due to the fact that STSs are more fine-grained than
PSMs, which subsume a guarded procedure call together with its post-conditions
on one transition. In STSs a transition corresponds to either an input action

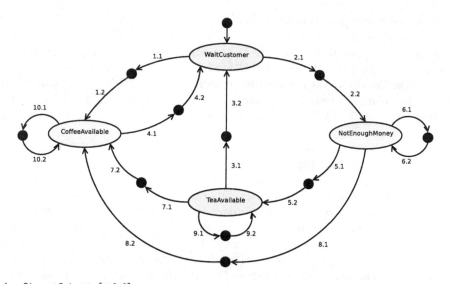

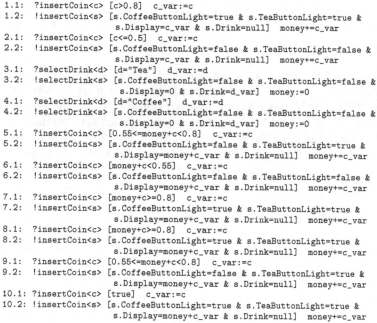

```
1.1:   ?insertCoin<c>  [c>0.8]  c_var:=c
1.2:   !insertCoin<s>  [s.CoffeeButtonLight=true & s.TeaButtonLight=true &
                        s.Display=c_var & s.Drink=null]  money+=c_var
2.1:   ?insertCoin<c>  [c<=0.5]  c_var:=c
2.2:   !insertCoin<s>  [s.CoffeeButtonLight=false & s.TeaButtonLight=false &
                        s.Display=c_var & s.Drink=null]  money+=c_var
3.1:   ?selectDrink<d>  [d="Tea"]  d_var:=d
3.2:   !selectDrink<s>  [s.CoffeeButtonLight=false & s.TeaButtonLight=false &
                        s.Display=0 & s.Drink=d_var]  money:=0
4.1:   ?selectDrink<d>  [d="Coffee"]  d_var:=d
4.2:   !selectDrink<s>  [s.CoffeeButtonLight=false & s.TeaButtonLight=false &
                        s.Display=0 & s.Drink=d_var]  money:=0
5.1:   ?insertCoin<c>  [0.55<=money+c<0.8]  c_var:=c
5.2:   !insertCoin<s>  [s.CoffeeButtonLight=false & s.TeaButtonLight=true &
                        s.Display=money+c_var & s.Drink=null]  money+=c_var
6.1:   ?insertCoin<c>  [money+c<0.55]  c_var:=c
6.2:   !insertCoin<s>  [s.CoffeeButtonLight=false & s.TeaButtonLight=false &
                        s.Display=money+c_var & s.Drink=null]  money+=c_var
7.1:   ?insertCoin<c>  [money+c>=0.8]  c_var:=c
7.2:   !insertCoin<s>  [s.CoffeeButtonLight=true & s.TeaButtonLight=true &
                        s.Display=money+c_var & s.Drink=null]  money+=c_var
8.1:   ?insertCoin<c>  [money+c>=0.8]  c_var:=c
8.2:   !insertCoin<s>  [s.CoffeeButtonLight=true & s.TeaButtonLight=true &
                        s.Display=money+c_var & s.Drink=null]  money+=c_var
9.1:   ?insertCoin<c>  [0.55<=money+c<0.8]  c_var:=c
9.2:   !insertCoin<s>  [s.CoffeeButtonLight=false & s.TeaButtonLight=true &
                        s.Display=money+c_var & s.Drink=null]  money+=c_var
10.1:  ?insertCoin<c>  [true]  c_var:=c
10.2:  !insertCoin<s>  [s.CoffeeButtonLight=true & s.TeaButtonLight=true &
                        s.Display=money+c_var & s.Drink=null]  money+=c_var
```

Fig. 7. STS model for the coffee machine example

(i.e. a procedure call), or an output action (i.e. the returned value of the procedure). Hence every interface method invocation corresponds to an input action and an output action. For instance, the `insertCoin(c: Coin): Status` method is mapped to an input action `?insertCoin<c: Coin>`, and an output action `!insertCoin<s: Status>`. This allows to specify an asynchronous message interchange, and has a number of consequences, for instance we have to remember the values given to procedures. To do so we store them in variables, an inherent concept of STSs. For instance take transition 1 of the PSM from Fig. 5. This transition is mapped to the transitions 1.1 and 1.2 in Fig. 7. Here the method invocation (i.e. input action) insertCoin(c) is executed with the restriction that c>0.8. We do so via the guarded transition 1.1, and store the parameter value c in an internal variable c_var (called location variable in STSs) to remember it. Next the SUT performs an output action, it returns a Status with certain settings. This is done via transition 1.2. Here we make use of the remembered parameter value of the preceding procedure call by referring to the internal variable via s.Display=c_var.

The challenging issue is the mapping of the special "get"-methods in the interface to STSs. The use of these methods corresponds to location variables in STSs. They are used to model state-dependent behavior, and they can be utilized in guards. In our example this concerns the getMoney() method, which is mapped onto a location variable money. After having inserted a coin, like in transition 1.1, we have to update the internal state. In the PSM this is expressed via getMoney()=getMoney@pre()+c. In the STS we can express this as money := money + c_var, shortly written as money += c_var in transition 1.2.

In so doing we can map the PSM into the given STS, which in turn allows us to use the existing **ioco**-based test theory and algorithm, which was adapted for STSs in [14].

Note that this transformation might not always be as easy as in the given example. One problem is that it is possible to partially specify methods like the getMoney() in a PSM. For instance we could have simply left out the update getMoney()=getMoney@pre()+c when applying the insertCoin(c) method in the PSM. Doing so we could not have developed the given STS without applying knowledge about this method which is not in the PSM. Hence in future research we will try to give exact restrictions to PSMs allowing for a guaranteed and automated translation process.

7.3   Automated Testing Based on STSs

In the remainder of this section we give a simple example run of the test generation algorithm as given in [14], which tests for **ioco**-conformance. It generates and executes test cases on-the-fly. That means that instead of firstly computing a set of test cases from the STS, and then applying them to the SUT, it generates a single input, applies it to the SUT, and continues w.r.t. the observed response of the system. As a consequence we avoid the state space explosion when generating test cases, see also [2].

First of all the system has to be initialized by giving initial values to the internal variables, in this case money and c_var. We assume both to be zero, i.e. no coin has been entered in the coffee machine, yet. At first the initial semantical state is computed. Such a state consists of a set of locations in which the SUT could currently be, and a valuation of the internal variables. In our case the STS is fully deterministic, therefore the set of locations will always be a singleton. The initial state here is (WaitCustomer, (money=0, c_var=0)).

The basic principle of the algorithm is to continuously choose nondeterministically one out of these three options:

- Stop testing and give the verdict `Pass`
- Give an input to the SUT
- Observe output (including quiescence) of the SUT (which may result in `Fail`)

Let's assume that first an input is given. The only specified input action in the initial location is `?insertCoin<c>`. The input constraint is computed for this action, which is a first order formula telling the condition for the parameters under which the action can be applied. To do so all outgoing switches with this specific action have to be taken into account. We get here $(c>0.8) \vee (c \leq 0.5)$. If a solution exists, one is chosen and applied to the system, e.g. `?insertCoin(0.5)`. Now the set of next possible locations is computed, which is only the one location where transition 2.1 leads. The new values of the variables are (`money=0`, `c_var=0.5`). Now the tester observes output, it receives the returned `Status` object saying that no drink is available and that the display shows 0.5. This is conformant with the specification, `money` is updated to 0.5 and we proceed to the semantical state (`NotEnoughMoney`, (`money=0.5`, `c_var=0.5`)). If we would have observed a different result, for instance a different display value, the test would have stopped with verdict `Fail`. Choosing next for another `?insertCoin<c>` action we get the input constraint $(0.55 \leq 0.5+c<8) \vee (0.5+c<0.55) \vee (0.5+c \geq 0.8)$, assembled from switches 5.1, 6.1 and 8.1. Again one solution is chosen for c, e.g. 1. We apply `insertCoin(1)` and observe in the returned status that coffee and tea are available, we end up in state (`CoffeeAvailable`, (`money=1.5`, `c_var=1`)). Now the algorithm may choose to stop the testing and give the verdict `Pass`. In practice the testing continues in this manner until either a fault is discovered via verdict `Fail`, or the testing is stopped after a predefined halting criteria.

For the audition of WSs it remains to be evaluated how such a halting criteria should be defined. It will also depend on the given application domain and its inherent security demands which specific halting criteria is considered sufficient. There are several well known halting criteria for model-based testing, mainly concerning coverage of the specification ingredients (locations, switches, evaluation criteria for the guards, etc.). Also more specific testing scenarios (called test purposes) might be of high value.

In Fig. 8 you find the test case corresponding to the exerted test run. We have abbreviated the returned `Status` object and we give it as a tuple representing the values of `CoffeeButtonLight`, `TeaButtonLight`, `Display`, and `Drink`, respectively. The abbreviation "qui" stands for observed "quiescence". As seen in the figure a test case formally corresponds to a tree-like LTS with distinguished terminal states `Pass` and `Fail`. When observing outputs such a test case must tell the tester how to proceed w.r.t. all possible outputs. For instance in our case the test case must specify this for all possible resulting `Status` objects. We have abbreviated this by the usage of an `else` transition. Given a system with a huge (let alone infinite) set of possible output actions, such a test case

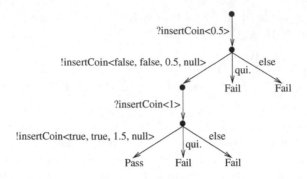

Fig. 8. An example test case

generation leads to an explosion of the state space. Due to the on-the-fly testing it is not necessary to generate such a complete test-case tree out of the specification, the tester just checks the single observed output for conformance, and continues accordingly.

This simple example does not reveal the hidden complexity within this process, like nondeterminism, or checking for quiescence. It is just presented to exemplify the basic principle. The detailed algorithmical tasks can be found in [14].

8   Conclusions and Future Work

Our research addresses the problem of testing a WS instance for conformance to a published specification, which could, for instance, be included in the UDDI registry. We have in fact conceived a possible framework for trustable WSs [4], in which a WS before UDDI registration undergoes sort of an "audition" to ascertain both whether it behaves conforming to the specifications when invoked, and also whether it in turn correctly invokes other published services.

The idea is that for widespread services within an application domain, the community agrees on some standard features and functions to be provided from any service provider who wishes to claim conformance to that standard. In this way interoperability between services provided by different companies can be achieved, and this is somehow what is being done by the WS-I initiative relatively to data and messaging conformance. Another important aspect of WS interoperability concerns how the service is used, i.e., the correct sequencing of invocations of the provided WS interface methods, and possibly the pre- and post-conditions to be guaranteed before and after each invocation. Hence, a key open issue in WSA research is currently how to augment the WSDL definition, so to provide a description of the intended usage for a "standard" service.

To obtain WS interoperability establishing a standardized protocol of usage *per se* is not enough: we also need sound approaches to assess that a WS implementation actually conforms to the corresponding standard specification. This is precisely the objective pursued here: we proposed in particular to exploit the extensive background in formal conformance testing of reactive systems, by adapting it to the peculiar features of WSs. On the other hand, to foster industrial adoption, we intend to start from a protocol specification written in the widespread UML notation. In particular, we have identified the PSM diagram of the UML2.0 as a suitable formalism for expressing how a WS has to be accessed. Then, to be able to readily apply the existing algorithms and tools for conformance testing, we envisaged to convert the PSM specification to a Symbolic Transition System model, which in principle possesses an adequate expressive power. Once the STS is derived, we intend to directly apply the test generation algorithm given in [14] which tests for **ioco**-conformance. As discussed, the advantage of this algorithm is that it generates and executes test cases on-the-fly, thus preventing state space explosion.

In this paper we have provided a preliminary overview of the approach and illustrated it through a simple example of a hypothetical coffee dispenser machine (admittedly coffee remains something quite difficult to produce via Internet, but the example is just to be seen as an intuitive illustration of client-server interaction). The latter was already sufficient to highlight the crucial point in the approach we propose: how to specify protocols of interaction between services without making any assumption on the internal implementation of the specific service instances.

We will continue investigating the specific issues raised by WS conformance in general, and the application of the **ioco**-test theory to it in particular. There are several issues which require further investigation. First, the use of the special "get"-methods to model internal state variables extend the visible interface, and they moreover put a requirement on the implementers to implement them correctly, and on the testers to test them. A question is whether there are alternatives to specify this in PSMs, e.g., using something analogous to location variables in STS. Second, a restriction of the formal testing approach currently is that only the providing interface of a WS is tested, and not the invocations to other WSs. Using the PSMs of the invoked services it seems possible to also consider the conformance of these invocations, both in isolation, or in combination with its own PSM. Third, a theoretical question is to what extent the test hypothesis that SUTs behave as input-output transition systems, really hold: can all methods always be invoked at any time? Finally, the translation from PSM to STS should, of course, be generalized, and automated in a tool.

Trustable services are the ultimate goal of our research: we wish to increase the interoperability and testability of WSA by fostering the application of rigorous model based testing methodologies. At present, a huge effort is taken by the various communities towards identifying common standard models for WSs, allowing for a smooth combination and inter-operation of WSs[1]. It is important to raise awareness within the same communities that also common standard methods for rigorous verification and validation of functional and nonfunctional properties of WS must be sought. In this sense, we hope that the

---

[1] This is for instance currently pursued within the EU Project TELCERT in the e-Learning domain.

approach proposed in this paper, although preliminary, provides first convincing arguments and interesting directions for further investigations.

References

1. G. Alonso, F. Casati, H. Kuno, and V. Machiraju. *Web Services – Concepts, Architectures and Applications*. Springer Verlag, 2004.
2. A. Belinfante, J. Feenstra, R.G. de Vries, J. Tretmans, N. Goga, L. Feijs, S. Mauw, and L. Heerink. Formal test automation: A simple experiment. In G. Csopaki, S. Dibuz, and K. Tarnay, editors, 12th *Int. Workshop on Testing of Communicating Systems*, pages 179–196. Kluwer Academic Publishers, 1999.
3. A. Bertolino. Knowledge area description of software testing. In *Guide to the Software Engineering Body of Knowledge SWEBOK*. IEEE Computer Society, 2000.
4. A. Bertolino and A. Polini. The audition framework for testing web services interoperability. In *Proceedings of the 31st EUROMICRO International Conference on Software Engineering and Advanced Applications*, pages 134–142, Porto, Portugal, August 30th - September 3rd 2005.
5. D. Booth et al. Web Services Architecture. http://www.w3.org/TR/ws-arch/, February 2004.
6. E. Brinksma and J. Tretmans. Testing Transition Systems: An Annotated Bibliography. In F. Cassez, C. Jard, B. Rozoy, and M. Dermot, editors, *Proceedings of the 4th Summer School on Modeling and Verification of Parallel Processes (MOVEP 2000)*, volume 2067 of *LNCS*, pages 187–195. SV, 2001.
7. L. Brandán Briones and E. Brinksma. A test generation framework for quiescent real-time systems. In J. Grabowski and B. Nielsen, editors, *Formal Approaches to Software Testing, FATES*, Linz, Austria, Sep 2004. Springer-Verlag GmbH.
8. M. Broy, B. Jonsson, J.P. Katoen, M. Leucker, and A. Pretschner, editors. *Model-based Testing of Reactive Systems: Advanced Lectures*, volume 3472 of *Lecture Notes in Computer Science*. Springer, 2005.
9. E. Christensen et al. Web Service Definition Language (WSDL) ver. 1.1. http://www.w3.org/TR/wsdl/, March 2001.
10. L. Clement et al. Universal Description Discovery & Integration (UDDI) ver. 3.0. http://uddi.org/pubs/uddi_v3.htm, October 2004.
11. H.E. Eriksson et al. *UML 2 Toolkit*. John Wiley and Sons, 2004.
12. K. Bellinger et al. WS-I - basic profile, ver. 1.1. http://www.ws-i.org/Profiles/BasicProfile-1.1-2004-08-24.html, August 2004.
13. H. Foster et al. Model-based verification of web services compositions. In *Proc. ASE2003*, pages 152–161, Oct., 6-10 2003. Montreal, Canada.
14. L. Frantzen, J. Tretmans, and T.A.C. Willemse. Test generation based on symbolic specifications. In J. Grabowski and B. Nielsen, editors, *FATES 2004*, number 3395 in LNCS, pages 1–15. Springer-Verlag, 2005.
15. X. Fu, T. Bultan, and J. Su. Analysis of interacting BPEL web services. In *Proc. of WWW2004*, May, 17-22 2004. New York, New York, USA.
16. David Garlan, Robert Allen, and John Ockerbloom. Architectural mismatch or why it's hard to build system out of existing parts. In *Proceedings 17th International Conference on Software Enginneering*, pages 179–185, April 1995.
17. H.G. Gross, I. Schieferdecker, and G. Din. *Testing Commercial-off-the-Shelf Components and Systems*, chapter Modeling and Implementation of Built-In Contract Tests. Springer Verlag, 2005.

18. M. Gudgin et al. Simple Object Access Protocol (SOAP) ver. 1.2. http://www.w3.org/TR/soap12/, June 2003.
19. R. Heckel and M. Lohman. Towards contract-based testing of web services. In *Proc. TACOS*, pages 145–156, 2004. Electr. Notes Theor. Comput. Sci. 116.
20. R. Heckel and L. Mariani. Automatic conformance testing of web services. In *Proc. FASE*, Edinburgh, Scotland, Apr., 2-10 2005.
21. C. Jard and T. Jéron. TGV: theory, principles and algorithms. In *IDPT '02*, Pasadena, California, USA, June 2002. Society for Design and Process Science.
22. B. Meyer. Applying design by contract. *IEEE Computer*, 25(10):40–51, October 1992.
23. Object Management Group. *UML 2.0 Superstructure Specification*, ptc/03-08-02 edition. Adopted Specification.
24. A. Orso, M. J. Harrold, and D. Rosenblum. Component metadata for software engineering tasks. In *Proc. EDO 2000*, LNCS 1999, pages 129–144, 2000.
25. A. Polini and A. Bertolino. *Testing Commercial-off-the-Shelf Components and Systems*, chapter A User-Oriented Framework for Component Deployment Testing. Springer Verlag, 2005.
26. J. Tretmans. Test Generation with Inputs, Outputs and Repetitive Quiescence. *Software – Concepts and Tools*, 17(3):103–120, 1996.
27. W. T. Tsai et al. Scenario-based web service testing with distributed agents. *IEICE Transaction on Information and System*, E86-D(10):2130–2144, 2003.
28. W.T. Tsai et al. Verification of web services using an enhanced UDDI server. In *Proc. of WORDS 2003*, pages 131–138, Jan., 15-17 2003. Guadalajara, Mexico.
29. XML Metadata Interchange (XMI) Specification ver. 2.0. http://www.omg.org/docs/formal/03-05-02.pdf, May 2003.

A Core Theory of Interfaces and Architecture and Its Impact on Object Orientation

Manfred Broy

Institut für Informatik, Technische Universität München,
D-80290 München Germany
broy@in.tum.de
http://wwwbroy.informatik.tu-muenchen.de

Abstract. We discuss – on the basis of a theory of components, architectures, refinement, and interfaces – object orientation with its notions of objects and classes aiming at interfaces of classes and of components as well as their specification. We define and analyze, in particular, concepts of components and interfaces for object oriented software systems and their architecture. We discuss "design by contract" as well as "specification by contract" and analyze their limitations. We discuss how to model interfaces. We treat a formal definition of class composition and analyze semantic complications. We outline, in particular, how we can extend concepts from object orientation towards components and more sophisticated ways to handle interfaces. Our approach is based on the notion of states, state assertions, and state machines.

1 Motivation

To master their complexity large software systems are typically built in terms of architectures, in a modular fashion, and hierarchically structured into components. The components are grouped together into software architectures. Such ideas of structuring software go back to "structured programming" according to Dijkstra, Hoare, Dahl, and, in particular, to Parnas (see [8]).

In the following, we introduce a simple theory of composition and interfaces. We apply the theory to object orientation. To do that we consider a very simple-minded concept of object orientation and deal mainly with classes that define attributes and methods, and cooperate exclusively by method invocation.

Basically we see the following principle ways to specify the behavior of classes and objects following the idea of interfaces (apart from writing code – which we do not see as a technique of specification):

- Predicates on the interaction between the objects, classes, and components in terms of streams of invocations and return messages
  - Message sequence charts (interaction diagrams)
  - Stream processing functions (see [3])
- State based specifications
  - Pre/post assertion specifications
  - State machines

R.H. Reussner et al. (Eds.): Architecting Systems, LNCS 3938, pp. 26–47, 2006.
© Springer-Verlag Berlin Heidelberg 2006

In this paper we try to develop a foundational approach to modular interface specifications of classes and components and their composition. Such a modular view is badly needed when trying to compose system parts to large, fairly complex systems. The architectural decomposition of systems into components and their systematic integration need interface specifications.

We introduce and discuss a theory of components, architecture, and composition. We relate this theory to object orientation considering generalizations of conventional classes to classes with export/import interfaces:

- As long as we consider only simple classes (without forwarded calls) such that method invocations can be understood to be synchronous and thus atomic state changes.
- "Design by contract" works in this case where specifying interfaces of classes, although this implies a kind of violation of the principles of encapsulation, information hiding, and data abstraction; the assertions have to refer to the local states defined by the attributes.

But such simple classes hardly can be seen as components. We need a concept of composition for components. Components are of interest in the context of architectures.

- Architectures have to cover distributed and concurrent systems. Supporting concurrency is a must for components.
- Components in architectures must be large, coarse grain building blocks with a lot of cohesion inside but minimal interfaces to the outside.
- Powerful abstractions are required for architectures that support tractable concepts of interfaces.

Our criticism of the object-oriented paradigm trying to use simple classes is as follows:

- Classes are a too small and, with respect to an interface given only by a set of (exported) methods not appropriate as a concept of a component.
- A notion of composition does not really exist for simple classes.

A better concept of a class being a component is obtained if we generalize the idea of an interface to sets of exported and imported methods and if we associate several of such interfaces with a class; but this makes only sense, however, if

- we deal explicitly with forwarded method calls, since invocation of exported methods in general may lead to invocations of imported methods and thus to forwarded method calls.
- we allow for call-backs where a method invocation of an exported method in turn leads to an invocation of imported methods and thus to forwarded method calls that in turn may lead to the invocation of an exported method and thus to call backs.

This manifests to the following view:

- A basic class is a simple form of a system with only an export interface.
- Generalizations of simple classes are classes with interfaces with export and import parts.
- Components are sets of classes with export and import parts.
- Composition of components is realized by matching and connecting their export/import interfaces.

Export/import interfaces, however, introduce a number of severe complications:
- Method calls are carried out by sequences of exchanged messages representing forwarded calls and returns.
- Simple pre/post specifications of method calls do no longer work.
- Classes have to be represented by state machines with input and output.
- The state spaces are formed by the data state of the objects of the classes (the valuations of their attributes) and the control states (including the call stacks).
- In the composition of components represented by state machines we get state machines with internal state transitions. An explicit abstraction from local step requires recursion to define the state machines.

The latter idea leads to a break down of the idea of design by contract. One solution would be to capture the complete effect of a method invocation even in the case of forwarded calls in the pre/post-assertions. This would, however, not only destroy the principles of encapsulation, information hiding, and data abstraction in a even more general sense, since we had to refer the states and attributes of other classes in the assertions. It would also obscure the concept of substitutability since we could not replace a class by another one that has completely different internal representations of its states, but the same observable behavior.

Giving up the model of synchronous method invocations and seeing method invocations consisting of at least two actions, issuing the call and issuing the return to the call, we gain a more flexible concept of observability onto the behavior of a class and its objects. However, then we have to deal with the more sophisticated question in which state an object is when it issues a forwarded call. This analysis leads to a critical conclusion:

- When modeling classes by state machines that receive calls of its export methods (and in turn issues return messages for these calls) and issue calls of its imported methods (and in turn receives return messages for these calls), then not only the states of its local attributes but also its call stack has to be dealt with as part of its state space.

The later fact is a methodological disaster for object orientation showing that the idea of method invocations like procedure calls is a concept of programming in the small that does not scale up to programming in the large.

In the following we discuss all these problems, concepts, and demonstrate all these complications by examples in detail and point out solutions.

2 Interfaces and Compatibility: The Principle of Substitutability, Modularity, and Observability

In this section we fix the essential notions of abstraction, interface and architecture. We describe the essentials of a basic theory (see also [1]).

2.1 Syntactic Framework

We assume some syntax to describe components and architectures. This means that we have a syntactic notion of components. Let LC be the formal language of components.

Every syntactic element $c \in LC$ represents a component. For our purpose, it does not matter whether we describe components by graphical languages (like UML) or by textual languages (like a programming language such as Java or C# or an architecture description language).

We in addition assume a *syntactic composition operator*. It is a partial operation on components that allows us to compose two components:

$$\otimes: LC \times LC \rightarrow LC \qquad \text{written in infix notation}$$

Here partial means that not for every pair $c1, c2 \in LC$ of components the operation yields a well-defined result. Only if two components $c1, c2$ fit together with respect to their syntactic properties (such as their types of their shared variables, their messages or method calls fit together) their composition is meaningful. For every pair $c1, c2 \in LC$ of components, $c1 \otimes c2$ is called the composed component, if the composition is defined for $c1$ and $c2$. In order to deal with the partiality we assume a relation

$$\Re: \wp(LC) \rightarrow \mathbb{B}$$

$\Re(C)$ holds for a family of components $C \subseteq LC$ if their composition is well-defined. So if and only if $\Re(\{c1, c2\})$ holds for components $c1, c2 \in LC$ (for simplicity we ignore here the case $c1 = c2$ and assume that $c1 \neq c2$ holds) we get that $c1 \otimes c2$ yields a well-defined result (we assume that $c \otimes c$ is not well-defined).

For finite sets of components $\{c_1, ..., c_k\} \subseteq LC$ with $\Re(\{c_1, ..., c_k\})$ we define

$$\prod \{c_1, ..., c_k\} = c_1 \otimes ... \otimes c_k$$

Using this notation we better assume that the operator $\otimes$ is commutative and associative. Whenever for $C \subseteq LC$ the proposition $\Re(C)$ holds, $\prod C$ is called an *architecture* with components from C.

Using the operation $\otimes$ we get a hierarchical concept of components – composing two components yields a component. Thus an architecture is again a component. A more restricted concept is obtained, if $\prod C$ is not seen as a component again. However, such a restriction is not substantial. Given two (disjoint) sets of components $C1, C2 \subseteq LC$ we easily define $C1 \otimes C2$ by $\prod(C1 \cup C2)$.

To keep our framework simple, we only introduced the concept of components here but not that of connectors as found in a couple of architecture description languages. Connectors are easily subsumed modelling them by special versions of components.

We assume that in the set of all components a subset $LS \subseteq LC$ is given that characterizes comprehensive self-contained systems.

2.2 Substitutability and Compatibility

When dealing with specifications and behaviours we are in particular interested in an essential semantic relation for components namely *substitutability* (see [15], [10]).

Definition. Substitutability and Compatibility
A component $c1$ is called substitutable for a component $c2$ if the following holds: in every system that is syntactically correct and in which $c2$ occurs as a component we can replace $c2$ by $c1$ which results in a system that is again syntactically correct and

the observable behaviour it shows is identical to (or a refinement of) the observable behaviour of the original system. In this case we also say that c1 is compatible to (or refined by) c2.   ❑

This definition is informal, since it does not provide a formal model of observable behavior. The concept of substitutability is closely related to that of interface specifications, as we will show in more detail below. Each interface specification has to characterize the set of components that can be used as replacements for the specified component. Thus an interface specification for a component defines the set of compatible components.

The essential concept that formalizes substitutability is observability. Looking at an entity from the outside we can observe certain actions and events. By such observations we filter out the relevant information about systems. If we restrict the concept of observations we obtain a more abstract view.

We give a more formal approach to observability in the following section.

2.3 Syntactic Compatibility

Our concept of syntactic composability formalized by the predicate $\Re$ introduces the idea of syntactic compatibility of components. Two components c1, c2 $\in$ LC are called *syntactically compatible* if we can use component c2 whenever we use c1 without running into syntactic problems.

To formalize this we introduce a relation

$$\triangleright \subseteq LC \times LC$$

with the following definition for components c1, c2 $\in$ LC

$$c1 \triangleright c2 \Leftrightarrow \forall\, C \subseteq LC \setminus \{c1, c2\}: \Re(C \cup \{c1\}) \Rightarrow \Re(C \cup \{c2\})$$

The proposition c1 $\triangleright$ c2 expresses that whenever component c1 can be used as a component in a system (leading to a syntactically correct system), c2 can be used instead, too. Component c1 can be syntactically replaced by c2. Of course, the system that we obtain by replacing component c2 for c1 may show a rather different behaviour. We only require that it be syntactically well formed.

Syntactic substitutability induces an equivalence relation

$$\sim\, \subseteq LC \times LC$$

on components that corresponds to mutually syntactically substitutability. This relation is defined as follows:

$$c1 \sim c2 \Leftrightarrow (c1 \triangleright c2 \land c2 \triangleright c1)$$

and called *syntactic equivalence*.

2.4 Observable Equivalence

Now, after we have introduced a basic syntactic framework of components and architectures we develop a semantic view onto components. This cannot be done without a precise semantic perspective. We introduce such a concept only for systems, to begin with by assuming that we have some idea of observations about systems.

To formalize *observable equivalence* we are interested in the question, under which conditions two systems are observable equivalent. Syntactic equivalence was introduced above. Observable equivalence is modelled by an equivalence relation on systems

$$\cong \subseteq LS \times LS$$

The equivalence relation expresses by the proposition $s1 \cong s2$ that two systems $s1$, $s2 \in SC$ are observably and thus semantically equivalent.

Theoretically and practically, there are of course many options to define observable equivalence. In the end, observability has to be related to the users' views onto a system making explicit which observations about a system are relevant for the users. Practically, what is a good notion of observation for system seems often obvious. In principle, we may include also non-functional aspects into observability such as reaction time or consumed resources. In the following, we are rather interested in observability of functional properties.

2.5 Refinement

On components we introduce the relation of semantic substitutability for components. We call this relation *refinement* and denote it by the relation

$$\succ \subseteq LC \times LC$$

The relation $\succ$ is assumed to be transitive and reflexive. Semantic substitutability for components has to be and can be directly related to observable equivalence of systems. In fact, we could define the relation $\succ$ formally based on the observability relation $\cong$. We rather keep the two relations independent to begin with and show, how they are and must be related then.

2.6 Compositionality and Modularity

Refinement for components has to be consistent with composition. This is called *compositionality*. With the introduced concepts we can formally define compositionality of refinement $\succ$ with respect to observabilty $\cong$.

Definition. Compositionality and modularity
The relation $\succ$ is called compositional (or modular) with respect to $\cong$, if for all components $c1, c2 \in LC$ we have:

$$c1 \succ c2 \Rightarrow \forall C \subseteq LC, s \in LS: \Re(C \cup \{c1\}) \wedge s \cong \Pi(C \cup \{c1\}) \Rightarrow s \cong \Pi(C \cup \{c2\}) \quad \square$$

This definition expresses that if $c1 \succ c2$ holds we can replace in any system s that uses the component $c1$ the component $c1$ by $c2$ and get an observably equivalent system.

By refinement $\succ$ we can extent the relation $\cong$ from systems to components $c1, c2 \in LC \setminus LS$ by the definition

$$c1 \cong c2 \Leftrightarrow (c1 \succ c2 \wedge c2 \succ c1)$$

This defines what it means that two components and two systems are observably equivalent. For systems $c1, c2 \in LS$, the formula is a straightforward theorem.

Of course, we expect that observable equivalence implies syntactic equivalence

$$c1 \cong c2 \Rightarrow c1 \sim c2$$

If $\succ$ is compositional, then for all components $c1, c2, c3, c4 \in LC$ we have

$$\Re(\{c1, c2\}) \wedge c1 \cong c3 \wedge c2 \cong c4 \Rightarrow \Re(\{c3, c4\}) \wedge c1 \otimes c2 \cong c3 \otimes c4$$

In this case we call the relation $\cong$ compositional, too, and we speak of a modular theory of components and architectures.

Refinement and substitutability is, of course, related to inheritance. Actually, refinement is the semantically more appropriate idea of inheritance – a relation which in object oriented languages, where inheritance is often just code reuse, is not always guaranteed.

Finally we consider the notion of what it means that refinement is fully abstract.

Definition. Full abstractness
The relation $\succ$ is called *fully abstract* for the equivalence relation $\cong$, if for all components $c1, c2 \in LC$

$$c1 \succ c2 \Leftarrow \forall C \subseteq LC, s \in LS: \Re(C \cup \{c1\}) \wedge s \cong \prod(C \cup \{c1\}) \Rightarrow s \cong \prod(C \cup \{c2\}) \quad \square$$

Full abstractness means that the refinement relation on components is the most abstract relation that guarantees modularity for the chosen concept of observability onto systems. There is a way to introduce refinement $\succ$ based on $\cong$ such that it is always fully abstract. This is achieved by taking the following formula as a definition of refinement:

$$c1 \succ c2 \Leftrightarrow \forall C \subseteq LC, s \in LS: \Re(C \cup \{c1\}) \wedge s \cong \prod(C \cup \{c1\}) \Rightarrow s \cong \prod(C \cup \{c2\})$$

If we introduce $\succ$ independently, this full abstractness is not guaranteed. If $\succ$ is fully abstract and compositional, however, this formula obviously holds and we have then also for all components $c1$ and $c2$:

$$c1 \cong c2 \Leftrightarrow \forall C \subseteq LC, s \in LS:$$

$$(\Re(C \cup \{c1\}) \wedge s \cong \prod(C \cup \{c1\})) \Leftrightarrow (\Re(C \cup \{c2\}) \wedge s \cong \prod(C \cup \{c2\}))$$

The relations $\cong$ and $\succ$ are called fully abstract, if for all components $c1, c2 \in LC$ we have

$$[\forall c \in LC: \Re(\{c1, c\}) \Rightarrow c1 \otimes c \cong c2 \otimes c] \Rightarrow c1 \cong c2$$

and respectively

$$[\forall c \in LC: \Re(\{c1, c\}) \Rightarrow \Re(\{c1, c\}) \wedge c1 \otimes c \succ c2 \otimes c] \Rightarrow c1 \succ c2$$

Full abstractness is a methodological essential concept, since only then we can replace a component by any of its refinements.

2.7 Interfaces and Specifications

For practical purposes it is difficult to work with an abstract notion of refinement and observable equivalence. It is better to introduce explicitly the concept of syntactic and semantic interfaces that characterize sets of components that can be used for a certain system. Interfaces are specifications of components.

The notion of a syntactic interface is straightforward. A syntactic interface defines a set of components. Formally, an interface is nothing but a predicate

$$\Im: LC \to \mathbb{B}$$

However, the predicate should fulfil certain properties. Formally, a syntactic interface is a predicate

$$\Im: LC \to \mathbb{B}$$

that is closed under the relation $\triangleright$. Formally, then for all components $c1, c2 \in LC$

$$\Im(c1) \wedge c1 \triangleright c2 \Rightarrow \Im(c2)$$

In other words, a syntactic interface $\Im$ characterizes a set of components, such that with every components that is syntactically fine with respect to $\Im$ all its valid syntactic replacements do also fulfil $\Im$.

Formally, a semantic interface is a predicate

$$\Im: LC \to \mathbb{B}$$

that is closed under the relation $\succ$. Then for all components $c1, c2 \in LC$ we assume

$$\Im(c1) \wedge c1 \succ c2 \Rightarrow \Im(c2)$$

In other words, a semantic interface $\Im$ characterizes a set of components such that with every component that is semantically fine with respect to $\Im$ all its valid refinements do also fulfil $\Im$.

The semantic interface $\Im$ characterizes a set of components. Logical implication induces a refinement relation on interfaces. This way notions such as compositionality or full abstractness carry over to interfaces.

A consequent methodological step is to consider interface specifications as non-operational components, too. Then in architectures specifications and realized components can be freely combined.

2.8 Final Remarks on the Theory

The introduced theory offers all the concepts introduced and fulfils all the rules given can be found for instance in the approach Focus (see [3]). Actually, such a theory does not exist so far for object orientation.

What we have described in this section is essential for a theory and methodology for the specification and modular design of architectures and their components. Of course, the theory alone is not enough for engineering. Obviously, we need, in addition, a useful syntax to represent interface specifications and architectures. The theory, however, provides a theoretical framework that gives hints which properties an approach with a concrete syntax has to fulfil.

3 Object-Oriented Components and Interfaces

Following the object oriented programming paradigm we introduce the essential syntactic and semantic notions of *method, method specification, interface, class,* and finally that of a *component.* We briefly analyze ideas of design by contract (see [7]).

We repeat the notion of a method, interface, class, and relate it to the concept of component based on the idea of design by contract and on state machines. Throughout this paper we work with only a few basic notations for state machines.

3.1 Methods, Invocations and Return Messages

In this section we introduce an approach to interfaces and components based on ideas used in object oriented software development.

3.1.1 Types, Methods and Invocation Messages

We work with interfaces that refer to the concept of data types. We deal with variable types and constant types. A constant type is basically a set of data values.

Definition. Types
A type is either a *constant* type or a *variable* type. Constant types denote basically sets of data values or class types (being names of classes used as types of the objects of that class). An identifier with constant type denotes a value of that set. A variable type is denoted by Var T where T is a constant type. An identifier with variable type denotes a variable (an attribute) that has assigned a value out of the set of elements of type T.   ❏

A method in object orientation consists syntactically of a method header and method body. Since we are not interested in programming as such nor in the particular code forming the method body we just deal with syntactic method headers in the following.

Definition. Method header
A method header has the syntactic form

$$\textbf{Method } m\ (p_1 : T_1, \dots , p_n : T_n)$$

where $p_1, \dots , p_n$ are identifiers for parameters and $T_1, \dots , T_n$ their types. Identifiers with constant types carry input and those with variable types serve for output (carrying results). To keep notation simple we consider only methods with one constant parameter w and one variable parameter v; thus the headers read

$$\textbf{Method } m\ (w : WT, v : Var\ VT)$$

where WT and VT are constant types. The set of method invocations INVOC(m) for the method m is defined by the following equation:

$$INVOC(m) = \{ m(b_1, b_2, w, v, v') : w \in WT, v, v' \in VT, b_1, b_2 \in Object \}$$

where the phrase $p \in T$ expresses that p is a value of type T and m(b1, b2, w, v, v') denotes a tuple of values. Here b1 denotes the caller and b2 the callee, v denotes the value of the variable parameter before and v' its value after the end of the execution of the method invocation.   ❏

In design by contract we treat method invocations as atomic state changes. Later we treat method invocations as sequences of state changes, starting with the method invocation and ending with the corresponding method return message. In the later case, the asynchronous case, method invocations correspond to two messages.

Definition. In- and Out-Messages for a method header
A method invocation consists of two interactions of messages called *the method invocation message* and the *return message*. Given a method header (for explanations see above)

$$\textbf{Method } m \ (w : WT, v : Var \ VT)$$

the corresponding set of invocation messages is defined by the following equation

$$SINVOC(m) = \{m(b_1, b_2, w, v): w \in WT, v \in VT, b_1, b_2 \in Object\}$$

Here we treat variables as call-by-value-return parameters. The v represents the value of the variable parameter before the call. The return message has the type (where v' is the value of the variable after the execution of the method invocation)

$$RINVOC(m) = \{m(b_1, b_2, v'): v' \in VT, b_1, b_2 \in Object\}$$

With each method we associate this way two types of messages, the invocation message and the return message.   ❏

Given a set of methods M we define

$$INVOC(M) \ = \ \bigcup_{m \in M} INVOC(m)$$

$$SINVOC(M) \ = \ \bigcup_{m \in M} SINVOC(m)$$

$$RINVOC(M) \ = \ \bigcup_{m \in M} RINVOC(m)$$

This way we denote the set of all possible invocations of methods that are in the set of methods M.

3.1.2 Specification by Contract
A method can be specified by contract as long as we can understand it as a definition of an atomic state change (see [7], [6], [12]). To do that we have to refer to the states of an object or more precisely to the states of an object oriented system before and after the invocation of a method.

Definition. States and their Attributes
The states of the objects of a class are determined by the valuations of the attributes of that class. An attribute is a typed identifier. An attribute set V is a set of the form

$$V = \{a_1 : T_1, \ldots , a_n : T_n\}$$

where $a_1, \ldots , a_n$ are (distinct) identifiers and $T_1, \ldots , T_n$ are their types. A type is either a constant type or a variable type. Variable types have the syntactic form **Var** T where T is a constant type. A valuation of the attribute set V is a mapping

$$\sigma: V \to UD$$

where UD is universe of data values. Of course, we assume for each valuation σ that for each attribute a the value σ (a) has the type given to the attribute. σ is also called a (data) state of V. By Σ (V) we denote the set of all states for V. In the following we consider for simplicity only classes with only one attribute a : Var AT.   ❑

Given the concept of a state of attributes and objects we now define what it means to write a specification by contract for a method.

Definition. Specification by contract for a Method
Let V = {a : Var AT} be an attribute set. A *specification by contract* for a method with header

Method m (w : WT, v : Var VT)

in a class with attribute set V is given by

> **Method** m (w : WT, v : Var VT)
>> **pre**   P(w, v, a)
>> **post**   Q(w, v, a, v', a')

Here P(w, v, a) and Q(w, v, a, v', a') denote predicates – more precisely formulas in predicate logic called *assertions* which contain w, v, a and w, v, a, v', a' as their free variables. We assume that each "primed" variable v' and a' denotes the value of that variable in the state after the termination of the invocation.   ❑

Example. Design by contract
The following section gives a syntactic interface of the class List. We consider only one method here and assume only one attribute

u : **Var** Seq Data

We give the following example of design by contract for a method that gets access ("reads") the ith element of sequence v:

> **Method** get (i : Nat, r : **Var** Data);
>> **pre** $1 \le i \le$ length(u)
>> **post**   r' = ith(i, u) $\wedge$ u' = u

Here we assume that the functions length (yielding the length of a sequence) and ith (yielding the i-th element of a sequence) are predefined for sequences, for instance, by an algebraic data type specification. It is essential to write also u' = u to express that the value of the attribute u is not changed by the execution of the method invocation.   ❑

It is important to emphasize that the design by contract approach requires knowledge about the local state structure of the respective class and object, determined by the attribute names and their types.

3.2 Object Oriented Interfaces

In this section we formalize the concept of an interface and that of the behavior of classes. We start with syntactic aspects and then go on treating behavioral aspects.

3.2.1 Simple Export Interfaces

We start with interfaces of conventional classes which we call *export classes*. An object oriented export interface is described simply by a collection of (exported) class names and the methods associated with them. The description of a syntactic class interface obviously is very simple. It is the collection of a set of syntactic method headers. Nothing is said about behavioral aspects.

Definition. Syntactic export interface

A *syntactic export interface* consists of a set of class types (names) and for each class a set M of method headers. Of course, we assume for simplicity that all methods have different names, since we do not want to deal with overloading.   ❑

Of course, we gain more flexibility, if we consider also sets of objects as part of the interface. Since we are rather interested in foundational issues, we do not do that. Nevertheless, the approach can schematically be extended into this direction.

In the following we discuss semantic, behavioral notions of interfaces in object orientation.

3.2.2 Specification by Contract for Export Interfaces

In this section we show how to express a specification by of classes contract. It is essentially based on the way to specify methods by contract as introduced above.

Definition. State transition assertion

Given a set of attributes $V = \{a : AT\}$ a *state transition assertion* is an assertion

$$R(a, a')$$

that restricts the state changes and also the set of reachable states. If the primed attributes a' do not occur in the assertion, we speak of a *state assertion*, otherwise of a state transition assertion.   ❑

We use state transition assertions and state assertions to provide behavioral specifications for classes in addition to the assertions given for methods in the design by contract. Now we give the definition of the specification of a class by design by contract.

Definition. Specification by contract of classes

For a *syntactic interface* consisting of a set of method headers a specification by contract is given by a set of typed attributes defining the class state and a specification by contract for each of its methods. In addition, a state transition assertion R may be given restricting the state changes and a state assertion defining the initial properties. R defines by the formula

$$\exists\, a' : R(a, a')$$

also an invariant.   ❑

An invariant R for an export interface expresses that each method call fulfills R. This means that $R(a, a')$ holds for every invocation where a is the attribute value before and a' is the attribute value after the invocation.

Example

For the attribute a the relation a' = a+1 used as an invariant expresses that each method invocation increases the value of a by one.   ❑

In the next section we show the relation to state machines.

3.2.3 Export Interfaces Described by State Machines

The specification by contract takes an atomic state transition view. Every method invocation results in an atomic state transition. The pre- and post-conditions characterize the states under which such an invocation can take place to guarantee a certain property of the generated state. In this section we show that this way essentially a state machine is defined (see [10]).

Definition. Class state machine for an export interface

Given an interface with an attribute set and a set of methods M the associated state transition function is a partial function of the form

$$\Delta: \Sigma(V) \times \text{INVOC}(M) \to (\Sigma(V) \cup \{\bot\})\ \textit{partial}$$

Here for $m \in \text{INVOC}(M)$ and $s, s' \in \Sigma(V)$ the equation $\Delta(s, m) = s'$ expresses that in state s the method invocation m is enabled and leads to the state s' (note that m includes the results of the invocation – thus if m is not enabled in state s it may simply mean that the results indicated in m of the method invocation cannot occur). If $\Delta(s, m)$ does not have a defined result, this means that the method invocation m is not enabled in state s. $\Delta(s, m) = \bot$ expresses that the method invocation does not terminate. In addition, we assume a set of initial states $I\Sigma \subseteq \Sigma(V)$.   ❑

The state machine associated with a class is easily defined via the specification by contract. Give a method invocation $m(c_1, c_2, w, v, v')$ for method m with precondition P(w, v, a) and post-condition Q(w, v, a, v', a'), we get (if the call terminates):

$$\Delta(\sigma, m) = \{\sigma': P(w, v, \sigma(a)) \land Q(w, v, a, v', \sigma'(a))\}$$

The difference between a state transition diagram specification of a class and a specification by contract is mainly a methodological one. In the first case we consider the states and define which method calls are possible in each state and to which successor state they lead. In the second case we specify for each method in which states they may be invoked leading to which successor states.

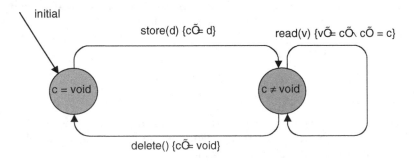

Fig. 1. State Transition Diagram for the Interface of the Cell

Mainly for demonstration purposes we introduce a simple example of a class called Cell. Let Data be a given type of data elements.

Example. Memory Cell

The memory cell is specified by contract easily as follows.

```
Class Cell =
{            c: Var Data | {void}
             initial c = void

             Method store (d: Data)
                pre   c = void
                post  c' = d

             Method read (v: Var Data)
                pre   c ≠ void
                post  c' = c ∧ v' = c

             Method delete ()
                pre   c ≠ void
                post  c' = void
}
```

This defines the interface of a very simple memory cell. Here there is no nontrivial invariant involved since all states are reachable.   ❏

It is easy to provide a state transition description for the state machine modelling a cell as it is shown in Fig. 1.

3.3 Closed View: Systems

By classes with export interfaces we get a closed view onto object oriented systems. Two systems with export-only interfaces cannot be composed in a nontrivial way since all we can do with these systems is to call their methods. Therefore we conclude that such classes describe systems, but not general components.

For closed system we get a very simple concept of observability. What we can observe is the sequences of method calls, and, in particular, whether method calls terminate and which results they produce.

4 Open View: Components

In this section we develop a concept of a component for object orientation. A component is a syntactic unit that can be composed.

4.1 Forwarded Method Invocations

To be able to compose two components in a way that they cooperate they have to exchange information. The only way to do this in object orientation is by mutual method invocation. The possibilities to allow for such forwarded calls and to compose components on this basis are discussed in the following.

The specification of export-only interfaces is particularly simple since it can rely on a very simple control flow. By each method invocation exactly one state transition is executed. The control is transferred to the component and returned at once. A method invocation is seen as an atomic possible huge state change this way. This is also called the synchronous view. This makes the execution model extremely simple – too simple for the component world.

The simplicity of this situation changes significantly if we allow and consider additional invocations of methods during the execution of methods. We speak of *forwarded method calls*. This way we get a considerably more complex execution model. A method invocation can be seen as an atomic state change then only, if we comprise also state changes for the objects affected by the forwarded method invocations in this state change. As a consequence the method invocations change not only the local attributes of the called object, but also those of other objects.

In this section we consider further invocations of methods during the execution of method calls. Then we need a more involved execution model. A method invocation can be seen as an atomic state change only, as long as we comprise also state changes for all the objects affected by the forwarded method invocations. As an effect we do no longer consider a single class or a single object with an encapsulated state changed by the method invocations. We consider a family of objects the encapsulated states of which are changed by a method invocation by forwarded method calls.

4.1.1 Interactive Method Invocation Illustrated by MSCs

In this section we do not understand method calls as events that result in atomic huge state changes for all the objects affected by forwarded message calls, but consider the addressed class and object in isolation. A message sequence chart can nicely represent an instance of the interaction behavior of an interactive method invocation. An example for a method get is shown in Fig. 2.

Here we simplify the representation of the method invocation messages and the return messages in diagrams. We do not list the identifier of the object in the

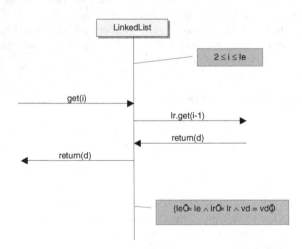

Fig. 2. Message sequence chart for the method get

invocations explicitly. The message return(d) stands for a return message with the return variable r with r = d. We can give or even generate a message sequence chart for each of the state transitions, however, the number of message sequence charts can be very high – even infinite. We study the situation of forwarded method invocations in a more systematic way in the following section.

4.2 Export/Import Interfaces

In general, in object orientation, a class uses other classes via their methods as sub-services to offer its interface behavior. Thus a class on one hand offers methods to its environment called an export method and on the other hand invokes methods of other classes called import methods. We speak of the *exported* methods and the *imported* methods of a class. This is captured by import/export interfaces.

In the following we deal with issues related to the import and export of interfaces in more detail.

4.2.1 Syntax of Export/Import Interfaces

In the case of forwarded calls we deal with classes dealing with two kinds of methods, imported and exported ones. This should be explicitly reflected in the syntactic and semantic interface. Every interface specification with an explicit import part and an explicit export part defines a so-called export/import interface.

Definition. Syntactic export/import interface

A *syntactic export/import interface* consists of two syntactic interfaces represented by two sets of method headers, the export and the import methods. For simplicity, we assume that all methods in the export and import interfaces have different names, since we do not want to deal with overloading. Given an export/import interface of a component c we denote by EX(c) its export interface and by IM(c) its import interfaces, both being simple one-way interfaces.   ❏

A syntactic export/import interface can easily be described graphically as it is shown in Fig. 3.

A class in object oriented programming, in general, uses other classes in forwarded method invocations and therefore in general has an export/import interface in spite of the fact that the idea of explicit imported interfaces is surprisingly not supported by most of the conventional object oriented techniques. Often the import interface is kept implicit for classes and not mentioned at all.

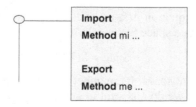

Fig. 3. Graphical representation of an export/import interface

4.2.2 Control Flow and the Call Stack

When dealing with export/import interfaces there may be call-backs, in general. In other words, a method invocation for object b may lead to a forwarded call that in turn may lead to invocation of methods of object b. We speak of a call-back. If the number of forwarded calls and possible call-backs is not statically bounded, we need additional attributes in the local state of the interface to be able to find the correct continuation for returned invocations (in the sense of the return addresses for subroutine calls in assembler languages).

In the general case, we use a full call stack. The call stack is the classical way to manage nested procedure calls or method invocations. Every time a procedure or method is called, the parameters and the return address are pushed onto the call stack. This way the call stack has to deal with control as well as data aspects. The call stack determines the continuation after the return of a forwarded call and provides the local state information providing the values of the parameters of the call under execution.

4.2.3 Export/Import Interfaces by State Machines with I/O

In this section we demonstrate how to describe the behavior of export/import interfaces by state machines. Since we have a set of in- and out-messages related to each of the method headers, this easily generalizes to class interfaces.

Definition. In- and Out-Messages of a syntactic class interface

Let c be a syntactic export/import interface with set $EX(c)$ of export methods in the set $IM(c)$ of import methods. It defines a set $In(c)$ of ingoing messages

$$In(c) = SINVOC(EX(c)) \cup RINVOC(IM(c))$$

and of a set of outgoing messages $Out(c)$ specified by

$$Out(c) = SINVOC(IM(c)) \cup RINVOC(EX(c)) \qquad \square$$

Since we have a set of in- and out-messages related to each of the method headers of an export/import interface, we construct a state machine that describes the behavior of the export/import interface. It uses the invocation messages in the export interface and the return messages in the import interface as input and the invocation messages in the import interface and the return messages in the export interface as output.

Definition. Export/import state machine

Given an interface c with an attribute set V and a set of methods, the associated state machine has the form (here we work with a total function)

$$\Delta: State \times In(c) \rightarrow ((State \times Out(c)) \cup \{\bot\})$$

Here for $m \in In(IF)$ the equation $\Delta(s, m) = \bot$ expresses that the method invocation does not terminate. The state space State is defined by

$$State = \Sigma(V) \times CS$$

Here CS is the control state space. Its members can be understood as representations of the control stack. Since we do not want to go deeper into the very technical discussion of control stacks, we do not further specify CS. Of course, we assume that a set of initial states $IState \subseteq State$ is given. $\qquad \square$

A convenient way to describe I/O state machines is a state transition diagram. In the case of asynchronous models of method invocations we work with state machines with input and output called Mealy machines.

It is not difficult to go - in the case of export-only interfaces - from such a Mealy machine

$$\Delta: \text{State} \times \text{In}(\text{IF}) \rightarrow (\text{State} \times \text{Out}(\text{IF})) \cup \{\bot\})$$

to the kind of state machines

$$\Delta': \Sigma(V) \times \text{INVOC}(M) \rightarrow (\Sigma(V) \cup \{\bot\})$$

we have introduced for export-only interfaces. In the case of export-only interfaces the only output messages that exist are return messages. Each transition $(s', y) = \Delta(s, x)$ determines a transition $z' = \Delta(z, c)$ and vice versa. From $(s', y) = \Delta(s, x)$ we easily construct the data states $z, z' \in \Sigma(V)$ from s and s' since in this case the control stack is trivial. The message $c \in \text{INVOC}(M)$ with $c = m(b_1, b_2, w, v, v')$ with $z' = \Delta(z, c)$ is determined by $x = m(b_1, b_2, w, v)$, $y = m(b_1, b_2, v')$.

4.2.4 Observability for Export/Import Interfaces

For an interface with export and import it makes an essential difference how a system is seen from the import/export point of view either making the import explicit or keeping it implicit. For a useful interface description, we have to make the export explicit. This leads to another idea of observability. Now we observe sequences of alternating input and output actions as well as the termination of method invocation.

Actually we have now two ways of non-termination. In one case an input message m in a state s may not lead to an output message. This is indicated by $\Delta(s, m) = \bot$. Moreover, a method invocation will lead to an infinite sequence of in- and out-messages under certain reactions of the environment.

In this model of observability using I/O state machines we can even do a step in the direction of concurrency using interleaving. Assume, we send a method invocation method to a component that triggers an invocation of an import method representing a forwarded method call. Then a sequential execution the next input message could only be another invocation message (triggered by a back-call) or the return message to the previous call. But nothing prevents us from giving an arbitrary invocation message (which cannot be distinguished from a back-call, anyhow) and thus to handle interleaved independent method invocations. We only have to place return messages at the right places in the input streams. Thus we get a restricted form of concurrency.

4.2.5 Concurrency and Multi-threading

So far we have mainly considered sequential control flow without concurrency. In more technical terms we did only consider executions of one thread. This kept our execution model simple. In large distributed systems a more complex situation is mandatory. There are several threads executed concurrently. Then it is no longer valid that a method invocation leads to a sequence of method invocations and return mes-sages that is completed before the next method invocation takes place. New method invocations from other threads may arrive before a method invocation sequence is completed. Several method invocations are executed, in general, in an interleaving mode.

Decomposing a method call into to complementary method exchanges, the invocation call and the return, which is done to be able to have open specifications of components and classes gives an interesting additional option: now we may (or may not) accept further method invocations before a method call has been completely executed – before is has sent back its return message. This forces us to freely introduce interleavings of calls and to introduce language constructs that allow us to avoid them in cases where calls should be completed before further calls are processed (mutual exclusion).

As a result of concurrency and multi-threading we get interleaving of single threaded invocation sequences. This leads also to issues of synchronization to be able to control the interleaving. Note that now the invocation stack has to be replaced by a individual stack for each thread.

4.3   Towards a Theory of Components and Architectures in OO

In this chapter we discuss where we are with a theory of components and architectures in object orientation. In this section we relate the introduced notion of object orientation to those of the theory introduced in section 3. We discuss the state of the art and methodological challenges.

4.3.1   What Is a Component in Object Orientation

In object orientation an obvious choice for the notion of a component is a class. Actually one can argue that objects should be considered components. We, however, prefer to see components as building blocks at design time in contrast to objects that are rather building blocks at runtime. So, for our purpose, classes or compounds of classes are an obvious choice. But is a class really a good choice for the notion of a component?

Obviously classes show a lot addressing the idea of components. There is a notion of interface, state encapsulation, and information hiding for classes as we would expect it for components. There at least two arguments, however, throwing some doubts on classes being good candidates for components:

- Classes are too small. Actually, of course, one may argue that we can write very large classes. But then we get unstructured huge entities. We need for components larger building blocks with additional hierarchical structuring concepts.
- Classes do not support concurrency.
- There is no tractable interface specification technique for classes with export and import.

This shows that classes, although they provide concepts close to what we need for components, fail to address necessary requirements for the notion of components.

4.3.2   What Is Composition in Object Orientation

There is no widely accepted concept of composition in object orientation. Never-theless, it is not so difficult to define a concept for composition in object orientation. Giving two classes with export and import methods (where import methods are related to objects of certain classes), we can compose them in a way, where classes may mutually call methods in their import signature that are in the export signature of the other class. We speak of internal calls. For simplicity, we ignore any problems that may arise with inheritance and method overloading where methods may be called for classes with names that do not occur in the export of the class or methods. So we concentrate on the method names and ignore any aliasing.

We start with the definition, when two classes can be defined. Given classes c_i with $i = 1, 2$, and export signature $EX(c_i)$ and import $IM(c_i)$ we define that $\Re(\{c_1, c_2\})$ holds, if there are no name conflicts. Then export signature EX and import IM of the result of the composition $c_1 \otimes c_2$ is defined by

$$EX(c_1 \otimes c_2) = (EX(c_1) \setminus IM(c_2)) \cup (EX(c_2) \setminus IM(c_1))$$

$$IM(c_1 \otimes c_2) = (IM(c_1) \setminus EX(c_2)) \cup (IM(c_2) \setminus EX(c_1))$$

In other words, in the composed class $c = c_1 \otimes c_2$ exports what is exported by one of the classes and not imported by the other one and imports what is imported by one of its component classes and not exported by the other one.

Next we consider the semantic composition of the two state machines associated with the classes ($i = 1, 2$)

$$\Delta_i: State_i \times In(c_i) \rightarrow (State_i \times Out(c_i)) \cup \{\bot\}$$

Now we define the composed state machine

$$\Delta: State \times In(c) \rightarrow (State \times Out(c)) \cup \{\bot\}$$

as follows

$$State = State_1 \times State_2$$

and for $x \in In(c)$ and $(s_1, s_2) \in State_1 \times State_2$ we define:

$$x \in In(c_1) \wedge (s'_1, y) = \Delta_1(s_1, x) \Rightarrow$$
$$y \in In(c_2) \Rightarrow \Delta((s_1, s_2), x) = \Delta((s'_1, s_2), y)$$
$$y \notin In(c_2) \Rightarrow \Delta((s_1, s_2), x) = ((s'_1, s_2), y)$$

$$x \in In(c_1) \wedge \Delta_1(s_1, x) = \bot \Rightarrow \Delta((s_1, s_2), x) = \bot$$

In other words, we give the input to that state machine to which the input fits. If the output is in the input of the other state machine, we do another state transformation. If this is done forever, then the state transition does not terminate, and thus $\Delta((s_1, s_2), x) = \bot$. In analogy we define the case where the input goes to the second component:

$$x \in In(c_2) \wedge (s'_2, y) \in \Delta_2(s_2, x) \Rightarrow$$
$$y \in In(c_1) \Rightarrow \Delta((s_1, s_2), x) = \Delta((s_1, s'_2), y)$$
$$y \notin In(c_1) \Rightarrow \Delta((s_1, s_2), x) = ((s_1, s'_2), y)$$

$$x \in In(c_2) \wedge \Delta_2(s_2, x) = \bot \Rightarrow \Delta((s_1, s_2), x) = \bot$$

This gives a recursive definition for the state transition function Δ. Actually, this way of definition results in a classical least fixpoint characterization of Δ.

4.3.3 What Is a System in Object Orientation

A system in terms of our theory in object orientation is a class (perhaps a composed one) with an empty import signature. A system nevertheless can actually be composed with a component in an interesting way. Consider a system s with export set EX(s) and import set IM(s) = $\varnothing$ and a component c with EX(s) $\subseteq$ IM(c). Then c $\otimes$ s describes a composed system where s is used as a local sub-system. For two systems composition degrades to the union of the signatures.

5 Conclusion

We have defined a first step of an instance of a theory of components, interfaces, and composition in object orientation. What we presented is certainly not sufficient for practical purposes. However, it gives a first idea what can be achieved and shows the limitations of existing approaches and unsolved problems.

Perhaps, it is worthwhile to draw a bottom line for what we have achieved by out theory and also to draw some conclusions:

- We defined a concept of component in OO as a generalization of the concept of a class: a component is a set of classes and their visible methods, divided into export, import and internal (hidden) ones.
- We described a model for this concept of components, namely state machines with input and output.
- We introduced composition for this concept of components.
- But we pay a (too) high price: we have to make the call stack explicit in the state space of the machine, in general.

There seems to be only one way out: introducing an explicit notion of a component, defining a wrapper for a set of classes and the methods (being the components in object orientation as we have introduced them), and connecting them by asynchronous message passing.

To be continued ...

Acknowledgement

It is a pleasure to thank Gerd Beneken, Bernhard Rumpe, Johannes Siedersleben, and Arnd Poetzsch-Heffter for discussions and feedback while writing this paper.

References

1. L. de Alfaro, T.A. Henzinger: Interface-Based Design. In: Engineering Theories of Software Intensive Systems, proceedings of the Marktoberdorf Summer School, Kluwer (2004)
2. M. Broy, C. Hofmann, I. Krüger, M Schmidt: A Graphical Description Technique for Communication in Software Architectures. In: Joint 1997 Asia Pacific Software Engineering Conference and International Computer Science Conference (APSEC'97/ ICSC'97)
3. M. Broy, K. Stølen: Specification and Development of Interactive Systems: Focus on Streams, Interfaces, and Refinement. Springer (2001)

4. D. Herzberg, M. Broy: Modelling Layered Distributed Communication Systems. To appear
5. H.-A. Jacobsen, Bernd J. Krämer: Modeling Interface Definition Language Extensions. TOOLS Pacific 2000, Sydney, (November 2000) 242–252
6. I. Krüger, R. Grosu, P. Scholz, M. Broy: From MSCs to statecharts. In: Proceedings of DIPES'98, Kluwer (1999)
7. B. Meyer: Object-oriented Software Construction, Prentice Hall (1988)
8. D. Parnas: On the criteria to be used to decompose systems into modules. Comm. ACM 15, (1972) 1053–1058
9. P. Müller, A. Poetzsch-Heffter: Modular Specification and Verification Techniques for Object-Oriented Software Components. In: Leavens, G. T. and Sitaraman, M. (eds.): Foundations of Component-Based Systems, Cambridge University Press (2000)
10. Oscar Nierstrasz: Regular Types for Active Objects. OOPSLA 1993: 1–15
11. A. Poetzsch-Heffter: Specification and Verification of Object-Oriented Programs. Habilitation thesis, Technical University of Munich (1997)
12. R. H. Reussner, H. W. Schmidt, I. Poernomo: Reliability Prediction for Component-Based Software Architectures. Journal of Systems and Software -- Special Issue of Software Architecture - Engineering Quality Attributes, 3:66 (2003) 241–252
13. B. Selic, G. Gullekson. P.T. Ward: Real-time Objectoriented Modeling. Wiley, New York (1994)
14. M. Spivey: Understanding Z - A Specification Language and Its Formal Semantics. Cambridge Tracts in Theoretical Computer Science 3, Cambridge University Press (1988)
15. P. Wegner, S. B. Zdonik: Inheritance as an Incremental Modification Mechanism or What Like Is and Isn't Like. In Proceedings ECOOP '88, ed. S. Gjessing and K. Nygaard, Lecture Notes in Computer Science 322, Springer-Verlag, Oslo, Aug. 15–17 (1988) 55–77.
16. G. Booch, J. Rumbaugh, I. Jacobson: The Unified Modeling Language for Object-Oriented Development, Version 1.0, RATIONAL Software Cooperation
17. Daniel M. Yellin, Robert E. Strom: Protocol Specifications and Component Adaptors. ACM Trans. Program. Lang. Syst. 19(2) (1997) 292–333

Making Specifications Complete Through Models

Bernd Schoeller[1], Tobias Widmer[2], and Bertrand Meyer[1]

[1] ETH Zurich, Switzerland
[2] IBM Research, Zurich, Switzerland

Abstract. Good components need precise contracts. In the practice of Design by Contract[TM], applications and libraries typically express, in their postconditions and class invariants, only a subset of the relevant properties. We present:

- An approach to making these contract elements complete without extending the assertion language, by relying on "model classes" directly deduced from mathematical concepts.
- An actual "Mathematical Model Library" (MML) built for that purpose
- A method for using MML to express complete contracts through abstraction functions, and an associated theory of specification soundness.
- As a direct application of these ideas, a new version of a widely used data structure and algorithms library equipped with complete contracts through MML.

All the software is available for download. The approach retains the pragmatism of the Design by Contract method, suitable for ordinary applications and understandable to ordinary programmers, while potentially achieving the benefits of much heavier formal specifications.

The article concludes with a discussion of applications to testing and program proving, and of remaining issues.

1 Introduction

Professional-quality components should be accompanied by precise specifications, or "contracts", of their functionality. Contracts as written today are often incomplete; we will discuss how to make them complete through the use of a model library.

The rest of section 1 discusses contracts and the problem of how to make them complete. Section 2 outlines the key element of our solution: the notion of model. Section 3 describes our application of this concept: the Mathematical Model Library (MML) which we have developed for this work. Section 4 explains how then to use MML to turn incomplete contracts into complete ones. Section 5 describes how we applied this approach to provide a completely contracted version of a widely used data structure and fundamental algorithms library. Section 6 presents a comparison with earlier uses of models for specification. Section 7 is a conclusion and presentation of future work.

R.H. Reussner et al. (Eds.): Architecting Systems, LNCS 3938, pp. 48–70, 2006.
© Springer-Verlag Berlin Heidelberg 2006

1.1   Contracts

Before they will accept a large-scale switch to Component-Based Development, organizations with a significant stake in the correct functioning of their software need some guarantee that the components they include in their applications will themselves perform correctly. The first step is to know what exactly each of these components is supposed to do.

The Design by Contract^{TM}techniques of Eiffel address this issue: every component is characterized by contract elements specifying its abstract relationship to other software elements. An individual operation (feature) has a *precondition*, stating what initial conditions it expects from its callers, and a *postcondition* stating what it provides in return; a group of operations (class) has an *invariant*, stating consistency conditions which each of these operations must preserve and each initialization mechanism (creation procedure) must ensure initially.

Design by Contract provides a number of advantages [21]: a methodological basis for analysis, design and implementation of correct software; automatic documentation, such as the class abstracters present in Eiffel environments extract from the class texts themselves; help for project management; a disciplined approach to inheritance, polymorphism and dynamic binding; and support for testing and debugging, including [8] component tests automatically generated and run from the contracts. An important characteristic of these techniques as available in Eiffel is that they are not for academic research but for practical use by developers, and indeed libraries such as EiffelBase [20,18,10] covering fundamental data structures and algorithms are extensively equipped with contracts. This distinguishes the context of the present study from extensions to Java or other languages (such as JML [16] or iContract [14]), which require the use of tools, libraries and language extensions different from what programmers actually use for real programs. We are closer in this respect to frameworks such as Spec# [2]

This pragmatic focus also explains why Design by Contract distinguishes itself from more heavy-duty "formal methods" in its attitude to specification *completeness*: you can benefit from the various advantages of contracts mentioned above even if your contracts express only part of the relevant specification properties. More precisely, in the practice of Design by Contract as illustrated by the Eiffel libraries:

- Preconditions tend to be complete. Specifying "**require** *cond*" enables the routine to assume that condition *cond* will hold on entry, and not to provide any guarantee if it doesn't. Clearly, this is safe only if the routine specifies such conditions exhaustively.
- Postconditions and class invariants, however, are often underspecified; the next section will give typical examples. Unlike with preconditions, there is no obviously disastrous consequence; operations simply advertise less than they guarantee or (in the invariant case) maintain. The same holds for other uses of contracts: loop invariants and loop variants.

Why are such specification elements incomplete? There are three common justifications:

- Economy of effort (or, less politely, laziness): expressing complete specifications would require more effort than is deemed beneficial.
- Limitations of the specification language: in the absence of higher-level mechanisms, such as first-order predicate calculus ("for all", and "there exists" quantifiers), some specifications appear impossible to express; an example would be "All the elements of this list are positive".
- The difficulty of expressing postconditions that depend on a previous state of the computation

This discussion will show that there is no theoretical impossibility, and will propose an approach that makes it possible to express complete specifications and apply them to practical libraries such as EiffelBase [10].

1.2   Incomplete Contracts

A typical feature exhibiting incomplete postconditions is *put* from class *STACK* of EiffelBase describing the abstract notion of stack, and its descendants providing various implementations of stacks. It implements the "push" operation on stacks (the name *put* is a result of the strict consistency policy of Eiffel libraries [18,20]). In its "flat" form taking inheritance of assertions into account, it reads

```
put (v: like item)
        -- Push 'v' onto top.
    require
        not_full: not full
    ... Implementation, or "deferred" mark ...
    ensure
        item_on_top: item = v
        count_increased: count = old count + 1
    end
```

The query *item* yields the top of the stack, and the query *count* its number of items; *full* tells whether a stack's representation is full (never true for an unbounded stack).

The precondition is complete: if the stack is not full, you may always push an element onto it. The postcondition, however, is not: it only talks about the number of items and the top item after the operation, but doesn't say what happens to the items already present. As a result:

- It leaves some questions unanswered, for example, what will get printed by
    ```
    create stack.make_empty
    stack.put (1)
    stack.put (2)
    stack.remove
    print (stack.item)
    ```

whereas the corresponding abstract data type specification [21] is sufficient to compute the corresponding mathematical expression: *item (remove (put (put (new, 1), 2)))*.

- It leaves the possibility of manifestly erroneous or hostile implementations, for example one that would push v but change some of the previously present items.

The specification of *STACK*, like most specifications in existing libraries, tells the truth, and tells only the truth; but it does not tell the whole truth.

For most practical applications of Design by Contract, these limitations have so far been considered acceptable. But it is desirable to go further, in particular to achieve the prospect of actual *proofs* of class correctness. Proving a class correct means proving that its implementation satisfies its contracts; this will require the specifications to be complete.

1.3   Approaches to Completing the Contracts

To address the issue of incomplete specifications, and obtain contracts that tell the whole truth, we may envision several possibilities.

A first solution is to extend the assertion language. In Eiffel and most other formalisms that have applied similar ideas, assertions are essentially Boolean expressions, with two important additions:

- The **old** notation, as used in the last postcondition clause (labeled count_increased:), making it possible to refer to the value of an expression as captured on routine entry (a "previous state of the computation" as mentioned in the earlier terminology).
- The **only** clause of ECMA Eiffel [24] (similar to the "modifies" clause of some other formalisms), stating that the modifying effect of a feature is limited to a specific set of queries; a clause **only** a, b, ... is equivalent to a set of clauses of the form $q = $ **old** q for all the queries q not listed in a, b, ...

This conspicuously does not include first-order predicate calculus mechanisms.

It is conceivable to extend the assertion language to include first-order constructs; the Object Constraint Language [30] for UML has some built-in quantifiers for that purpose. We do not adopt this approach for several reasons. One is that first-order calculus is often insufficient anyway; it doesn't help us much to express (in a graph class) an assertion such as "the graph has no cycles". Another more practical reason is that it is important in the spirit of Design by Contract to retain the close connection between the assertion language and the rest of the language, part of the general **seamlessness** of the method. In particular, for applications to testing and debugging — which will remain essential until proofs become widely practical — it is important to continue ensuring that assertions can be evaluated at reasonable cost during execution. This rules out properties of the form "For all objects, ..." or "For all objects of type T, ...". Properties of the form "For all objects in data structure D, ...", on the other hand, are easy to handle through Eiffel's **agent** mechanism [9,25]. For example, we state that "all values in the list of integers *il* are positive" through the simple Boolean expression

$il.for\_all$ (**agent** *is_positive*)

using a simple query *is_positive*. In the absence of an agent mechanism, it would be still possible, although far more tedious and less elegant, to write a special function for any such case, here *all_positive* applying to a list of integers.

A second solution is to rely on extra features that express all the properties of interest. *all_positive* is a simple example, but we may extend it to more specific features; for example a class such as *STACK* may have a query *body* yielding the stack consisting of all the items except the top one (the same that would result from a "pop" command). We can then add to put a postcondition

$body === $ **old** *Current*

where $===$ is *object equality*. This technique works and has the advantage that it is not subject to the limitations of first-order predicate calculus; in our graph example we may write a query *acyclic* — a routine in the corresponding class — that ascertains the absence of cycles. The disadvantage, however, is to pollute classes with numerous extra features useful for specification only. In addition, we must be particularly careful to ensure that such features can produce no state change. The solution retained below is in part inspired by this approach but puts the specification features in separate classes with impeccable mathematical credentials.

A third solution would be to refer explicitly, in contracts, to internal (non-exported) elements of the objects' state. This is partially what a query such as *body* does, in a more abstract way. But the need for complete specification is not a reason to break the fundamental rules of information hiding and data abstraction.

For the record, we may mention here a fourth solution, as used in some specifications of the ELKS library standard [29], based on [26] and relying on recursive specifications. In the absence of a precise semantic theory it is not clear to us that the specifications are mathematically well-founded.

2   Using Models

The approach we have adopted for specifying libraries retains some of the elements of the second and third solutions above, but through a more abstract technique for describing the state.

2.1   The Notion of Model

The basic idea is to consider that a software object — an instance of any particular class — is a certain computer representation of a certain mathematical entity, simple or complex, called a *model* for the object, and to define the semantics of the applicable operations through their effect on the model.

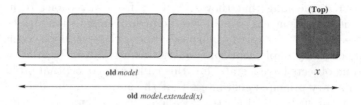

Fig. 1. Sequence model of a stack

As model for a stack, for example we may choose a *sequence*, with the convention that the last element of the sequence corresponds to the top of the stack (although the reverse convention would work too). Figure 1 illustrates this.

Then the effect of *put* can be specified through the model: *put* simply adds the new element at the end of the sequence. We will express this below and see that the existing postconditions (*count* increased by one, *item* denoting the new element) become immediate consequences of this property.

2.2   A Model Library

The model for a software object, as noted, is a mathematical object, such as a set, a sequence, a number, or some combination of any such elementary objects. But we still want to preserve the seamlessness of the approach; this would not be the case if we expressed contracts in a separate mathematical notation, for example a mathematical specification language.

It turns out that a language such as Eiffel is perfectly appropriate to express such concepts. For example we can write a class *MML_SEQUENCE [G]* that directly models the mathematical notion of sequence, and use it in lieu of the mathematical equivalents, as long as we observe a golden rule:

Model Library Principle
Model classes may not have commands.

A *command* (as opposed to *query*), also called a procedure, is a feature that modifies the object state; this is also excluded for purposes of specification. ("Creation procedures" will, however, be permitted, as they are necessary to obtain the mathematical objects in the first place.) For example the *MML_SEQUENCE* class may not have a procedure *extend*, which would modify a sequence by adding an element at the end; but it has a query *extended* such that *s.extended (v)* denotes another sequence with the elements of *s* complemented by an extra one, *v*, at the end.

In Eiffel a query may be implemented as either a *function* ("method" in some programming languages' terminology) or an *attribute* ("field", "data member", "instance variable"). The "Principle of Uniform Access" implies that the difference is not visible from the outside. As detailed below, the basic model classes will be deferred, meaning that they stay away from any choice of implementation; this is how client classes will see them. Implementation classes are also provided (section 3.7) for testing purposes; these classes, representing mathematical objects, may implement some queries as attributes. In other words the corresponding objects have a state, but this causes no conceptual problem since the Model Library principle guarantees that the state is immutable.

Our library of such model classes is called the *Mathematical Model Library* (MML). It is important to note that MML is couched in the programming language — Eiffel — for purposes of expressiveness, convenience and seamlessness only; underneath the syntax, it is a direct expression of well-known and unimpeachable mathematical concepts as could be expressed in a mathematical textbook or in a formal specification language such as Z [33] or B [1].

Instead of relying on explicit knowledge of the state, the contracts will rely on abstract properties of the associated model. We add to every relevant class a query

$$model: SOME\_MML\_TYPE$$

and then rely on *model* to express complete contracts for the class and its features. Taking advantage of the "selective export" facility of Eiffel [19,25], we declare *model* in a clause labeled

feature {*SPECIFICATION*}

which implies that, depending on the view they choose, client programmers will, through the documentation tools in the environment, either see it or not. For simple-minded uses, it is preferable to ignore it; as soon as one is interested in advanced specification, tests or proofs, it is preferable to retain it.

The model describes a kind of abstract implementation of the concept underlying a class. As an implementation, however, it is purely mathematical and does not interfere with the rest of the class. In particular, the approach described here has no effect whatsoever on performance in normal operational circumstances, where contract monitoring is usually disabled. If contract monitoring is on (for debugging or testing), options should be available to include or exclude the extra "model contracts".

2.3   Model Example

Let us now express how to use the notion of model on our earlier example of an unbounded stack. We use an *MML_SEQUENCE* as model for a stack. To this effect we add to class *STACK* a query:

feature {*SPECIFICATION*} -- Model

$$model: MML\_SEQUENCE\ [G]$$
  ensure
    not_void: **Result** $/ =$ **Void**

Based on this model, we can complete the contract of *put* by adding the model-based properties:

> *put (v:* **like** *item)*
>> -- Push 'v' onto top.
>
>> *require*
>>> not_full: **not** *full*
>>
>> **do**
>>> ... *Implementation* ...
>>
>> **ensure**
>>> model_extended: *model* === **old** *model.extended (v)*
>>> item_on_top: *item* = *v*
>>> count_increased: *count* = **old** *count + 1*
>
>> **end**

The assertion *model* === **old** *model.extended (v)* states that the model after the feature invocation is the same as the model before the feature invocation except that *v* has been added to the end of the sequence. In a formalism such as Z it would be expressed as the following before-after predicate (where :: is the operator for appending a value to a sequence):

$$model' = model :: v$$

We now have a completely contracted version of *put*: the postcondition specifies the full effect, without revealing details about the implementation [35].

2.4 Theories and Models

As detailed in section 6 (devoted to the comparison with earlier work), models have already been used in several approaches to program specification and verification, notably Larch and JML.

In general, these approaches treat models as additions to the *specification framework*, each created in response to a particular specification need. The model classes themselves have to be contracted in the existing specification language (without model features); the meaning of the model is based solely on its own contracts. We again get into the problems of underspecification, this time within the model library.

MML does not integrate the models into the specification framework, but into the *specification language*. We postulate that the models correctly reflect their theoretical counterparts which, as a consequence, define their semantics. To reason about assertions using models, we translate them into the underlying theory. The contracts of model classes directly reflect axioms and theorems of the associated theory, assumed to have been proved (often long ago, and documented in mathematical textbooks), so we can just take them for granted.

As our basic theory, we choose typed set theory. It is a well-defined formalism, easy to understand for the average software developer; the typed nature of modern programming languages such as Eiffel makes types a familiar concept.

A formalization intended for software modelling purposes can be found in the language of the B method [1] (whose program refinement aspects, studied in [31] in relation to contracts, are not relevant for this work). The availability of theorem provers for this theory [28,34] is an added advantage.

3   Model Library Design

The model library is designed around a set of deferred classes describing the interfaces of the modeling abstractions.

3.1   Model Classes

Eiffel's inheritance and genericity mechanisms enable us to model the definition of powersets, relations, functions, sequences, bag and graphs in terms of sets and pairs. The result reflects the definitions of [1]. Inheritance in particular provides a direct way to represent the subtype relation.

Figure 2 is a BON diagram of the inheritance structure of the principal deferred classes. The top type is *MML_ANY*, with two direct heirs *MML_SET* and *MML_PAIR*. (All the class names have the *MML_* suffix, omitted in the figure except for *MML_ANY*.)

3.2   Specifics of Model Objects

Mathematical objects are different from software objects:

- Mathematical objects are normally immutable: the operation $5 + 1$ does not change 5, but instead describes another number. Similarly, we cannot "add"

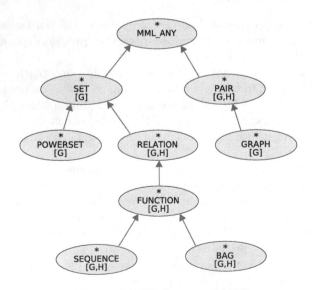

Fig. 2. A BON diagram of MML

an element to a set; rather, we describe new sets by union or intersection of existing sets like in $\{a, b, c\} \cup \{d\} = \{a, b, c, d\}$.
 - They have no notion of identity distinct from their value.

Software objects do not have these properties: they have a mutable state, and an identity independent from their value. MML classes, although expressed in Eiffel, represent mathematical objects and hence must satisfy immutability and not rely on object identity.

3.3   Immutability

Enforcing immutability means that an instance of an MML class, once created, will never change its state. All features of the class other than creation procedures are *pure* (side-effect-free) queries.

3.4   Comparing Mathematical Objects

Not relying on object identity means that comparison operations will never apply to references, but to objects.

Object equality in Eiffel has a predefined version, *default_is_equal*, which compares objects field-by-field, and a redefinable version, *is_equal*, whose semantics also governs the   equality operator. Neither is adequate, however, for defining the equality of model objects, because two Eiffel objects cannot be equal unless they have the same type; in mathematics this is too strong a requirement, even with the type approach we are following. For example an object of type *MML_RELATION [X, Y]* can never be equal, in the Eiffel sense, to an object of type *MML_SET [MML_PAIR [X, Y]]*, whereas mathematically they may represent the same concept (a relation is a set of pairs).

For that reason, *MML_ANY* introduces a special query *equals* to represent mathematical object equality. Its descendants redefine it to describe their specific notions of equality. Every comparison of MML objects should use equals, not *is_equal*. To guarantee this and avoid mistakes, *MML_ANY* and descendants do not export *is_equal*.

Here is the specification of equal in *MML_ANY*:

> *equals* **alias** *"==="* *(other: MML_ANY): BOOLEAN*
> > -- Is *other* mathematically equivalent to current object?
> > **require**
> > > other_not_void: *other* / = **Void**
> > **ensure**
> > > symmetric: **Result implies** *(other.equals (***Current***))*
> > > yes_if_equal_as_objects: *is_equal (other)* **implies Result**

The first postcondition clause expresses symmetry, the second that object equality implies mathematical equality (although, as noted, not necessarily the other way around).

The precondition refers to **Void** values, which will not arise with mathematical objects. This clause will go away thanks to the ECMA Eiffel standard [24] which deals with this issue statically; all MML types will be attached [23] and hence statically guaranteed non-void.

The **alias** clause makes it possible to use $a === b$ as shorthand for $a.equals$ (b).

3.5   Class Overview

Here are some of the features of the MML classes in the top part of the hierarchy as shown in figure 2.

MML_SET is the basic class for the definition of sets as models. It implements most basic operators. Examples of available predicates on sets are *is_member* $(x \in A)$, *is_subset* $(A \subseteq B)$, *is_proper_subset* $(A \subset B)$ or *is_disjoint* $(A \cap B = \emptyset)$. Other operators include *united* $(A \cup B)$, *intersected* $(A \cap B)$, *subtracted* $(A - B)$, *cartesian_product* $(A \times B)$ and so on. The class also provides a non-deterministic choice operator called *any_item*.

MML_PAIR represents tuples of cardinality two. All other types can be described in terms of *MML_PAIR* and *MML_SET*.

MML_RELATION describes relations viewed as sets of pairs. Thanks to inheritance we adapt set operations into operations on relations.

The class then adds another substantial set of relation-specific features: queries such as *is_reflexive* and *is_transitive*, transformations such as *image* and *inversed*.

Relational composition causes the only problem with using the language's type mechanisms to model set-theoretical type rules. The notion of relation involves two generic parameters, representing the types of the source and target sets. But the expression *r1.composed (r2)* requires a third generic type, the target set of *r2*. This cannot be modelled directly since only classes, not features, may have generic parameters.

Our solution is to take *ANY* as the type of the second argument. This has sufficed for the examples we have encountered so far, but we may have in the future to add a third generic parameter to the class just for the sake of the composition operator.

MML_FUNCTION describes possibly partial functions, viewed as a special case of relations. It defines such concepts as partiality and surjectivity.

MML_SEQUENCE, MML_BAG, MML_GRAPH provide the library with a richer set of modeling concepts. Sequences in particular provide part or all of the model for many concepts, including lists, strings, files and others for which the ordering of data is important.

3.6   Quantifiers

To model quantifiers, we use Eiffel's *agent* mechanism. Agents are objects encapsulating features, and hence functionality. These objects are immutable, so the introduction of agents does not affect the "pure" (side-effect-free) requirement on the model library.

The agents we use for our model-based specifications represent predicates. For example $\forall x \in S.P(x)$ will appear as *S.for_all(***agent** *P(?))* where the question mark represents the bound variable — "open argument"' in Eiffel terminology; an agent expression like **agent** *P(?)* where all arguments are open can be abbreviated into just **agent** *P*.

For modularity and ease of use, all the basic quantifier mechanisms based on this technique are grouped into a specific class (a "facet" abstraction [35]) called *MML_QUANTIFIABLE*, with the following two features.

feature -- Quantifiers

> *there_exists (predicate: FUNCTION [ANY, TUPLE [G], BOOLEAN]):*
> *BOOLEAN* **is**

>> -- Does *current* contain an element which satisfies
>> -- *predicate* ?

> **require**
>> predicate_not_void: *predicate* / = **Void**

> **deferred**

> **ensure**
>> definition: **Result** =
>>> (**not** *for_all* (**agent** *negated (?, predicate)))*

> **end**

> *for_all (predicate: FUNCTION [ANY, TUPLE [G], BOOLEAN]):*
> *BOOLEAN* **is**

>> -- Does *current* contain only elements which satisfy
>> -- *predicate* ?

> **require**
>> predicate_not_void: *predicate* / = **Void**

> **deferred**

> **ensure**
>> definition: **Result** =
>>> (**not** *there_exists* (**agent** *negated (?, predicate)))*

> **end**

The contracts capture the relations of $\forall$ and $\exists$. *negated* is a feature from the class *MML_FUNCTIONALS* offering generic functionals such as negation and composition on predicates defined by agents. We may note in passing that this class and *MML_QUANTIFIABLE* achieve — thanks in particular to agents — the side goal of providing, within the Eiffel framework, a substantial subset of the mechanisms of functional languages such as Haskell.

3.7   Implementing the Model Classes

MML classes as seen so far are all deferred (abstract). A deferred class may have no direct instances; correspondingly, it need not provide any implementation for its features. Non-deferred (concrete) classes, directly describing software objects, are called *effective* [21].

If we are interested in completely contracted classes for proving purposes, deferred classes are clearly sufficient. There is no need for direct instances of model objects, for implementation of model features, or more generally for execution.

If, on the other hand if we are also interested in equipping classes with complete contracts for the purpose of *testing* them more effectively, we will need implementations — effective versions of the original classes.

As a result of these observations, MML includes a set of reference implementations, one provided (as an effective descendant) for each of the directly usable deferred classes.

All implementations assume that the sets are finite and small enough to be represented through *ARRAY* or *LINKED_LIST* data structures. This is sufficient for the problems we have tackled so far.

Most of the work for the default implementation is done in the two classes *MML_SET* and *MML_PAIR*. *MML_SET* uses the *ARRAYED_SET* data structure of EiffelBase. *MML_PAIR* just defines two variables *one* and *two* to represent the values of a pair.

Because typed set theory allows describing all other structures (bags, sequences etc.) in terms of these two, their implementation builds on implementations of sets and pairs.

4   Using Models to Achieve Complete Contracts

The model library as sketched in the previous section enables us to reach our original goal of equipping realistic, practical classes with complete contracts. We now explore this process and its application to some important classes of the EiffelBase library.

4.1   Devising a Model

The first step in equipping a class with model-based complete contracts is to choose a model that will adequately capture the state of its instances; in the *STACK* example the choice was sequences.

As with the basic object-oriented design issue of of finding the right inheritance or client relation, there is no general, infallible process. [35] gives some hints.

For example, a mathematical relation is probably the right model for classes describing hash tables or other dictionary-like structures. As another hint, the EiffelBase placement of the random number generator class as as a descendant of *COUNTABLE_SEQUENCE* suggests sequences as the model for this notion.

4.2   The Abstraction Function

We may call the relationship between a concrete software object and its MML model its "abstraction function" (a notion introduced in [13] in the form of the "representation function", its inverse, actually multi-valued). For the *AR-RAYED_STACK* class we use the following model:

feature{*SPECIFICATION*} -- Model

> *model: MML_SEQUENCE [G]* **is**
>> -- Model of the stack
>> **local**
>>> *l: LINEAR[G]*
>> **do**
>>> **create** {*MML_DEFAULT_SEQUENCE [G]*}**Result**.*make_empty*
>>> *l := linear_representation*
>> **from**
>>> *l.start*
>> **until**
>>> *l.off*
>> **loop**
>>> **Result** := **Result**.*prepended (l.item)*
>>> *l.forth*
>> **end**
> **end**

Model queries always return an attached (non-void) result in the sense of ECMA Eiffel. They have no feature-specific contracts (preconditions or post-conditions), but may have associated constraints as part of the class invariant. Any implementation of the abstraction function (potentially useful, as noted, for applications to testing) may only rely on the invariant.

4.3   Composite Models

In many of the more advanced examples it is not realistic to capture the complete state of a data structure through an atomic model built directly from one of the classes of MML, such as a single sequence in the examples above. As an example, consider the EiffelBase class *LINKED_LIST*, describing a sequence of values equipped with a *cursor* to facilitate traversal and manipulation (figure 3).

To describe the full state, we may use a tuple of a sequence s and a cursor position n, yielding an abstraction function of type:

$$model : LINKED\_LIST[G] \Rightarrow SEQUENCE[G] \times \mathbb{N}$$

To build this abstraction function into the class we first define an abstraction for each component of the model:

feature{*SPECIFICATION*} -- Model

> *model_index: INTEGER* **is**
> > -- Model of the cursor position
>
> **do**
> > **Result** := *index*
>
> **end**

> *model_sequence: MML_SEQUENCE [G]* **is**
> > -- Model of the list when regarded as a sequence
>
> **do**
> > . . .
>
> **end**

Then we create a common model by pairing the two components:

> *model: MML_PAIR [SEQUENCE [G],INTEGER]* **is**
> > -- Model of the list
>
> **do**
> > **create** {*MML_DEFAULT_PAIR*}**Result**.
> > *make(model_sequence,model_index)*
>
> **end**

Our experience shows that this is a convenient practice. In particular we have retained the technique, illustrated in all the above examples, of always using a single *model* query expressing the entire abstraction function and yielding a single object; if the model conceptually involves several components — in the last example, a sequence and an integer — we turn them into a single one by taking advantage of the MML classes for pairs and sets. This rule yields a consistent style and enables us to refer for any class to "the model" and "the abstraction function".

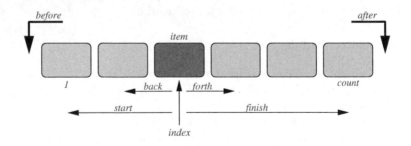

Fig. 3. *LINKED_LIST* with active cursor

4.4   Classic and Model Contracts

Most Eiffel classes, especially in libraries, are equipped with some contracts expressing important elements of their intended semantics. We will call them *classic contracts* in contrast to contracts relying on the model library, called *model contracts.*

Classic contracts are usually easy to understand for programmers, even those who may be put off by more formal approaches. But, as noted, they are often incomplete, especially postconditions and invariants. With the help of model contracts we should be able to check that they are at least *sound*, according to the following definition:

Definition: Soundness of a Model

A classic contract for a model-equipped class is sound if:

1. Every classic precondition implies the corresponding model precondition.
2. Every model postcondition implies the corresponding classic postcondition.
3. Every model invariant implies the corresponding classic invariant.

In the informal terms used at the beginning of this discussion: model contracts give us "all the truth"; classic contracts, the only ones that less advanced or less interested programmers will see, are sound if what they tell, while perhaps not the full truth, is still "the truth".

To this effect, condition 1 guarantees that every call that appears correct to a client programmer working on the sole knowledge of the classic contracts will indeed satisfy all the required conditions — even if it might satisfy more than strictly needed.

Condition 2 guarantees that every call will, on return, deliver every condition promised to clients - even if it might deliver more than classically advertised.

Condition 3 guarantees that the consistency constraints expected of instances of a class actually hold.

On the basis of this definition, let us examine the soundness of the *STACK* specification extract. The interesting part is the postcondition, consisting of three clauses, two classic and one model-related:

ensure
    model_is_extended: $model === $ **old** $model.extended\ (v)$
    item_pushed: $item = v$
    count_increased: $count = $ **old** $count + 1$

From the invariant, we know that

invariant
    count_defined_through_model: $count = model.count$
    item_defined_through_model: $item = model.last$

By combining the assertions of the postcondition and the invariant, we can derive the following two proof obligations to verify the soundness of the classical contracts:

> *(model === **old** model.extended (v))* **and**
> *(item = model.last)*
>> **implies**
> *(v = item)*

> *(model === **old** model.extended (v))* **and**
> *(**old** count = **old** model.count)* **and**
> *(count = model.count)*
>> **implies**
> *(count = **old** count + 1)*

Both properties can be easily verified using a theory for sequences. The notion of soundness is particularly interesting in combination with inheritance. It is possible to prove soundness at an abstract level, in a deferred class such as *STACK*, without having to redo the proof in effective descendants such as *ARRAYED_STACK*. This point was discussed in [22].

5   Specification of a Full Library

As a testbed for the approach described here, and a major application of interest in its own stake, we considered EiffelBase [10], a reusable, open-source library of data structures provided with the Eiffel environment. Making heavy use of multiple-inheritance and genericity,the classes of EiffelBase include not only implementations of the data structures but also offer a rich set of deferred classes that capture useful concepts such as abstract containers, common traversal strategies, and mathematical structures such as "ring" and total order. The full design of the library is discussed in [20].

5.1   Overall Structure

We produced a fully contracted version of the structural classes of EiffelBase; a significant endeavor since that part of the library includes 36 classes totalling 1853 exported (public) features.

The process of completing the specifications brought to light numerous inconsistencies in the library. Using model specifications, we were able to come up with a cleaned up hierarchy for EiffelBase. Figure 4 on the facing page presents a BON diagram of this hierarchy. A full specification for each class appears in [35].

5.2   Models of DYNAMIC_LIST

As an illustration of the work involved in this reengineering of EiffelBase for complete contracts, we consider a typical class. *DYNAMIC_LIST* is the parent for

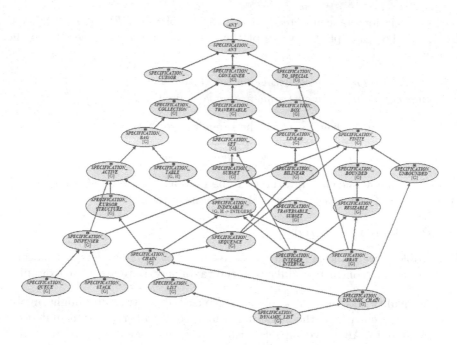

Fig. 4. The inheritance hierarchy of EiffelBase

the implementation of lists through arrays (*ARRAYED_LIST*) and linked structures *LINKED_LIST*. Dynamic lists, like EiffelBase lists in general (see figure 4) are "active": they contain a movable cursor with a current cursor position.

The classes of our reengineered library bear the names of the corresponding EiffelBase classes prefixed by *SPECIFICATION_*, for example *SPECIFICATION_DYNAMIC_LIST*.

Four different models are available to describe the state of the dynamic list. They are inherited from the parent classes and describe different possible views of lists:

feature{*SPECIFICATION*} -- Model
    model_bag: MML_BAG [G]
        -- Bag model for the list
        -- (from SPECIFICATION_BAG)
    model_indexable: MML_RELATION [INTEGER,G]
        -- Table model for the list
        -- (from SPECIFICATION_TABLE)
    model_cursor: INTEGER
        -- Cursor model for the list
        -- (form SPECIFICATION_TRAVERSABLE)
    model_sequence: MML_SEQUENCE [G]
        -- Sequence model for the list
        -- (from SPECIFICATION_TRAVERSABLE)

All four relations are connected by the invariant of *SPECIFICATION_DYNA-MIC_LIST*. For example the value of the cursor is limited by the size of the sequence:

$$model\_cursor >= model\_sequence.lower\_bound - 1$$
$$model\_cursor <= model\_sequence.upper\_bound + 1$$

The domain of the bag has to be the range of the sequence:

$$model\_bag.domain === model\_sequence.range$$

This shows how the class invariant can be used as a so-called *gluing invariant* between the different mathematical abstractions of the list.

5.3   Problems Discovered

Most problems we found in EiffelBase were caused by heavy underspecifications, contradictions in contracts and flaws in the taxonomy. Here are some examples:

- The equality relation of "active" (cursor-based) data structures might involve not only elements of the structure, but also a cursor position and other internal data. All active data structures were missing a clear specification of whether they should be regarded equivalent if they have the same data but different cursor positions.
- The class *TRAVERSABLE_SUBSET* does not inherit from class *TRAVERSABLE*, even though it implements all features offered by *TRAVERSABLE*. This design decision prohibits polymorphic use.
- The features *prune* and *prune_all* in class *SEQUENCE* move the cursor to off, even if the element to be pruned is not present in the sequence.
- The feature *wipe_out* in class *ARRAY* is marked as obsolete. Obsolete feature clauses are not the proper way to declare a feature as inapplicable.
- The class *BILINEAR* inherits twice from *LINEAR* to implement bi-linearity. This makes specification difficult, as it is not always clear which iteration features are derived for which inheritance relation.
- Internal cursors and functionals such as *for_all*, *there_exists* and *do_all* do not represent the same concept and should be distinguished. The linearity is not necessary for an implementation of logic quantifiers.

A full list of problems discovered can be found in [35].

6   Related Work

Models have been used before for software specification. Early work by Hoare [13] suggested the use of models. The Larch language and toolset [12] relies on models for program verification. In contrast to our approach, Larch introduces a special language for the specifications of models. This creates a conceptual separation between the model-based specifications and the programming language. Special projects provide embedding mechanisms of Larch models into such languages as Smalltalk [6] and C++ [15].

JML [16,5] applies models to the domain of modular specifications of Java programs. JML includes an extensive model library for the specification of object-oriented programs, offering more than a hundred Java classes describing very diverse specification mechanisms. The core of the library comprises structural classes such as *JMLSequence* and *JMLValueSet*. The technique presented in this paper is strongly related to the *model variables* of JML [7]. The major difference is that JML model variables introduce the notion of state into the contractual specification. We view models as abstraction functions, without model variables. In addition, as explained earlier, we treat models as an extension to the contractual language and not as part of the surrounding framework.

Müller, Poetzsch-Heffter and Leavens [27] extend the use of model variables and procedures to the field of *frame properties*. We have not explicitly addressed this important issue here. Our working hypothesis is that to the extent that the model expresses all the properties of interest any effect the software's operations may have on properties not covered by the model is irrelevant. (Eiffel can, as noted, express frame properties through the newly introduced **only** postcondition clause, but the precise relation between models and the **only** clause still needs to be explored).

The Spec# programming language [2] currently offers predefined sets and sequences as value types. In [17], Leino and Müller suggest a general approach for model fields that employs the Boogie methodology for object invariants. This promises a major simplification for reasoning on model fields and model field updates.

ASMs [11] and AsmL [3] use the concept of models and introduce model variables with a related notion of model programs. This yields *executable* specifications since one may treat the model as an abstract program that operates on the abstract state denoted by the model variables. By this, AsmL can provide executable specifications. The verification process consists of showing that the implementation is a behavioral subtype of that executable specification.

Also, ASMs define a set of *background* constructs [4], like sets, tuples, arrays and lists. These constructs are defined "ahead of time" used by algorithms as a variable working space.

The Z specification language [33,32] and the B method [1] have both been used to apply set theory to specify software in conjunction with before-after predicates. Our work is intended to provide Eiffel contracts with the same expressive power.

Mitchell and McKim [26] introduced models in the context of Eiffel and Design by Contract.

7   Conclusion

The framework described here appears to allow the development of libraries with complete contracts, not too difficult to write yet still understandable by any programmer who cares to learn a few basic concepts. We are continuing to apply this process to the EiffelBase library, which lies at the core of many applications and hence plays a major practical role. Research work that will immediately benefit from this effort includes:

- Our ongoing effort to produce proofs that the classes indeed satisfy their contracts.
- Complementary work on entirely automatic ("push-button") tests of components based on their contracts [8], evidently made all the more interesting if the contracts are more extensive.

So far we have mostly applied our model-based techniques to libraries such as EiffelBase describing fundamental computer science concepts. Although we believe they can also be fruitfully applied to more application-oriented classes, or to graphical libraries such as EiffelVision, this remains to be demonstrated and is one of the next challenges.

The effort of producing complete contracts for EiffelBase has already born fruit: while the library has been carefully designed and is reused in many commercial and non-commercial applications, the process has uncovered a number of technical and conceptual flaws. These will be reported and fixed in the "classic" EiffelBase, although we definitely hope that — in line with the applied nature of this work and its intention, thanks to Eiffel's built-in contracts, to serve the direct needs of operational developments — the version with complete contracts will become the reference.

The mere process of writing the complete contracts and the resulting improvements to classic EiffelBase has already shown that more complete specifications improve the Design by Contract process and lead to clearer abstractions.

References

1. Jean-Raymond Abrial. *The B-Book – assigning programs to meanings.* Cambridge University Press, 1996.
2. Mike Barnett, K. Rustan M. Leino, and Wolfram Schulte. The Spec# programming system: An overview. In *CASSIS 2004*, LNCS 3362. Springer, 2004.
3. Mike Barnett and Wolfram Schulte. The ABCs of specifications: AsmL, behavior, and components. *Informatica*, 25(4):517–526, November 2001.
4. Andreas Blass and Yuri Gurevich. Background, reserve, and gandy machines. In Peter Clote and Helmut Schwichtenberg, editors, *Proceedings of CSL'2000*, volume 1862 of *LNCS*, pages 1–17. Springer-Verlag, 2000.
5. L. Burdy, Y. Cheon, D. Cok, M. Ernst, J.R. Kiniry, G.T. Leavens, K.R.M. Leino, and E. Poll. An overview of JML tools and applications. Technical Report R0309, NIII, 2003.
6. Yoonsik Cheon and Gary T. Leavens. The larch/smalltalk interface specification language. In *ACM Transactions on Software Engineering and Methodology*, volume 3, pages 221–253. ACM Press, July 1994.
7. Yoonsik Cheon, Gary T. Leavons, Murali Sitaraman, and Stephen Edwards. Model variables: Cleanly supporting abstraction in design by contract. Technical Report 03-10, Iowa State University, April 2003.

8. Ilinca Ciupa and Andreas Leitner. Automatic testing based on design by contract. In *Proceedings of Net.ObjectDays 2005*. tranSIT Thüringer Anwendungszentrum für Software-, Informations- und Kommunikationstechnologien GmbH, 2005. (to be published).

9. Paul Dubois, Mark Howard, Bertrand Meyer, Michael Schweitzer, and Emmanuel Stapf. From calls to agents. *Journal of Object-Oriented Programming*, 12(6), 1999.

10. Eiffel Software. *EiffelBase*, August 2005. `http://archive.eiffel.com/products/base/`.

11. Yuri Gurevich. Sequential abstract state machines capture sequential algorithms. *ACM Transactions on Computational Logic*, 1(1):77–111, July 2000.

12. John V. Guttag, James J. Jorning, S. J. Garland, K. D. Jones, A. Modet, and J. M. Wing. *Larch: Languages and Tools for Formal Specifications*. Springer-Verlag, New York, N. Y., 1993.

13. C.A.R. Hoare. Proof of correctness of data representations. *Acta Informatica*, 1(4): 271–281, 1972.

14. R. Kramer. iContract - the Java(tm) Design by Contract(tm) tool. In *TOOLS '98: Proceedings of the Technology of Object-Oriented Languages and Systems*, page 295, Washington, DC, USA, 1998. IEEE Computer Society.

15. Gary T. Leavens. Larch/C++, an interface specification language for C++. Technical report, Iowa State University, Ames, Iowa 50011 USA, August 1997.

16. Gary T. Leavens, Albert L. Baker, and Clyde Ruby. Preliminary design of JML: A behavioral interface specification language for Java. Technical Report 98-06t, Department of Computer Science, Iowa State University, June 1998.

17. K. R. M. Leino and P. Müller. A verification methodology for model fields. In *European Symposium on Programming (ESOP)*, Lecture Notes in Computer Science. Springer-Verlag, 2006.

18. Bertrand Meyer. Tools for the new culture: Lessons from the design of the eiffel libraries. *Communications of the ACM*, 33(9):40–60, September 1990.

19. Bertrand Meyer. *Eiffel: the language*. Object-Oriented Series. Prentice Hall, New York, NY, 1992.

20. Bertrand Meyer. *Reusable software: the Base object-oriented component libraries*. Prentice-Hall, 1994.

21. Bertrand Meyer. *Object-Oriented Software Construction*. Prentice Hall, 2 edition, 1997.

22. Bertrand Meyer. A framework for proving contract-equipped classes. In Egon Börger, Angelo Gargantini, and Elvinia Riccobene, editors, *Abstract State Machines 2003, Advances in Theory and Practice, 10th International Workshop, Taormina (Italy), March 3-7, 2003*, pages 108–125. Springer-Verlag, 2003.

23. Bertrand Meyer. Attached types and their application to three open problems of object-oriented programming. In Andrew Black, editor, *ECOOP 2005 (Proceedings of European Conference on Object-Oriented Programming, Edinburgh, 25-29 July 2005)*, number 3586 in LNCS, pages 1–32. Springer Verlag, 2005.

24. Bertrand Meyer, editor. *Eiffel Analysis, Design and Programming Language*. ECMA International, June 2005. As approved as International Standard 367.

25. Bertrand Meyer. Eiffel: The language. Third Edition, ongoing work as published at `http://se.ethz.ch/~meyer/ongoing/etl/`, August 2005.

26. Richard Mitchell and Jim McKim. *Design by Contract, by example*. Addison-Wesley, 2002.

27. P. Müller, A. Poetzsch-Heffter, and G. T. Leavens. Modular specification of frame properties in JML. *Concurrency and Computation: Practice and Experience*, 15: 117–154, 2003.

28. Tobias Nipkow, Laurence C. Paulson, and Markus Wenzel. *Isabelle/HOL - A Proof Assistant for Higher-Order Logic.* Springer, 2004.
29. Nonprofit International Consortium for Eiffel (NICE). *The Eiffel Library Standard,* June 1995. TR-EI-48/KL.
30. Object Management Group. *UML 2.0 OCL Specification,* November 2003. adopted specification, ptc/13-10-14.
31. Bernd Schoeller. Strengthening eiffel contracts using models. In Hung Dang Van and Zhiming Liu, editors, *Proceeding of the Workshop on Formal Aspects of Component Software FACS'03,* number 284 in UNU/IIST Report, pages 143–158, September 2003.
32. J. M. Spivey. An introduction to Z and formal specifications. *Software Engineering Journal,* 1989. January.
33. J. M. Spivey. *The Z Notation: A Reference Manual.* International Series in Computer Science. Prentice-Hall, second edition edition, 1992.
34. Steria, Aix-en-Provence, France. *Atelier B Interactive Prover User Manual.*
35. Tobias Widmer. Reusable mathematical models. Master's thesis, ETH Zürich, July 2004.

Bus Scheduling for TDL Components

Emilia Farcas, Wolfgang Pree, and Josef Templ

Department of Computer Science, University of Salzburg, Austria
firstname.lastname@cs.uni-salzburg.at

Abstract. This paper describes a solution for bus scheduling of distributed multi-mode TDL (Timing Definition Language) components. The TDL component model is based on the concept of Logical Execution Time (LET), which abstracts from physical execution time and thereby from both the execution platform and the communication topology. The TDL component model allows the decomposition of hard real-time applications into modules (= components) that are executed in parallel. A TDL module runs in one particular mode at a time and may switch to another mode independently from other modules. This is in contrast with global modes as introduced by other available hard real-time systems and introduces new challenges for bus scheduling.

1 Introduction

Traditionally, the development of software for embedded systems is highly platform specific. However, with more powerful processors available, there is a shift of functionality from hardware to software and the requirements are becoming more ambitious. A luxury car, for example, comprises about 80 electronic control units interconnected by multiple buses and driven by more than a million lines of code. In order to cope with the increased complexity of the resulting software, a more platform independent "high-level" programming style becomes mandatory. In case of real-time software, this applies not only to functional aspects but also to the temporal behavior of the software. Dealing with time, however, is not covered appropriately by any of the existing component models for high-level languages.

A particularly promising approach towards a high-level component model for real time systems has been laid out in the Giotto project [5][8][9][10] at the University of California, Berkeley, by introduction of Logical Execution Time (LET), which abstracts from the physical execution time on a particular platform and thereby abstracts from both the underlying execution platform and the communication topology. Thus, it becomes possible to change the underlying platform and even to distribute components between different nodes without affecting the overall system behavior.

This paper refers to a component model, named TDL (Timing Definition Language) [15], which has been developed in the course of the MoDECS[1] project at the University of Salzburg, as a successor of Giotto. It shares with Giotto the basic idea of LET but introduces additional high-level concepts for structuring large real time systems.

---

[1] The MoDECS project (www.MoDECS.cc) is supported by the FIT-IT Embedded Systems grant 807144 (www.fit-it.at).

R.H. Reussner et al. (Eds.): Architecting Systems, LNCS 3938, pp. 71–83, 2006.

In the following, we shall start with an explanation of LET and proceed with an overview of the TDL component model. Then, we focus on the distribution of TDL components and describe the problems related to independent mode switches. The description of our approach to automatic bus schedule generation for these requirements is the core contribution of the paper.

2 Logical Execution Time (LET)

LET means that the observable temporal behavior of a task is independent from its physical execution [8]. It is only assumed that physical task execution is fast enough to fit somewhere within the logical start and end points. Fig. 1 shows the relation between logical and physical task execution.

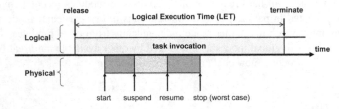

Fig. 1. Logical Execution Time

The inputs of a task are read at the release event and the newly calculated outputs are available at the terminate event. Between these, the outputs have the value of the previous execution.

LET introduces a delay for observable outputs, which might be considered a disadvantage. On the other hand, however, LET provides the cornerstone to deterministic behavior, platform abstraction, and well-defined interaction semantics between parallel activities [11]. It is always defined which value is in use at which time instant and there are no race conditions or priority inversions involved. LET also provides the foundation for what we call transparent distribution [3] (see Section 4).

3 TDL Component Model

Based on the concept of LET, Giotto introduces the notion of a *mode* as a set of periodically executed activities. The activities are task invocations (according to LET semantics), actuator updates, and mode switches. All activities can have their own rate of execution and all activities can be executed conditionally. Actuator updates and mode switches are considered to be much faster than task invocations, thus they are executed in *logical zero time*. The set of all modes reachable from a distinguished start mode constitutes the Giotto *program*.

Our successor of Giotto, named TDL (Timing Definition Language), extends these concepts by the notion of the *module*, which is a named Giotto program that may import other modules and may export some of its own program entities to other client modules. Every module may provide its own distinguished start mode. Thus, all modules execute in parallel or in other words, a TDL application can be seen as the parallel composition of a set of TDL modules. It is important to note that LET is always preserved, that is, adding a new module will never affect the observable temporal behavior of other modules. It is the responsibility of internal scheduling mechanisms to guarantee conformance to LET, given that the worst-case execution times (WCET) and the execution rates are known for all tasks.

Parallel tasks within a mode may depend on each other, that is, the output of one task may be used as the input of another task. All tasks are logically executed in sync and the dataflow semantics is defined by LET.

Modules support an export/import mechanism similar to modern general purpose programming languages such as Java or C#. A service provider module may export a task's outputs, which in turn may be imported by a client module and used as input for the client's computations. All modules are logically executed in sync and again the dataflow semantics is defined by LET. Modules are a top-level structuring concept that serves multiple purposes:

1. a module provides a name space and an export/import mechanism and thereby supports decomposition of large systems,
2. modules provide parallel composition of real time applications,
3. modules are the unit of mode switching, that is, every module executes in its own mode and may switch to a different mode independently from other modules,
4. modules serve as units of loading, that is, a runtime system may support dynamic loading and unloading of modules, and
5. modules are the natural choice as unit of distribution, because dataflow within a module (cohesion) will most probably be much larger than dataflow across module boundaries (adhesion).

The fact that modules are the unit of mode switching implies that an application consisting of multiple TDL modules is not in a single global mode. This is in contrast to state-of-the-art systems, which support only global mode switches. Furthermore, the possibility to distribute TDL modules across different computation nodes leads us to the notion of *transparent distribution* as explained in more detail in Section 4 and in [3].

Example TDL Modules
The following TDL source code shows two modules M1 and M2. M1 exports three named constants and two tasks, and M2 imports M1 and may therefore access the exported entities. Module M1 defines two modes of operation, f11 and f12, where f11 is the start mode. Both modes invoke two tasks inc and dec and check the mode switch condition once per mode period, which in both cases is 10ms. The difference between the two modes is that in f12 the task dec will be invoked twice as fast as in f11. Module M2 defines a single mode, which uses the outputs of tasks inc and dec in order to calculate the sum and update an actuator. Depending on the mode of M1, the output will be a constant value or it will change over time. As a developer specifies only the timing behavior in TDL, the functionality of the tasks has to be implemented in another programming language. The functions invoked by the tasks, the drivers for reading sensors and updating actuators, and the guards for conditional execution can be implemented in any imperative programming language such as C. The external functionality code is indicated by the keywords uses and if.

```
module M1 {

public const
  c1 = 50; c2 = 200; refPeriod = 10ms;

sensor
  int s uses getS;

public task inc {   // wcet=1ms
  output int o := c1;
  uses incImpl(o);   // inc. by step 10
}


public task dec {   // wcet=1ms
  output int o := c2;
  uses decImpl(o);   // dec. by step 10
}

start mode f11 [period=refPeriod] {
  task
    [freq=1] inc(); // LET of task inc is 10/1 = 10ms
    [freq=1] dec();
  mode
    [freq=1] if switch2m2(s, inc.o) then f12;
}

mode f12 [period=refPeriod] {
  task
    [freq=1] inc();
    [freq=2] dec();   // LET of task dec is 10/2 = 5ms
  mode
    [freq=1] if switch2m1(s, inc.o) then f11;
}
}
```

```
module M2 {

import M1;

actuator
  int a := M1.c2 uses setA;

public task sum {   // wcet=1ms
  input int i1; int i2;
  output int o := M1.c2;
  uses sumImpl(i1, i2, o);
}

start mode main [period=M1.refPeriod] {
  task
    [freq=1] sum(M1.inc.o, M1.dec.o);
  actuator
    [freq=1] a := sum.o;

}
}
```

Fig. 2 shows the outputs of module M1's inc and dec tasks, and module M2's sum task. Module M1 is in mode f11 at the beginning, therefore the sum task is producing a constant output. After pushing the sensor button, a mode switch occurs and task sum produces the corresponding output pattern. The delay between the output of the sum task and the output of the inc and dec tasks is due to the LET semantics.

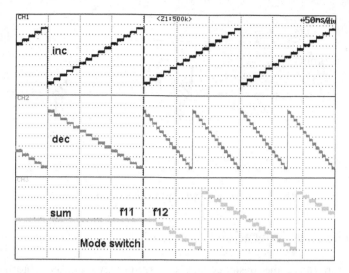

Fig. 2. Functional and temporal behavior of modules M1 (mode f11 and then f22) and M2

4 Transparent Distribution

The term transparent distribution in the context of hard real-time applications is defined with respect to two points of view. Firstly, at run-time a TDL application behaves exactly the same, no matter if all modules (that is, components) are executed on a single node or if they are distributed across multiple nodes. The logical timing is always preserved, only the physical timing, which is not observable from the outside, may be changed. Secondly, for the developer of a TDL module, it does not matter where the module itself and any imported modules are executed. The TDL tool chain and run-time system frees the developer from the burden of explicitly specifying the communication requirements of modules. The mapping of modules to computation nodes is defined separately in a platform configuration file, which also contains the physical properties of the communication infrastructure (e.g., bandwidth, protocol overhead and payload size). It should be noted that in both aspects transparency applies not only to the functional but also to the temporal behavior of an application.

In order to illustrate the importance of LET for transparent distribution, we consider an example of two modules M1 and M2, located on two different nodes. For the sake of simplicity, we assume that each module has a single mode of operation, which invokes a single task. task1 runs within module M1 and task2 runs within module M2 using as input the output of task1. In other words, module M2 imports module M1, and task2 has as input the output port of task1. For this example, we further assume that task2 runs twice as often as task1, that is, the LET of task1 is twice the LET of task2.

Fig. 3 shows an example for the communication required between the two tasks. In order to implement this exchange of information, we assume a communication layer on both nodes that we call TDL-Comm [3]. Its purpose is to send and receive messages at *appropriate* times so that the LET constraint of task1 is met. This means that the output value of task1 has to arrive at node2 before LET1 ends.

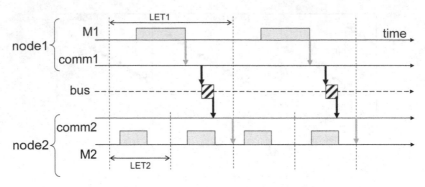

Fig. 3. Sample communication between two tasks

5   Bus Schedule Generation

This section presents the basic concepts, terminology and the algorithm which generates the bus schedule for the TDL component model. The bus schedule is generated at compile time. We do not describe how the TDL tasks are scheduled on the particular node where a TDL module is executed.

5.1   Preliminaries for Bus Scheduling

We assume a network infrastructure based on broadcast semantics, that is, a frame sent by one node can be received at the same time by all other nodes. Furthermore, we assume that packets sent by different nodes cannot be combined into a single packet but are sent as individual network frames according to some protocol. This rules out special support for systems such as EtherCAT, where a frame can be shared by multiple nodes.

The access to the shared communication medium is collision free via a TDMA (Time Division Multiple Access, [12]) approach. In order to support this, we rely on a mechanism for clock synchronization over the network. Furthermore, we adhere to the Producer/Consumer model. This means that the nodes that generate information—the producers—trigger the sending of information over the network. The nodes that need the information—the consumers—do not send any requests to the producers as it is the case in the Request/Response model.

5.2   Mode Switch Instants Per Module

TDL restricts mode switches such that task invocations are never interrupted by a mode switch. Thus, mode switches are said to be *harmonic*, that is, a mode switch must not occur during the LET of every task invocation of the currently active mode. Therefore, the period of a mode switch must be a multiple of the LCM (least common multiple) of the period of tasks invoked in this mode. This check is done during compilation. Furthermore, the mode period is always a multiple of the periods of task invocations and mode switches.

For a given module M, we define $mspGCD_M$ as the GCD (greatest common divisor) of mode periods and mode switch periods in all modes in M. We know that within the time span $[N*mspGCD_M$ .. $(N+1)*mspGCD_M]$ there will not be a mode switch within module M. In other words, we can express the mode switch instants as an integer multiple of $mspGCD_M$.

5.3 Bus Period

As we generate a static schedule, the size of the schedule needs to be finite. Thus, the schedule is repeated periodically. We call the time span covered by the schedule the *bus period*.

As each mode in every module may have its specific communication requirements, an obvious candidate for the bus period is the longest time span without a mode switch in any module. Thus we calculate the bus period as GCD of the $mspGCD_M$ of each module M which communicates on the bus.

Each mode period consists of an integer multiple of bus periods and we introduce the term *phase* in order to distinguish these mutually exclusive parts of a mode.

5.4 Messages

We define the term *message* as the collection of all values of the task output ports produced by a task invocation. Each task invocation produces one message. Note that if a task is invoked N times per mode period, N messages are produced.

As an optimization, task output ports that are not used by any client are ignored. Furthermore, tasks that are not public or that have no clients produce no messages.

A message has a unique *tag*. The reason for that is explained below. The tag defines the node, module, mode, task invocation, and the phase of the mode in which the message has been produced.

The size of a message is measured in bytes as the sum of the size of the contained values and the size of the tag.

Each message has individual timing constraints. The *release* constraint is the earliest time instant message sending can be started. The *deadline* constraint of the message is the latest time instant when the message sending must be finished.

A simple approach is to set the release constraint to the release time of the task invocation that produces that message plus its worst case execution time (wcet). The deadline constraint results from the end of the LET of the producer task invocation. The release and deadline of a message are relative to the phase where the task invocation ends.

5.5 Frames Per Module

In order to use the communication medium efficiently, we map the messages of a phase to one or more reserved communication windows within the bus period such that these communication windows can be used for all phases of a module. A reserved communication window corresponds to a *frame*, which is the unit of information to be sent on the bus. The exact point in time when the frame will be scheduled within this communication window is computed later, see Sect.5.7

The schedule generator determines the frames and binds each message to exactly one frame. At run-time, the phase of a module determines which subset of the messages bound to a frame is actually sent. As the content of a frame varies at runtime, we need a means to identify messages. For that purpose we have introduced the message tag as described above.

The *release (r)* constraint of a frame is the maximum of the release constraints of the bound messages. The *deadline (d)* constraint of a frame is the minimum of the deadline constraints of the bound messages. The schedule generator guarantees that the frame size and constraints are sufficient for the communication requirements of all phases.

To exemplify this, we consider a module with a mode of execution that has three phases, and we assume that it produces a message of 4 bytes in phase0, a message of 3 bytes in phase1, and two messages of 1 byte each in phase2. Depending on their size and timing constraints, all messages may be bound to the same frame in the schedule, as seen in Fig. 4. The left and right bounds of the message and frame boxes represent the release and deadline constraints.

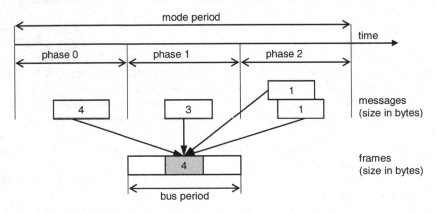

Fig. 4. Sample binding of several messages to one frame

The following pseudo code shows how messages are extracted and bound to frames. We assume that the bus period is globally available.

```
createFrames(Module M) returns Set {
    let frames be an empty set
    for each mode m of module M {
        for each phase p of m {
            let msgs be an empty set
            for each task invocation instance t that ends in p {
                add new Message(M, m, t, p) to msgs
            }
            bindMsgs(msgs, frames)
        }
    }
    return frames
}
```

The following pseudo code refines bindMsgs, which associates a message with an existing frame if possible. Otherwise a new frame is created and the message is bound to the new frame. The method createFrame creates a frame, binds the message to that frame, sets the size of the frame to the size of the message, and adds the frame to the set frames. It also checks if the size does not exceed the maximum allowed on the network and if the frame transmission time fits in the bus period.

The decision of binding a message to a frame depends on the result of metric computation and on how many bytes we still have available from the size of the frame. We define for each frame the instance variable *available*, which is reset at the beginning of each phase to the size of the frame. The method bind binds a message to a frame and reduces the available bytes of the frame by the message size. The concept of computing metrics is explained below.

```
bindMsgs(Set msgs, Set frames) {
    reset the available bytes of all frames to the size of each frame
    for each msg in msgs {
        if (frames is empty) {
            createFrame(msg, frames)
        } else {
            for each frame in frames {
                computeMetric(msg, frame)
            }
            select the frame selFrame with the highest metric
            if (selFrame.metric > threshold) {
                bind(msg, selFrame)
            } else {
                createFrame(msg, frames)
            }
        }
    }
}
```

5.6 Heuristics

The method computeMetric calculates a real number between 0 and 1 and stores that number in the instance variable metric of a frame. For each message, we choose the frame that has the highest value for the metric, and if that value is higher than a threshold (e.g, equal to 0.5), then we bind the message to the frame. The allocation of messages to existing frames introduces a tradeoff between saving bandwidth and tightening the timing constraints. Hence, the topic is subject to further optimizations and heuristics.

The metric measures the degree of overlapping between the message and frame windows. We define the *window*, for a message or a frame, as the time interval between the release and deadline. If we allocate the message to this frame, then the new timing constraints for the frame will be the window of the overlapping section. Therefore, we want this to be as close as possible to the message and to the existing frame, otherwise the timing constrains would be too restrictive and we reduce the chance to find a feasible schedule. The overlapping and the metric as an average percentage are defined by the following formulas:

$$overlapping = Min(frame.d, msg.d) - Max(frame.r, msg.r) \qquad (1)$$

$$metric = \frac{\dfrac{overlapping}{frame.d - frame.r} + \dfrac{overlapping}{msg.d - msg.r}}{2} \qquad (2)$$

5.7 Bus Schedule

For each module in the system, we have identified the required messages and mapped them to frames, but the communication windows of different frames could overlap. Therefore we collect the frames required by all modules and apply on this global set a variation of the Reversed EDF scheduling algorithm, that is, the Latest Release Time (LRT) [13].

This decides when each frame must be sent on the network, depending on the release, deadline and worst case transmission time of each frame. Furthermore, the bus scheduler has additional constraints that result from the physical properties of the communication infrastructure. For example, it includes gaps in the schedule, because it has to align the sending time according to the inter frame gaps and the clock resolution on the computing nodes. The bus scheduler also generates extra frames, for example for time synchronization. Furthermore, it merges adjacent frames in the sorted list of frames if they are sent by the same node. This leads to the remapping of the corresponding messages to the merged frame.

6 Related Work

The state-of-the-art methods and tools for the development of distributed systems support at most global mode switches. By our knowledge, there is no other available system that allows real-time components to switch modes independently. Furthermore, the LET abstraction is the only model that leads to predictable real-time applications in both value and time determinism [11], thus we will emphasize the distribution approach in Giotto. Then we will present an example of static off-line scheduling, the TTP/C protocol. Another scheduling approach, especially in the automotive industry (DaVinci [18], dSPACE[2]) is to use a real-time kernel with dynamic scheduling (e.g. OSEK[14]) and a communication system based on static priorities (e.g., CAN[1]), therefore the system cannot be predicted and it has to be simulated as whole.

The Giotto language [8][9][10] focuses on task distribution, therefore it provides support only for global modes, and only one program runs in the system. [6] presents a methodology for distributed real-time code generation, thus multiple suppliers can independently compile different parts of a Giotto program to run on multiple CPUs. A system integrator assigns each task a particular host and supplier, by annotating the Giotto source code. Each supplier receives a part of the Giotto program, and a timing interface specifying the time slots that can be used for the task and communication scheduling. Given these, each supplier produces code, and then the integrator checks the interface compliance and the time safety, that is, if the code meets the Giotto timing requirements (e.g., release and deadlines) on a given platform. The schedule is generated off-line in form of virtual machine code, that is, S code [7]. The timing interface provides the exclusive time windows for scheduling, but not exactly when to perform the actions within the windows, so the supplier still has some flexibility. However, these timing interfaces are currently generated manually. Furthermore, the approach [6] is described by means of a single mode Giotto program. So it is unclear if a distributed multi-mode Giotto system has ever been implemented, though that would still stick to the global mode switch approach.

The time-triggered protocol (TTP) [12] is a communication protocol for fault-tolerant distributed hard real-time systems. It provides time-triggered communication, distributed clock synchronization and a membership service. The communication on the bus is done with static, periodic TDMA rounds. In TTP/C [17] the schedule is implemented as a message description list (MEDL), specifying exactly when a node has to send a certain message and when it has to receive messages from other nodes. A TTP cluster cycle consists of multiple TDMA rounds and the messages sent in a TDMA round can differ throughout the cluster cycle. A task descriptor list describes the cyclic scheduling of application tasks, thus at run-time the scheduler is a simple dispatcher. The TTTech [16] tool chain consists of two main tools for application development. The TTPplan tool generates the bus schedule (cluster level design). The TTPbuild tool generates the task schedule (node level design). The developer must specify in TTPplan every message that is sent from any node, and then in TTPbuild every periodic task and the messages it consumes. This is in contrast to our approach where the required messages are automatically identified from the TDL code. Furthermore, the TTP/C protocol supports global mode switches. The length of the cluster cycle can be changed from cluster mode to cluster mode and the messages transferred in the rounds of each node can be changed as well. However, although the protocol is designed for mode switches per subsystem, the current limitation of the TTTech tools is that they only support a single global mode of execution.

Regarding off-line scheduling and flexibility in real-time systems, [4] describes algorithms to support also aperiodic messages and to switch modes at run-time. When the condition for a mode change is enabled, the mode change request is communicated within a message on the network. All nodes receive the request at the same time, and perform the mode switch at the same time (that is, there is a consistent view of the mode switch requests). The duration of the mode switch results from the delay in the current schedule until it gets to a slot where the switch is feasible, and the duration of a transition schedule. This mode switch delay can be computed off-line and tested to be lower than some deadline set at design time.

7   Conclusions

The LET abstraction invented in the realm of the Giotto project paved the way for transparent distribution in real-time systems. We think this novel approach will lead to significantly more robust embedded software and will reduce the costs of integration testing. The TDL component architecture implies that modes may switch independently in each component, which is a radical innovation in real-time systems. We presented a scheduling algorithm for message communication, to support these independent mode switches, while maintaining transparent distribution. Future research and implementation efforts are required to show the scalability of transparent distribution and the scheduling algorithm. Another set of challenges comprises optimizations, improved heuristics and metrics for generating the communication schedules, considering the feedback from the time safety check for task execution, and strategies for avoiding the re-generation of schedules when components are added or modified.

Acknowledgements

We thank the MoDECS project team at the University of Salzburg for providing valuable input during informal discussions and group meetings. This research was supported in part by the FIT-IT Embedded Systems grant 807144 provided by the Austrian government through its Bundesminsterium für Verkehr, Innovation und Technologie.

References

1. Bosch, 1991, *CAN Specification, Version 2*. Robert Bosch GmbH, http://www.can.bosch.com/docu/can2spec.pdf
2. dSPACE GmbH: http://www.dspace.de
3. E. Farcas, C. Farcas, W. Pree, J. Templ. Transparent Distribution of Real-Time Components Based on Logical Execution Time, *Proc. of ACM SIGPLAN/SIGBED Conference on Languages, Compilers, and Tools for Embedded Systems* (LCTES), ACM Press, 2005, pages 31-39
4. G. Fohler, Flexibility in Statically Scheduled Real-Time Systems, PhD Thesis, Technisch-Naturwissenschaftliche Fakultaet, Technische Universitaet Wien, Austria, April 1994
5. Giotto Project, http://www-cad.eecs.berkeley.edu/~fresco/giotto/
6. T.A. Henzinger, C.M. Kirsch, and S. Matic, Composable Code Generation for Distributed Giotto, *Proc. of ACM SIGPLAN/SIGBED Conference on Languages, Compilers, and Tools for Embedded Systems* (LCTES), ACM Press, 2005, pages 21-30
7. T.A. Henzinger, C.M. Kirsch, and S. Matic. Schedule carrying code, *Proc. of the Third International Conference on Embedded Software* (EMSOFT), LNCS, Springer-Verlag, 2003
8. Thomas A. Henzinger, Benjamin Horowitz, and Christoph M. Kirsch. Giotto: A time-triggered language for embedded programming. *Proceedings of the First International Workshop on Embedded Software* (EMSOFT), Lecture Notes in Computer Science 2211, Springer-Verlag, 2001, pp. 166-184.
9. Thomas A. Henzinger, Benjamin Horowitz, and Christoph M. Kirsch. Embedded control systems development with Giotto. *Proceedings of the International Conference on Languages, Compilers, and Tools for Embedded Systems* (LCTES), ACM Press, 2001, pp. 64-72.
10. Thomas A. Henzinger, Christoph M. Kirsch, Marco A.A. Sanvido, and Wolfgang Pree. From control models to real-time code using Giotto. *IEEE Control Systems Magazine* 23(1):50-64, 2003.
11. C.M. Kirsch, 2002, Principles of Real-Time Programming. *In Proceedings of EMSOFT 2002, Grenoble* LNCS, 2491.
12. H. Kopetz, 1997, *Real-time Systems: Design Principles for Distributed Embedded Applications*. Kluwer, 1997

13. Jane W. S. Liu. *Real-Time Systems*. Prentice-Hall, 2000
14. OSEK Group, 2001, OSEK/VDX Time-triggered Operating System Specification, Version 1.0, http://www.osek-vdx.org/mirror/ttos10.pdf
15. J. Templ, 2004, TDL Specification and Report. Technical Report C059, Department of Computer Science, University of Salzburg, http://www.cs.uni-salzburg.at/pubs/reports/T001.pdf
16. TTTech - Time-Triggered Technology http://www.tttech.com
17. TTTech. Time-Triggered Protocol TTP/C High-Level Specification Document. Edition 1.0.0, July 2002.
18. M. Wernicke: New Design Methodology from Vector simplifies the Development of Distributed Systems, *Vector Informatik Press Release*, June 2003, http://www.vector-informatik.com/pdf/press/PND_DaVinci_PressRelease_200306_EN.pdf

Refinement and Consistency in Component Models with Multiple Views

Heike Wehrheim

Institut für Informatik, Universität Paderborn
33098 Paderborn, Germany
wehrheim@uni-paderborn.de

Abstract. In a step-wise design of systems, models of components are being developed on several levels of abstractions. In such a design process *model transformations* are used to change or replace (parts of) models. Model transformations are required to be *behaviour preserving*: component models at lower levels should adhere to the descriptions given in higher levels thus achieving *substitutability*. Moreover, for complex components, models usually consist of descriptions of different *views* or aspects (e.g. data and protocols). Consequently, different kinds of transformations take place on different views, and together they should guarantee behaviour preservation.

In this paper we discuss the applicability of formal methods concepts to model transformations. Formal methods come with build-in notions of transformations between models, or more precisely, with *refinement* and *subtyping* concepts which provide means for comparing component models on different levels with respect to their behaviour. Moreover, refinement and subtyping concepts for *different* views can be shown to neatly fit together. This is achieved by giving a common semantics to all views, which furthermore opens the possibility of checking *consistency*.

Keywords: Modelling of components, refinement, substitutability, consistency.

1 Introduction

The OMG's (Object Managemant Group's) standard for model-driven architecture defines *models* to be the core concept in software development. *Model transformations* are intended to provide the means for getting from high-level platform independent to lower level platform specific models. Model transformations are expected to be *behaviour preserving*: lower-level models should reflect the behaviour of higher-level models.

When modelling complex systems consisting of several components, there are usually multiple different aspects to be taken into account. A complex system has to fulfill several orthogonal requirements: on the static behaviour (data and operations), on its dynamic behaviour (adherence to protocols, scenarios), its timing behaviour, etc. Thus a model of a component will usually

R.H. Reussner et al. (Eds.): Architecting Systems, LNCS 3938, pp. 84–102, 2006.

consist of descriptions of several *views*. As a consequence, a modelling language has to supply the designer with facilities for modelling multiple views and with (at the best *formal*) concepts supporting a stepwise design with multiple views. This does in particular apply to model transformations which should operate on all views, but concerns questions of consistency between views as well.

The UML partly fulfills these requirements on modelling languages. It offers possibilities for describing multiple views: the static behaviour can be modelled using class diagrams, protocols are denotable as state machines, scenarios in sequence diagrams. Concepts supporting a model-driven stepwise design with multiple views, in particular formal concepts, are however less developed. In this paper we will therefore discuss which concepts developed in the context of formal methods can be applied to a model-driven development with multiple views. It turns out that in particular *refinement* concepts, which play a central rôle in a formal approach to software development, can be seen to tightly match (certain forms of) model transformations. Refinement guarantees that the desired criterion of behaviour preservation (and thus subsitutability) is met. Thus a model transformation involving a change of a data type or a protocol, a splitting of an activity or an extension with new operations can be evaluated wrt. a definition of refinement. Furthermore, questions of consistency between views (and its preservation under a transformation of the model) can be precisely studied in a formal framework.

The main focus of this paper lies on illustrating the applicability of formal methods to a model-driven design. We will therefore most often refrain from giving a precise definition of the formal concepts and instead explain where the concepts can be used. To this end we sketch some examples of model transformations on UML diagrams. For every transformation we provide a corresponding concept from formal methods covering this case. The concepts are all variations of *refinement* [6, 4, 39], a notion of transformation correctness being central in formal methods. Definitions of refinement can both be found in state-based and process-oriented formalisms, and are thus applicable to different views. In Section 3 we will discuss how transformations on different views can be brought together and what their effect on the semantics of the overall model is. Finally, we show what concepts from formal methods can be used to define consistency, and whether this kind of consistency is preserved under model transformations.

Related work. There is a huge amount of work to be found on model transformations and refactorings, see for instance [14, 38, 35, 18, 23]. The OMG's focus is currently on the *description* of model transformations: its QVT request [14] aims at defining (standardising) a language for model transformations. A main issue in this area is the choice of language; aspects of formal correctness play a minor role. Formal underpinnings of model transformations can especially be found in the area of graph transformations [22, 2], a relational approach in [1] and an overview on formal approaches to refactoring in [27]. The work most closest to ours is that of [10] which uses the process algebra CSP and its refinement concept for model transformations. That work studies consistency as well, however, not between static and dynamic diagrams. Concerning the formal methods side, refinement and its variations is an intensively studied topic as well. For modelling systems by different views a number of *integrations* of formal methods have recently been proposed [21, 31, 13, 11], one of which we will use in this paper. Refinement in integrated specification techniques is for instance studied in [3, 33]. The issue of substitutability in component-based designs is (among others) studied in [20, 25, 19].

2   Model transformations

In the following we will sketch some rather small examples of different kinds of model transformations on different views of a component. As a modelling language we employ the UML. It offers various diagram types to model different aspects of complex system models, in particular diagrams for a static view (data and operations) and for a dynamic view (process behaviour).

In order to apply formal concepts to UML diagrams we need a formal semantics for them. For this, we first of all have to choose a semantic domain, and afterwards define a translation of the diagram to this domain. The semantic domain (or formal method) should most closely reflect the modelling domain of the particular sort of diagram, i.e. a diagram for describing static behaviour should be given a semantics in terms of a state-based formal method whereas a diagram for protocols or interactions should be translated to a formal method good at modelling dynamic behaviour.

The examples of different views and model transformations elaborated on in the sequel are described by class diagrams, protocol state machines and sequence diagrams. The semantic domains for them are *Object-Z* (for class diagrams) and *CSP* (for state machines and sequence diagrams). Object-Z [32] is an object-oriented extension of Z [34], a state-based specification language for describing states and operations on them. CSP [30, 16] is a process algebra developed for modelling parallel communicating systems by means of process descriptions. The actual translation from the diagrams to the semantic domains is not of interest for the study undertaken in this paper and will therefore only be exemplified here, for details see [24]. Of interest are the formal concepts coming with these languages, and whether and how they are applicable in a model-driven development.

The following model transformations will be studied. On the static model, i.e. class diagrams, we look at classes with

- changes of data types (and corresponding operations),
- splitting of operations, and
- extension with new operations.

On the dynamic model, i.e. protocol state machines, we look at corresponding transformations which are

- changes of protocols,
- splitting of transitions, and
- extension with new transitions.

Change of a data type. Figure 1 shows a class A being part of a class diagram of one model and a corresponding class C of a different model. Attributes and operations are described in a mathematical notation, close to Z. The change made in the model transformation concerns the type of the attribute *buffer* and consequently the definition of the method *choose* operating on this attribute. In class A attribute *buffer* is of type *set* (of some elements) and *choose* chooses just any element of this set, whereas in C *buffer* is of type (injective) *sequence* and *choose* always chooses the first element in the sequence.

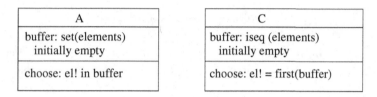

Fig. 1. Model transformation changing a data type

The question of interest for the correctness of the model transformation is the following:

Is every behaviour of C a behaviour of A?

The requirement on this type of transformation is that C should not show a behaviour which has not been possible in A, thus preventing unexpected surprises. The formal concept which can be used for answering the above question is that of *data refinement* coming from Object-Z [33, 6]. Data refinement is concerned with describing the allowed changes for attributes and operations when the externally observable behaviour is required to be preserved, or more precisely, when every behaviour of C has to have a corresponding behaviour in A.

For applying this concept to UML diagrams we have to give an Object-Z semantics to it. For our example the resulting Object-Z classes can be found in Figure 2. An Object-Z class specification starts with a schema (box) describing the state space, i.e. the attributes of the class. The *Init* schema declares restrictions on initial values of attributes. Then a number of operation schemas can be used to define methods. The Δ-list appearing in operation schemas lists the variables which are allowed to be modified by an execution of the operation.

A data refinement relationship between classes is achieved by imposing the following conditions (which are the downward simulation conditions of Object-Z data refinement) on the two classes A and C with state $AState$ and $CState$, operations AOp and COp and initialisation $AInit$ and $CInit$, respectively:

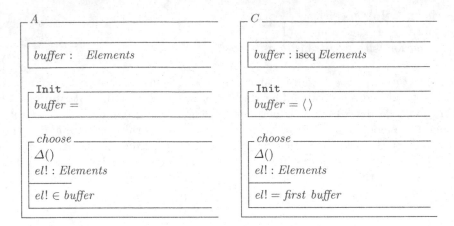

Fig. 2. Object-Z classes for UML classes

1. A *representation relation* $R : AState \leftrightarrow CState$ has to be given, which relates the attributes in A with corresponding ones in C. For the example, R is

$$buffer_A = \bigcup_{1 \; \leq \; i \; \leq \; \#buffer_C} buffer_C[i]$$

(the set *buffer* in A consists of the elements in the sequence *buffer* in C).

2. *Initialisation:* Every initial state in C must have a corresponding (via R) initial state in A:

$$\forall \, CInit \bullet (\exists \, AInit \bullet R)$$

(which holds since an empty sequence is related to an empty set),

3. Corresponding operations must have corresponding behaviour:
   - *Applicability: choose* in A is applicable iff *choose* in C is applicable:

$$\forall \, AState; \; CState \bullet R \Longrightarrow (\text{pre} \, AOp \Longleftrightarrow \text{pre} \, COp)$$

   (which is true since both are applicable when the set/sequence, respectively, is non-empty),

   - *Correctness:* Whenever *choose* is applied in C, the result (concerning outputs and next state) corresponds with an application of *choose* in A:

$$\forall \, AState; \; CState; \; CState' \bullet R \wedge COp \Longrightarrow (\exists \, AState' \bullet R' \wedge AOp)$$

   (which holds since the first element of the sequence in C is an element of the corresponding set in A as well and thus can be chosen as output).

In model transformations data refinement is usually applied for transfering abstract data types (like sets) to more concrete ones (like arrays, which the sequence is almost) which are closer to actual data types used in an implementation.

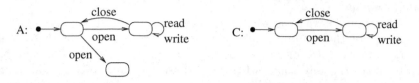

Fig. 3. Model transformation changing a protocol

Change of protocol. Figure 3 shows two protocol state machines belonging to classes A and C, respectively, which are part of different models, however, where C is the class corresponding to A. The state machines describe the ordering of operations which are allowed for a file. The state machine of A belongs to a higher-level model, it is nondeterministic and also models the case where the file to be opened is non-existent (and thus no read/write might be possible after *open*). In C, the nondeterminism has been resolved, possibly by ensuring applicability of open on existing files only.

The correctness criterion for such kind of changes is again:

Is every behaviour of C a behaviour of A?

and the formal concept applicable here is that of *process refinement* [30] coming from the process algebra CSP. For applying this we now have to translate the state machine to the semantic domain CSP. On our example the translation gives us the following process descriptions:

$$proc_A = open \rightarrow Open_A$$
$$\qquad \square \; open \rightarrow STOP$$
$$Open_A = read \rightarrow Open_A$$
$$\qquad \square \; write \rightarrow Open_A$$
$$\qquad \square \; close \rightarrow proc_A$$

$$proc_C = open \rightarrow Open_C$$
$$Open_C = read \rightarrow Open_C$$
$$\qquad \square \; write \rightarrow Open_C$$
$$\qquad \square \; close \rightarrow proc_C$$

Here $\rightarrow$ is the prefix operator of CSP (for sequencing) and $\square$ is the external choice.

Process refinement allows to reduce nondeterminism in a process. Depending on how discriminating the notion should be one can either use trace or failures refinement. The traces describe the possible sequences of operation execution, e.g. *open; read; write; close* $\in traces(A)$; failures give additional information, they describe the traces plus sets of operations which cannot be executed after a trace, i.e. are refused. The failures of A for instance include the pair $(open, \{read\})$: after executing trace *open* the class A might reach a state where operation *read* is not possible next. Based on these two notions the two versions of refinement are defined.

1. *Trace refinement:*
   The traces of C have to be a subset of those of A: $traces(C) \subseteq traces(A)$. This holds for the example since the state machine of C is contained in that of A.

2. *Failures refinement:*

The failures of C have to be a subset of those of A: $failures(C) \subseteq failures(A)$. This holds for the example but would for instance not hold for the reverse direction: the failures of A are not a subset of the failures of C since A might refuse *read* after *open* whereas C does not. Failures give additional information about the availability of operations and thus provide a more discriminating view on processes.

In model transformations, process refinement is used to reduce the nondeterminism in a model and thus again to improve implementability. In an initial model a designer might want to specify the system in a highly nondeterministic manner thus leaving room for different kinds of implementations. Successive model transformations might then step by step reduce the nondeterminism, and thus make the decisions as to how the system is concretely behaving.

Splitting of operation in static model. Figure 4 shows two classes with operations for sending messages over a network. While class A contains a single operation *send*, class C uses two operations for one send, the first one being responsible for preparing the message for sending (e.g. adding certain headers) and the second one for actual transmission. (We refrain from actually specifying them since this gets a bit complex.)

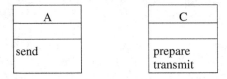

Fig. 4. Model transformation splitting an operation into two

The question to be asked on this type of model transformation is slightly different since the classes have different operations:

Has every behaviour of C a corresponding behaviour in A?

Here, corresponding means that the execution of *prepare* and *transmit* should have the same effect as that of *send*. The formal concept to be used in this case of that of *non-atomic data refinement* [5, 7] from Object-Z. The conditions to be checked can be seen as an extension of those of ordinary data refinement. We assume A to be the abstract class with state $AState$, initialisation $AInit$ and operation(s) AOp, and C to contain $CState$, $CInit$ and split the operation into COp_1 and COp_2.

1. Again a representation relation $R : AState \leftrightarrow CState$ has to be given.
2. With this R the usual data refinement conditions have to hold, which are initialisation:

$$\forall\, CInit \bullet (\exists\, AInit \bullet R)$$

and applicability and correctness of *prepare; transmit* with respect to *send*: *send* is applicable iff *prepare* is applicable, and the execution of *prepare; transmit* corresponds to one of *send*:

$$\forall\, AState;\ CState;\ CState \bullet (COp_1 \,\S\, COp_2) \wedge R \Rightarrow \exists\, AState \bullet R \wedge AOp$$
$$\forall\, AState;\ CState \bullet R \Rightarrow (\text{pre}\, AOp \Longleftrightarrow \text{pre}\, COp_1)$$

3. Furthermore, there are additional conditions for ruling out new behaviour in C which did not occur in A: 1) *Continuation*: once *prepare* has been executed *transmit* is applicable, and 2) *Proper starting*: *transmit* cannot be executed without prior execution of *prepare*. Since the definitions are quite technical we refrain from giving them here (see [7]).

Such transformations might be used when the system is developed with models on different levels of abstraction: what may be a single operation on an abstract level might be more complex when looking at the system in more detail.

Splitting of operation in dynamic model. Figure 5 shows a similar example of the splitting of an operation in a state machine. This time sending of messages is part of a simple protocol involving the receipt of messages as well.

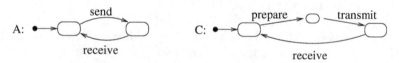

Fig. 5. Model transformation splitting a transition of a protocol

Again sending is divided into preparation and transmission, in this case by splitting a transition into two. The question is again

Has every behaviour of C a corresponding behaviour in A?

The formal concept applicable in this case is that of *non-atomic process refinement* [8] from CSP. The translation of the state machines is straightforward:

$$proc_A = send \rightarrow receive \rightarrow proc_A$$
$$proc_C = prepare \rightarrow transmit \rightarrow receive \rightarrow proc_C$$

Correspondence of behaviours in this setting is declared via an operation ↑ on traces and failures of processes which (roughly) maps the sequence *prepare; transmit* in traces to *send*. The following formal definition assumes that an operation AOp^i (with index $i \in I$ ranging over the operations of class A) is replaced by a sequence of two operations $COp_1^i;\ COp_2^i$ from class C (e.g. *send* is replaced by *prepare; transmit*).

$$tr \uparrow = (tr \restriction \{COp_2^i \mid i \in i\})[COp_2^i \mapsto AOp^i, i \in I]$$
$$X \uparrow = (X \setminus \{COp_2^i \mid i \in i\})[COp_1^i \mapsto AOp^i, i \in I]$$

Here, $\lceil$ is a projection function and $\mapsto$ is renaming. The abstraction operator on traces removes all COp_1s and then replaces COp_2s by $AOps$. For an example: $(prepare;\ transmit;\ receive;\ prepare;\ transmit)\ \uparrow=\ send;\ receive;\ send$. On failures, the abstraction operator ignores COp_2s and replaces COp_1s by $AOps$. As an example: $\{prepare, receive\}\ \uparrow=\ \{send, receive\}$ and $\{transmit\}\ \uparrow=\quad$.

Technically, the conditions to be checked are an extension of ordinary process refinement:

1. Depending on whether traces or failures are to be used we either check $traces(C)\ \uparrow\ \subseteq\ traces(A)$ or $failures(C)\ \uparrow\ \subseteq\ failures(A)$ (and both of them hold in our example) .
2. In addition, two conditions corresponding to those of non-atomic data refinement have to be checked: 1) *Continuation:* after a trace of C in which *prepare* has occured but *transmit* not, *transmit* may not be refused; 2) *Proper starting:* There are no traces in C in which *transmit* occurs without a prior *prepare*.

The application scenario of this type of transformation is the same as that of non-atomic data refinement: the granularity of operations change when moving to a more detailed level of abstraction.

Extension of static model. The model transformation in Figure 6 replacing class A by class C is concerned with an extension of the class with new methods. The classes model buffers with methods *put* and *get*, and class C in addition with a method *empty* querying the contents of the buffer.

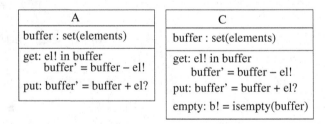

Fig. 6. Model transformation extending a class with new operations

It is obvious that class C now cannot have exactly the same behaviour as A anymore (since *empty* cannot be called on A). The question to be asked for correctness of the transformation is thus slightly rephrased. Instead of requiring behaviour preservation, we require *substitutivity.*

Can a user of A use C as if it were A?

If a client uses C as if it were A (i.e. on A's interface only), then no difference to A should be detectable. The formal concept achieving this kind of substitutivity is *subtyping* [20], in case of classes it is state-based subtyping from Object-Z [36]. Again, we thus translate the two classes to Object-Z.

┌─ A ─────────────────────────   ┌─ C ─────────────────────────

| ┌──────────────────────────── | | ┌──────────────────────────── |
| $buffer :$ $Elements$ | | $buffer :$ $Elements$ |

┌─ put ──────────────────────   ┌─ put ──────────────────────
$\Delta(buffer)$ $\Delta(buffer)$
$el? : Elements$ $el? : Elements$
───────────────────────────   ───────────────────────────
$buffer = buffer \cup \{el?\}$ $buffer = buffer \cup \{el?\}$

┌─ get ──────────────────────   ┌─ get ──────────────────────
$\Delta(buffer)$ $\Delta(buffer)$
$el! : Elements$ $el! : Elements$
───────────────────────────   ───────────────────────────
$el! \in buffer$ $el! \in buffer$
$buffer = buffer \setminus \{el!\}$ $buffer = buffer \setminus \{el!\}$

                                   ┌─ empty ────────────────────
                                   $\Delta()$
                                   $b! :$
                                   ───────────────────────────
                                   $b! \Leftrightarrow (buffer = \quad)$

Subtyping can be seen as a combination of refinement and inheritance: as far as existing methods and attributes are concerned they may be changed according to the data refinement rules and in addition functionality is allowed to be added. For the new methods it is required that they

- either do not modify attributes at all (which is the case in our example since *empty* is a query method),
  or
- they only modify *new* attributes. This allows them to access values of attributes already defined in A, but not to change them.

Formulated in terms of the Z schema calculus, we thus require:

$$\forall\, AState, CState, CState \bullet R \wedge COp \Rightarrow \exists\, AState \bullet R \wedge \Xi\, AState$$

In model transformations this type of change is applied when additional functionality is to be added to an existing model. This is for instance the case if software (and their models) is incrementally constructed, starting with a small protoype which is then gradually extended.

Extension of behaviour model. The last model transformation to be considered is the case of extension on the dynamic model. Figure 7 gives the behaviour-oriented version of the extension described in the previous example, however, in this case restricting the allowed ordering of method execution (only *put* and *get*

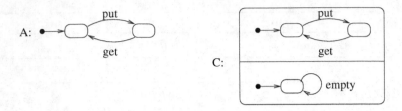

Fig. 7. Model transformation extending a protocol with new transitions

in turn). A state machine is extended with a parallel component independently executing the method *empty*.

The question is again that of substitutivity:

Can a user of A use C as if it were A?

The formal concept applicable here is the behaviour-oriented version of subtyping: when the state machines are given a CSP semantics they can be compared via *behaviour-oriented subtyping* [37]. The CSP processes of the two state machines are the following:

$$proc_A = put \rightarrow get \rightarrow proc_A \qquad proc_C = C_1 \,|||\, C_2$$
$$C_1 = put \rightarrow get \rightarrow C_1$$
$$C_2 = empty \rightarrow C_2$$

Here, $|||$ is the *interleaving* operator of CSP, setting two processes in parallel without any communication between them.

Technically, subtyping is defined on the failure sets of the processes for C and A:

$$failures(C) \subseteq failures(A \,|||\, CHAOS(empty))$$

The process *CHAOS* in this definition allows any behaviour over the method *empty*, refusing as well as executing it. A weaker notion can be defined by using the traces of processes instead of the failures (see [26]). The definition says that the behaviour of C has to be a process refinement of the behaviour of A interleaved with executions of *empty* at any time. Hence execution of *empty* in C may not interfere with the "old" behaviour modelled in A.

3 Transformations and Views

These rather small examples have sketched how concepts from formal methods can be applied for evaluating model transformations once the diagrams have been supplied with a formal semantics. The question still to be answered is, however, what is the relationship between these different concepts being applied to different views? What is the impact of transformations on separate views on the overall system? In order to formally define this, *one* semantic domain has to be chosen into which all views of one model can be translated. An appropriate combination of the semantics of separate views then gives the semantics of the system model. For class diagrams and state machines a possible common semantic domain is CSP. The semantics can be obtained by translating Object-Z to CSP, and afterwards combining the CSP semantics of the state machine with that of the class diagram:

$$CSP(ClassDiagram) \parallel_{\text{joint methods}} CSP(StateMachine)$$

The two CSP processes are combined with parallel composition, this time not with an arbitrary interleaving of the operations but with synchronisation on joint methods. That is, if both the class diagram and the state machine give a specification of a method then both restrictions have to be obeyed. This is achieved by synchronising on these methods: execution is only possible if both the class description and the state machine currently allow it.

Applying this technique to the last example of the previous section (buffer with put and get) we get the following. The CSP process of the class C is

$$ClassC = \bigsqcap_{buf:\mathbb{P}\ Elements} C(buf)$$
$$C(buf) = nonempty(buf) \ \& \ \bigsqcap_{el\ buf} get.el \rightarrow C(buf \setminus \{el\})$$
$$\square \ put?el \rightarrow C(buf \cup \{el\})$$
$$\square \ empty!isempty(buf) \rightarrow C(buf)$$

In this definition the guard (&) and internal choice ($\sqcap$) of CSP are used. The guard really works as a guard to the execution of the method, get can only be executed when the buffer is nonempty. The internal choice is used to internally choose a value, for the initial value of the buffer (since there is no $Init$ schema restricting it) or for the output of operation get. The CSP process $proc_C$ for the state machine has been given in the last section. Thus the semantics of class and state machine together is $ClassC \parallel_{put,get,empty} proc_C$.

The idea of combining Object-Z and CSP part in this way follows an approach taken in CSP-OZ, a combination of CSP and Object-Z [11]. As a consequence, all Object-Z concepts which have been used for model transformations need to be mapped to CSP. Fortunately, this works quite well. For all three kinds of model transformations (change, splitting, extension) correspondence results between the state-based and the behaviour-oriented definitions have been proven. More precisely, the following result has been shown for data and process refinement [15, 17], adapted to Object-Z in [33]:

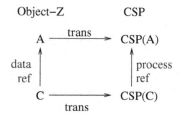

Theorem 1. *Let A, C be Object-Z classes such that C is a data refinement of A. Let furthermore $CSP(A)$ and $CSP(C)$ be their corresponding CSP processes. Then $CSP(C)$ is a failures refinement of $CSP(A)$.*

Whenever a class C is a data refinement of a class A then the corresponding CSP processes of C and A (obtained via a translation from Object-Z to CSP) are in a process refinement relationship. This result carries over to the cases of non-atomic refinement [8]

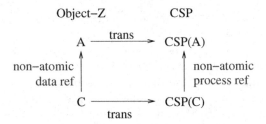

as well as subtyping [36]:

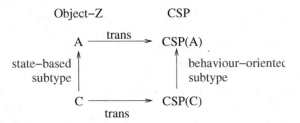

Moreover, all three notions of refinement/subtyping can be shown to be preserved under parallel composition, which is the operator used to combine the semantics of views. For instance, for ordinary data and process refinement we have (leaving out a precise formalisation of the synchronisation set in parallel composition):

Theorem 2. *Let A be an Object-Z class with a state machine SM_A, and C and SM_C class and state machine, respectively, in another model. If C is a data refinement of A and $CSP(SM_C)$ a failures refinement of $CSP(SM_A)$, then $CSP(C) \parallel CSP(SM_C)$ is a failures refinement of $CSP(A) \parallel CSP(SM_A)$.*

As a consequence, it is possible to separately apply the state-based concepts on the class diagrams and the behaviour-oriented concepts on the state machines while still achieving a correct transformation on the complete model.

4   Consistency and Transformations

Correctness of model transformations is sometimes also referred as *vertical consistency*. In this section we are concerned with *horizontal consistency* between views. Views partially define the behaviour of a system. The parts they define might not necessarily be disjoint, thus the question arises whether the views within one model specify contradictory requirements. A formal semantics for views is useful for answering this type of question as well.

Again, we only sketch this on very small examples. The first example concerns classes and associated state machines.

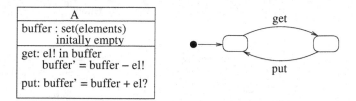

A
buffer : set(elements) initally empty
get: el! in buffer   buffer' = buffer − el!
put: buffer' = buffer + el?

A model with a class diagram and state machines has two partially overlapping views: the state machines restrict the order of method executions, and preconditions of methods specified in class diagrams might restrict it as well. These requirements might be contradictory in that the two specifications cannot be fulfilled at the same time (and therefore no execution of methods is possible at all). In the above example, the class diagram specifies the buffer to be empty initially and the method *get* to require that at least one element is in the buffer. The state machine on the other hand only allows *get* as the first operation, which the class diagram forbids.

For checking whether such contradictory requirements are in the model, the semantics of the whole system can be checked [28]:

- Set the system semantics to $S = CSP(ClassDiagram) \parallel CSP(StateMachine)$,
- check whether there is a *deadlock* in S but none in $CSP(ClassDiagram)$ and $CSP(StateMachine)$. If the answer is yes, then the class diagram and the state machine impose conflicting requirements on method executions.

Formally (again leaving out the synchronisation set in the parallel composition),

Definition 1. *A class specification A and its associated state machine are consistent iff the CSP process $CSP(A) \parallel CSP(StateMachine)$ is deadlock free.*

This check for consistency can be performed automatically using the CSP modelchecker FDR [12]. On our example it indeed claims to have found a deadlock after the empty trace, i.e. initially. The designer can then be confronted with this example and can change the model in one or the other way. The result of such analysis can thus be used to enhance the consistency of models with multiple views.

The second example concerns consistency in a system model consisting of a state machine and a class diagram plus a sequence diagram describing a possible scenario. The following example describes (part of) an automatic teller machine with a specification of the interface towards clients. The state machine states that initially a *pin* has to be typed in, which is then checked. When correct, the client can either choose *withdraw* (with a successive issue of *money*) or *view account* (with a successive *show account*). When the pin is wrong the procedure starts again. The scenario described in the sequence diagram show a successful withdrawl of money.

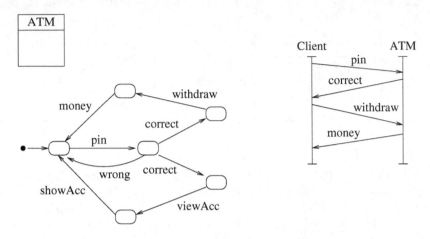

The class diagram and state machine are consistent with the sequence diagram if the scenario is possible in the model, i.e. there is one run of the model which shows the behaviour of the scenario. This can be checked as follows:

- Again set $S = CSP(ClassDiagram) \parallel CSP(StateMachine)$,
- take $P = CSP(SequenceDiagram)$,
- and check whether $traces(P) \subseteq traces(S)$, i.e. whether the behaviour described in the sequence diagram is part of the behaviour of the system. Again this can be checked with FDR.

The CSP process of the sequence diagram is obtained by composing the CSP processes of the lifelines in the diagram in parallel. In our example these are $SDClient = pin \rightarrow correct \rightarrow withdraw \rightarrow money$ and $SDATM = pin \rightarrow correct \rightarrow withdraw \rightarrow money$. They are the same because all messages in the sequence diagram involve both actors (and we have not included input and output parameters here which could show the direction of communication). The process for the complete diagram is then

$$CSP(SD) = SDClient \parallel_{pin,correct,withdraw,money} SDATM \ .$$

Definition 2. *A class specification A and its associated state machine are consistent with a sequence diagram iff* $traces(CSP(SequenceDiagram)) \subseteq traces$ $(CSP(A) \parallel CSP(StateMachine))$.

A more elaborate definition of consistency between sequence diagrams and UML models can be found in [29].

Preserving consistency under model transformations. Furthermore, a formal semantics can be used to study what types of consistency are preserved under what model transformations. For the two examples given above the theory from the process algebra CSP immediately gives us the following results. Consistency between classes and state machines is preserved under refinement: If A and C are both models comprising a class and a state machine, the model A is consistent and there is a refinement relationship between the corresponding views of C and A, then C is consistent as well. Formulating it for one of the refinement relationships discussed in this paper:

Theorem 3. *Let A and C be classes with state machines SM_A and SM_C, respectively, and let C be a data refinement of A and $CSP(SM_C)$ a failures refinement of $CSP(SM_A)$. Then the following holds: If A is consistent with its state machine then C is consistent with its state machine.*

A similar result can, however, not be obtained for consistency with scenarios. Consistency between a system model and a scenario might not be preserved under refinement: Refinement allows for a reduction of behaviour, thus a scenario possible in A might not be possible in C anymore, even if C is a refinement of A.

As an example, consider the following state machine which is a failures refinement of those of the *ATM*.

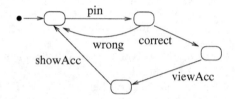

The above depicted scenario between a client and the ATM is not possible here anymore because the branch with *withdraw* has been cut off. This is allowed by refinement because a refusal of *withdraw* after the trace *pin; correct* was also possible before. Actually, the inital specification of the ATM's state machine was wrong, there should not be two transitions labelled *correct*. This can, however, not be detected by a consistency analysis; this falls into the area of property verification.

5 Conclusion

The purpose of this paper was to illustrate on several small examples from the UML what concepts coming from the area of formal methods can be applied to what questions arising in a model-based design of complex systems. In particular, several kinds of model transformations on different views as well as consistency between views has been considered. As future work we plan a more systematic study of these issues, in particular on preservation of consistency under model transformations. Furthermore, more complex types of model transformations are needed. Here, we focussed on single entities which are transformed, essentially keeping the structure of the model. It would be interesting to look at structure-building transformations as well, or transformations which cross the borders of views (as in [9]). In this respect, there is still work to be done on the formal methods side.

In order to have a designer of a model apply these techniques on his/her models it would furthermore be important to have *graphical transformation patterns* on UML models which guarantee a refinement relationship on the underlying formal semantics.

Acknowledgement. I am grateful to John Derrick and Holger Rasch for joint work which became part of this paper.

References

1. David H. Akehurst and Stuart Kent. A relational approach to defining transformations in a metamodel. In Jean-Marc Jézéquel, Heinrich Hussmann, and Stephen Cook, editors, *UML 2002 - The Unified Modeling Language. Model Engineering, Languages, Concepts, and Tools. 5th International Conference, Dresden, Germany, September/October 2002, Proceedings*, volume 2460 of *LNCS*, pages 243–258. Springer, 2002.
2. Paolo Bottoni, Francesco Parisi-Presicce, and Gabriele Taentzer. Coordinated distributed diagram transformation for software evolution. In Reiko Heckel, Tom Mens, and Michel Wermelinger, editors, *Electronic Notes in Theoretical Computer Science*, volume 72. Elsevier, 2003.
3. A. Cavalcanti, A. Sampaio, and J. Woodcock. A Refinement Strategy for Circus. *Formal Aspects of Computing*, 15(2-3):146–181, 2003.
4. W.-P. de Roever and K. Engelhardt. *Data Refinement: Model-Oriented Proof Methods and their Comparison*. Cambridge Tracts in Theoretical Computer Science 47. Cambridge University Press, 1998.
5. J. Derrick and E. Boiten. Non-atomic refinement in Z. In J. Woodcock and J. Wing, editors, *FM'99, World Congress on Formal Methods*, number 1709 in LNCS, pages 1477–1496. Springer, 1999.
6. J. Derrick and E. Boiten. *Refinement in Z and Object-Z, Foundations and Advanced Application*. Springer, 2001.
7. J. Derrick and H. Wehrheim. Using coupled simulations in non-atomic refinement. In *ZB 2003: Formal Specification and Development in Z and B*, number 2651 in LNCS, pages 127–147. Springer, 2003.
8. J. Derrick and H. Wehrheim. Non-atomic refinement in Z and CSP. In *ZB2005*, LNCS. Springer, 2005.
9. John Derrick and Graeme Smith. Structural Refinement of Systems Specified in Object-Z and CSP. *Formal Aspects of Computing*, 15(1):1 – 27, July 2003.
10. Gregor Engels, Reiko Heckel, Jochen Malte Küster, and Luuk Groenewegen. Consistency-preserving model evolution through transformations. In Jean-Marc Jézéquel, Heinrich Hussmann, and Stephen Cook, editors, *UML 2002 - The Unified Modeling Language. Model Engineering, Languages, Concepts, and Tools. 5th International Conference, Dresden, Germany, September/October 2002, Proceedings*, volume 2460 of *LNCS*, pages 212–226. Springer, 2002.
11. C. Fischer. CSP-OZ: A combination of Object-Z and CSP. In H. Bowman and J. Derrick, editors, *Formal Methods for Open Object-Based Distributed Systems (FMOODS '97)*, volume 2, pages 423–438. Chapman & Hall, 1997.

12. Formal Systems (Europe) Ltd. *Failures-Divergence Refinement: FDR2 User Manual*, Oct 1997.
13. A. J. Galloway and W. Stoddart. An operational semantics for ZCCS. In M. Hinchey and Shaoying Liu, editors, *Int. Conf. of Formal Engineering Methods (ICFEM)*. IEEE, 1997.
14. T. Gardner, C. Griffin, J. Koehler, and R. Hauser. A review of OMG MOF 2.0 Query / Views / Transformations Submissions and Recommendations towards the final Standard. OMG document.
15. J. He. Process simulation and refinement. *Formal Aspects of Computing*, 1(3): 229–241, 1989.
16. C. A. R. Hoare. *Communicating Sequential Processes*. Prentice-Hall, 1985.
17. M.B. Josephs. A state-based approach to communicating processes. *Distributed Computing*, 3:9–18, 1988.
18. J. Koehler, R. Hauser, S. Kapoor, F. Wu, and S. Kumaran. A Model-Driven Transformation Method. In *EDOC 2003*, pages 186–197. IEEE Computer Society, 2003.
19. Bernd J. Krämer, Ralf H. Reussner, and Heinz W. Schmidt. Predicting properties of component based software architectures through parameterised contracts. In Martin Wirsing, editor, *Monterey Workshop 2002 – Radical Innovations of Software and Systems Engineering, Venice, Italy, October 7–11*, Lecture Notes in Computer Science, 2002.
20. B. Liskov and J. Wing. A behavioural notion of subtyping. *ACM Transactions on Programming Languages and Systems*, 16(6):1811 – 1841, 1994.
21. B. P. Mahony and J.S. Dong. Blending Object-Z and Timed CSP: An introduction to TCOZ. In *The 20th International Conference on Software Engineering (ICSE'98)*, pages 95–104. IEEE Computer Society Press, April 1998.
22. T. Mens, N. Van Eetvelde, D. Janssens, and S. Demeyer. Formalising Refactorings with Graph Transformations. *Journal of Software Meintenance and Evolution.* submitted.
23. T. Mens and T. Tourwé. A Survey of Software Refactoring. *IEEE Transactions on Software Engineering*, 30(2), 2004.
24. M. Möller, E.-R. Olderog, H. Rasch, and H. Wehrheim. Linking CSP-OZ with UML and Java: A Case Study. In *Integrated Formal Methods*, number 2999 in Lecture Notes in Computer Science, pages 267–286. Springer, March 2004.
25. O. Nierstrasz. Regular types for active objects. In O. Nierstrasz and D. Tsichritzis, editors, *Object-oriented software composition*, pages 99 – 121. Prentice Hall, 1995.
26. E.-R. Olderog and H. Wehrheim. Specification and inheritance in CSP-OZ. In F.S. de Boer, M. Bonsague, and W.P. de Roever, editors, *Formal Methods for Components and Objects*, volume 2852 of *LNCS*, pages 361–379. Springer, 2003.
27. J. Philipps and B. Rumpe. *Refactoring of Programs and Specifications*, pages 281–297. Kluwer Academic Publishers, 2003.
28. H. Rasch and H. Wehrheim. Checking Consistency in UML Diagrams: Classes and State Machines. In *FMOODS 2003: Formal Methods for Open Object-based Distributed Systems*, number 2884 in LNCS, pages 229–243. Springer, 2003.
29. H. Rasch and H. Wehrheim. Checking the validity of scenarios in UML models. In *FMOODS 2005: Formal Methods for Open, Object-based Distributed Systems*, LNCS. Springer, 2005.
30. A. W. Roscoe. *The Theory and Practice of Concurrency*. Prentice-Hall, 1997.
31. G. Smith. A semantic integration of Object-Z and CSP for the specification of concurrent systems. In J. Fitzgerald, C. B. Jones, and P. Lucas, editors, *Proceedings of FME 1997*, volume 1313 of *LNCS*, pages 62–81. Springer, 1997.

32. G. Smith. *The Object-Z Specification Language*. Kluwer Academic Publisher, 2000.
33. G. Smith and J. Derrick. Refinement and verification of concurrent systems specified in Object-Z and CSP. In M. Hinchey and Shaoying Liu, editors, *Int. Conf. of Formal Engineering Methods (ICFEM)*, pages 293–302. IEEE, 1997.
34. J. M. Spivey. *The Z Notation: A Reference Manual*. Prentice-Hall International Series in Computer Science, 2nd edition, 1992.
35. Gerson Sunyé, Damien Pollet, Yves Le Traon, and Jean-Marc Jézéquel. Refactoring UML models. In Martin Gogolla and Cris Kobryn, editors, *UML 2001 - The Unified Modeling Language. Modeling Languages, Concepts, and Tools. 4th International Conference, Toronto, Canada, October 2001, Proceedings*, volume 2185 of *LNCS*, pages 134–148. Springer, 2001.
36. H. Wehrheim. Relating State-based and Behaviour-oriented Subtyping. *Nordic Journal of Computing*, 9(4):405–435, 2002.
37. H. Wehrheim. Behavioral subtyping relations for active objects. *Formal Methods in System Design*, 23:143–170, 2003.
38. Jon Whittle. Transformations and software modeling languages: Automating transformations in UML. In Jean-Marc Jézéquel, Heinrich Hussmann, and Stephen Cook, editors, *UML 2002 - The Unified Modeling Language. Model Engineering, Languages, Concepts, and Tools. 5th International Conference, Dresden, Germany, September/October 2002, Proceedings*, volume 2460 of *LNCS*, pages 227–242. Springer, 2002.
39. J. Woodcock and J. Davies. *Using Z - Specification, Refinement, and Proof*. Prentice Hall, 1996.

A Taxonomy on Component-Based Software Engineering Methods

Christian Bunse[1], Felix C. Freiling[2], and Nicole Levy[3]

[1] Fraunhofer Institut Experimentelles Software Engineering, Fraunhoferplatz 1,
67663 Kaiserslautern, Germany
`Christian.Bunse@iese.fraunhofer.de`
[2] Universität Mannheim, Informatik 1, 68131 Mannheim, Germany
[3] PRiSM, University of Versailles, 45 Av. Des Etats-Unis,
78035 Versailles, Cedex, France

Abstract. The component paradigm promises to address many of the productivity and quality problems currently faced by the software industry. However, its correct application requires systematic, methodological support. A wide range of theoretical and practical methods have been developed in the context of the component paradigm. A taxonomy of these methods can provide a tool for increasing the understanding of the ways in which component-based development is currently addressed and directions for future development. This paper outlines a taxonomy based on the fundamental criteria and definitions, and provides examples to justify this classification. It can therefore serve as a first orientation for new researchers interested in the area of component-based software engineering.

1 Introduction

Software is of growing importance in human society since it is contained at the core of nearly any modern product or service. However, the development processes of such software is undergoing a tremendous change due to market requirements for time-to-market and cost. This has been the major reason for the development of object technology and subsequently component-based software engineering techniques. These promise that software systems can be created with significantly less effort than in traditional approaches, simply by assembling the appropriate prefabricated parts. In popular computer terminology this is captured by the "plug and play" metaphor. As soon as the relevant parts have been "plugged" together, they should be able to "play" with each other in the resulting system.

To obtain the goals of the component paradigm, systematic methodological support is required. For this reason, over the years there has been a vast amount of research and development which incrementally established a large body of knowledge, known as Component-based Software Engineering (CBSE). Unfortunately, the number of available approaches is rapidly growing, and often developers are disoriented and unable to select and adopt the appropriate tools that can best facilitate their work.

This paper offers a coherent and comprehensive view of methods and technologies supporting CBSE activities. According to [14] any attempt to provide an abstract view

R.H. Reussner et al. (Eds.): Architecting Systems, LNCS 3938, pp. 103–119, 2006.

of a complex and composite entity is inevitably exposed to risks: on the one hand, it is possible to oversimplify or confuse different issues and topics; on the other, there is a risk of providing a flat presentation with limited insight and abstraction. The approach presented in this paper is pragmatic, and tries to attempt to find a reason-able and useful compromise between these two opposite forces.

The paper is organized as follows. Section 2 shortly sketches existing approaches to the classification of software engineering methods. Section 3 illustrates the classification scheme that has been adopted in this paper by defining the basic terms, providing characterization criteria, briefly discussing the chosen approach, and introducing a simple approach for visualizing and analyzing the results. Section 4 describes the main existing methods that support and guide component-based software development activities. However, these only represent a small sample of the existing methods. Section 5 presents the results of applying the proposed taxonomy and briefly sketches some important topics that will likely have an impact to future research on methodological support for component-based software development. Finally, Section 6 proposes some concluding remarks.

2 Related Work

The field of software development methodologies is large and still rapidly growing. For example a popular link-list [7] contains links to more than 50 different methodologies. Even if the focus is narrowed to methods suitable for component-based development, the number of methods is still remarkably large. Therefore, several attempts have been made in the past to provide an overview of the field, the goal being threefold:

1. To inform those interested in understanding the technology (e.g., [7]).
2. To justify avoidance or acceptance of the technology (e.g., [11], [13], [17]).
3. To reveal open research issues (e.g., [4], [14]).

Unfortunately, these surveys are either outdated and/or address the field of (object-oriented) software development in general. No surveys, specifically targeted at open research issues, are currently available which present an in-depth analysis of component-based software development methods. This might be due to the fact that objectively evaluating methodologies is a difficult and complex task because of several reasons:

1. Comparing methodologies is often like comparing apples and oranges (e.g., differences in terminology which have a significant impact on the appropriateness and application).
2. Many methods are targeted or strongly influenced by specific context constraints (e.g., programming languages). Thus, the evaluation of methods requires an understanding of the target platform for which the methodology is intended.
3. Certain methodologies assume a "greenfield" development context (i.e., the project is separate, stand-alone, and has no need to integrate with existing applications). This assumption removes certain constraints the methodology may have to deal with [4].

4. The completeness of various methodologies varies drastically (i.e., some methods simply describe a process, others present a graphical notation, while still others combine both graphics and a process). The depth and completeness of each of these components varies significantly from method to method.

Thus, on the one hand, an in-depth comparison or survey requires an understanding of the culture underlying a particular development approach. However, on the other hand, before such a comparison may start a general taxonomy is needed to classify existing methods. First applications of such a taxonomy may already reveal some open research issues, but only an in-depth examination may reveal limitations and restrictions of methods and can be used as a basis for a research agenda in component-based software development.

3 Taxonomy

The goal of this paper is to present a taxonomy for classifying component-based development methods as a basis for further analysis. Each method presented in this and the following sections can be regarded as an attempt for formalizing the process of software development following specific principles. The taxonomy is based on experience, user needs, and the published state of the art/practice. In addition, following [4], as technology changes, methods will evolve. Consequently, a taxonomy flexible enough to capture the dynamic nature of development methods must avoid rigid and precise definitions. Its structure, will depend more on judgment than on scientific objectivity [4]. This means that the taxonomy will remain partly subjective.

3.1 Definitions

Component-based software development methods aim at enabling *humans* to perform software engineering *processes* to produce software *products* that are of value to their customers. Thus, the integration of people, processes and products is a key enabler and has to be reflected in a taxonomy of such methods. However, although terms like method, process, or product are widely used in software engineering there are many conflicting definitions. In the following we define the major terms used in the context of this chapter.

- *Method:* Following [21] a method is a systematic approach for developing a product which provides a definition of the activities to be performed and the artifacts (requirements specification, design, etc.) to be developed. In other words, a method is a codified set of practices (i.e., a series of steps, to build software) that may be repeatable carried out to produce software, and which are accompanied by additional material such as templates, tools, best-practice know-how, etc. In this sense, a method can be seen as a combination of consistent process and product models, enriched by experience.
- *Process model:* In general, a process model describes the tasks that are undertaken within a software project, and it shows how and what information needs to be communicated between tasks [6]. Typically, a process model is instantiated from a software life-cycle model (e.g., waterfall) and can be used to

expose the manner in which the defined development activity is going to be conducted. In the context of component-based software development, the process defines basic development steps as well as the composition of components, their quality, assurance, and deployment.

- *Product Model:* In general, the Product Model is the entire product information resource that describes the product completely and unambiguously. According to [21], a software product model includes any of the artifacts generated during a software project: those that are delivered (e.g., manuals or code) and those that are usually not delivered (e.g., specifications, design, etc.). For each of these there can be a variety of models (including notations) that characterize attributes of the product. In general, product models can be broken down into several categories, with static (i.e., based on static properties or structure) and dynamic models (i.e., based on the execution behavior) being the most important ones. Together they provide a comprehensive view of a software product. In the context of component-based software development, products are viewed as a composition of components, whereby some components are atomic and some are composed of simpler components. In addition, software components of various kinds exhibit tangible properties that impact the quality of software.
- *Framework:* In object-oriented systems a framework represents a set of classes that embodies an abstract design for solutions to a number of related problems [21]. Transferred to the component-based development, a framework can be viewed as a collection of components with extension and composition mechanisms regarding a certain type of application

3.2 Criteria

Software development is a complex task which requires experience and knowledge. In order to systematically obtain valuable results it therefore has to be based on solid methodological grounds. It is simply impossible to develop component-based systems effectively by simply "writing code". In this sense the term "component-based software engineering methods" means all concepts, notations, guidelines, and techniques that can be used in creating better and more effective software systems. Many of these are embedded in or supported by a specific technology (e.g., design and coding toolsets). In other cases, methods are just concepts and knowledge that software developers have to in their daily work.

According to [14] methods include four different entities: principles, development techniques, meta-methods, as well as styles and patterns. Principles are essential ingredients of all software engineering methods and include concepts such as modularity, flexibility, robustness, interoperability, and quality. In order to obtain modularity other principles (e.g., information hiding, hierarchical decomposition, cohesion and decoupling) have to be in place. Flexibility in turn, also known as design for change, requires properties like extensibility, and scalability. Quality is represented by principles such as usability, reliability, or efficiency.

Software development activities are carried out according to a number of different development techniques. They can be roughly organized in three classes:

- *Informal* approaches are not based on any formal syntax or semantics. They simply state a number of guidelines and principles that should be followed in software development activities.
- *Semi-formal* approaches are techniques that include some more formal concepts. Typically, they exploit notations that do have syntax, but lack formal semantics.
- *Formal* approaches not only exploit formal notations but also use formal semantics based on mathematics and logic.

Strongly related to the formality of a method is the level of abstraction it typically operates on. On a rough scale three different levels (i.e., low, medium, and high) can be distinguished, corresponding to the level of detail typically obtained in different life-cycle phases (e.g., *high* corresponds to the requirements/analysis phase whereby *low* corresponds to the implementation phase.).

Another important property, especially in the area of component-based development, is the underlying development strategy of a method. Here we simply can distinguish between top-down and bottom-up strategies or a mixture of these two. In the component domain the strategy describes in which order components are specified and assembled.

The goal of each method is to support humans in developing a product. However, software systems are diverse in nature and have specific needs concerning methodological support. Therefore it is important to know which properties of a system are addressed. Here we can distinguish between system properties such as support for functional and non-functional properties, or development properties such as process and product.

Finally, it is important to mention the domain a method is targeted at. A method domain represents a scientific classification of software systems [26] which are targeted by a method, and should not be confused with the application domain of a system (e.g., logistics). Typically different domains have specific requirements concerning documentation, modeling languages, standards, and concepts. Following the SEI classification schema [26], domains can roughly be organized in the following groups:

- *General* – This group contains those methods which are more a process framework than a concrete method (e.g., Unified Process) and which claim to support software development in every domain.
- *Artificial Intelligence* – Systems concerned with basic models of behavior and the building of virtual and actual machines to simulate animal and human behavior.
- *Information Systems* – Systems concerned with file systems, database systems, and database models.
- *Human-Computer Interaction* – Systems concerned with user interfaces, computer graphics, and hypertext/hypermedia.
- *Numerical and Symbolic Computing* – Systems concerned with methods for efficiently and accurately using computers to solve equations for mathematical models.

- *Computer Simulation* – Systems concerned with the basic aspects of modeling and simulation (i.e., statistical models, queuing theory, variable generation, discrete simulation, etc.).
- *Real-Time Systems* – Systems concerned with knowledge about the development of real-time and embedded software systems (e.g., automotive).

In summary, Fig. 1 presents an overview on the proposed taxonomy for component-based software engineering methods.

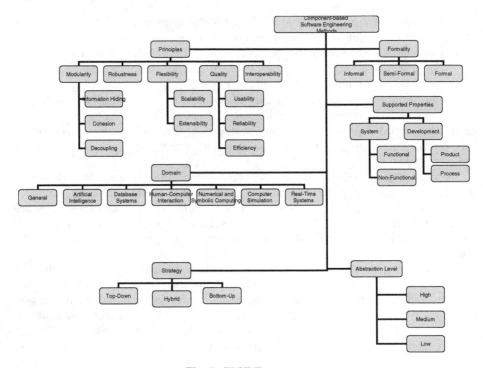

Fig. 1. CBSE Taxonomy

3.3 Applying the Taxonomy

In the previous subsections, basic definitions and criteria have been given to characterize component-based software development methods. Together these define the dimensions of the taxonomy and provide a schema to characterize every available method. However, it is important to stress that the taxonomy should not be considered exhaustive or a finished work. In the first instance, it deliberately did not address all possible aspects of component-based development. In the second instance, the taxonomy itself is subject to continuous evolution, since the elements that it classifies continue to evolve, due to scientific and technological advances in the field. In the following it is discussed how to apply the taxonomy to position some concrete methods, and how to draw conclusions and recommendations from the collected data.

In principle, the taxonomy will be applied to the methods presented in section four. These methods have been selected because of their different nature and coverage of the field. As such, this should also be reflected in their comparison based on the taxonomy. This comparison can then be used to identify to which extent the methods complement each other. Another typical use of the taxonomy is to compare methods that share the same or a similar purpose. This allows the identification of differences, strengths and weaknesses.

3.4 Presentation

The goal of a taxonomy is not only to provide a comprehensive overview (e.g., in form of tables) but also to identify white-spots and areas where future work should take place. The latter requires a simple and easy to compare representation of the collected and characterized data. This can be achieved by the application of radar or spider-web charts (see Fig. 2 for an example). These are not only useful to look at several different factors related to one item, but also to overlay several of them to have a quick overview on multiple items.

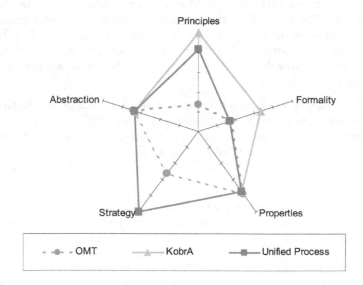

Fig. 2. Spider-Web Chart Example

Spider-web charts have multiple axes along which data can be plotted. A point close to the center on any axis indicates a low value, and a point near the edge a high value. Within this paper we define a general spider-web chart which has an axis for each taxonomy criteria. The single values are then plotted along these axes and connected by a single line, resulting in an individual shape for each characterized method. By placing the single charts on top of each other a common method chart is created which allows to quickly identifying white-spots and areas which warrant future research.

4 Methods for Component-Based Software Development

4.1 First Generation Object-Oriented Methods

Almost all modern software development approaches have roots in the first generation of object-oriented methods. The explosion in the number of object-oriented methods in the early 1990's, and the subsequent cross-fertilization of ideas, makes it very difficult to trace the precise influence and contribution of each method. Other well known first generation methods such as Shlaer/Mellor [28], Objectory [18], Booch [5] and Coad/Yourdon [9] are not discussed explicitly because their influence has been less direct. Since they were developed relatively early in the history of object technology, none of these methods directly considers components, design patterns and product lines. Nevertheless, they all embody important ideas that can be helpful in using these technologies.

4.1.1 OMT

Probably the single most influential method in the evolution of object-oriented development methods is the OMT (Object Modeling Technique) method developed by Rumbaugh et al. [25]. Many of its ideas have been adopted in ensuing generations of methods and notations. Its two most significant legacies are the UML [23], whose notational concepts are primarily based on OMT and its approach to analysis. In detail, OMT identifies three distinct but overlapping models to be generated during the development of a system:

- Object Model, which identifies the user visible data abstractions that the system manipulates, and the relationships between them.
- Dynamic Model, which describes the dynamic behavior of the system in terms of states, events and object interactions.
- Functional Model, which shows the computations or data transformation performed by the system.

The analysis phase is followed by a design phase in which the system is divided into subsystems and algorithms are designed for the methods of the identified classes. Although it is the strongest part of the method, OMT's analysis approach has one major weakness. The functional model is difficult to be kept consistent with the other analysis models. In practice, therefore, OMT users often ignore this model. The design process is the major shortcoming of OMT as a general purpose method. It is much less well defined than the analysis process, and lacks any kind of support for incremental development.

4.1.2 Fusion

Fusion [10] is a descendent of OMT, which fixed some of the problems with OMT's analysis approach, and significantly enhanced the design process. Fusion also pointed the way towards increased rigor and prescriptiveness in object-oriented development.

The analysis phase adopts the same three basic viewpoints as OMT, but with slightly different models and terminology. One of the main innovations was to require that textual operation schemata describe the effects of system operations in terms of the concepts in the object model. This improved the presentation of the functional model and introduced a set of consistency rules between the functional and object model.

The other main contribution of Fusion was the use of interaction modeling. It showed that the design process could be organized in a highly systematic fashion based on the elaboration and documentation of interaction scenarios on an operation-by-operation basis. The basic idea in the Fusion design phase is to create a collaboration diagram that documents how each system operation is realized in terms of lower level interactions. Unfortunately, Fusion suffers from the same problem as OMT in having a "flat" waterfall-based process model.

4.1.3 ROOM

The Real-Time Object-Oriented Modeling (ROOM) [27] method views software systems based on the concept of interacting processes. The basic building blocks of ROOM, known as actors, are active "logical machines", rather than simple ADTs, and typically encapsulate an active thread or process as well as state information. At the language level they therefore correspond to active constructs such as tasks in Ada or threads in Java.

Although ROOM was published before component-based development became a buzzword and dedicated component technologies (e.g., JavaBeans) became available, it contains all the basic characteristics of a classic run-time component model. Actors represent self-contained, autonomous components that can be realized as hardware elements as well as software elements, ports represent independently defined interfaces that allow components to be connected together in arbitrary configurations, and bindings represent concrete connectors that link components together to solve particular problems.

The main problem with ROOM is its lack of integration with data-modeling. Although ROOM defines an advanced and highly systematic way of using state machine diagrams, it makes little use of the core object modeling concepts such as associations, attributes and multiplicities etc. and gives little indication of how they fit in. This is a symptom of the fact that ROOM is more process (i.e., thread) oriented than data oriented.

4.1.4 HOOD

The Hierarchical Object-Oriented Design (HOOD) method [16] is largely limited to the European Space Agency (HOOD's creator) and its contractors. However, it has powerful and unique concepts not found in any other methods.

HOOD views a system as a community of objects organized in terms of two hierarchies: the seniority and the usage hierarchy. The first reflects the containment of objects within one another, and always yields a tree structure. The second reflects the usage of one object by another, in the sense of a client-server relationship. The key idea is to organize the development steps around the containment hierarchy (or seniority hierarchy). The overall development approach is thus one of recursive, top-down refinement in which progressively smaller objects are identified, modeled and implemented.

4.1.5 OORAM

OORAM [24] introduced some important ideas relating to the way in which systems can be modeled. The key innovation is to focus on roles throughout the modeling process as a way of tying different perspectives of a system together. A role essentially defines how a client object sees a server object, including its operations, behavior and needs.

Unfortunately the overall lifecycle process adopted in OORAM is essentially a waterfall model, although there is a high level of iteration within the major phases such as analysis and design. Object containment and hierarchical development play no part in the process, and thus it is essentially a "flat" method like OMT and Fusion.

4.2 Component-Oriented Methods

In view of the importance of the component paradigm, most modern methods aim to accommodate them in one form or another, but generally components are viewed as just a convenient implementation tool rather than an integral part of the overall software development cycle. In the last few years, however, methods have emerged which orient the whole development process around components and view them as richer abstractions than just binary code modules.

4.2.1 Catalysis
Catalysis [12] was one of the first methods developed specifically to leverage the UML [23] in connection with component based development, and embraces many of the other reuse technologies (i.e., architectural styles, design patterns and frameworks). The method either introduced or popularized many of the ideas that today are considered natural ingredients of component-based development, and several of these have been explicitly adopted in the UML.

Catalysis uses an iterative and incremental process based on cleanly defined abstraction and refinement mechanisms. These mechanisms are applied throughout system development from early analysis to implementation and set up the basis for recursive relationships between models, which then support forward- and re-engineering of systems. Catalysis makes use of the UML [23] with strong semantic consistency and completeness criteria based on a small set of 'core' constructs.

4.2.2 KobrA
The KobrA method [1], developed at Fraunhofer IESE, propagates the use of components throughout all phases of the software life cycle. This goal is achieved by integrating the three most important software-engineering paradigms today: Components, Product Lines, and Model Driven Architectures (MDA). In addition, the KobrA method comes equipped with powerful means to achieve continuous, model-driven quality assurance. So far the KobrA method has only mainly been developed for system engineering in the domain of ERP systems. A common problem in all component-based development methods is their complete lack of capability to support the non-functional requirements.

4.2.3 MARMOT
MARMOT (Method for Component-Based Real-Time Object-oriented Development and Testing) [22], a descendant of KobrA, is specifically geared towards embedded and real-time system development in an object and component-oriented context. It subsumes the powerful principles of the KobrA, but provides additional features, that

are particularly important in embedded, real-time application construction. MARMOT is based upon fundamental principles (i.e., software/hardware integration, aspect-orientation, real-time specification and scheduling, etc.) that are fully in line with the KobrA method's meta-model.

4.2.4 Select Perspective

Select Perspective [2] emphasizes the importance of business process modeling as the starting point of development, and follows a clean process that transforms system-independent business processes into implementation-oriented models of the system of interest in a step-by-step way. This includes the explicit identification of components, as well as the potential integration of legacy systems.

Select Perspective is particularly rich in practical recommendations and guidelines. It defines most of the essential ingredients needed for component-based development in the early stages of the software life cycle, and provides some useful guidelines for their application. Unlike other methods, it also explains the role that component technology can play in integrating legacy systems into new applications, and suggests how this can be achieved. However, its main weakness is that it is not always clear which aspects of the underlying business objects are being described by which models. In other words, the distribution of the information describing a business object is somewhat arbitrary.

4.2.5 UML Components

UML Components [8] focuses on the specification of components using the UML [23]. The method identifies two main phases (or workflows): the requirements work-flow which captures the basic needs that the system must fulfill in terms of use cases and high level business classes, and the specification workflow which documents the business types, interfaces, and components that have been chosen to satisfy these requirements.

In essence, UML components offer a subset of Catalysis concepts but with a much simpler, UP-flavored process. This is both its strength and weakness. On the one hand it packages a core subset of the Catalysis concepts in a more accessible and prescriptive way, but on the other, it loses some of the key ideas of Catalysis, including the nesting of components to arbitrary depths, the recursive application of development concepts, and the use of frameworks to package larger-grained reusable structures than interface and components. Nevertheless, the early emphasis on the definition of component architectures in terms of component instances and their connections, and the enhancement of the idea of focusing diagrams on individual components or interfaces, represent valuable insights.

4.3 Product-Line Oriented Methods

With the possible exception of Catalysis, the methods described to this point are focused on the development of single systems. The creation of system variants takes place as part of the maintenance activity, and is generally viewed as a repeated application of the method rather than an integral part of the method itself. With the growing recognition of the value of a product line approach to the software life cycle, several methods have emerged in recent years that focus on product-line oriented software development and maintenance. Catalysis can support such an approach thanks to its advanced framework concepts, but product-lines are not its main focus. The product-line oriented methods vary in their degree of customizability, and the level of abstraction at which they address the variability's and commonalities in a product family.

4.3.1 FODA

Feature-Oriented Domain Analysis (FODA) [19], published by the Software Engineering Institute, relies on the basic idea that a domain is analyzed to identify the features which a system in this domain must or may provide. These features are hierarchically represented within a feature model. Features are recursively composed of other features, with some features being optional or alternatives to other features. A feature model thus serves as a useful input to the designers of a reference architecture for the domain.

Unfortunately, FODA is not described in sufficient detail to be easily applied without guidance. Nevertheless, the feature model is a useful way of capturing commonality and variability within a system family, and adds value to methods that focus on software reuse and product lines.

4.3.2 FAST

The core of FAST [29] is the commonality analysis to identify commonalities in a family of systems in terms of general textual statements. This is used as the basis for "implementing the domain", which involves the creation of domain-specific languages, architectures, generators, etc. to facilitate the low-effort creation of new members of the product family.

One problem of FAST is that it only addresses the product line issues at a very high level of abstraction, akin to the analysis level in conventional development methods. The critical connection to concrete implementation technologies is not directly addressed. Moreover, the guidelines provided for the domain analysis process are vague and unprescriptive.

4.3.3 PuLSE

PuLSE [3], developed at Fraunhofer IESE, splits the life-cycle of a system into four phases: initialization, product line infrastructure construction, usage, and evolution. It provides technical components for the different deployment, which itself are customizable to the context. Unfortunately PuLSE suffers from the same basic problem as other approaches due to its focus on the description of family properties at a very high-level of abstraction without giving concrete guidance on how the required flexibility should be realized at the implementation level.

4.4 Object-Oriented Method Frameworks

Object-oriented methods have come a long way since the early approaches mentioned above. Not only have they become more sophisticated, they have had to embrace a significant set of new concepts, such as components, architectures, frameworks, use cases and incremental development. One strategy for accommodating all these ideas in a coherent way is to raise the level of abstraction in which a process is described and make it more generic. This leads to methods that are compatible with a large number of specific development strategies, but are not ready to use "out of the box". They must consequently be tailored to the needs of specific projects. Such approaches, of which there are two main examples, are therefore often characterized as method frameworks.

4.4.1 Unified Process

The Unified Software Development Process [20] has been developed to provide a unified process to support the full power of the UML [23]. It can be characterized as a component-based, use-case-driven, architecture-centric, iterative, and incremental software development method. In principle the Unified Process iterates a series of cycles, whereby a cycle consist of four phases: Inception, Elaboration, Construction, and Transition. In addition, the Unified Process defines various workflows, the most prominent being Requirements, Analysis, Design, Implementation, and Test, which are carried out to a specific extent in each phase of a cycle. In general the Unified Process focuses more on management (e.g., workflows planning, evaluation, business modeling, etc.) than on technical issues, and provides most support, due to its origins in OMT, the Booch method, and Objectory, to modeling with only a high-level add-on for other phases of development.

4.4.2 OPEN

OPEN (Object-Oriented, Process, Environment and Notation) [15] initially encompassed a unified notation, known as the OML as well as a process, but the former has been subsumed by the UML standardization effort. In its current form OPEN can be characterized as a highly generic process framework oriented towards development with the UML.

Like the Unified Process, the generic nature of OPEN is a double edged sword. On the one hand it means that the ideas of OPEN are applicable, when properly instantiated, to a very wide range of domains. On the other hand, it means that much of the difficulty in using the method is wrapped up in the instantiation process. Poor or incorrect instantiation can easily lead to an incoherent process with very little chance of success. Unfortunately, the instantiation of the OPEN process is still one of its least well-developed parts. Also, in trying to integrate all acclaimed object-oriented techniques, including components, architectural styles and design patterns, OPEN suffers from the same "feature overload" problem as the Unified Process.

5 Results

The methods presented in the previous section represent only a small sample of all available development methods, although the list seems to be quite complete concerning component-based development. However, even this small selection shows that the knowledge required to analyze existing methods and to identify areas for future research is large and quite diverse. The taxonomy presented in Section 3 was used to get a first overview by applying it to the methods presented in the previous section.

Instead of presenting large tables we use a two-part radar chart based on the highest level taxonomy items (i.e., principles, formality, abstraction, strategy and properties).

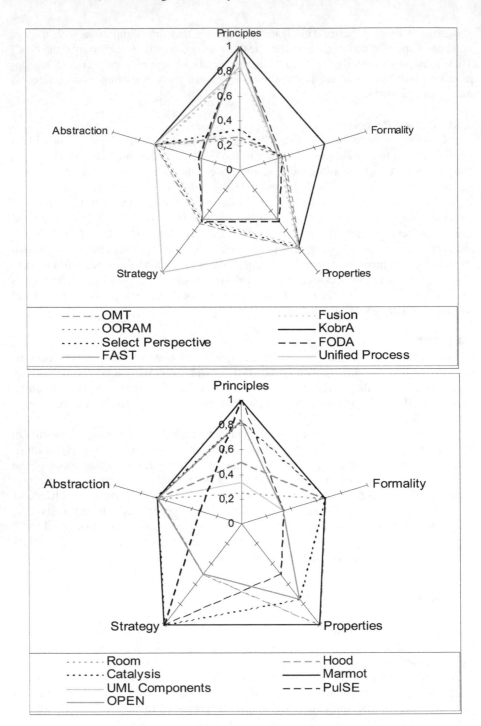

Fig. 3. Spiderweb - Development Methods

The two parts of this chart with together 15 methods are presented in **Fig. 3**. To obtain values for the top-level items the following process was applied: (1) Atomic values have been assigned a 0 if non-existent or 1 if existent. (2) For all sub-items (i.e., modularity) the mean of its atomic values was calculated. (3) Finally, the mean of all sub-items for each of the top items was calculated and the visualized in the radar chart.

For example, for the OMT method, we assigned for Formality the following values: 1 for Informal and 0 for Semi-formal and Formal. Therefore, the value assigned to OMT for the Formality axis is the average of these 3 values, which is 0.33.

At a first glance **Fig. 3** shows that the required properties, principles and strategies for component-based development are covered. Especially component specific methods such as Catalysis or KobrA have made significant advances. However, most methods fail when it comes to non-functional properties or support for the lower levels of abstraction. The latter might be based on the fact that methods tend to focus on the early phases of development (i.e., requirements, analysis, and design), neglecting the link to the implementation phase. Often this link is seen as a responsibility of tools (code generation) or developers. However, the recent advent of the Model-Driven-Architecture (MDA) approach has shown models and code can be tightly linked and that this not only increases development speed but also has a positive impact on the overall quality.

Software becomes more and more prominent also in domains such as aviation, automotive, or even consumer-electronics. However, these systems, often characterized as embedded systems, have specific requirements concerning safety, performance, or timing. These non-functional properties dominate the development of such systems to a large extent. Therefore, systematic development methods have to provide support for handling and quality assurance of such properties. In the area of component-based development this becomes even more important. Assembling systems out of pre-fabricated components requires mechanisms to assess specific non-functional properties as well as actions to optimize and handle them properly.

6   Summary and Conclusions

This paper has briefly presented a taxonomy for classifying component-based software engineering methods on a high level of abstraction. This taxonomy has then been applied on a small selection of published methods. However, it has to be stated that the paper focused on some key criteria in order to identify areas which warrant future research, rather than presenting specific features of a method in detail.

In summary the taxonomy showed that methodological support for component-based software development has made significant advances, compared to early methods, such as OMT. However, the methods available today are no silver-bullets and sensitive against the requirements of different domains and system types. More specifically, the area of safety-critical systems requiring formal development and support for addressing non-functional properties warrants future research. Another problem is the level of detail or abstraction covered by single methods. It seems that methodological support is missing for the lowest abstraction levels (e.g., implementation). The reason might be that the link between models, as used in analysis and design, and the corresponding source-code is weak. The advent of the MDA paradigm might offer a solution.

However, it must be clear that, as in any similar effort, this is just one step forward in a never-ending process. New results in technology development as well as in software engineering theory require further extensions and enhancements concerning the studied methods. Thus, the classification attempt made in this chapter may have to be revised and, eventually, deeply changed.

Following [14] it must be stated, that software engineering is a dynamic and challenging discipline, where novel approaches and technologies emerge as our understanding of software increases and deepens. Thus the classification of methods is an essential aid to researchers and practitioners.

References

1. Atkinson, C., Bayer, J., Bunse, C. et al. Component-Based Product Line Engineering with UML. Pearson, 2001.
2. Aonix A.: Service and component based development: using the select perspective. Addison-Wesley Longman Publishing Co, Inc., Boston, MA, 2003 ACM Computing Reviews 9 (2003)
3. Authors: Bayer, J., Flege, O., Knauber, P., Laqua, R., Muthig, D., Schmid, K., Widen, T., DeBaud, J.M., Proceedings of the Fifth ACM SIGSOFT Symposium on Software Reusability (SSR'99), (Los Angeles, CA, USA), May 1999, pp. 122-131
4. Blum, B.I., A Taxonomy of Software Development Methods, Communication of the ACM Vol 37, No. 11, 1994
5. Booch. B., Object Oriented Analysis and Design with Applications. Benjamin/Cummings, Redwood City, California, 2nd edition, 1994.
6. Bunse, C., von Knethen, A., Vorgehensmodelle Kompakt, Spektrum Verlag, 2001
7. Links on Objects & Components, Pages at the WWW last visited June 2005, http://www.cetus-links.org/
8. Cheesman, J. and Daniels, J., UML Components: A simple Process for Specifying Component-Based Software, Addison-Wesley, 2000.
9. Coad, P., Yourdon. E., Object-Oriented Analysis. Prentice Hall, 1991.
10. Coleman, D. Arnold, P., Bodoff, S., Dollin, C., Gilchrist, H., Hayes, F., Jeremaes, P. Object-Oriented Development: The Fusion Method. Prentice Hall, 1993.
11. J. Cribbs, C. Roe, and S. Moon, An Evaluation of Object-Oriented Analysis and Design Methodologies, SIGS Books, New York, New York, 1992. 75 pages.
12. D'Souza, D. F. and Wills A. C., Objects, Components and Frameworks with UML: The Catalysis Approach, Addison-Wesley, 1998.
13. R.G. Fichman and C.F. Kemerer, Object-Oriented and Conventional Analysis and Development Methodologies: Comparison and Critique, Center for Information Systems Research, Sloan School of Management, M.I.T., CISR WP. No. 230, 1991. 38 pages.
14. Fuggetta, A., Sfardini, L., Software Engineering Methods and Technologies, Technical Report, Cefriel, 2004
15. Graham, I., Henderson-Sellers, B., and Younessi, H., The OPEN Process Specification, Addison Wesley 1997.
16. HUM Working Group, HOOD User Manual, HOOD User Group, July 1994
17. Hutt, T.F. (ed.), Object Analysis and Design – Description of Methods, OMG Press, 1994
18. Jacobson, I., Christerson, M., Jonsson,P. Object-Oriented Software Engineering - A Use Case Driven Approach, Addison-Wesley, 1992

19. Kang, K,C., Cohen S.G., Novak, W.E,. Peterson, A.S., Feature-Oriented Domain Analysis (FODA) Feasibility Study, Tech. Report CMU/SEI-90-TR-21, Software Engineering Institute (SEI), November 1990
20. Kruchten, P. B., The Rational Unified Process. An Introduction, Addison-Wesley, 2000.
21. Marciniak, J.J. (Ed.), Encyclopedia of Software Engineering (2nd ed.), John Wiley & Sons, 2002
22. MARMOT homepage. to be found at www.marmot-project.org, 2005.
23. Object Management Group. Unified Modeling Language Specification. 2000.
24. Reenskaug, T., Wold, P., Lehne, O., Working with Objects: The OOram Software Development Method, Manning/Prentice Hall 1996.
25. Rumbaugh, J., Blaha, M., Premerlani, W., Eddy, F., Lorensen, W. Object-Oriented Modeling and Design. Prentice Hall, 1991.
26. Software Engineering Institute. Software Engineering Body of Knowledge Version 1.0, available at www.sei.cmu.edu/publications/documents/99.reports/99tr004/99tr004sd.html
27. Selic, B., Gullekson, G. and Ward, P.T., Real-Time Object-Oriented Modeling, John Wiley & Sons, 1994.
28. Shlaer, S., Mellor, S.J.. The shlaer-mellor method. Pages on the WWW which can be found at: http://www.projtech.com/, 1998.
29. Weiss, D. M. and Lai, C. T. R., Software Product Line Engineering: A family Based Software Engineering Process, Addison-Wesley, 1999

Unifying Hardware and Software Components for Embedded System Development

Christian Bunse[1] and Hans-Gerhard Gross[2]

[1] Fraunhofer Institute for Experimental Software Engineering (IESE),
Sauerwiesen 6, 67661 Kaiserslautern, Germany
`Christian.Bunse@iese.fraunhofer.de`
[2] Delft University of Technology, Faculty EWI/Software Technology, Mekelweg 4,
2628 CD Delft, The Netherlands
`h.g.gross@tudelft.nl`

Abstract. Model-driven and component-based software development, using the UML, has become one of the dominant development paradigms, particularly in business and web application engineering. Unfortunately, model-driven and UML-based development methods are still inferior to conventional software development approaches when it comes to component-based embedded system development. One important aspect is the heterogeneity of embedded systems: they contain both, hardware and software components. Although, component-based development in embedded systems (with hardware components) has a long tradition, there is still a problem of combining it with component-based software development. One reason is the inability of contemporary component technologies to cope with the specific non-functional requirements of embedded systems (e.g., timing, resource consumption). Thus, the major question is how both approaches can be successfully combined.

The goal of this chapter is to discuss the problems of embedded systems engineering in the context of a component-based development approach, and to identify specific requirements for a development process under this paradigm. In addition, the chapter proposes an approach to specify software and hardware components in a uniform way, concerning their functional and non-functional properties, so that they can be applied in embedded system development. The method proposed is not yet solving all the problems associated with component-based embedded systems development, but it addresses important issues like hardware/software integration, and how timing and resource issues can be dealt with.

1 Introduction

In the past, embedded systems used to be highly specialized, custom designed, and primarily targeted toward mission critical applications. Today, embedded systems are ubiquitous, controlling almost everything from mobile phones to cars, from household appliances to global positioning systems, and entire production environments. The development of embedded systems requires multidisciplinary knowledge of the involved parties ranging from physics, through mechanical engineering and electronics, to computer science, in general, and software engineering, in particular. The driving

R.H. Reussner et al. (Eds.): Architecting Systems, LNCS 3938, pp. 120–136, 2006.

factor behind contemporary embedded system engineering has become software. Software accounts by far for most of the new functionality, for competitive distinction and market share, and for integration and internetworking of increasingly smart devices.

In the domain of embedded systems we can currently observe the same trend that has turned the business computing world upside-down some ten years ago: the advent of the Internet. This had generated a huge momentum toward the development of the e-business applications that we now take for granted, and it led to an exponential growth in the need for new software. For embedded systems, this leap forward comes in the form of a tremendous shift from the more traditional custom hardware implementation to more and more functionality being realized purely through software that is running on and controlling cheap standard hardware components.

Component-based development and reuse are as attractive in the embedded domain as they are in other areas of the software industry, and they may be considered the single most important foundational technologies to appease the ever increasing demand in new and more complex systems. Component-based development methodologies, technologies, and tools have come a long way in the past years to meet the increasing demands of most contemporary information systems. However, software engineering principles, in general, and component technology, in particular, are not successfully exploited in embedded systems development. The disciplines that are dealing with the design of such systems, mechanical engineering, electrical engineering, and software engineering, are not in sync. This situation cannot really be attributed to one of these fields alone. As a matter of fact, engineers are struggling hard to master the pitfalls of modern, complex embedded systems, but they only approach the problems from their individual perspectives. What is really lacking in embedded system development is a vehicle to transport the recent advances in software engineering and component technologies into the hardware world in a way that all the stakeholders can communicate and understand each other. In other words, the techniques and tools in each of the three disciplines involved are now sound and applicable, but there are no obvious methods to transfer ideas and concepts between the various stakeholders in one single project.

This chapter introduces and explains a methodology, referred to as MARMOT, which is intended to provide all the ingredients to master the multi-disciplinary effort of developing component-based embedded systems. It does this by extending an existing methodology, the KobrA method, to incorporate the views and artifacts that typical mechanical and electrical engineers would apply with the views of a typical software engineer. The aim of MARMOT is to enable engineers from the three disciplines to work in tandem in a single project, rather than in separation and ignorance.

2 Related Work

2.1 Model-Based Approaches to Embedded System Development

The Unified Modeling Language (UML) [13], in its most recent version (i.e., UML 2.0) already has the capability to model the most relevant real-time system features, such as performance (using tagged attributes or OCL statements), resources (using Component or Deployment Diagrams), and time (using timing diagrams, classifiers and tagged attributes). Unfortunately, the absence of a standard and 'unified' approach for applying UML in embedded system development, the same embedded system properties may be modeled in several different ways, leading to problems in the composition and reuse of software components. Thus, how to use UML for modeling real-time and other embedded system features, has become recently an active area of research and several proposals have been made.

The Real-Time UML profile [16], developed and standardized by the OMG, defines a unified framework to specify timing, scheduling and performance aspects of a system. The profile is based on a set of modeling elements that can be used by developers to build models of real-time systems annotated with relevant 'Quality-of-Service' (QoS) parameters. Based on these models, external tools can perform different analyses and provide information on the system's performance and schedulability before it is actually built. The profile standardizes an extended UML notation to support the interoperability of modeling and analysis tools, but it says little about platform representation [4].

UML-RT [15] is a profile that extends UML with stereotyped active objects, known as capsules, in order to represent system components. The internal behavior of a capsule is defined using state-diagrams, whereby the interactions of capsules are specified by 'protocols'. These protocols define the sequence of signals exchanged through ports (i.e., stereotyped objects). The UML-RT profile is able to capture the behavior of an embedded system, and it provides support for simulation or synthesis tools, due to its precise execution semantics. However, UML-RT has only limited architecture and performance modeling capabilities. Thus, it should be considered complementary to the Real-Time UML profile [16].

HASoC [7, 8] is a design methodology based on the UML-RT profile, which provides a development process for embedded system development. First, the behavior of a system is described from an external point of view using 'standard' use case diagrams. In a second step, these are transferred to a UML-RT-compliant version including annotations with mapping information.

Other approaches such as that presented in [11] aim at combining UML Diagrams with the formal semantics of SDL specifications to model embedded systems. Typically, the high-level system specification is defined through use-case diagrams, whereby system components and their interactions are specified through block diagrams and message sequence charts, respectively. The behavior of each module is specified using SDL. This specification can be executed and simulated, allowing for early verification of the specific properties of embedded systems.

2.2 CBSE Methods

Catalysis [5] was amongst the first methods to use or integrate the UML, contemporary component technologies, and modern re-use techniques. However, Catalysis defines a large number of principles, techniques, and artifacts without systematically defining their relations, and their application and use throughout the entire development process. Developers therefore have to rely on their experiences in configuring and applying Catalysis. In addition, the development of technical systems with their specific non-functional characteristics is not addressed sufficiently.

The Unified Process [12] represents an attempt to integrate methods such as OMT [14], Booch [3], and Objectory [10]. However the Unified Process, defined as a standard, is only vaguely applying rules and guidelines that help developers or application programmers to achieve their daily tasks. For example, they require the development and application of models without stating how to perform the modeling, how to incorporate non-functional requirements, or how to assure the overall quality of the resulting system.

The KobrA method [1] propagates the use of components throughout all phases of the software life cycle. This goal is achieved by integrating the three most important software-engineering paradigms today: Components, Product Lines, and Model Driven Architectures (MDA). In addition, the KobrA method comes equipped with powerful means to achieve continuous, model-driven quality assurance. The more recent advances in aspect oriented software development such as those proposed in [6], are not yet part of the KobrA method.

2.3 Summary

In summary, existing component-based development methods provide little guidance on how to achieve their promises under stringent constraints of developing embedded systems. In particular, quality requirements are often completely ignored, and they are later burdened upon the testing phase, or it is simply taken for granted that the component-based methods, by definition, lead to high quality software units right from the beginning of a project. Such practices and assumptions are utterly detrimental. Quality must be built into the components on purpose, and this principle must be followed right from the very start of the project. In doing so, existing techniques, methods, and tools need to be tailored and used for achieving this overall goal. However, quality-enhancing technologies are often limited to conventionally structured development methods.

3   Embedded Systems

Embedded systems are systems comprising both, hardware and software. They take control over a considerable portion of our everyday lives since they are ubiquitous in most technical devices such as cars, cellular phones, household appliances, etc., with their importance steadily growing. Due to their dual nature, the design of hardware and software parts cannot be done in isolation but should be treated uniformly.

Unfortunately, there is no generally agreed and comprehensive definition of embedded systems, due to their large spread over many domains. On an abstract level, an embedded system can be defined as:

> A special purpose computer system comprising a combination of hardware and software (and optionally mechanical, electrical or other parts) designed to perform a dedicated function, and which is inseparably interconnected with, and embedded in a larger product.

Most embedded systems are reactive systems operated by a micro-controller. Thus, they have to receive signals from their environment, process them and implement

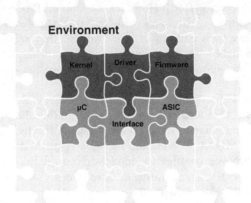

Fig. 1. Abstract structure of an embedded system

corresponding actions, e.g., again in their environment. Figure 1 shows a more abstract structure of an embedded system. A system can be divided horizontally in software (Kernel, Driver, and Firmware), and hardware (µC, Interface, and ASIC) and vertically in micro-controllers (µC), user-specific hardware components (ASIC) and interfaces (Interface) between the individual components and the environment (see **Fig. 1**). These parts of a system are elaborated in the following paragraphs.

3.1 Hardware vs. Software Components

In hardware engineering, the reuse of pre-existing building blocks or components is a common way for rapid system development. The main goal is to reduce the high costs of hardware development by using existing building blocks. In practice, there are large libraries or catalogues providing lists of available components together with their specifications or even their 'source-code' or realization (i.e., detailed electronic circuit descriptions). From a historic point of view this reuse process has evolved over time, from transistors and registers to complex microcontrollers, which today expands into the software world (i.e., building blocks perform complex tasks and are systems in their own right). Thus, they can be seen as components, and, in fact, they are. Here, the idea of component-based development of embedded systems, comprising hardware and software components, is quite natural. Unfortunately, there are some conceptual differences between hardware and software components, which complicate the task of a unified development.

According to Szyperski , "a software component is a unit of composition with contractually specified interfaces and explicit context dependencies. A software component can be deployed independently and is subject to composition by third-parties [17]." Thus, a software component can be characterized as being standardized, in that it follows a standard component model, being independent, in that it is usable without adaptation, being composable, in that external interactions use its public interface, deployable, with components as stand-alone entities, and, additionally, having a documentation. Most of these principles have their analogy in the hardware world.

For hardware components, there are "runtime" composition standards available, e.g. plug-and-play hardware and bus protocols such as PCMCIA, USB, and the like. However, the hardware world is not providing a model for creating component instances dynamically and for connecting such instances in a uniform way. Such a model would define not only component interfaces, but also additional information on a higher level of abstraction that can be used for run-time instantiation, integration, and for the deployment in a broader context. Information, at a higher level of abstraction is either not existing or does not follow a standard. Put it that way, the documentation of hardware components, usually consisting of textual descriptions and datasheets on a low level of abstraction, i.e., voltages, currents, temperatures, etc, so that uniform high-level software and hardware composition and deployment is hugely difficult. The primary problem is the dependence between interface and implementation in hardware.

In order to treat hardware and software components in system development in a uniform way and in order to bridge the apparent conceptual gap between the two worlds, a 'generic' or abstract view on hardware components is needed. This would allow the composition of systems from high-level components. Therefore, hardware components are wrapped and hidden inside software-like interfaces which provide the required level of abstraction, and can then be combined with other software components at the same abstraction level during development. As analogy, we could look at these additional artifacts in the same way as device drivers in operating systems, only that here, we are concerned with development-time "device drivers", rather than runtime artifacts.

3.2 Component-Based Development of Embedded Systems

Reuse is a key success factor in industry today and a major driving force in hardware and software development pushed forward by the growing complexity of systems. This chapter introduces a new methodology for the component-based development of embedded systems, referred to as MARMOT (Method for Component-Based Real-Time Object-Oriented Development and Testing). This methodology is an extension of the KobrA [1] method and its aim is to provide support and guidelines for assembling embedded systems from existing building blocks of known quality at a high level of abstraction. The main concept is that on high level of abstraction component and system developers do not need to be aware of anything about a component's, or its associated components' implementations, or about the type of a component, such as whether it is hardware, software, or a mixture of both. In addition, MARMOT supports hierarchical development, and thus allows the reuse of more complex systems in the form of them being components in their own right.

3.2.1 Principles
Most existing component-based development methods only regard an entity as a component if it is implemented through a specific construct (e.g., a Java Bean), or modeled by using a particular abstraction (e.g., a component icon). In other words, being a component is regarded as an absolute property. But, quite in contrast, being a component is a relative term rather than an absolute one. The term "component" indicates that one artifact (the component) may be a part of another artifact (another component), and certainly not that it is described in some particular form or abstraction. It only needs

to come equipped with the right features that permit the tools to integrate it with other such entities. Composition is a key activity in component-based development. Methods such as MARMOT recognize this fact in that they advocate composition as the single most important engineering activity. A system can thus be viewed as a tree-shaped hierarchy of components, in which the parent/child relationship represents development-time composition (i.e., a super-ordinate component is composed out of its contained sub-ordinate components). Another form of composition is the acquisition of a component during run-time according to the client-server model.

Another, long established principle of software engineering is the separation of the description of what a software unit does (e.g., "specification", "interface" and "signature") from the description of how it does it (e.g., "realization", "design", "architecture", "body", and "implementation"). This facilitates a "divide-and-conquer" approach to modeling, in which a component can be developed independently. It also allows new versions of a component to be interchanged with old versions provided that they do the same thing and abide by the same interface.

This principle is as important when modeling architectural components as it is when implementing them. A component that is modeled according to this principle is essentially described at two levels of detail - one representing a component's interface (i.e., what it does) and the other representing its body (i.e., how it fulfills the specified interface). Following this principle, each component within a system can be described through a suite documents, for example UML diagrams, as if it was an independent system in its own right. This is shown in **Fig. 2.** A MARMOT component is equivalent with a KobrA component plus additional artifacts that are essential for embedded systems. The arrows indicate consistency rules [1] ensuring that the various models describe the same entity from different points of view. The separation between specification and realization allows developers who want to use an existing component, or to replace one component with another one, to concentrate on the interface, neglecting the details of the body.

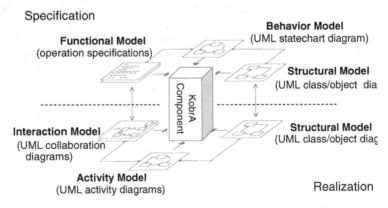

Fig. 2. MARMOT Component Model (extends the KobrA component model)

3.2.2 Embedded Components

The idea of modeling the components of a system using a standard suite of documents or artifacts seems to be applicable in general, so that hardware components may be described in the same way, only perhaps through different types of documents. In particular, this means that software and hardware components are treated in the same logical way. In principle, hardware components in an embedded system typically consist of the hardware itself and a device driver to communicate with the software. For component-based development, however, an additional interface definition is required which follows the same standard as that for software components (i.e., a uniform specification for all component types). Therefore, a "hardware wrapper" must be devised that provides such an interface, and that triggers the events concerning hardware interrupts, and that passes calls and parameters to the hardware's device driver. In this sense, the wrapper and the device driver hide hardware-specific details (e.g., port access) and allow the component to participate in remote method calls. From the view point of the software system, this will turn a hardware component into any odd software component.

Components within an embedded system belong to one out of three groups or types: (1) Software, (2) Hardware (divided into electronics, mechanics, and mechatronics components), and (3) Software/Hardware components, which have a software and a hardware realization. Due to the wrapper concept, each component type can be described at the interface level using a standard set of UML diagrams. Fig. 3 shows the meta-model for these diagrams.

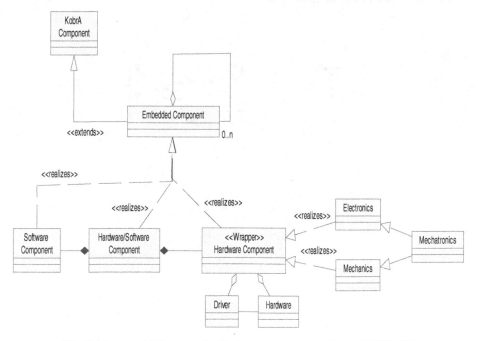

Fig. 3. Meta-model for an embedded component according to MARMOT

3.3 MARMOT Process Model

The core principle of MARMOT is separation of concerns, so it associates its main development effort with two basic dimensions that map to four basic activities [1].

These are illustrated in Fig. 3. The third dimension (Genericity/Specialization) is only used in product-line developments, when a generic component framework (product line) is instantiated according to decision models to form a final concrete product of that product line. The other, more important two dimensions are

–   Composition/Decomposition dimension.
    Decomposition follows the "divide-and-conquer" paradigm, and it is performed to subdivide the entire embedded system into smaller parts that are easier to understand and control. Composition represents the opposite activity, which is performed when the individual components have been implemented, or some others reused, and the system is put together.
–   Abstraction/Concretization dimension.
    This is concerned with the implementation of a system and a move toward more and more executable representations. The activity is called embodiment, and it turns the abstract system represented by models into more concrete representations that can be executed by a computer. The move back is called validation. This activity checks whether the concrete representations are in line with the abstract ones.

The following paragraphs explain the individual activities along the primary two development dimensions in more detail.

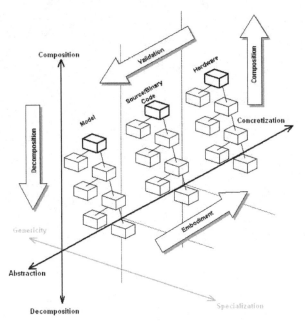

Fig. 4. Two main development dimensions of MARMOT with activities

3.3.1 Decomposition

An embedded system development project always starts above the top left-hand side box in **Fig. 4.** The box represents the entire system to be built. Before the specification of the box, we have to determine the concepts of the domain, or the physical world in which the system is supposed to operate. This comprises descriptions of all entities relevant in the domain including standard hardware components that will eventually appear on the right-hand side towards concretization. In embedded systems these implementation-specific entities often determine the way in which a system is broken up into smaller parts [9].

During decomposition we attempt to map newly identified logical parts of the system to existing components. Whether these are hardware or software does not play a role at this early phase because of the way all components are treated in terms of collections of descriptive artifacts, as said before. Decomposition always requires a good understanding of the domain under consideration, and it is always directed toward already existing pre-fabricated parts. After all, everything is about reuse. Channeling all the constraints of a component-based project into a logical decomposition is one of the most difficult engineering challenges and it can be seen as the single most important determining factor for a good resulting system architecture.

3.3.2 Embodiment

During decomposition we define the shapes of each identified individual component in an abstract and logical way. The system, or its parts thereof, can then be moved toward more concrete representations, some of which will turn out to be program code, some others hardware realizations. This depends on the constraints of the domain and the type of existing entities that can be identified. If functionality exists, it needs to be integrated into the logical architecture through (hopefully) existing and reusable abstract descriptions. If no existing abstractions can be identified, engineers have to decompose the system further until they find a suitable reusable comopnent, or, in the worst case, they have to develop functionality from scratch.

3.3.3 Composition

After we have implemented some of the boxes and some others reused, we can start to put the system together according to our abstract model. By doing this we have to interconnect the subordinate with their respective super-ordinate boxes, or other dynamically acquired boxes in a way that exactly follows our component standard previously described. Hard- and software components are treated in a uniform way, because they have a uniform abstract component model. Dynamically acquired external components may require adapters.

3.3.4 Validation

A final activity, validation, is carried out in order to check, whether the concrete composition of the embedded system corresponds to its abstract description. Validation is not necessarily the last activity in this cycle. We do not have to fully decompose the system in order to implement a single box. Because KobrA and, as a consequence, MARMOT are recursive, each box can be seen as a system in its own right, which passes through all steps individually. The advantage of complete initial decomposition is that all the system dependencies of recursive containment of instances can be resolved from bottom up. This facilitates testing, since components at a higher level of decomposition are usually depending upon components at lower levels of decomposition.

3.4 The Basic MARMOT Product Model

MARMOT is an extension of the KobrA method [1] that adds concepts particularly aimed at embedded systems development to an otherwise restricted model that has initially only been devised for information-type systems. MARMOT fully subsumes KobrA's principles and component model, and it extends both. According to the MARMOT method, components are built on the same fundamental principles that are coming from object technology. Therefore MARMOT components follow the principles of encapsulation, modularity and unique identity that most component definitions put forward [2, 13, Szy99], and these lead to a number of properties that are obligatory for MARMOT components:

– Composability is the primary property of a MARMOT component, and it can be applied recursively: components make up components, which make up components, and so on.
– Reusability is the second key property that can be separated into development *for reuse*, which deals with how components have to be specified and treated, so that they can be reused, and development *with reuse*, which refers to the way in which existing individual components need to be combined in order to make up an embedded system. Both strategies are fully described in [1].
– Having unique identities requires that a component may be uniquely identifiable within its development environment as well as within its runtime environment. KobrA provides the principles for that.
– Modularity and encapsulation refer to a component's scoping property as an assembly of services, which is also true for a hardware component, and as an assembly of common data, which is true for the hardware and the software parts of an embedded component. Here, the software part only represents an abstraction of the hardware part that essentially provides the memory for the data.
– An additional important property is communication through interface contracts, which becomes feasible in the hardware or embedded world through typical software abstractions. Here, the additional hardware wrapper of MARMOT realizes that the typical hardware communication protocol is translated into a typical component communication contract.

Composition along the Composition/Decomposition dimension turns a MARMOT project into a tree-shaped structure with consecutively nested abstract component representations. Such a tree is called containment tree. Each of the boxes in the tree, that represents an instance of a component or a system in its own right, is made up of a component specification and a component realization. The specification is a suite of descriptive artifacts that collectively define everything externally knowable about a component. These descriptions fully specify a component in a way that it can be assembled in a system and used by the system. The realization is a suite of descriptive artifacts that collectively define how a component is internally realized. And according to the composition principles, components can be made up of other components which, in our case, can even be hardware components or combinations of hardware and software components. Any component instance in a MARMOT containment tree can therefore be a containment tree in its own right, and, as a consequence, another MARMOT project. These principles are subsumed from the KobrA method. The only difference in MARMOT is the type of artifacts that can or must be used to describe a specific type of component. MARMOT components can be software, hardware, mechanics, or a combination of everything. This organization is explained in the following paragraphs.

3.5 Hardware/Software Integration in MARMOT

A component specification is a collection of models that describe the externally visible features of a MARMOT component, such as a structural model that shows the immediate external neighbors, and other interacting components, a behavioral model that shows the reactions to externally generated stimuli and how these may change the component's state, and a functional model that describes externally accessible individual functionality, etc. These are common for all components. In addition, each specific component type, distinguishable through the stereotypes <<Electronics>>, <<Mechanics>>, and <<Mechatronics>>, will have their own specific document types that are common and understood in the domain of that component.

In this way, each component that is somehow related to one or several of the domains involved in a project will be equipped with the right documents, so that each stakeholder of each domain can understand its specification. The software engineer will most probably concentrate more on the UML abstraction of the component, whereas the electrical engineer will probably be more interested in the data sheets of the encapsulated hardware entities and the electrical signals that they provide and require. The interface between the two worlds is realized through a wrapper that, in

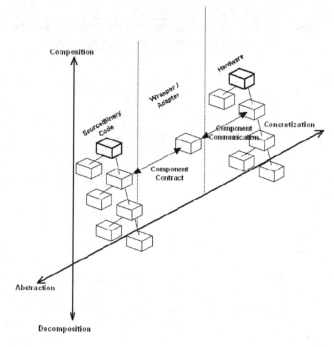

Fig. 5. Component wrapper along the embodiment dimension

terms of a specification, represents operation invocations and parameter communication along the lines of a component contract. In terms of a realization, this would be represented as electrical signals. The wrapper corresponds to an interface between the source/binary code (software) and the hardware, as depicted in **Fig. 5.**

The wrapper component in the adaptor abstraction in **Fig. 5.** explicitly communicates with the hardware component in the hardware abstraction in terms of signals. The abstract source code component will talk to the wrapper component in terms of a component contract, e.g., through operation invocations and pre- and post-conditions.

The following paragraphs provide examples of which documents can be used in the various component types and according to the various stakeholders of the domains.

<<Electronics>> components, such as microprocessors, microcontrollers, sensors, and actuators, in addition to the standard descriptive artifacts like behavioral and structural model, will provide data sheets (**Table 1**) and technical drawings (**Fig. 6.**). These documents, in tandem with the other standard MARMOT specification artifacts, provide a sufficient black-box view on such components.

Table 1. Data sheet template

Type	Type of the <<Electronics>> component.
Name	Name of the <<Electronics>> type, from the containment hierarchy, or realization structural model
Description	Standard name/type of the component, or specific vendor name/type
Interfaces	List of the external interfaces that the <<Electronics>> Component requires or provides
Physical Properties	Electrical and other physical properties that of the component (data sheet of the physical component)

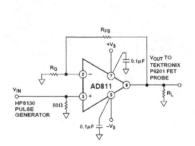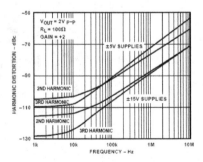

Fig. 6. Example technical drawing and technical specification

<<Mechanics>> components are pieces of hardware that are fully governed by their physical properties. It is arguable, whether the properties of mechanical components will have an effect on the software system. This becomes more apparent when we look at <<Mechatronics>> components that are made up of mechanical elements and electronics. The mechanical properties of a component may have a substantial

effect on its electrical properties, which, in turn, define the way the software needs to be designed. Component-based development is supposed to separate the three domains, although their views have to be incorporated. MARMOT deals with this separation and combination issue through the component wrapper that essentially realizes an abstract device driver. We can separate the view on a component in terms of mechanical engineering, electronics and software documents, but, at the same time, they are part of the same abstraction, so that we can combine these views into one individual building block.

MARMOT's specification level provides a simplified view on the entire system through component abstractions. At the realization level, this simple view has to be specialized and made more concrete. In practice, the system architects, and this may include roles from the three domains under consideration, must decide, which existing component will most likely satisfy its abstract specification requirements, and needs to adapt the wrapper according to the abstract specification. Currently, this would be a manual negotiation and adaptation effort, but automation is also perceivable.

4 Non-functional Properties

Non-functional, or so-called quality-of-service (QoS), requirements are typically derived from user-level abstractions in very early stages of system development. Within the two-dimensional development model of the MARMOT method this would be a stage that is even above the left-hand side top box in **Fig. 7.** However, in embedded system development, most QoS attributes are coming from requirements of the physical world in which the software system is embedded and which it is supposed to monitor and control. In other words, here, the non-functional requirements are in fact coming from above the upper right hand side box (hardware abstraction) in **Fig. 7.** The dilemma is that it is not initially clear how to distribute the QoS requirements among the boxes along the decomposition hierarchy at the abstract (model) level. The question here is: how much budget of a QoS requirement will be implemented by one lower-level box? A customer of a system is interested in that the system as a whole satisfies its non-functional requirements. However, systems are decomposed into finer-grained parts that are easier to deal with. So, the implementation of the non-functional requirements takes place at the lowest-level of decomposition and at the lowest level of abstraction. This can be regarded as a semantic gap between high-level and low-level composition entities.

The fact that MARMOT represents a spiral approach (in contrast to a waterfall model) to embedded system development may alleviate this distribution problem to some extent. In other words, how much budget of memory or execution time will be "used up" by each of the boxes, so that, in combination, they can satisfy their high-level memory or timing requirements, for example? In our opinion, this is not entirely solvable unless there is a direct one-to-one mapping between high-level decomposition abstract and low-level decomposition concrete entities. What we can do is to decompose the system vertically, box by box, in terms of functionality and assess how well the QoS requirements are met by each individual part and then compose the system box by box until the budgets of the QoS requirements are fully "used up". If we have decomposed and composed our system completely in the way it was planned, we are finished. Otherwise, we still have uncompleted boxes, for which we do not have any more budgets left over in terms of QoS requirements. And we have to go back to the other boxes and optimize and gain some budgets that we can use for other boxes. This must be repeated until all boxes as a composition satisfy all the high-level QoS requirements.

As discussed earlier, MARMOT's specification level provides a simplified view on the entire system through component abstractions. These, in turn, are specified in form of UML diagrams, and, in case of non-software components, accompanying additional documents. Therefore, the question is how to describe the non-functional properties of a component already at the specification level? One approach, following the ideas of different UML profiles, is to provide a meta-model of specific non-functional aspects in form of a UML class diagram.

Fig. 8. shows such a simple model concerning reliability. In this example reliability can be estimated low, medium and high, which depend on other attributes such as *portability* and *developer*. The system or a component (i.e., a robot) can then have specific non-functional requirement asking for a high reliability.

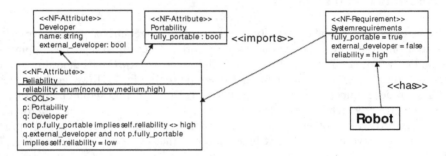

Fig. 7. Reliability Model

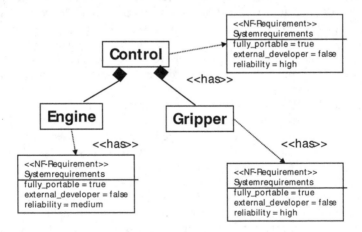

Fig. 8. Refined Reliability Model

In the context of a MARMOT development project, such a high-level requirement can be refined as components and subcomponents.

Fig. 8. shows the refinement of the Control component into two subcomponents and how the reliability properties of these components are specified. During the composition process it can then be evaluated, whether the non-functional requirements of a super-component can be met, taking the properties of the subcomponents into account.

5 Summary and Conclusions

The phenomenal interest in the Unified Modeling Language provides a unique opportunity to increase the amount of modeling work performed in the software development industry, and to increase quality standards. UML 2.0 promises new opportunities to apply object-oriented and model-based development techniques throughout embedded systems engineering. However, this chance will be lost, if developers are not given effective and practical means for handling the complexity of such systems, and if they are lacking guidelines for systematically applying them.

This chapter has outlined the UML modeling practices, which are needed in order to fully leverage the component paradigm in the development of embedded software. Following the principles of encapsulation and uniformity - separating the description of what a system unit does (e.g., "specification", "interface" and "signature") from the description of how it does it (e.g., "realization", "design", "architecture", "body", and "implementation"), and describing both levels with a standard set of models – it becomes feasible to model hardware and software components of an embedded system in a uniform way. This facilitates also a "divide and conquer" approach to modeling, in which a system unit can be developed independently. It also allows new versions of a unit to be interchanged with old versions provided that they do the same thing. The MARMOT method supports this approach to modeling by providing embedded system developers with step-by-step guidelines throughout a complete development project. The principles of the MARMOT method are currently being tried out in real industrial case studies, and adapted to various embedded systems domains. The next step will be the provision of a tool suite.

References

1. C. Atkinson, et al.: Component-Based Product Line Engineering with UML. Addison-Wesley (2002)
2. G. Booch. Software Components with ADA: Structures, Tools and Subsystems. Benjamin-Cummings (1987)
3. G. Booch: Object-Oriented Analysis and Design with Applications. Benjamin-Cummings (1994)
4. Rong Chen, Marco Sgroi, Grant Martin, Luciano Lavagno, Alberto Sangiovanni-Vincentelli, Jan Rabaey: Embedded System Design Using UML and Platforms. Proceedings of the Forum on Specification & Design Languages 2002 (FDL'02), Marseille, France, September 24-27 (2002)
5. D. D'Souza, A. Wills: CATALYSIS practical rigor and refinement - extending OMT, fusion, and objectory. Technical report, ICON Computing Inc. (1995)

6. R.E. Filman and others: Aspect-Oriented Software Development. Addison-Wesley (2005)
7. P.Green, M. Edwards, S. Essa: UML for System-Level Design, Forum on Design Languages, Proceedings of FDL 2001, Lyon, France, Sept. 3-7 (2001)
8. P. N. Green, M. D. Edwards: The modeling of Embedded Systems Using HASoC, Proceedings of Design, Automation and Test in Europe (DATE 02).
9. H.-G. Gross: Component-Based Software Testing with UML. Springer, Heidelberg (2005)
10. I. Jacobson: Object-Oriented Software Engineering. Addison-Wesley (1992)
11. G. de Jong: A UML-Based Design Methodology for Real-Time and Embedded Systems, Proceedings of of Design, Automation and Test in Europe (DATE 02).
12. P. Kruchten: The Rational Unified Process. An Introduction. Object Technology Series. Addison-Wesley (1998)
13. Object Management Group: Unified Modeling Language Specification (2000)
14. J. Rumbaugh and others: Object-Oriented Modeling and Design, Prentice-Hall (1991)
15. B. Selic, J. Rumbaugh: Using UML for Modeling Complex Real-Time Systems, White paper, Rational (Object Time) (March 1998)
16. B. Selic: A Generic Framework for Modeling Resources with UML, IEEE Computer Society (June 2000)
17. C. Szyperski: Component Software, Beyond Object-Oriented Programming. Second Edition. Addison-Wesley, London (1999)

On the Composition of Compositional Reasoning

Felix C. Freiling[1] and Thomas Santen[2]

[1] Universität Mannheim, Informatik 1,
D-68131 Mannheim, Germany
[2] Technische Universität Berlin, Softwaretechnik,
FR 5-6, Franklinstr. 28/29, D-10587 Berlin, Germany

Abstract. We survey compositionality results for three classes of system properties: invariance/safety properties and liveness properties (based on work by Abadi and Lamport), and confidentiality properties (based on work by Mantel). We then analyse the difficulties which occur when trying to apply the compositionality results of these classes of properties simultaneously.

1 Introduction

In many areas of engineering, compositional reasoning is a key to master the complexity of practical applications. Briefly spoken, compositional reasoning allows to derive properties of a complex system from the individual properties of it's components. In civil engineering, the structural integrity of a building for example is calculated from the properties of the used materials (stiffness of steel, thickness of concrete, etc.) plus the structure of the overall construction plan.

Since complexity is one of the fundamental problems of modern software systems, the idea of compositional reasoning has also been applied in software engineering. The growing area of component-based systems (for an overview see Szyperski [17]) can be regarded as a witness for the importance of this issue. However, compositional reasoning is no silver bullet. Reasoning about the composition of systems is nothing which can be taken lightly because it needs to pay careful attention to the subtle and often surprising ways in which components may interact.

There are many ways in which it is possible to investigate compositional reasoning. On the one hand, the component-based system community has documented many efforts in this direction, often under the heading of component *predictability* (see for example recent work by Crnkovic *et al.* [7]). The focus of this stream of work lies on particular practical system properties (like reliability and performance) and their compositionality. Thus, the models used are tailored to a specific setting and context. On the other hand, there is a more theoretical view which is closer to the work in the software verification community. There, compositional reasoning is based on an (often rather general and) rigorous (i.e., formal) theory of system semantics. Both streams of work (the predictability stream and the verification stream) focus on orthogonal issues of compositionality: While the verification community wishes to obtain results which are as general as possible (within the respective semantic domain), the predictability

R.H. Reussner et al. (Eds.): Architecting Systems, LNCS 3938, pp. 137–151, 2006.
© Springer-Verlag Berlin Heidelberg 2006

community strives for concrete formulas from which the behavior of a composed system may be forecast.

Based on the background of the authors, in this paper we follow the path of the verification community. Several theories of composition and for distinct classes of properties have been proposed. But while being rather general, most of the theories available today are far from universal. Instead of aiming at a (complex) "meta theory" of composition comprising all types of system properties, it seems more promising to ask the question whether and in what way existing methods of compositional reasoning for different types of system properties are themselves compositional.

In this paper we look at three domains of system properties and their compositionality results and ask whether these results can be applied in the same system context simultaneously. The classes of system properties considered are:

1. *Assertional properties* of the system state, i.e., properties which hold or which do not hold in the history (the "past") of a system execution. Examples for this kind of property are *partial correctness*, i.e., the property that the termination state of a system satisfies a certain input/output relation, or *mutual exclusion*, i.e., the property that no two processes in the system access a shared resource simultaneously. Assertional properties are often called *safety properties*. The characteristic of such properties is that their violation occurs in finite time.

2. *Liveness properties* of systems, i.e., properties which demand that the system will do something in the "future" of a system execution. Examples of such properties are *termination*, i.e., that eventually the system reaches a termination state, or many types of *fairness* properties, e.g., every process which requests access to a shared resource will eventually be able to access it in finite time. The characteristic of such properties is that their violation occurs in infinite time.

3. *Confidentiality properties* of systems, i.e., properties which assert that an observer of the system is not able to deduce information about the occurrence or non-occurrence of certain types of internal system events. The characteristic of such properties is that they cannot be judged by observing an individual system execution but require an analysis of the actual system behavior in relationship to alternative behaviors the system might have exhibited instead. As an example, consider a hospital information system where patients can usually access their medical files but are denied access in case a doctor has added a terminal diagnosis (in order to convey it to the patient in the presence of medical staff). Knowing this rule (i.e., the complete system behavior) and observing an access restriction a patient is able to conclude that he has a terminal diagnosis without observing this directly. So the system does not satisfy confidentiality.

Our selection of properties was made partly based on their prominence in the verification literature and partly based on the background of the authors. The classes of safety and liveness properties are well-established in classical verification of reactive systems [11, 12, 5] while the particular class of confidentiality properties investigated here is part of an increasingly popular stream of work within the security community. It should be noted, however, that there are also other streams of work which we could have considered, for example work by Charpentier and Chandy [6] which, in contrast to the work considered here, does not use automata-based models of computation.

Our notion of compositional reasoning for a class of properties $\mathcal{P}$ basically is the following: Given a set of components $\{\Pi_1, \ldots, \Pi_n\}$. Each component Π_i satisfies property $P_i \in \mathcal{P}$. Now consider the composition Π of the Π_i (written as $\Pi_1 \| \Pi_2 \| \ldots \| \Pi_n$). We would like to derive the property P which Π satisfies from the properties of the Π_i. The class of properties admits compositional reasoning if P is expressible as a function of P_i, i.e., $P = F(P_1, \ldots, P_n)$. A composition theorem for the class of properties generally has the form: Given Π_i which satisfy properties P_i. Under some hypothesis H there exists a function F such that $\Pi = \Pi_1 \| \ldots \| \Pi_n$ satisfies $P = F(P_1, \ldots, P_n)$.

In the following Section 2, we survey basic compositionality results for the previously described classes of properties, namely Abadi and Lamport's composition principle for safety and liveness properties [1] and Mantel's compositionality results for the domain of confidentiality properties [14]. In Section 3 we examine the difficulties which occur when trying to apply these compositionality results simultaneously. The main results of this examination are the following:

1. The compositionality theorems are mutually compatibe in the sense that the system models are equivalent and their hypotheses are — in general — not inconsistent.
2. Certain types of confidentiality properties imply the absence of certain types of safety properties. This means that a system specification which requires both properties to hold may not be implementable.
3. In contrast to safety properties, liveness properties do not contain a potential conflict with confidentiality properties. However, this insight may be of little help in practical settings where the problem is to find a proper decomposition that ensures the preconditions of the individual compositionality theorems simultaneously.

We conclude the paper in Section 4.

2   Classes of System Properties and Compositional Reasoning

In this section we review the fundamental compositionality results for the domains of safety and liveness properties on the one hand and the domain of confidentiality properties on the other.

2.1   Safety and Liveness Properties

In 1993, Abadi and Lamport [1] discussed the composition of safety and liveness properties at a semantic level. Followup work by the same authors [2] investigated composition using a particular logic (TLA). We now briefly revisit their system model and the main results.

Semantic Model. The model is state based with the addition of *agents*. For a component, basically two agents are distiguished: the component and its environment. Agents are responsible for state changes.

A *behavior* is a sequence of alternating state and agents meaning that the next state is reached by the agent executing some action. Concurrency is modeled using interleaving semantics. Two behaviors are *stuttering equivalent* if they are equal after sequences of stuttering steps (where the state does not change) are replaced by the single state. A *property* is a set of behaviors closed under stuttering equivalence.

A property is a *safety property* if it is closed under prefixes. A property is a *liveness property* if every finite behavior prefix is a prefix of a behavior in that property. The *specification* of a system is the property consisting of all behaviors in which the system is considered to perform correctly.

Using results from topology, Alpern and Schneider [3] proved that every property (in the above sense) can be represented as the intersection of a safety property and a liveness property. In a sense, safety and liveness properties are therefore universal for the domain of properties which are sets of behaviors. For a survey of safety and liveness see Kindler [9].

Types of Specifications Considered. A system we specify cannot control its environment. Therefore a specification must be written such that it does not constrain the environment. A good specification asserts that the system behaves correctly *if* the environment behaves correctly. A specification is called *unrealizable* if it constrains the environment and therefore is unimplementable. We now describe this concept more precisely.

A behavior is the outcome of a two-player infinite game played between the system and its environment. The environment chooses the initial state. Then system and environment take turns in extending the behavior. The system can add at most one step, the environment any finite number of steps. The system wins if the resulting behavior satisfies the specification. A specification is *realizable* if the system always has a winning strategy, i.e., the system can always make the behavior satisfy the specification no matter what the environment does.

The *realizable part* of a specification is the set of behaviors in which the environment never had the chance to win. Abadi and Lamport [1] consider only the realizable part of a specification.

Programs. A program consists of a set of states, a set of initial states, a next state relation and a progress property (often called a fairness property). Initial states and the next state relation define a safety property. The semantics of a program is the intersection of the safety property of the program (defined by the set of initial states and the next state relation) and the progress property.

A pair of properties (M, P) is *machine-closed* iff M equals the safety closure of P. Machine closure of (M, P) means that P does not imply any safety property not implied by M. Let S be the safety property of the program and L be its progress property. Then Abadi and Lamport demand that $(S, S \cap L)$ should be machine-closed. All published forms of progress properties (strong/weak fairness, progress, maximality) are machine-closed for any program.

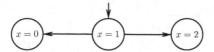

Fig. 1. Example system for which the liveness property "eventually $x = 2$" is not machine closed.

As an example, consider the system depicted in Fig. 1. Consider the safety property S defined by the transition relation of that system: the state $x = 1$ is the initial state and only two subsequent state transitions are possible (either to $x = 0$ or $x = 2$). Once that state is reached, the system remains in that state. Let the liveness property L be "eventually $x = 2$". Now the pair $(S, S \cap L)$ is not machine-closed. To see this, observe that requiring the system to satisfy L implies that it never takes the state transition from $x = 1$ to $x = 0$. So $S \cap L$ implies the safety property "never $x = 0$" which is not part of S.

Normal Forms of a Specification. A specification has the canonical form

$$I \cap E_S \cap E_L \Rightarrow M_S \cap M_L$$

where I is an initial state predicate, E_S is the safety property of the environment and M_S is the safety property of the system. The properties E_L and M_L should be machine-closed with respect to their respective safety properties, i.e., E_S and M_S.

Abadi and Lamport prove [1–Theorem 1] that the progress properties M_L and E_L can be combined to one and the specification be written as:

$$I \cap E_S \Rightarrow M_S \cap (E_L \Rightarrow M_L)$$

Composition Principle. For simplicity, we just consider the composition Π of two systems Π_1 and Π_2. We assume that they refer to the same state space and they "contain" different agents. Composition of two properties is interpreted as conjunction (or intersection) of the properties. Property S implements property S if the realizable part of S is a subset or equal to S.

Given two components Π_1 and Π_2 with specifications $E_i \Rightarrow M_i$ and let the composition Π of Π_1 and Π_2 have specification $E \Rightarrow M$. Here, E, E_1, and E_2 are assumed to be safety properties.

The composition principle has three hypotheses:

1. Π guarantees M if each component Π_i guarantees M_i. This basically means that $M = M_1 \cap M_2$.
2. If Π satisfies E and Π_j satisfies M_j then E_i is satisfied for all Π_i. Basically this means that $E \cap M_1 \cap M_2 \Rightarrow E_1 \cap E_2$.
3. Every component Π_i guarantees M_i under environment assumption E_i. Basically this means that each Π_i satisfies its specification $E_i \Rightarrow M_i$.

The conclusion of the composition principle states that Π satisfies $E \Rightarrow M_1 \cap M_2$. Note that the composition principle is very general in that it does not restrict the way in which components interact, i.e., the components can mutually influence each other.

Example. The following example is directly taken from Abadi and Lamport [1]. Assume you are given two components Π_1 and Π_2 as depicted in Fig. 2. A

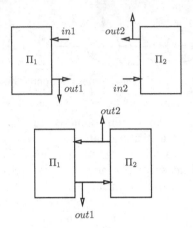

Fig. 2. Example for the composition principle [1–p. 75]

split wire outputs the same value at both heads of an arrow. The specification of the two components is as follows:

- Π_1 guarantees that it never sends a "1" on *out1* (M_1), assuming that its environment never sends it a "2" on *in1* (E_1).
- Π_2 guarantees that it never sends a "2" on *out2* (M_2), assuming that its environment never sends it a "1" on *in2* (E_2).

Note that the composed system Π does not receive values from its environment and so it has no environment assumption E.

If we consider the two components above as two people, the specifications can be metaphorically rephrased as "if you never do X then I will never do Y" for the first person and "if you never do Y then I will never do X" for the second. Intuitively, it should be clear that the resulting system satisfies the property that X and Y never happen (like in a nonaggression treaty). So let's check the hypotheses of the composition principle for Π, the composition of Π_1 and Π_2: Firstly, E_1 and E_2 as well as $E_1 \cap E_2$ are safety properties. Secondly, if $M_1 \cap M_2$ holds, then $E_1 \cap E_2$ are satisfied. Thirdly, each component satisfies its specification in isolation. So, alltogether Π satisfies $E_1 \cap E_2 \Rightarrow M_1 \cap M_2$.

Now we change the specifications of Π_1 and Π_2 by exchanging the word "never" to the word "eventually" as follows:

- Π_1 guarantees that it eventually sends a "1" on *out1* (M_1), assuming that its environment eventually sends it a "2" on *in1* (E_1).
- Π_2 guarantees that it eventually sends a "2" on *out2* (M_2), assuming that its environment eventually sends it a "1" on *in2* (E_2).

Intuitively, this means that one component says "if you start doing X I will start doing Y" and the other "if you start doing Y then I will start doing X". Here, the conclusion of the composition principle would be that Π satisfies $M_1 \cap M_2$, i.e., eventually a "1" is output at *out1* and a "2" is output at *out2*. But it should be clear that as in politics of deterrence the result is stagnation (neither X nor Y happen). Formally, the composition principle is not applicable here.

The hypothesis is violated which states that the environment assumptions are safety properties.

2.2   Confidentiality Properties

We now investigate confidentiality properties and their compositionality. More precisely, we consider *possibilistic information flow* properties. These properties require that, given the system can perform a certain behavior, it can also perform certain other behaviors. A system satisfying such a property keeps unobservable differences between those behaviors confidential. Mantel's thesis [14], on which the presentation is based, presents a comprehensive overview over different types of confidentiality properties and fundamental compositionality results.

Information flow properties like the ones investigated by Mantel are usually discussed using examples from the area of multi-level security. Confidentiality of events should be ensured regarding two types of users which are named *High* and *Low* after their corresponding security levels. User High is assumed to manipulate confidential information whereas user Low also has access to the system but should not be able to deduce certain types of confidential information.

Note that in the context of confidentiality properties, the term *property* has a slightly different formal interpretation (as will be describes below). Also, the term *trace* is used instead of the term *behavior*. A trace is a sequence of events, whereas a behavior is a sequence of agents and states. Technically, traces and behaviors can be mapped to each other.

System Model. The system model on which the definitions of information flow properties is based describes the possible traces over a given set of events, which are classified as inputs, outputs, and internal events.

An *event system* is a tuple (E, I, O, Tr), where E is the set of all possible events, $I \subseteq E$, $O \subseteq E$ are disjoint sets of input and output events, and Tr is a prefix closed set of *traces*, i.e., sequences of events. The set E comprises all finite traces. The set E additionally includes the infinite ones.

A property Q of sets of events is a *closure property* if for all $Tr \subseteq E$ there is a set $\overline{Tr} \supseteq Tr$ with $Q(\overline{Tr})$.

All properties of traces can be expressed as properties of sets of traces (using their characteristic sets). Conversely, a property of sets of traces can be expressed by an equivalent property of traces if the property is closed under subsets and has a maximal element. Therefore, closure properties cannot be reduced to equivalent properties of traces [14]. McLean [16] has proved a similar theorem.

Basic Security Predicates. Mantel's *Modular Assembly Kit for Security Properties* (MAKS) identifies basic properties that can be conjoined to produce different information flow properties. These *basic security predicates* (BSP) are related to a *view* $\mathcal{V} = (C, N, V)$ partitioning the events E of a system into confidential ones C, visible ones V, and non-visible but not confidential ones N. Each BSP has the following form, where the predicate $S\ (\tau, \beta, c, v)$ implies that β is a prefix of τ.

$BSP\ (Tr)\ \Longleftrightarrow$

$$\forall \tau : Tr; c : C; v : V; \beta : E\ .S\ (\tau, \beta, c, v) \implies \exists \tau\ : Tr.T\ (\tau, \tau, \beta, c, v) \quad (1)$$

Thus, a BSP basically requires that, under certain conditions, there exists some trace $\tau \in Tr$ for a each $\tau \in Tr$. All basic security predicates hold for E, i.e., $BSP\ (E)$ is true. Therefore, a BSP is a closure property.

Constructing τ from τ can be considered a two step process: first, some τ is *disturbed* by adding or deleting one or more confidential events, which produces a sequence of events that not necessarily is a trace in Tr; second, that sequence is *corrected* to produce τ by adding or deleting events in N.

Standard information flow properties such as *generalized noninterference* [15] and *forward correctability* [8] formally capture the intuition that observing only the visible events of a system trace does not allow an adversary to gain information about the confidential events of that system trace. Such properties can be expressed as conjunctions of BSPs in MAKS.

A view determines which events are considered confidential. The question who "owns" events is a motivation for that distinction. Usually, the *Low* part of a system is considered the one against whom the *High* part needs to be protected. Therefore, it is obvious that all events directly accessible to Low are considered visible. Often, only high *inputs* are considered confidential because low events may influence high outputs (if High computes outputs based on data gained from Low). Then, the high outputs are not visible (to Low) but also not confidential, i.e., they make up the set N of a view.

Forms of Composition. The *general composition* $ES_1 \parallel ES_2$ of two event systems ES_1 and ES_2 is defined by

$$E = E_1 \cup E_2$$
$$I = (I_1 \setminus O_2) \cup (I_2 \setminus O_1)$$
$$O = (O_1 \setminus I_2) \cup (O_2 \setminus I_1)$$
$$Tr = \{t \in E\ |t|_{E1} \in Tr_1 \wedge t|_{E2} \in Tr_2\}$$

The events of E not in I and O are the internal communication events of the composed system. Depending on the possible directions of communications between the subsystems, one can distinguish the following special cases of general composition:

- In a *product*, both subsystems work completely independently.
- A *general cascade* allows only unidirectional communication between the subsystems, i.e., outputs of ES_1 become inputs of ES_2 but not vice versa.
- A *proper cascade* is a general cascade where $I = I_1$ and $O = O_2$, i.e., it pipes inputs through ES_1 to ES_2, which produces the system outputs.

Figure 3 shows a general cascade $\Pi_3 \parallel \Pi_3$ of two identical components Π_3. That component receives confidential events from the set

$$\{c_k | k = pq, p \neq q, prime(p), prime(q)\}$$

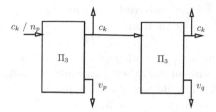

Fig. 3. Cascaded Leaking of a Prime Factor

or non-visible but unobservable events from the set $\{n_p|prime(p)\}$. Each event represents the natural number which is its index. An event c_k thus represents a natural number with exactly two prime factors. The component forwards events c_k but it suppresses events n_p. In any case, it produces an observation from these inputs.

For each c_k it receives, Π_3 produces a visible event v_p, where p is an arbitrary prime factor of k. If it receives an event n_p then Π_3 produces the visible event v_p corresponding to the same prime number p.

The cascade $\Pi_3 \parallel \Pi_3$ produces *two* visible events v_p and v_q for each c_k, where p and q are – not necessarily distinct – prime factors of k. If the cascade receives an event n_p, then it produces only one observation, the corresponding v_p.

A single Π_3 keeps the occurrence of c_k confidential: For each observed v_p, there is an infinite number of c_k that could have caused this observation, indeed it could also have been caused by the non-confidential event n_p.

The cascade $\Pi_3 \parallel \Pi_3$, however, does *not* keep products of two prime numbers confidential: if $k = pq$ and the two components choose to reveal v_p *and* v_q then it is clear that c_k must be the confidential event that caused those observations.

Separation of Views. The different forms of composition are made up by varying the relationship of inputs and outputs of the subsystems. They do not consider views associated to the systems.

To come up with a compositional verification of a BSP for a composed event system with a given view $\mathcal{V}$, this view must be decomposed to views $\mathcal{V}_1$ and $\mathcal{V}_2$ on the subsystems. The latter two form a *proper separation* of $\mathcal{V}$ if $V \cap E_1 = V_1$, $V \cap E_2 = V_2$, $C \cap E_1 \subseteq C_1$, $C \cap E_2 \subseteq C_2$, and $N_1 \cap N_2 = \emptyset$.

The separation of views for the cascade in Figure 3 is straight forward. Note that $N_1 = \{n_p|prime(p)\}$ for the left component, whereas $N_2 = \emptyset$ for the right component.

Well-Behaved Composition. As mentioned above, a basic security predicate always requires corrections of certain pertubations to exist in the trace set of a system. When composing systems, those requirements for the components may contradict each other: a correction necessary for one component may be a perturbation for the other, requiring another correction, which in turn may be a perturbation in terms of the first component, and so on. For two components Π_1 and Π_2, there are four conditions each of which is sufficient to avoid this kind of situation. If one of those conditions holds, the composition is *well-behaved*. The most simple condition for well-behavedness requires the set of confidential events of one component to be disjoint from the set of non-visible events of the other, i.e., $N_1 \cap E_2 = \emptyset \wedge N_2 \cap E_1 = \emptyset$. If only Π_1, say, satisfies this condition, e.g., $N_1 \cap E_2 = \emptyset$ holds, then it may be sufficient to require that Π_1 also can accept (or produce) non-visible events of the other component at any time ($total(ES_1, C_1 \cap E_2)$) and that it satisfies an additional information flow property, saying that it can correct certain insertions of confidential events. The latter condition ensures that Π_1 can correct perturbations caused by Π_2. The third condition is similar to the second with the roles of Π_1 and Π_2 exchanged. The remaining fourth condition handles the case that both components can produce perturbations for the other. It is considerably more complex than the other conditions are.

Although the composition in Figure 3 is well-behaved (the second condition holds), the composition does not protect the events c_k, as we have seen above. The reason is that the instance of Π_3 at the right-hand side does *not* protect c_k with respect to a view that has no non-visible events. This shows that a proper separation of views is established "after the fact": The separated views are derived from the composed system, they are not an independent part of the description of the components.

Well-behavedness is a *necessary* condition for compositionality of all known information flow properties, but for most properties it is not sufficient. Additional conditions need to ensure that the specific requirements of how perturbations may be corrected for a given information flow property are compatible for the two components.

Verification of Compositionality. The essential tool to verify compositionality of information flow properties is Mantel's *Generalized Zipping Lemma*, which generalizes a lemma used by Johnson and Thayer [8] to prove compositionality of forward correctability. The Generalized Zipping Lemma states that, given a proper separation of views and a well-behaved composition, the following must always be possible: If both components can extend a trace τ of the composed system independently such that they do not produce confidential events and they agree on the visible events, then there is an extension of τ in the composed system that contains the same visible events but no confidential events.

Classification of Compositionality Results. Mantel classifies compositionality results by distinguishing the workings of components with respect to well-behavedness: Locally correcting perturbations, a *polite* component will not produce perturbations that the other component needs to correct, whereas a *tolerant* component can correct any perturbation that the other component may produce. If the composition is a general cascade and the non-visible events of Π_1 do not contain input events of Π_2, then Π_1 is polite. If it is also tolerant, i.e., satisfies an appropriate information flow property, then there is no need to further restrict the behavior of Π_2. This is the case for generalized noninterference, which is compositional under general cascade. The most liberal alternative is to make both components tolerant. To make this composable, the components must satisfy a strong information flow property, such as forward correctability [8] or Mantel's weakened forward correctability [14].

2.3   Summary

In this section we surveyed basic compositionality results for the classes of safety/liveness properties on the one hand and confidentiality properties on the other. In the next section we investigate the compatibility of these results, i.e., the question whether the results can be applied to reason about safety/liveness and confidentiality simultaneously.

3   Composing Compositional Reasoning

In this section we examine the difficulties which occur when trying to apply the compositionality results of Abadi/Lamport [1] and Mantel [14] simultaneously.

3.1   Basic Considerations

Given two domains of system properties $\mathcal{T}_1$ and $\mathcal{T}_2$. We want to reason about two components in Π_1 and Π_2 in both theories simultaneously. Assume that both theories allow to express Π_1 and Π_2.

Compatibility of System Model. Here, $\mathcal{T}_1$ is the domain of safety and liveness properties, and $\mathcal{T}_2$ is the domain of confidentiality properties as discussed in Section 2. We consider the basic system models (state-based for safety/liveness and event-based for confidentiality) as equivalent. An event can be modeled as a state change and a state can be modeled as an equivalence class of sequences of events [1–p. 77]. We regard the restriction of confidentiality properties to finite traces as merely technical. For example, McLean [16] provides a theory of possibilistic information flow properties which is based on infinite traces. The expressiveness of the types of properties however is different. Safety properties are sets of traces whereas confidentiality properties are sets of sets of traces, and, being closure properties, cannot be reduced to sets of traces. But what is a liveness property in the system model of traces?

A property Q, e.g., stating that some event x will eventually occur, is a liveness property if every finite trace τ can be extended by some (possibly infinite) sequence of events t such that $Q(\tau.t)$ holds. In other words, the set of all finite prefixes of all traces σ satisfying $Q(\sigma)$ comprises *all* finite sequences, i.e.,

$$\{\tau \in E \mid \exists \sigma \in E \ .Q(\sigma) \wedge \tau \leq \sigma\} = E \tag{2}$$

Now, let Tr be the trace set of an event system (with possibly infinite traces). In general, the finite traces of Tr are a proper subset of E, because Tr satisfies not only liveness but also safety properties. By definition, Tr is prefix closed. Therefore Q constrains Tr in that all traces in Tr are extensible to traces satisfying Q.

$$L_Q(Tr) \iff \forall \tau \in Tr \cap E \ .\exists t \in E \ .Q(\tau.t) \wedge \tau.t \in Tr \tag{3}$$

Although Q essentially determines L_Q, L_Q cannot be reduced to a property of traces, because it is not closed under subsets: Suppose L_Q holds for Tr and let $\tau \in Tr$ be a finite trace not satisfing Q. Then $Tr \setminus \{\sigma \in E \mid \tau < \sigma\}$ does not satisfy L_Q.

On the other hand, L_Q also is not a closure property, because $L_Q(E)$ need not hold: Let σ_0 be an infinite trace not satisfing Q. Then, there is no way to extend the singleton $\{\sigma_0\}$ to a set satisfying L_Q.

Compatibility of Hypotheses. In $\mathcal{T}_1$ the components satisfy properties P_1 and P_2 and the composition $\Pi_1 \| \Pi_2$ satisfies property $F_1(P_1, P_2)$ under hypothesis H_1. The hypothesis H_1 for safety/liveness is mainly that the liveness property is machine-closed with respect to the safety property. As argued above, F_1 is conjunction, i.e., the composition satisfies $P_1 \cap P_2$.

Similarly, in $\mathcal{T}_2$ the components satisfy properties Q_1 for view $\mathcal{V}_1$ and Q_2 for view $\mathcal{V}_2$, and the composition $\Pi_1 \| \Pi_2$ satisfies property $F_2(Q_1, Q_2)$ under hypothesis H_2. The hypothesis H_2 for confidentiality properties mainly concern the notion of well-behaved composition, as discussed above. The property $F_2(Q_1, Q_2)$ of the composition then is an appropriate information flow property for a view $\mathcal{V}$, for which $\mathcal{V}_1$ and $\mathcal{V}_2$ make up a proper separation.

Hypothesis H_1 guarantees the existence of F_1, and H_2 guarantees the existence of F_2. The hypotheses H_1 and H_2 are consistent, i.e., there are safe/live *and* secure systems which are composed from components with the respective properties. Therefore, if H_1 and H_2 hold and the respective properties of the components hold, then the two composition theorems can be applied and the composition satisfies both, $F_1(P_1, P_2)$ and $F_2(Q_1, Q_2)$.

First Summary. Safety, liveness and information flow are three different kinds of properties. Being properties of sets of traces that cannot be reduced to properties of traces but also are not closure properties, liveness properties seem to have a conceptual complexity between the relatively simple safety properties and the quite complex information flow properties.

Because the system models are equivalent and the hypotheses of the composition theorems are consistent, there is no fundamental reason why the results could not be applied simultaneously. However, there are some possible conflicts in the details of the models which we now explain.

3.2   Possible Conflicts Between Safety and Confidentiality

There is a possible conflict between confidentiality properties and safety properties. A confidentiality property may disallow certain safety properties. If the system specification for domain $\mathcal{T}_1$ requires these properties, then there exists no implementation for such a system.

As observed by Mantel [13–p. 192ff], the specification of a secure system usually consists of two parts:

1. A part which specifies the functional aspects of the system. This part can conveniently consist of a safety and a liveness property, i.e., a set P of traces.
2. A part which specifies the security requirements of the system. This part can conveniently consist of a closure condition C for the set of traces P.

In general, P need not be closed with respect to C. Simply constructing the closure of P with respect to C is no solution because this adds traces that were not considered correct regarding P. The task is to find a subset P of P which is closed with respect to C. However, this set may be empty and therefore not be suitable as a system specification.

Mantel [13–p. 193] defines the notion of *compatibility* between P and C to formalize this issue. The set P is compatible with C if the closure of P with respect to C is equal to P. Otherwise, P and C are incompatible.

As an example, consider a system which immediately audits low level events at the high level. Thus observing a low level event admits the conclusion that the corresponding high level event has happened after a certain time. Security properties that disallow this form of information flow are incompatible with the functional requirements of the auditing system.

3.3   Possible Conflicts Between Liveness and Confidentiality

Section 3.1 showed that there is no principal hindrance in applying both compositionality results for liveness and confidentiality simultaneously. If there are two components with exactly the desired liveness and information flow properties, then composing them yields a live and secure system.

From an engineering point of view, this "bottom up" result is not very helpful. Usually, a system development would start with required liveness property L_{sys} and an information flow property C_{sys} for the system to be built. Then engineers would try and find decomposisions $L_{sys} = F_1(P_1, P_2)$ and $C_{sys} = F_2(Q_1, Q_2)$ of those properties such that it is possible to build (or find) components Π_1 and Π_2 satisfying $P_1 \wedge Q_1$ and $P_2 \wedge Q_2$, respectively.

In this setting, two problems arise: First, the decomposition of the properties may be inconsistent, i.e., it may be impossible to satisfy P_i and Q_i simultaneously. This does not necessarily mean that there is no system which would satisfy both L_{sys} and C_{sys}. Rather the decomposition is inadequate. Although the general forms of both properties (c.f., formulas (1) and (3)) are similar, the traces of Tr they relate, i.e., τ and τ in (1), and τ and $\tau.t$ in (3) are structurally different. The "alternative" τ of τ in (1) usually is not an extension of τ but a modification at the last occurrence of a confidential event in τ or τ . Thus, the differences in traces required by liveness and information flow concern different "dimensions" of the set of system traces. As a consequence, a trace required to be in Tr by liveness, say, may require the presence of another trace in Tr to satisfy the information flow property.

Second, the hypotheses H_1 and H_2 of the composition theorems may not be satisfied. This means, although both components are "live and secure", their composition is not guaranteed to be, because they do not satisfy the additional requirements that make the composition theorems applicable. For safety and liveness, the hypotheses (H_1) require the environmental assumptions to be safety properties. For information flow properties, the hypotheses (H_2) require a well-behaved composition.

To determine the possible interference of those two types of hypotheses, it is useful to rephrase the possible instances of H_2 as environment conditions for the components.

1. Conditions of the form $N_1 \cap E_2 = \emptyset$ can be interpreted as an environment condition of Π_1: "Π_2 does not produce events in N_1".
2. Totality conditions $(total(ES_1, C_1 \cap E_2))$ are environment conditions of Π_2: "Π_1 can always accept (output) events in $C_1 \cap E_2 \cap O_2$, and it can always produce (input) events in $C_1 \cap E_2 \cap I_2$".
3. The remaining information flow properties that a well-behaved composition must satisfy do not have sensible interpretations as environment conditions, i.e., they must be considered part of M_i for Π_i.

Condition (1) clearly is a safety condition, as is Condition (2). Therefore, there is no general contradiction between H_1 and H_2. Nevertheless, specific environment assumptions to ensure liveness may be inconsistent with a well-behaved composition with respect to information flow.

In summary, to ensure applicability of both compositionality theorems, it is necessary to design the decomposition in such a way that the safety conditions the single components impose on their environment for liveness and information flow are consistent. Only after this is established it is useful to consider the liveness and information flow properties that the two theorems require the single components to fulfill.

4   Summary and Conclusion

We investigated the problems which may arise if compositional reasoning for different types of properties is applied simultaneously to a system. We considered three distinct classes of system properties, namely safety, liveness and confidentiality properties. We found that Abadi and Lamport's [1] and Mantel's [14] compositionality results *can* work together. However, difficulties arise in the compatibility of individual system properties (like safety and confidentiality) and in certain engineering aspects of system decomposition.

Our findings emphasize that compositionality of compositional reasoning exists and is a promising direction of further work, but it requires new interdisciplinary efforts within computer science to bring together different domains of research. For example, the safety/liveness framework in the area of concurrency theory has remained unnoticed by the security community for quite some time. Similarly, many members of the concurrency theory community are still trapped in the safety/liveness world and think that there are no properties beyond it.

Furthermore, we have only investigated three classes of system properties. There are many more, for example the complex field of system (hardware) reliability [4] or software reliability [10]. Especially in the area of non-functional properties there are many areas which still do not have sound compositionality results of their own. Thus, our findings can only be seen as a starting point for further investigation.

Acknowledgments

We wish to thank the members of the breakout group "Limits of Predictability" during the Dagstuhl seminar 04511 "Architecting Systems with Trustworthy Components" for inspiring this work. Thanks also to the anonymous reviewers for constructive comments.

References

1. M. Abadi and L. Lamport. Composing specifications. *ACM Transactions on Programming Languages and Systems*, 15(1):73–132, Jan. 1993.
2. M. Abadi and L. Lamport. Conjoining specifications. *ACM Transactions on Programming Languages and Systems*, 17(3):507–534, May 1995.
3. B. Alpern and F. B. Schneider. Defining liveness. *Information Processing Letters*, 21:181–185, 1985.
4. A. Birolini. *Reliability Engineering: Theory and Practice*. Springer Verlag, third edition, 1999.
5. K. M. Chandy and J. Misra. Parallel Program Design: A Foundation. Addison-Wesley, Reading, Mass., 1988.
6. M. Charpentier and K. M. Chandy. Theorems about composition. In Proceedings of the International Conference on Mathematics of Program Construction (MPC), pages 167-186, 2000.
7. I. Crnkovic, M. Larsson, and O. Preiss. Concerning predictability in dependable component-based systems: Classification of quality attributes. In R. de Lemos, editor, Architecting Dependable Systems III, number 3549 in Lecture Notes in Computer Science, pages 257-278. Springer-Verlag, 2005.
8. D. M. Johnson and F. J. Thayer. Security and the composition of machines. In *Proc. IEEE Computer Security Foundations Workshop*, pages 72–89, 1988.
9. E. Kindler. Safety and liveness properties: A survey. EATCS-Bulletin, (53), June 1994.
10. M. R. Lyu, editor. Handbook of Software Reliability Engineering. McGraw-Hill and IEEE Computer Society, 1996.
11. Z. Manna and A. Pnueli. The temporal logic of reactive and concurrent systems: Specification. Springer-Verlag, 1991.
12. Z. Manna and A. Pnueli. Temporal verification of reactive systems: safety. Springer-Verlag, 1995.
13. H. Mantel. Possibilistic definitions of security - An assembly kit. In Proceedings of the 13th IEEE Computer Security Foundations Workshop (CSFW 2000), Cambridge, England, July 2000. IEEE Computer Society Press.
14. H. Mantel. *A Uniform Framework for the Formal Specification and Verification of Information Flow Security*. PhD thesis, Universität des Saarlandes, 2003.
15. J. McLean. A general theroy of composition for trace sets closed under selective interleaving functions. In *Proc. IEEE Symposium on Research in Security and Privacy*, pages 73–93, 1994.
16. J. McLean. A general theory of composition for a class of "possibilistic" properties. *IEEE Transactions on Software Engineering*, 22(1):53–67, Jan. 1996. Special Section—Best Papers of the IEEE Symposium on Security and Privacy 1994.
17. C. Szyperski, D. Gruntz, and S. Murer. Component Software: Beyond Object-Oriented Programming. ACM Press and Addison-Wesley, New York, NY, second edition edition, 2002.

Trustworthy Instantiation of Frameworks

Uwe Aßmann, Andreas Bartho, Falk Hartmann,
Ilie Savga, and Barbara Wittek

Institut für Software- und Multimediatechnik,
Technische Universität Dresden
{uwe.assmann, andreas.bartho, falk.hartmann, ilie.savga,
barbara.wittek}@inf.tu-dresden.de

Abstract. Frameworks are large building blocks of systems, encapsulating the commonalities of a family of applications. For reuse of these common features, frameworks are instantiated by smaller-sized components, *plugins*, to specific products. However, the framework instantiation process is often difficult, because not all aspects of the interplay of the framework and its plugins can be captured by standard type systems. Application developers instantiating a framework often fail to develop correct applications. Thus, this paper surveys several typical framework instantiation problems. A simple facet-based classification of the problems is given. It is shown how the different problem classes are related to phases of the software process and how they can be tackled appropriately. Finally, the paper derives several research challenges, in particular, the challenge to define appropriate framework instantiation languages.

1 Introduction

The use of frameworks eases the creation of large software systems and leads to lower overall production costs. However, the instantiation of a complex framework still requires a lot of resources: besides the time required for training, it is necessary to dedicate person power exclusively, sometimes even a specific team, for the treatment of all issues. Complex frameworks turn out to be hard to instantiate, because the dependencies between the numerous extension points hamper finding and understanding of valid instantiations. Hence, the process of framework instantiation should be made as easy and reliable as possible.

A framework is instantiated by specifying values at predefined *extension points*. Technically, different forms of frameworks are established, which implies that different kinds of extension mechanisms exist [1]. *White-box* frameworks are extended towards applications by subclassing framework classes to application classes. *Black-box* frameworks are extended by delegating functionality from framework classes to application classes. *Generic* frameworks provide several generic classes with parameter types, the *framework parameters*, which must be instantiated towards application types. More general forms are possible; for instance, Model-Driven Architecture (MDA) defines *platform-independent models*, model frameworks, that are instantiated towards applications by model transformations [2]. Other frameworks apply the concept of extension points not only to

R.H. Reussner et al. (Eds.): Architecting Systems, LNCS 3938, pp. 152–168, 2006.
© Springer-Verlag Berlin Heidelberg 2006

code, but also to intrinsic data, resources, or GUI-elements [3]. Then, extension points do not directly correspond to classes, but comprise more elements.

In the following, we speak in all of these different cases uniformly of framework instantiation at extension points. In particular, we are interested in the assumptions the framework makes about its extensions. These assumptions, both about single extension points or between them, will be considered as constraints that must be fulfilled in order to validly instantiate a framework. In Section 2, some examples of constraints will be given together with a classification that can be used to decide how a constraint should be treated by the framework designer. In Section 3, several techniques for the treatment are given, e.g., for the removal or for static checking of a constraint. In the concluding Section 4, an outlook including open research questions is given.

2   Framework Instantiation Problems

In order to successfully instantiate a framework, the properties that separate the valid instantiations from the invalid ones must be known. These properties are usually described by constraints. A simple constraint may only restrict the instantiation of a single extension point (such as "The value used to instantiate this extension point must not be null"), whereas others, *multi-point constraints*, span several extension points (e.g., "The value used to instantiate extension point A must be different from the one used for extension point B"). Frameworks are hard to instantiate if they constrain their valid instantiations; the more constraints are exposed by the framework, the harder it is to find a valid instantiation.

2.1   Some Examples

In order to understand the problems raised by the instantiation of frameworks, some examples are given in the following. They cover the range between hypothetical, academic and practical frameworks. The problems illustrated by the examples will be classified in Section 2.2.

Example 1. Car Configurator
Imagine a car configurator, a component of many car manufacturer websites. Usually, when configuring a car, you first choose a base model. Afterwards, you are able to add extra features to the car. The configurator checks whether a feature you want to add fits your configuration. Sometimes, one feature enforces or rules out some other feature. A good example is the dependency between the catalytic converter and the engine. If you are configuring a car with a diesel engine, you need to use the appropriate converter.

When the car configuration is developed as a framework, car models, engines etc. can be defined as base classes. The car has the extension points *engine* and *catalytic converter*; however, in valid instantiations, engine and converter type must match, which is a typical multi-point constraint.

Example 2. SalesPoint Framework
Domain-specific multi-point constraints occur in many frameworks. As an example, take the SalesPoint framework, a Java framework for sales applications,

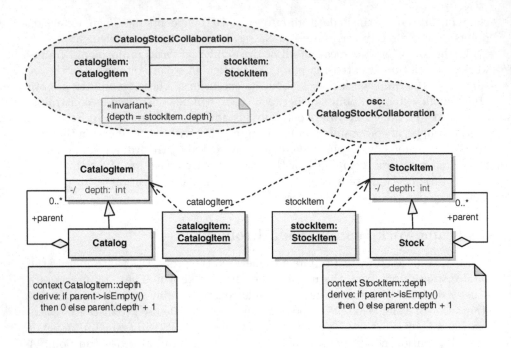

Fig. 1. A constraint in the SalesPoint Framework

used to teach students about framework-based applications [4]. Applications, typically instantiated from the framework by a student project group, consist of a *shop*, the main controlling entity and several *points of sale*, each of which is used for business transactions, for instance, buying goods or managing the inventory. SalesPoint also supports data management, user management, logging and simple GUI components, such as tables and forms. The framework is documented extensively, making the access easier for novices [5], but nevertheless, often instantiation problems are reported.

One multi-point constraint of SalesPoint has to do with its built-in data management. SalesPoint provides data structures essential for warehouse and order management, e.g., so-called `Catalog` and `Stock` classes (Fig. 1). `Catalogs` contain `CatalogItems`, which are descriptions of potentially available objects. `CatalogItems` store attributes such as name, price, size, or weight of an object. `Stocks` contain `StockItems`, which, in contrast, describe attributes of the actually available objects. To ensure data integrity of catalogs and stocks, there are strict rules to be adhered to. As `StockItems` of the same kind always have common attributes, they always refer to a `CatalogItem`, while on the other hand, properties differing between `StockItems`, like serial numbers, are stored individually in the `StockItem` itself. Similarly, a `Stock` must always refer to a `Catalog`. A `StockItem` can only be added to a `Stock`, if the corresponding `CatalogItem` is contained in the `Catalog` to which the `Stock` refers. If this is not the case, adding the `StockItem` to the `Stock` is being refused [5].

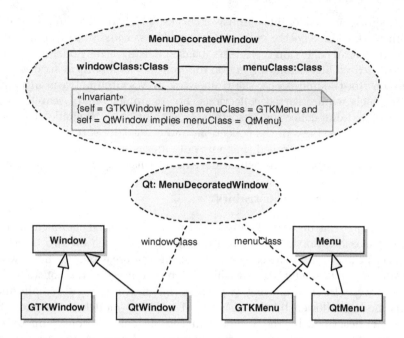

Fig. 2. The Window/Menu collaboration

The data management of SalesPoint has been implemented using the Composite pattern, so that `Catalogs` and `Stocks` can be nested. The abovementioned constraint of a `StockItem`'s parent `Stock` referring to the appropriate `Catalog-Item`'s parent `Catalog` implies that the `Catalog` and `Stock` hierarchy have to match (see the invariant in Fig. 1). A common mistake is that students try to set up the `Stock` hierarchy before the associated `Catalog` hierarchy is created.

Example 3. Window/Menu collaboration
When implementing a framework for applications using multiple widget sets, such as Qt [6] and GTK+ [7], one often ends up with a component in the framework that implements the mere collaboration between a window and its (main) menu. This component exposes a quite simple constraint: the instantiation with a Qt-window (resp. a GTK-window) implies the use of a Qt-menu (resp. a GTK-menu). Such a collaboration, which is called a "parallel class hierarchy" in [8], is shown in Fig. 2 as a UML collaboration.

Example 4. Fulfilment of Dynamic Assumptions
Verification of many constraints can be supported by reasoning over types. In some cases, however, the static type information is not enough to preserve consistency of the instantiated framework. For example, changes of object states at run-time can invalidate some operations which previously could be applied. Checking of such constraints requires checking of the value or state of the object.

Perhaps the best-known dynamic assumption is the absence of `null` values, preventing the code from any erroneous access to non-existing objects. This usually requires a considerable number of checks, which are scattered throughout the framework code. Another example are *sortedness constraints*. If a framework works with several collection types (sets, bags and lists), it may offer an extension point for a search algorithm, relying on different key comparison strategies. Depending on run-time decisions, the framework may switch between algorithms, some of which require sorted collections. For example, binary search requires that the underlying collection is sorted. As a solution, a dynamic checker can determine the sortedness of the collection, and eventually sort it.

In general, it can be argued that virtually any non-trivial framework makes assumptions about extensions, which have an intrinsically dynamic nature.

2.2   Classification of Constraints

The constraints that underly the presented problems can be classified in several ways. The classification proposed in the following is based on two facets. The first facet is the *cause* of the constraint. During the creation of a framework, a constraint might basically occur within different phases of the software development process. In the following, a process that first creates a domain and an analysis model, followed by the creation of a design model, is assumed. Such a process is described by the V-model in Fig. 3. Then, a constraint occuring during the domain or the analysis modeling is called *domain-specific*, whereas a constraint introduced during the design is called a *technical* constraint.

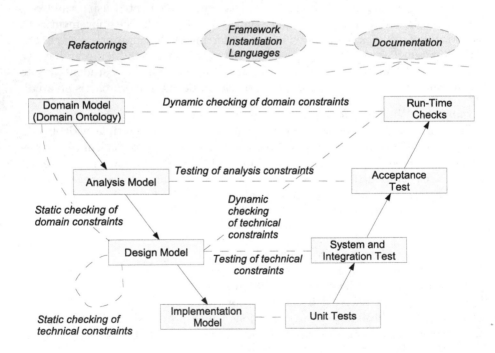

Fig. 3. Safe framework instantiation mechanisms in a V-model-like software process

The second facet is the *stage* of the constraint, i.e., whether it can be checked statically or needs to be checked dynamically. Static checking in this case means checking of types: a constraint is *static*, if it is merely a statement about the classes of its participants. On the other hand, a dynamic constraint involves properties of instances: a constraint is *dynamic*, if it involves instances, their states, and values.

The two facets lead to four categories of constraints, which can be mapped to the four examples given above. An example for the class of domain-specific static constraints is Ex. 1. Obviously, it is a domain-specific constraint, because it is a statement about the domain *engineering of cars*. Furthermore, it is static, because the constraint itself only states something about the type of engine parts that can be combined.

Ex. 2 is an example for a domain-specific dynamic constraint. It is dynamic, because the final structure of `Catalogs` and `Stocks` can be set during runtime. Furthermore, it is domain-specific, because the `Catalogs` and `Stocks` and their nesting are not a design issue, but rather originate from the domain modeling.

An example for a technical static constraint is given in Ex. 3. Obviously, the constraint is technical because it deals with the suitability of classes from several widget sets. Moreover, it has been modeled as a static constraint: the framework is instantiated by binding classes to the extension points.

Last, Ex. 4 shows a technical dynamic constraint: the sortedness predicate is technical by being defined in the framework design model, and it has inherently dynamic nature by operating on run-time object values.

The constraint classes are not entirely unrelated. For instance, it is possible to model a domain-specific constraint using technical means, e.g., in Ex. 1, you could use the design pattern Marker Interface [9] to designate the suitability of the diesel catalytic converter for the diesel engine. In this pattern, interfaces are used to model unary predicates of classes, i.e., if their invariants obey a unary predicate, it should inherit from the corresponding marker interface. On the other hand, we believe that such workarounds are often not a good idea. In this specific example, the concept of interfaces is abused for a matter that does not have to do something with interfacing.

It is usually also possible to turn a static constraint into a dynamic constraint by using object instances instead of classes for the instantiation. However, an advice on whether a static constraint should be replaced by a dynamic one can hardly be given.

Based on this classification, we show in the next section how the validity of different classes of constraints should be checked by different mechanisms.

3   Supporting Safe Instantiation

There are several ways to support safe instantiation—all based on some treatment of the constraints exposed by a framework. Fig. 3 gives an overview. We assume as underlying software process a simple V-model. Several of the methods can be attached to a specific phase of the software process, others are ubiquitous.

First, and under all circumstances, both simple constraints as well as multi-point constraints should be documented well. The often-used approach to utilize some JavaDoc-like API documentation tool can be improved with user-defined metadata annotations, to be exploited by additional tools, such as code generators. Second, one can try to remove a constraint by means of refactoring, an approach that should be used in particular, if the overall design of the framework benefits from the refactoring. Third, static constraints can be verified, once they are specified in a logic that cohabitates with class models. We suggest to employ UML collaborations and OCL constraints here. Fourth, static as well as dynamic constraints can be described using framework instantiation languages, domain-specific languages that can be used to validate plugins. Fifth, when a dynamic instantiation constraint is violated, a framework should behave conveniently, which can be ensured by negative testing. Finally, conformance with a dynamic constraint should be checked at run time, which can be done in several ways, e.g., using aspects.

3.1   Documentation

One of the simplest possibilities to prevent instantiation problems is a thorough documentation of framework's extension points and their requirements on plugins. Documentation describes how the application developer has to work with the framework and which constraints are to consider. One way to share the necessary knowledge are *cookbooks*, informal descriptions explaining how to instantiate a framework. Cookbooks divide the instantiation process into subtasks, for which step-by-step solutions are presented. Therefore, they can be seen as a collection of recipes that describe how typical framework usage problems are solved.

It is important that the framework documentation follows the pyramid principle [10]. This principle structures the documentation into three levels. At the top level, the framework selection level, the application domain of the framework is described, so that an application developer can decide whether she wants to use the framework. The second level, the standard usage level, answers the question how to use the framework. Documentation at the third, so-called detailed design level, describes the design of the framework and its technical aspects in depth, so that a framework developer can maintain and evolve it.

The SalesPoint framework can be taken as an example. A "Technical Overview" [5] constitutes the top level of the framework documentation pyramid. For the other levels, there are two cookbooks, the so-called "Hooks" and "How To" documents. While the "How To" cookbook covers a very limited but often sufficient set of code examples, the "Hooks" cookbook provides an extensive and rather formal approach. As a consequence, the "How To" is preferred of beginners (standard usage level), whereas the "Hooks" are of greater use to advanced programmers, also covering the detailed design level. With a pyramid-based documentation, students can find solutions for their problems easily.

In recent years, programming environments have started to employ *metadata annotations* for documentation and tool support. Java documentation tags and C# annotations enable users to define tag structures, write tools that exploit the tags, and generate code from them. On the one hand, these tag structures provide excellent documentation information, so that they are quite popular among programmers. On the other hand, tagging tools such as XDoclet [11] provide extensible code generators that help to adapt frameworks towards their extensions. For instance, XDoclet can adapt Enterprise Java Beans when they are embedded into application frameworks, because it can generate transaction code, serialization code, and many other forms of critical glue code. Since metadata annotations do not belong to the programming language per se, but offer a second, a metalevel of descriptions, one could characterize this approach as a form of semi-automatic documentation tool, which can also be helpful to increase the reliability of framework instantiation.

The usage of different forms of documentation for trustworthy instantiation of frameworks is not a new but rather down-to-earth approach. However, the methods can never give assistance for all aspects of using the framework. Furthermore, the application developer typically has the responsibility and the freedom of choice between many solutions.

3.2   Refactoring Multi-point Constraints

Often constraints between extension points evolve from technical issues inside the framework. Such constraints are—even when documented appropriately—a constant source of instantiation problems. However, in many cases, these constraints can be removed from the framework by refactoring it in a way that hides them inside.

An example for a design that is exposing a technical constraint has been given in Ex. 3. That framework can be refactored to a form where the constraint between the extension points lies inside the framework: instead of exhibiting two extension points for the classes of the window and of the menu, the latter one can be removed. To this end, the responsibility of determining the menu class must be moved to the subclasses of Window, which is implemented by declaring an abstract factory method in the Window class. The refactored example framework is shown in Fig. 4.

Before applying refactorings to move constraints from outside the framework to the inside it should be carefully evaluated, whether this makes the framework easier to understand. No general rule can be given on this, but usually a comparison of the states before and after the refactoring should show, whether refactoring is worth the effort. In the given example, the refactoring should definitely be made—especially since a real-world example would incorporate more collaboration parties. Most probably, it would be better to introduce a new abstract factory class that needs to be implemented once for the various widget sets, capturing which widget classes belong together.

3.3   Static Checking of Multi-point Constraints

Contracts are a well-known mechanism for achieving trustworthy software [12]. In a *required contract*, a client describes its expectations to a service, whereas a service offers functionality in a *provided contract* [13]. Required and provided

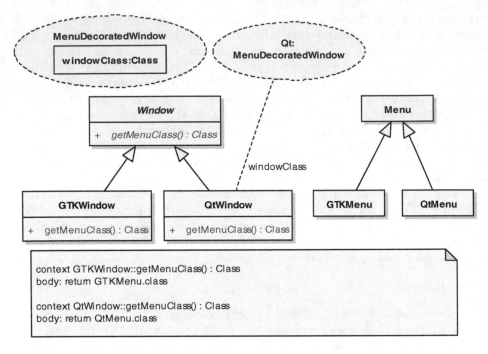

Fig. 4. The framework from Fig. 2 after refactoring

contracts can be specified as pre-conditions, post-conditions and invariants using some logic, but also with state- or protocol-based models [14]. In all cases, required and provided contracts are verified to match in a process called *contract checking* by a contract verifier, be it a theorem prover or a model checker. So far, research has mainly focused on procedure- and class-oriented contracts. Here, contracts are presented in the context of frameworks, both to static and dynamic instantiation constraints (*framework instantiation contracts*).

Example 5. Generic Frameworks with Generic Classes
In languages with genericity, a set of generic classes can be regarded as a generic framework. Additionally, some languages allow for the specification of inheritance bounds for formal class parameters, which specify a simple required contract of a generic class, the compiler has to check at every instantiation point. For instance, in the Java 5 framework, parameters of collection classes can be bound by the interface `Comparable`, which means that the collection elements are comparable using a compare function [15].

In general, if an instantiation constraint deals with information about types and is given in a decidable logic, it is a static instantiation constraint and can be verified with a verification tool at instantiation time. The instantiation process can assemble all instantiation constraints, bind formal parameters in the constraints to actual parameters, and then verify the entire constraint specification.

For multi-point constraints, UML collaborations turn out to be useful, because they describe the constraint in a closed form (Ex. 2 and 3 have already used UML collaborations). Originally, this technique has been proposed in the Catalysis approach [16], but its standardization in UML 2.0 makes the technique available for CASE tools and integrated development environments. However, UML collaborations differ slightly from Catalysis collaborations. In Catalysis, a collaboration *is* a framework, i.e., specifies all framework classes and constraints together. Catalysis does not distinguish instantiation constraints from internal framework invariants, which hampers comprehensibility, because both groups deal with different concerns. Instead, instantiation constraints should be separately specified. Then, they can further be distributed over several collaborations, for instance, collaborations describing domain-specific and collaborations describing technical constraints. In this way, constraints of all classes of our classification can be specified separately, orthogonalizing their handling. For large frameworks, this is very important for documentation purposes, and UML 2.0 follows this trend.

Once specified with OCL, the constraints can be assembled and checked by appropriate tools [17], which ensures trustworthy instantiation already on the modelling level [18]. On the other hand, in the future, domain-specific analysis constraints will probably be specified with ontology languages. The reason is that software processes will be based on standardized domain ontologies [19]: development will start with the domain ontology and enrich it with requirements and design information, until the implementation can be delivered. In such an ontology-aware software process, the domain-specific constraints are automatically shared with all designs and implementations; a verifier can check the constraints in all development phases. This holds in particular when product lines are constructed based on domain ontologies. For all products in a line, an ontology reasoner is able to verify the domain constraints. Ex. 1 provided an illustrative example: the car configuration constraints can be described in a domain ontology and verified in an ontology-based software process using an ontology reasoner. Hence, it is likely that ontology languages, such as OWL [20, 21], will play a major role in the trustworthy development of product lines [19].

3.4   Framework Instantiation Languages

In order to support the safe instantiation of frameworks, not only constraint languages can be used. Since a framework may deal with other resources than classes or objects, e.g. files, data or widget resources, other concepts need to be included when talking about extension points. This suggests to define domain-specific languages for framework instantiation, *framework instantiation languages*, which should not only provide a good way to specify the code extension points, but also verify assertions over all kinds of resources.

A well-known example for a simple framework instantiation language is the plugin language of the universal tool platform Eclipse [3]. Eclipse provides extension points into which components, so-called *plugins*, can be dynamically loaded on demand. In this way, both the original platform as well as other plugin

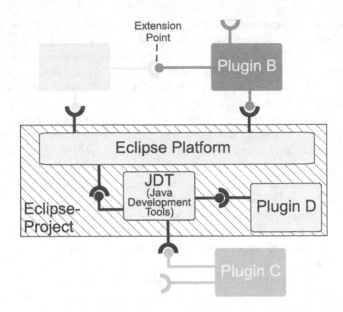

Fig. 5. A structural overview about the Eclipse platform

components can be extended easily, and new applications can be built (Fig. 5). Eclipse itself consists of the core platform and some set of plugins, including, for example, the Java Development Tools (JDT).

The Eclipse extension mechanism is based on the specification of extension points with the standard markup language XML. Each plugin for Eclipse contains a so-called *manifest file* `plugin.xml` with extensibility information. For every extension point, the file references an extended XML schema definition (in *extensions schema language (exsd)*), describing the structure of a extension. Whenever an extension is programmed, its content has to be described according to this schema definition (Fig. 6), and XML tools can be used to check the validity of the specifications. In this way, Eclipse can control, whether all extensions of a plugin fill the specification of their extension points. In Fig. 6, the mechanism is illustrated. A plugin description `extended` is typed by two schema files. Most of the specification is typed by the plugin schema file `plugin.xsd` that defines standard plugin tags, such as `plugin` or `extension-point`. An extension point `example`, however, references another schema file `example.exsd` typing all possible extensions of this extension point. Since different extension points must be extended differently (extensions can refer to code, menu actions, and other resources), their extensions must be typed by a particular extension schema.

This plugin specification mechanism supports trustworthy instantiation of frameworks, because the plugin description is machine-processable and can be used to check whether technical constraints are met, both of static and dynamic nature. However, since XML is used, only constraints expressible in XML types can be formulated and processed, such as tree-structure constraints, or type constraints on the basic XML data types. Nevertheless, since XML is standardized

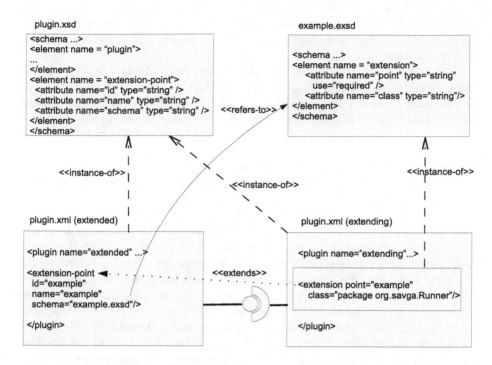

Fig. 6. The XSD/XML mechanism of the Eclipse plugin concept. On the top: schema files. On the bottom: plugin descriptions.

and supported by tools, checking of plugins becomes much simpler than in an ad-hoc approach.

The Eclipse plugin language seems to be one of the first specification languages for framework extension points. Eclipse shows that in a framework, extensibility does not only refer to code alone, but also to resources, such as widgets, views, repositories, transaction policies and others. However, this requires that for instantiation, domain-specific framework instantiation languages have to be developed that allow for reasoning about all of these artifacts. These languages must provide the concepts of frameworks, extension points, and plugins, to reason about variability, extensibility, and consistency of instantiations. In the long run, such a language must go beyond XML and build on a form of logic that is apt to handle context-sensitive constraints, so that multi-point instantiation constraints can be specified and handled. Clearly, such a domain-specific, logic-based language for framework instantiation could be defined as an extension of OCL or OWL.

3.5   Framework Instantiation Testing

So far, we dealt with the checking of static constraints, but turn now to the role of dynamic constraints in framework instantiation. Although testing is generally advised, it needs to be mentioned in this context that framework testing is crucial to prevent misinstantiations. The testing process for frameworks has to be much more censorious than a usual testing process: it has not only to serve *positive functional testing*, but has also to ensure that a framework is not abused, i.e., must stress *negative testing*.

To specify negative test cases, several methods are available. *Misuse case diagrams*, dually to use case diagrams, specify actions that should not be performed, but prevented by the system [22]. Although mainly applied in the specification of requirements for security-critical systems, misuse diagrams can specify abnormal use cases in general, in particular erroneous attempts to instantiate frameworks. However, misuse case diagrams are only the first step to find negative test cases, because they abstract from many important details. Before a test class can be derived, they have to be refined by scenario analysis, as in scenario-based use case realization [23].

Starting from use and misuse case diagrams, *test case tables* are elaborated [24]. Such tables may have positive test case entries that stem from use cases and describe functional test cases, as well as negative entries that stem from misuse cases and describe cases of absent behavior. Usually, erroneous inputs have to be specified for a negative test case, along with the expected behavior of the application. In case of framework instantiation, instead erroneous instantiation conditions have to be described, as well as the expected reactions of the framework. Since violated dynamic instantiation constraints typically generate run-time exceptions, instantiation testing should show that these are handled appropriately and that generated error messages are comprehensible not only for the programmers, but also for the end-users.

Finally, test case entries are usually transformed by hand into test case methods or test case classes, e.g., as extensions of unit testing frameworks such as JUnit [25]. Alternatively, automatic derivation methods are being researched [26]. The derived test cases for misinstantiation have the same structure as other, positive test cases.

3.6   Run-Time Checks

If a framework instantiation contract cannot be described in a statically decidable logic, it must be checked dynamically. This section presents two best practices, *contract layers* and *contract aspects*.

While tests allow for checking of dynamic constraints before deployment of the application, there are dynamic constraints, which must be checked at runtime of the application, because not all inputs and application states can be foreseen. Framework instantiation constraints that cannot be checked statically nor tested exhaustively, should be checked at the border of the framework, i.e., whenever the flow of control moves from the application code into the framework code. Then, the inner parts of the framework are protected against contract violations. Hence, a framework should be protected by a *contract layer* which checks for all dynamic instantiation constraints.

Example 6. Checking Sortedness with Contract Layer
Reconsider Ex. 4 from Section 2.1, in which a binary search algorithm should run solely on a sorted collection. Before searching on a collection, its sortedness

has to be checked and, eventually, it has to be sorted. Such a constraint can be encapsulated into a contract checking procedure at the border of the framework:

```
class Collection {
  public boolean sorted() { ... /* sortedness predicate */ }
  public Element searchBinary(ElementKey key){
    // contract checking
    if(!sorted())
      sort();
    // calling the inner layer
    return searchBinaryInternal(key);
  }
  // inner layer
  protected Element searchBinaryInternal(ElementKey key){
    .. binary search algorithm ...
  }
}
```

In this code, the methods of the framework class are divided into a group of methods that solely check the dynamic constraints, and methods that do the real work. From the application, only the contract checking methods are visible; they ensure the validity of the dynamic constraints and call the internal group that takes the contract for granted. In our example, searchBinary belongs to the first group, searchBinaryInternal belongs to the second group.

Contract layers have other advantages. Because from inside the framework, the inner layers can be used directly, the contract checks can be saved so that the application runs faster. This is not possible if contracts are intermingled with arbitrary framework code. Secondly, contract layers encapsulate the contract concern. According to the principles of aspect-oriented programming [27], they form a *contract aspect* and can be specified separately. Such a separate specification of contract aspects is important for multi-point instantiation constraints and for simple instantiation constraints that refer to many extension points. The implementation of such constraints will be scattered throughout the framework; the contract checks crosscut the program structure. By increasing the code interdependencies, this crosscutting can complicate the framework instantiation considerably. The following example shows a contract aspect written in the AspectJ language [28], an aspect-oriented extension of Java.

Example 7. Testing for null objects
Testing for invalid parameters is one of the main tasks of contract checking. Usually, checks for null objects are distributed all over the framework methods. Such checks can be factored out of the code into a *contract aspect* that is woven as a contract layer into the framework accessor methods.

```
before(Menu m): call(* framework.*.*(Menu)) && args(m) {
    if (m == null) {
        throw new Exception ("Null Menu parameter passed when " +
            thisJoinPoint.getThis() + " was called ");
    }
}
```

The aspect specifies that before a method of a class in package `framework` is called, a parameter of type `Menu`, designated in the aspect as `m`, should be checked on a null value. Since window classes provide many functions to which menus are passed as parameters, these checks, if they were implemented by hand, would be scattered all over the framework. Encapsulated as an aspect, the Aspecjt/J aspect weaver is responsible to distribute the checks over the framework.

Aspects can also be used to implement the collaborations of Section 3.3. Because collaborations encapsulate the interplay of objects or classes, they can be regarded as a simple form of aspects without crosscutting. The relation between a formal collaboration parameter and an actual type is *1:1*, whereas aspect specifications can express crosscutting, i.e., $n{:}m$ relations. Hence, with aspects, also more general framework instantiation contracts can be specified.

4   Conclusions

This paper surveyed some typical framework instantiation problems, classified them with regard to cause and stage, and summarized several techniques, which can be used along the software process to achieve trustworthy instantiation. From real-world examples, such as SalesPoint and Eclipse, it can be derived that both human-readable and machine-processable documentation of constraints lead to frameworks that are easier to instantiate. The paper has discussed the expressive power of UML-2.0-collaborations for the modelling of frameworks, especially when used in conjunction with OCL expressions. Framework instantiation contracts can be specified with aspects, even if they span framework extension points. Because framework instantiation is such a multidimensional problem space, it has been suggested that domain-specific languages should be developed for framework instantiations. Those should integrate contract checking with plugin descriptions, for instance, combine approaches such as UML collaborations with Eclipse extensions.

However, the paper has left many questions for future research. How shall future framework instantiation languages look that go beyond standard contract languages, providing expressive concepts for variablity, extensibility, and consistency among the different resources of the framework? How can these languages help to improve the systematic documentation of frameworks? How can collaborations and aspects be embedded into these languages for better specification of consistency constraints? How can the framework instantiation languages help to automate the code generation for test suites and run-time monitoring?

Because the benefit of a framework, whether developed with a commercial focus or not, strongly depends on a widespread usage, trustworthy instantiation is the key to its success. So, spending some thoughts on how to simplify framework instantiation is always worth the effort.

References

1. Schmidt, H.W.: Systematic framework design by generalization. Communications of the ACM **40** (1997) 48–51
2. OMG: MDA Guide. (2003) http://www.omg.org/mda (visited 2006, January 16).
3. Eclipse Foundation: Eclipse Documentation. (2005) http://www.eclipse.org (visited 2005, December 31).
4. Demuth, B., Hußmann, H., Zschaler, S., Schmitz, L.: Erfahrungen mit einem frameworkbasierten Softwarepraktikum. In Schulz, C., Weber-Wulff, D., eds.: Software Engineering im Unterricht der Hochschulen SEUH '99 Workshop, Wiesbaden, Februar 1999, Tagungsband, Teubner (1999) 21–30
5. Zschaler, S., Bartho, A., et al.: Salespoint Documentation, Technische Universität, Dresden. (2002) http://www-st.inf.tu-dresden.de/SalesPoint/v3.1/documentation/index.html (visited 2005, December 31).
6. Trolltech AS: Qt Documentation. (2005) http://doc.trolltech.com/3.3/index.html (visited 2005, December 31).
7. The GTK+ Team: GTK+ Documentation. (2005) http://www.gtk.org/api/ (visited 2005, December 31).
8. Gamma, E., Helm, R., Johnson, R., Vlisside, J.: Design Patterns: Elements of Reusable Object-Oriented Software. Addison-Wesley, Reading, Massachusetts (1995)
9. Grand, M.: Patterns in Java: A Catalog of Reusable Design Patterns Illustrated with Uml,Volume 1. John Wiley & Sons, Inc., New York, NY (2002)
10. Meusel, M., Czarnecki, K., Köpf, W.: A model for structuring user documentation of object-oriented frameworks using patterns and hypertext. In: Proceedings of the European Conference on Object-Oriented Programming (ECOOP 97). Lecture Notes in Computer Science. Springer, Heidelberg (1997)
11. Walls, C., Richards, N., Oberg, R.: XDoclet in Action. Manning Publications Co., Greenwich, CT, USA (2003)
12. Meyer, B.: Object-Oriented Software Construction. Prentice Hall (1988)
13. Wing, J.M.: Writing Larch interface language specifications. ACM Transactions on Programming Languages and Systems **9** (1987) 1–24
14. de Alfaro, L., Henzinger, T.A.: Interface automata. In: ESEC/FSE-9: Proceedings of the 8th European Software Engineering Conference held jointly with 9th ACM SIGSOFT International Symposium on Foundations of Software Engineering, New York, NY, USA, ACM Press (2001) 109–120
15. Sun Microsystems: Java Development Kit Version 5. (2004) http://www.javasoft.com (visited 2005, December 31).
16. d'Souza, D.F., Wills, A.C.: Objects, Components and Frameworks with UML – The Catalysis Approach. Addision-Wesley (1998)
17. Demuth, B., Hußmann, H., Löcher, S.: OCL as a specification language for business rules in database applications. In Gogolla, M., Kobryn, C., eds.: UML 2001 - The Unified Modeling Language. Modeling Languages, Concepts, and Tools. 4th International Conference, Toronto, Canada, October 2001, Proceedings. Volume 2185 of Lecture Notes in Computer Science., Springer (2001) 104–117

18. Rumpe, B.: Agile Modellierung mit UML - Codegenerierung, Testfälle, Refactoring. Springer-Verlag (2005) ISBN: 3-540-20905-0.
19. Aßmann, U.: Reuse in semantic applications. In Eisinger, N., Maluszynski, J., eds.: Summer School of REWERSE (Reasoning on the Semantic Web). Number 3564 in Lecture Notes in Computer Science, Berlin, Springer (2005)
20. Smith, M.K., Volz, R., McGuiness, D., Welty, C.: Web Ontology Language (OWL) guide version 1.0. Technical report, W3C World Wide Web Concortium (2002) http://www.w3.org/TR/2002/WD-owl-guide-20021104/ (visited 2005, December 31).
21. Möller, R., Haarslev, V.: High performance reasoning with very large knowledge bases: A practical case study. In: Seventeenth International Joint Conference on Artificial Intelligence, IJCAI-01. (2001)
22. Sindre, G., Opdahl, A.L.: Eliciting security requirements with misuse cases. Requirements Engineering **10** (2005) 34–44
23. Jacobson, I., Booch, G., Rumbaugh, J.: The Unified Software Development Process. Object Technology Series. Addison Wesley Longman, Reading, Mass. (1999)
24. Rätzmann, M.: Software-Testing und Internationalisierung - Rapid Application Testing, Softwaretest, Agiles Qualitätsmanagement. Gallileo Press (2004)
25. Beck, K., Gamma, E.: Test infected: Programmers love writing tests. Java Report **3** (1998) 51–56 http://members.pingnet.ch/gamma/junit.htm (visited 2006, January 16).
26. Stotts, D., Lindsey, M., Antley, A.: An informal formal method for systematic JUnit test case generation. In: XP/Agile Universe. Volume 2418 of Lecture Notes in Computer Science. Springer (2002) 131–142
27. Kiczales, G., Lamping, J., Mendhekar, A., Maeda, C., Lopes, C., Loingtier, J.M., Irwin, J.: Aspect-oriented programming. In: Proceedings of the European Conference on Object-Oriented Programming (ECOOP 97). Volume 1241 of Lecture Notes in Computer Science. Springer, Heidelberg (1997) 220–242
28. AspectJ Project: Home Page. (2005) http://eclipse.org/aspectj/ (visited 2005, December 31).

Performance Prediction of Component-Based Systems
A Survey from an Engineering Perspective

Steffen Becker[1], Lars Grunske[2], Raffaela Mirandola[3], and Sven Overhage[4]

[1] Software Engineering Group, University of Oldenburg,
OFFIS, Escherweg 2, 26121 Oldenburg, Germany
steffen.becker@informatik.uni-oldenburg.de
[2] School of Information Technology and Electrical Engineering, University of Queensland,
Brisbane, QLD 4072, Australia
grunske@itee.uq.edu.au
[3] Dipartimento di Elettronica e Informazione,
Politecnico di Milano, Italy
mirandola@elet.polimi.it
[4] Dept. of Software Engineering and Business Information Systems,
Augsburg University, Universitätsstraße 16, 86135 Augsburg, Germany
sven.overhage@wiwi.uni-augsburg.de

Abstract. Performance predictions of component assemblies and the ability of obtaining system-level performance properties from these predictions are a crucial success factor when building trustworthy component-based systems. In order to achieve this goal, a collection of methods and tools to capture and analyze the performance of software systems has been developed. These methods and tools aim at helping software engineers by providing them with the capability to understand design trade-offs, optimize their design by identifying performance inhibitors, or predict a systems performance within a specified deployment environment. In this paper, we analyze the applicability of various performance prediction methods for the development of component-based systems and contrast their inherent strengths and weaknesses in different engineering problem scenarios. In so doing, we establish a basis to select an appropriate prediction method and to provide recommendations for future research activities, which could significantly improve the performance prediction of component-based systems.

1 Introduction

In many application domains such as avionics, automotive, production-control, bioinformatics and e-business, software systems must meet strict performance goals in order to fulfill their requirements. Consequently, designers must address performance as a fundamental issue during the design and construction of software systems. This requires annotating component-based architectures with known performance qualities, and choosing fast and scalable component implementations and infrastructures. However, without an upfront effort to produce a flexible architecture during the design phase, it is rarely possible to retrofit component-based systems to significantly improve their performance.

R.H. Reussner et al. (Eds.): Architecting Systems, LNCS 3938, pp. 169–192, 2006.

Especially decisions taken in a late development stage, such as increasing the size of a thread pool or deploying replicated components on different hardware platforms, typically lead to a limited system performance improvement only. For that reason, unwise decisions at design-time probably render it impossible to achieve the required performance level once the system has been composed.

Current industrial practice to evaluate the performance impact of early design decisions involves the construction of prototypes, which are executed on the target deployment platform in order to measure performance properties. In this way, prototyping can help to give confidence in the resulting system performance being adequate for its needs. Prototyping is, however, expensive and time-consuming, and the results will not be valid if substantial design changes are made during implementation. Consequently, software engineering practices could be improved if software architects were able to predict the performance of the final system based on design documents without implementation details. This would reduce the effort and costs of performance prediction.

There is a substantial amount of research devoted to creating performance prediction techniques for software systems. A leading example, the software performance engineering community (SPE) [1, 2] has spent a number of years to integrate design and performance modeling activities. The developed methods are based on use case models, object and functional modeling mostly using UML-based notations. Other techniques combine analytical models with benchmarking or support model-based prototype generation. Regardless of their approach, techniques for the performance prediction of component-based systems should exhibit the following basic characteristics:

- **Accuracy.** The prediction must be accurate enough in order to provide useful results. On the other hand, a compromise between the accuracy of predictions and the analysis effort must be found in order to enable the efficient evaluation of complex applications.
- **Adaptability.** Prediction techniques should support efficient performance prediction under architecture changes where components are added/modified or replaced by different type of components.
- **Cost effectiveness.** The approach should require less effort than prototyping and subsequent measurements.
- **Compositionality.** Prediction techniques should be able to make performance predictions based on the performance characteristics of the components, which together build the system. Since component-based systems usually are structured hierarchically and consist of composite components, performance prediction techniques should be able to exploit this structure by using the analysis results on lower abstraction layers to enable the performance prediction of composite components.
- **Scalability.** Component-based systems are typically built either with a large set of simple components or utilize a few large-grain, complex components. To predict performance attributes, analysis techniques need to be scalable to handle both cases.
- **Analyzability.** Prediction techniques should not only reveal performance bottlenecks, but also give insights into possible flaws in architecture designs that are causing problems.
- **Universality.** The approach should be applicable to different component technologies with minimal modification. This enables the performance prediction of an integrated system with multiple component technologies involved.

In this paper, we analyze the applicability of existing performance prediction techniques in various software engineering problem scenarios. The aim is to highlight the strengths and weaknesses of the approaches, and reveal areas where further research is required. We start by describing a set of practical concerns which should be taken into account by performance prediction methods in section 2. Afterwards, we introduce current performance prediction methods in section 3 and classify them according to their underlying prediction technique. In section 4, we examine the individual strengths and weaknesses of the different prediction methods with respect to the before-mentioned basic characteristics and the practical concerns provided in section 2. Based on the examination of existing performance prediction techniques, we derive a variety of recommendations to improve the performance prediction of component-based systems in section 5. Finally, we conclude the paper in section 6.

2   A Taxonomy of Practical Concerns

In addition to the basic characteristics of component-based performance prediction techniques, which are mentioned in the previous section, we want to highlight some practical concerns in this section. The result will be a taxonomy of concerns, which have to be considered by performance prediction methods and their underlying prediction models. Additionally, the introduced taxonomy should also guide system architects to identify appropriate performance prediction methods with respect to their practical concerns. Both topics are investigated in detail in later sections of this paper.

It is important to stress that the problems listed in the following paragraphs are not merely scientific cases but have practical relevance. The mentioned concerns emerge in industrial scale development scenarios. This is being illustrated by the case study of an experimental Web server, which has been implemented by the Palladio group at Oldenburg University with a set of C# components. The Web server has been developed with the aim to compare and validate performance prediction methods. It supports handling basic HTTP GET and POST requests and provides an interface for the generation of dynamic HTML pages, e.g., by returning data stored in a connected database. Despite this restricted functionality and the fact that it has not that many lines of code (LOC), many concerns with today's performance prediction methods can be demonstrated by using this server. Especially, the concerns listed below emerged during the Web server development.

Third-party deployment. A major concept when looking at the performance evaluation of component-based systems is reasoning about the system properties based on the properties of the constituting components. This concept is a prerequisite to enable scalable prediction methods. Additionally, when considering Szyperski's definition [3] of a component, it is mentioned that components have to be third-party deployable. It becomes difficult to reason about extra-functional properties of components that can be deployed by third-parties, because the QoS of a component service can be only determined at run-time and only ex-post. This means that the QoS of a component service only can be determined by running the program and by measuring the QoS in question. This results from the fact that the QoS is not solely dependant on the *executable code* of the component but also on the *run-time dynamics* and the *environment* in which the component is executed in. In the web server example we have used a component accessing a database. Its QoS is significantly different if the component is deployed on the back-end server hosting the database or if it is run on a laptop with limited memory and processing power.

Third-party deployment can be regarded as super-concern, in a sense that it has an impact on all the other concerns. Thus, third-party deployment is not independent of the other concerns. Nevertheless, it is worth looking at some of the following concerns in more detail. The concerns regarded below are the usage of external services, the deployment environment, resource usage and congestion, the operational profile, and interdependencies caused by these aspects.

The third-party deployment paradigm raises an additional issue that will be elaborated later on: Approaches specifying extra-functional properties of components as constant figures will fail. This is obvious: One can only specify QoS when fixing the environment, e.g. using a reference platform, which supports the QoS figures. But then, it is only possible to deploy the component on exactly the same environment if we want to get the same QoS which is a major restriction of independent deployment. Thus, it is necessary to use specification languages and methods which are able to specify the QoS of components depending on every possible environment. During our survey, we will consequently also examine the applicability of existing approaches to QoS specification (section 3.3).

In the following, the introduced example system is investigated further to highlight the afore mentioned concerns.

External Services. The QoS of a component's service depends on the QoS of the external services called by this service. Consider for example the response-time of the component handling HTTP requests. We observe that the QoS of the `HandleRequest` method depends on the QoS of the external services the component calls, i.e., the performance of this call will never exceed the performance of the external method. For example, the attached HTML reader component (retrieving Web pages from the hard disk) needs to open a HTML file, read the data and close the file again. If opening and closing takes 200ms and processing the required data take another 100ms then the initial request will never be processed faster than 500ms. Additionally, when the request processor component is deployed in a different context, perhaps the file stream is replaced by a component delivering a network stream, it will likely perform its tasks slower due to the different QoS of the external service.

Deployment. It is not solely the constituent components of a component-based system have an impact on the component's performance, the hardware and middleware platform on which the component is deployed can make a significant difference (as already mentioned above). A component which is executed on a fast CPU will perform better than the same component which is executed on a slower CPU. Other well known influential factors are memory availability, network bandwidth, number of CPUs, performance of external storage devices (e.g. disks, optical media), and so on. Equivalent concerns apply with component-based systems that utilize software infrastructures such as middleware platforms or virtual machines. With such environments, for example, the performance of the byte code interpreter or bandwidth of the middleware server are crucial performance factors.

Given the Web server example there is a difference if its components are deployed on the .NET runtime installed on a high performing back-end server or on a desktop PC. Additionally, we have also measured that the performance of a component deployed on the Mono runtime environment (www.mono-project.com) is different from the deployment on the Microsoft implementation. This demonstrates the mentioned influences of hard- and middleware.

Resources. Software infrastructures have resource limits that constraint the performance of a component-based system. For example, the amount of threads (thread pool size), software caches/ buffers, semaphores, database connections and locking schemes must be understood in order to predict the behavior of component-based systems. Some of these factors, e.g. thread pool size, can be configured for the example Web server and their impact can be measured. Further, as a part of the deployment decisions, we could consider deploying the component redundantly on several hosts and using a load balancer to spread and monitor application load.

In general, any resource acquisition takes a certain amount of time, depending on the number of resources available. If many components have to use a rare resource it is more likely that resource conflicts will occur. In this case the component has to line up itself into a queue of components requesting the resource. Consequently, this delay due to resource conflicts need to be considered, as it influences the performance of a service call. As a result a performance prediction model has to include somehow the shared resources in environment with (virtual or physical) concurrent control flows. Additionally, the priority inversion problem could occur, where a high priority process is blocked by a low priority process, because this low priority process uses a resource which is needed by the high priority process [4].

Operational Profile. The previous section highlights additional obstacles in performance engineering. Considering the resource acquisition example, as long as the software architecture has to deal with only a single user calling its services, it is unlikely that resource conflicts will be an issue. This situation changes as soon as the component is deployed to service multiple concurrent requests. The system will have to deal with many simultaneous requests, making resource contention a major issue in terms of performance. This kind of dependency is called operational profile [5, 6].

There are additional important aspects, namely the probability of supported use cases occurring, the size and value of input parameters (which may also lead to different usage scenarios), the rate with which requests for a certain service are being made. Note the distinction between use case occurrence and request rate for a specific service. The first is from the viewpoint of the user of the system and might be translated into calls to services offered by the whole application. The second is from the viewpoint of the single components of the system. The request rate is important at every component in the system architecture even at those which cannot be called by the user directly. The translation of the usage profile in service request rates is an open field of research.

In the web server example the type of the request determines the response time. Retrieving a static HTML page stored on the hard drive is faster than retrieving a dynamic page which has to be computed from database queries. So, it is important to capture the relationship between the request types quite accurately or to model the two cases in separate use cases. Additionally the frequency and the amount of requests per unit of time have to be taken into account, especially as many concurrent requests lead to contention of the CPU resource(s). Finally, also the size of the return type is important. Retrieving and streaming a small HTML page is faster than the retrieval of a large image.

Interdependencies. Note that there are certain interdependencies between the different aspects of a component's context. The usage of the component results in a load on the hard- and software resources as well as external services, for example the amount of concurrent threads/requests, request frequency of certain mutually exclusive resources locks, and so on. It is a major challenge to predict - utilizing the operational profile of a single service call - the operational profiles of the components which actually are involved in the handling the request. For example, a single HTTP request for a yellow page application creates several queries of the yellow page database to generate the descriptions of the matching companies for the initial query. Another example of the dependencies on external service calls can be seen in an authentification server. If this component is used on a website it mostly has to serve plain password challenges. In an enterprise context the same server might be also challenged by certificate requests.

There are two challenges arising from the preceding discussion:

– The aspects discussed above must be considered by performance evaluation techniques. Every time a certain technique abstracts one of these aspects, the prediction becomes less accurate or in certain cases totally wrong.
– If we want to support QoS prediction in the context of third-party deployable components there has to be a large specification of the respective components. There has to be a specification of the component which allows the estimation of QoS in *different* contexts. Usually this kind of specifications contain a lot of information enabling the component user to evaluate the performance and contextual aspects in a parametric way. The information can only be specified by the component producer. This is a strong assumption and appears infeasible without extensive tool support.

3   Classification of Approaches

As already outlined in the introduction, the integration of quantitative evaluation into the software development processes is an important activity to meet extra-functional, and in particular performance requirements. Balsamo et al. [7] presents a survey of different approaches for model-based performance evaluation. The proposed classification is based on the type of the performance model (Queueing Networks, Petri Nets, Process Algebras, Markov Processes), the applied evaluation method (analytical or simulative) and the presence of automated support for performance prediction. Some of these approaches have also been extended to deal with component-based systems.

In this section, we present a (short) survey of the existing approaches for predictive performance analysis of component-based systems. We distinguish between quantitative (section 3.1) and qualitative (section 3.2) analysis. Furthermore, quantitative

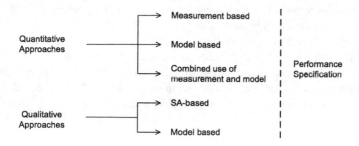

Fig. 1. *Approaches overview*

techniques are categorized by the kind of techniques used (measurement-based, model-based, combination of measurement-based and model-based). Figure 1 visualizes the different approaches together with the cross-cutting aspect of performance specification (dealt with in section 3.3), whose existence plays a key role for a successful application of performance prediction techniques.

A comparison of these approaches with respect to the characteristics and concerns described in sections 1 and 2 will be presented in the next section.

3.1   Quantitative Approaches

Measurement-Based. Measurement-based approaches are suitable and useful, if the focus is on quantitative evaluation of performance. In [8] (**M1**) a discussion is given about how component-based system properties may influence the selection of methods and tools used to obtain and analyze performance measures. Then, a method is proposed for the measurement of performance distinguishing between application-specific metrics (e.g., execution time of various functions) and platform-specific metrics (e.g., resource utilization). The automation of the process of gathering and analyzing data for these performance metrics is also discussed. The major drawbacks of this approach are that it is only suitable for already implemented systems and the obtained results do not show general applicability of the approach.

A different approach that partially overcomes these difficulties is presented in [9] (**M2**), where starting from a specific COTS middleware infrastructure, in a first step, performance measures are collected empirically. Afterwards, in a second step, the obtained results are elaborated to extend their validity to a more general setting. The proposed approach includes a reasoning framework for understanding architectural trade-offs and the relationship between technology features and the derivation of a set of mathematical models describing the generic behavior of applications using that specific COTS technology. An inherent limitation of this approach is that it leads to sound results only for a specific hardware platform.

Denaro et al. [10] (**M3**) describes and evaluates a method for testing performance of distributed software in the early development stages. Their method takes into account the impact of the middleware used to build a distributed application. To this end the authors use architecture designs to derive application-specific performance test cases. These test cases are then executed on the available middleware platform and used to improve performance prediction in the early stages of the development process.

Model-Based. An approach, which includes predictability of performance behavior of component-based systems is presented in [11] (**MB1**). The basic idea of this approach is that the "behavior of a component-based system must be compositional in order to be scalable". To fulfill this requirement, in addition to the descriptions of the functional behavior, performance specifications are also included in component specifications. The paper outlines, how classical techniques and notations for performance analysis are either unsuitable or unnatural to capture the performance behavior of generic software components, and points out that, "performance specification problems are so basic that there are unresolved research issues to be tackled even for the simplest reusable components". A first attempt towards a compositional approach to performance analysis is then presented, mainly based on the use of formal techniques. However, as the authors argue, an engineering approach to predictability on performance is a necessary ingredient to ensure predictable components.

The papers [12, 13, 14] (**MB2**) propose a prototype enabled prediction technology, called PECT that integrates component technology with analysis models. The main goal of PECT is to enable the prediction of assembly level properties, starting from certifiable components, prior to component composition. In fact PECT is described as a "packaging of engineering methods and a supporting technical infrastructure that, together enable predictable assembly from certifiable components".

Bertolino and Mirandola introduce in [15, 16] (**MB3**) the CB-SPE framework: a compositional methodology for component-based performance engineering and its supporting tool. CB-SPE is based on the concepts and steps of the SPE technology, and uses OMG's SPT profile [17]. The technique is compositional: It is first applied by the component developer at the component layer, achieving a parametric performance evaluation of the components in isolation; then, at the application layer, the system assembler uses a step-wise procedure for predicting the performance of the assembled components on the actual platform.

In [18, 19] (**MB4**) a specific performance evaluation technique, layered queueing networks, is applied to generate performance models for component-based systems. To achieve this goal an XML-based language is defined that describes performance models of both software components and component-based systems. A model assembler tool starting from component sub-models automatically generates a layered performance models that can be solved by use of classical techniques.

In [20] (**MB5**), Balsamo and Marzolla present a simulation environment, where starting from Use Case, Activity and Deployment diagrams with RT-UML annotations (augmented, in some cases, to better fit performance features) a discrete-event C++ simulation program is derived. The transformation methodology is close to a one-to-one mapping from elements of UML model to elements of the simulator, so that the structure and the dynamics of the simulator closely follow the structure and the behavior of the UML model.

Eskenazi et al. [21] presents a method for the "Analysis and Prediction of Performance for Evolving Architectures" (APPEAR) that combines both structural and statistical techniques in a flexible way. It allows a choice of, which parts of the component are structurally described, modeled and simulated, and which parts are evaluated statistically. Additionally, the same authors present in [22] (**MB6**) a stepwise approach to predict the performance of component compositions. "The approach considers the major factors influencing the performance of component compositions sequentially: component operations, activities, and composition of activities. During each analysis step, various models - analytical, statistical, simulation-based - can be constructed to specify the contribution of each factor to the performance of the composition. The architects can choose which model they use at each step."

A simulation-based approach for predicting real-time behavior of an assembly based on models of its contained components is proposed by Chaudron et al. in [23] (**MB7**). The presented method deals with the main aspects of real-time systems such as: mutual exclusions, combinations of periodic and aperiodic tasks and synchronization constraints. Additionally, the simulator provides data about the dynamic resource consumption and real-time properties like response time, blocking time and number of missed deadlines per task.

In [24] (**MB8**) a compositional component performance model based on parametric contracts is presented. The approach allows for parameterization with context dependencies in order to model the performance of a single component that depends on the performance properties of the environment by using so-called service effect automata. These automata describe the call sequence of the external services on which a component service depends.

Combined Use of Measurement and Model-Based Approaches. Menasce et al. [25] (**MBM1**) proposes a QoS-based approach to distributed software system composition and reconfiguration. This method uses resource reservation mechanisms at the component level to guarantee soft (i.e., average values) QoS requirements at the software system level. Different metrics can be used for measuring and providing a given QoS property, such as response time, throughput, and concurrency level. Specifically, the method relies on the definition of QoS-aware components, where a client component can request a service with a certain QoS level. In case the server is able to provide this QoS level, it commits itself to do so; otherwise a negotiation is started until an agreement on a new QoS level is reached. The method implementation is based on the combination of queueing models and measurement techniques.

In [26] (**MBM2**) a methodology is presented, which aims for predicting the performance of component-oriented distributed systems both during development and after the system have been built. The methodology combines monitoring, modelling and performance prediction. Specifically, performance prediction models based on UML models are created dynamically with non-intrusive methods. The application performance is then predicted by generating workloads and simulating the performance models.

In [27] (**MBM3**) an approach to predict the performance of component-based applications during the design phase is presented. The proposed methodology derives a quantitative performance model for a given application using aspects from the underlying component platform, and from a design description of the application. The results obtained for an EJB application are validated with measurements of different implementations. Using this methodology, it is possible for the software architect to make early decisions between alternative application architectures in terms of their performance and scalability.

3.2 Qualitative Approaches

In this section we shortly describe some approaches which evaluate the quality of component-based systems either based on the affinity between software architecture and software components or exploiting the principles of the model driven engineering. The common characteristic of these approaches is to consider qualitative analyzes that are derived from an attribute-based style or trough "screening questions" and are meant to be coarse-grained versions of the quantitative analysis that can be performed when a precise analytic model of a quality attribute is built.

SA-Based. A qualitative approach to performance analysis of component-based systems is undertaken in [28], where the affinity between Software Architecture (SA) and Software Component (SC) technology is outlined and exploited. This affinity is related to different aspects: (i) the central role of components and connectors as abstraction entities, (ii) the correlation of architectural style and component model and frameworks, (iii) the complementary agendas followed by the SA and SC technologies: enabling reasoning about quality attributed, and simplifying component integration. Therefore, the basic idea of these approaches is to develop a reference model that relates the key abstractions of SA and component-based technology, and then to adapt and apply some existing SA analysis methods, such as SAAM, ATAM and QADP.

Model-Based. The basic idea of model-driven engineering (MDE) is to create a set of models that help the designers to understand and to evaluate both the system requirements and its implementation. A key point for a successful application of an MDE-based process is the integration of orthogonal models taking into account cross-cutting aspects such as the application's performance. The following approaches are mainly descriptive and focus on paths leading to the construction of different performance models. A crucial issue for the application of MDE techniques is the existence of automatic tools allowing model transformations from design models to analysis-oriented models.

Solberg et al. [29] outlines the need to incorporate QoS specification and evaluation within a MDA-based approach at a more abstract level and at the platform-specific level. In this view, the model transformations, the code generation, the configuration and deployment should be QoS-aware. Ideally the target execution platform should be also QoS-aware.

Grassi and Mirandola [30] present an approach for the predictive analysis of extra-functional properties of component-based software systems. According to a model-driven perspective, the construction of a model that supports some specific analysis methodology is seen as the result of a sequence of refinement steps, where earlier steps can be generally shared among different analysis methodologies. The focus is mainly on a path leading to the construction of a stochastic model for the compositional performance analysis, but some relationships with different refinement paths are also outlined.

To facilitate extra-functional analysis in the design phase, automatic prediction tools should be devised, to predict some overall quality attributes of the application without requiring extensive knowledge of analysis methodologies to the application designer. To achieve this goal, a key idea is to define a model transformation system that takes as input some "design-oriented" model of the component assembly and (almost) automatically produces as a result an "analysis-oriented" model that lends itself to the application of some analysis methodology. However, to actually devise such a transformation, one must face both the heterogeneous design level notations for component-based systems, and the variety of extra-functional attributes.

In this perspective, the work in [31, 32] describes an intermediate model called Core Scenario Model (CSM), which can be extracted from an annotated design model. Additionally a tool architecture called PUMA is described, which provides a unified interface between different kinds of design information and different kinds of performance models, for example Markov-models, stochastic Petri nets and process algebras, queues and layered queues. Petriu et al. [33] proposes a transformation method of an annotated UML model into a performance model defined at a higher level of abstraction based on graph transformation concepts, whereas the implementation of the transformation rules and algorithm uses lower-level XML trees manipulations techniques, such as XML algebra. The target performance model used as an example in this paper is the Layered Queueing Network (LQN).

A different approach is described in [34]. This approach defines a kernel language with the aim to capture the relevant information for the analysis of extra-functional attributes (performance and reliability) of component-based systems. Using this kernel language a bridge between design-oriented and analysis-oriented notations could be established, which enables a variety of direct transformations from the former to the latter. The proposed kernel language is defined within a MOF (Meta-Object Facility) framework, to allow the exploitation of MOF-based model transformation facilities.

3.3 Performance Specification

A key point for a successful application of quantitative validation of performance properties during component-based software development is the existence of languages allowing performance specification when designing a component-based system both at component and at assembly level.

A UML Profile for Schedulability, Performance and Time (SPT Profile) has been proposed and adopted as an OMG standard [17] as a response to the exigencies of introducing in UML diagrams quantifiable notions of time and resources usage. The SPT Profile is not an extension to the UML meta model, but a set of domain profiles for UML. Basically, the underlying idea is to import annotations in the UML models, which describe the characteristics relative to the target domain viewpoint (performance, real-time, schedulability, concurrency). In this a way various (existing and future) analysis techniques can usefully exploit the provided features. In fact, the SPT profile is intended to provide a single unifying framework encompassing the existing analysis methods, still leaving enough flexibility for different specializations.

Zschaler in [35] investigates the possibility to define a framework, which can be used to provide semantics for extra-functional specifications of component-based systems, by explaining also how the different parts of a component-based system cooperate to deliver a certain service with certain extra-functional properties. The claimed objectives are "To allow application developers to use Component-Based Software Engineering to structure their applications and thus lower the complexity of the software development process while at the same time enabling them to make use of proven and tested theories for providing extra-functional properties of those applications."

In [36], the authors define a simple language, based on an abstract component model, to describe a component assembly, outlining which information should be included to support compositional performance analysis. Moreover, a mapping of the constructs of the proposed language to elements of the UML Performance Profile is outlined, to give them a precisely defined "performance semantics", and to get a starting point for the exploitation of proposed UML-based methodologies and algorithms for performance analysis.

In [37] the QoS modeling language (QML) is described. The QML is used to specify QoS attributes for interfaces, operations, operation parameters, and operation results. It is based on the fundamental concepts of contract types, contracts and profiles. Contract types are utilized to specify the metrics used to determine a specific QoS concept. Contracts are used afterwards to specify a certain level of the metrics of a contract type. The linking between contracts and interface methods, operation parameters or results is done via QML profiles. There is a conformance relation defined on profiles, contracts, and constraints. The conformance is needed at runtime, so that client-server connections do not have to be based on an exact match of QoS requirements with QoS properties. For example, if the client requests a response time of less than 5ms the server has to provide exactly a response time of less than 5ms. Nevertheless, instead of exact matches, a service is allowed to provide more than what is required by a client. In the example, the server is also allowed to provide a response time of less than 2ms as this is conforming to the required 5ms requested by the client.

4 Abstract Comparison

Table 1 relates the different performance prediction approaches described in section 3 with (a) the concerns to component-based systems described in section 2 (columns C in the table) and (b) with general characteristics of performance (prediction) techniques described in section 1 (columns A in the table). The comparison has been carried out only for quantitative approaches since qualitative methods pose themselves on the different perspective to give only qualitative insights about the performance of component-based systems.

Each row in the table refers to a specific methodology. The considered methods are grouped according to the categories introduced in section 3 (first column) and each methodology is identified by the assigned labels (second column), by the author's names (third column) and by the reference paper(s)(fourth column).

To quantify the fulfillment of the concerns C (columns 5-9) and the characteristics A (columns 10-16) we have adopted a coarse-grained classification, i.e.,: High, Medium, Low, Absent, since the considered methods are often described with a low level of detail. Moreover, in some cases, the description is carried out at an high abstraction level that is not sufficient to quantify the relationships for the factors A and C. In these cases we have inserted in the table an educated guess followed by a question mark. Additionally, dealing with aspect A7, we have considered the existence of an automated tool or framework for the derivation of performance characteristics as a good starting point.

In the remaining part of this section we describe in some details each row of table 1 presenting how each methodology deals with factors A and C.

Table 1. Performance prediction of Component-Based Systems - comparison of quantitative approaches

Category	Method	Authors	Reference	Third party deployment C1	External services C2	Deployment and resources C3	Usage Profiles C4	Interdependencies C5	Accuracy A1	Adaptability A2	Cost-effective A3	Compositionality A4	Scalability A5	Analyzability A6	Universality A7
Measurement	M1	Yacoub	[8]	M	L	L	M	L	M	L	L	L	L	A	A
	M2	Chen et al.	[9]	M	L	H	M	M-L	M	L	M	M	L	L	A
	M3	Denaro et al.	[10]	M	L	H	M	M	M	L	L	L	L	L	A
Model-based	MB1	Sitaraman et al.	[11]	M	L	L	M	M	L	M	L	M	L	M	A
	MB2	Hissam et al.	[12,14]	H	H	M	M	H	M-H	H	H	H	M	M	M
	MB3	Bertolino et al.	[15,16]	H	M	M	M	M	M?	H	H	H	M-L	H	M
	MB4	Wu et al.	[18,19]	M	L	M	L	M	M?	H	H	M	M	H	M
	MB5	Balsamo et al.	[20]	M-L	M	L	M-L	L	M-L?	M	H	M	M	H	M
	MB6	Eskenazi et al.	[22]	M	M	M	L	L	M?	M?	M	M	H	H	L
	MB7	Bondarev et al.	[23]	M	H	H	L	M	L?	M?	M	H	L	M	L
	MB8	Reussner et al.	[24]	M	M	L	M-L	A	M?	L	M	H	L	H	M
Model and Measurement	MBM1	Menasce et al.	[25]	M	M	H	H	L	H	M	M	M	L	H	M
	MBM2	Diaconescu et al.	[26]	H	M-H?	H	H	M?	H?	L	L	M	L-M?	H	M
	MBM3	Liu et al.	[27]	H	M	H	H	M	H	L	M	M	M	H	A

Legend:

H= High, M= Medium, L= Low, A= Absent, the ? denotes an educated guess

Let us consider, for example, the measurement based approaches (M1-M3): M1 is a introductive study and is simply based on the monitoring of single applications, while M2 and M3 seem more promising to deal with component-based systems. Both of them take middleware details into account and consider J2EE application with EJB containers. To deal with the concerns factors C4 and C5, M2 defines application-specific behavioral characteristics through the design of a set of test-cases. The performance of the server side is characterized using these tests with parameter settings concerning the transaction type and frequency, the database connection, and the pool size. Instead M3 tries to model usage scenarios relevant to performance through the modeling of workload in terms of number of user and frequency of inputs. The interactions among distributed components and resources are studied according to whether they take place between middleware and components, among components themselves or to access persistent data in a database.

Considering the general foreseeable characteristics of prediction techniques, the methods based on measurements show good value for the accuracy aspect, while they exhibit quite low values for all the other features. Actually, since they require already implemented systems their cost effectiveness is low. Moreover, they are often platform-specific and this fact limits the adaptability, the scalability and the analyzability. The universality facet in these approaches is completely absent, because the implementation and the analysis are completely manual and no automatic support is provided.

The weak point of model-based approaches is the lack of empirical studies for the validation of the predicted results. As a consequence the column A1 regarding the accuracy of the obtained results is filled-in only with educated guesses.

MB1 is one of the first papers addressing the importance of a performance engineering approach for component-based systems, and this paper specifically outlines issues like compositionality, performance specification and usage profile definition (as shown by the quite good values in the table). However, the proposed formal approach is not supported by an automated framework and seems to be only a good reasoning tool rather than a method to be applied in an industrial software development context.

MB2's aim at integrating component technology with analysis models, allowing analysis and prediction of assembly-level properties prior to component composition. It is based on the definition of an analytic interface, that takes into account the component technology, but spans aspects related to the use of some analysis methodology to support predictions about quantitative properties of the system. This approach is very attractive and shows high values in the table. It is supported by an automatic framework as well as it includes also a first "measurement and validation environment" to validate the analysis results and to give informed feedback to the design team. A weak point is that the performance model does take usage profiles and resource contention aspects into account.

MB3, MB4 and MB5 are based on the use of UML models as design notation augmented with performance annotations compliant to the SPT profile [17]. These approaches are all supported by (semi-)automatic frameworks and provide good (also very good) values for general properties of prediction techniques. They differ in the type of performance models (queueing network, layered queueing network and simulation, respectively) and in the way of addressing the concerns that arise when developing component-based systems. MB3 and MB4 consider (even if in simple way) most aspects related to component-based models, while MB5 has been conceived for a traditional software development process and scores therefore not so well for component-based systems.

In MB6 component composition is considered in terms of concurrent activities that invoke a number of component operations. At first, a detailed analysis of performance models for component operations is carried out; then an activity model is constructed through a flow graph and finally a model of the concurrent activities is obtained. The first step is based on the combination of different methods and deals well with the concerns that occur with component-based development. The second step uses traditional techniques related to flow graphs, while the third step is not detailed enough, which making the overall understanding of the characteristics of this prediction technique difficult.

MB7 assumes as starting point Robocop component models that include resource, function, behavior and executable models. The following step combines the behavior and resource consumption models with an application model constructed for possible critical execution scenarios. This combination is performed taking into account the application static structure and its internal and external events. This model serves as an input to a simulation tool, which outputs the execution behavior of the assembly with its timing properties (latency and resource utilization). Therefore, MB7 shows quite good scores for component-based development concerns, but it is specifically targeted for the Robocop component model and this fact decreases its adaptability and scalability values.

MB8 uses components described in the Palladio component model, which includes service effect specifications (gray box component view) with service effect automata. Additionally, annotations of the probability density distribution of the response times of the external service calls and the internal calculations are used. Consequently, it gets good marks for the inclusion of external dependencies and compositional reasoning. Nevertheless, in so doing it regards hardware dependencies only implicitly. Also the usage profile is used solely to estimate probabilities of certain control flows. Multiple threads or concurrent resource utilization is disregarded.

The methods based on the combination of measurement and modeling seems to have the capabilities to combine the different concerns Cs and As in Table 1, however a weak point is represented by a low level of adaptability and scalability due to the specifics of the selected platform.

MBM1 focuses on component specifications rather than on the analysis, it consists of the definition of component QoS-aware capable of engaging QoS negotiation with other components in a distributed environment. This approach seems to be very promising, because it allows to cope with external services, deployment and usage profile in a good way. The accuracy of the obtained results are validated in an experimental environment and the presence of an automated tool for performance model generation and analysis increases the value/ attractiveness of this approach. The major drawback is the low scalability, due to the simplicity of the treated models. The models are hardly able to cope with complex systems.

MBM2 presents a framework composed of a module, which collects run-time performance information on the software components and on the software application execution environment. This module is implemented for J2EE applications and EJB container and allows also the execution of performance analyses. This is achieved with an instrumentation of the software components by a proxy layer that lowers the cost-effectiveness of the approach. Additionally, there is also a partially implemented adaptation module, which aims to solve performance problems through the selection of different, functionally-equivalent, components. The two modules are supposed to operate in an automated feedback-loop. Currently, this framework is only partially implemented and automated. This is reflected by some low (or guessed) values in the table. However, it is the first automated framework including both component and application layer, which contains an optimization module. Consequently this approach get high values for both aspects: As and Cs.

MBM3 is based on the modeling of an application in terms of component interactions and demands placed on the component container; its parameterization is carried out based on the definition of a performance profile of the container and the underlying platform obtained through benchmarking. In this way the factors Cs can be fulfilled in a quite satisfactory way. The accuracy of the obtained results is validated in a real setting and thus theoretically justified. In addition, the other A factors show medium to high values, except for the adaptability, because the method is only presented and validated in an EJB context. Furthermore, the universality of the approach can be questioned, since the method has to be applied manually and thus the results are based on the expertise and skills of the design team.

To summarize, figure 2 depicts the different scores of the discussed techniques with respect to concerns As and Cs. Roughly speaking, we can observe how measurement-based methods show low values for characteristics A while deal quite well with concerns Cs. On the contrary, the model-based approaches deal quite well with A factors while show Low or Medium values handling factors C. The joint use of models and measurement techniques combine the potentialities of both methods. A detailed comparison of different techniques would require performing some common validation experiment with the various tools and methodologies. Our feeling is that working

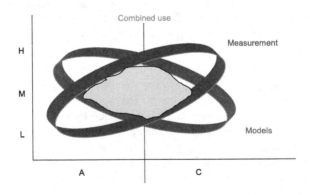

Fig. 2. Models and measurement techniques

on simple examples could lead to misleading results because of lacking of critical aspects inherent to component-based systems. To overcome this problem we are working towards the definition of a reference system including the main characteristics and concerns of a typical component-based applications and our long-term goal is to use this system to compare and validate the various performance approaches.

Although several approaches have been proposed and applied we are still far from seeing performance analysis as an integrated activity into component-based software development, both for the novelty of the topic and for the inherent difficulty of the problem.

5   Recommendations

In the last sections, we have stressed the importance of performance predictability in component-based development approaches as "the ability to reason about application behavior from the quality attributes of the components and the components' interconnections" [38]. In the following we summarize the lessons learned from the review of the current performance predictions techniques and we offer some suggestions for improvement of the performance predictability of component-based systems.

Component-based development is a new paradigm for the development of large complex software-intensive systems, but while the functional properties of the systems have been extensively dealt with both from industrial and academic communities, the quality (performance) aspect of the software products are not adequately addressed [7]. As described in section 3, in the last few years some attention has been paid also to include quantitative performance validation within component-based software development processes. The existing approaches are based on models, which has proven good predictive qualities, but they are often not considering the characteristics of component-based systems; on the other hand, measurement-based approaches are able to tackle the component-based development concerns but are frequently related to a single environment and lack of generality. Table 1 summarizes how different methods deal with the different aspect of component-based systems and could be used as a first guide in the selection of an appropriate methodology for the objective of the study/ project.

However, since the ability to predict the performance characteristics of the assembled system should be applied as early as possible to reduce the costs of late problem fixing [2], it becomes crucial to determine from the design phase whether the component-based product will satisfy its requirements. This goal can be obtained only via a rigorous design discipline and by accepting standard modelling notations as well as strict documentation and design rules, so that independently constructed components can be effectively connected and properly interact. This basic notion is central to the Design-by-Contract discipline [39], originally conceived for object-oriented systems, but even better suited for component-based development [3].

To obtain performance predictability of a component-based system several factors must be available. We devise three main features as crucial for performance prediction of component-based systems:

1. Necessity of component technology providing the means for specification of component performance taking into account its dependency both on the environment (middleware and hardware platform) and on different software resources;

2. Component selection based on the exposed performance characteristics;
3. Combination of measurement and modeling techniques embedded in an automated framework.

Considering issue 1 we devise parametric performance contracts as a good way to model the dependency of a component on the "external world" and in the following we describe the form of a parametric contract, we conceive for each service offered by a given component. Let us suppose that a given component C_i offers h   1 services S_j (j=1, ..., h). Each offered service can be carried out either locally (i.e., exploiting only the resources of the component under exam) or externally (i.e., exploiting also the resources of other components). A service S_j is defined with a set of parameters/attributes $(a_1, ..., a_m)$ that define/are related to its resource usage, i.e., S_j $(a_1, ..., a_m)$; among these attributes we can distinguish:

– constant (or non parametric attributes) such as, for example, the kind of resources required
– "stand-alone" parametric attributes that depend only on the kind of metric we are interested in for the performance measurement (e.g., a number, if we are considering "average" metric, a range of numbers if we are interested in best-worst case analysis);
– "external" parametric attributes that depend also on other services.

We consider a user management component with `Login` and `Logout` methods to give examples for the above mentioned categories. The component is implemented for the J2EE platform running on a Java virtual machine. Hence, `J2EE` and `JavaVM` can be seen as constant parameters. The performance influence of the J2EE middleware platform for example was investigated in [40]. Information on the duration of the execution of the code of each of the user management services is part of the stand-alone parameters, e.g., the average execution time of the methods or a distribution of their response times. Additionally, the `Login` method calls an external database to verify any given username and password combination. As this call's response time adds to the `Login` method's response time the call has to be considered as external parametric attribute. Further examples for the inclusion of external service calls into a performance prediction model can be found in [41].

In a performance prediction model capable of modeling situations as in the example above, each component's service should be accompanied by a performance parametric contract $PerfC_i(S_j(...))$ whose form depends on the kind of service parameters.

For example, if S_j is a simple service with constant attributes $(a_1, ..., a_i)$ and stand-alone parametric attributes $(a_i + 1, ..., a_m)$ then it can be characterized as

$$PerfC_i S_j (a_1, ..., a_m) = f_{S_j}(a_i + 1, ..., a_m)$$

where f_{S_j} denotes some kind of internal dependency. Otherwise, if S_j is a composite service with constant attributes $(a_1, ..., a_i)$, stand-alone parametric attributes $(a_i + 1, ..., a_j)$ and external parametric attributes $(a_j + 1, ..., a_m)$ then it can be characterized as:

$$PerfC_i S_j (a_1, ..., a_m) = f_{S_j}(a_i + 1, ..., a_j) \oplus g_{S_j}(a_j + 1, ..., a_m)$$

where $\oplus$ represents some kind of composition operator.

Considering issue 2, it is obvious that to fulfill performance requirements, the system assembler will choose those components among multiple component implementations providing the same functional behavior that best fit the performance requirements.

Let us describe how the above introduced characterization can help the system assembler in the service pre-selection step where one chooses, among components offering the same service, those that provide the best performance. In fact, one can instantiate the generic $PerfC_iS_j$ $(a_1, \ldots, a_m)$, with the characteristics of the adopted (or hypothesized) environment, so obtaining a set of values among which the best ones can be selected. Obviously, this kind of selection does not consider the impact of contention with other services for the use of a resource. To this end it should be necessary to define an order ($\prec$) between the $PerfC_iS_j$ $(a_1, \ldots, a_m)$ indices that depends on the adopted measurement framework (i.e., what kind of measurement we are interested in: mean, distribution, best/worst case) and on the execution environment and then select the components following this order.

Finally, taking into consideration issue 3, a trustworthy performance prediction methodology should consider the integrated use of models and measures to exploit the inherent advantages of both methods and to handle the complexity of component-based systems. Moreover, the process of performance analysis should be automated as best as possible to avoid errors and increase the efficiency of performance prediction. This applies both to the derivation of the performance model as well as the model solution. Another, often neglected, important aspect that should be included in the prediction methodology is the assessment of the *goodness* of a model, i.e., how close the model is to the real system. This involves a verification step ensuring that the model is correctly built and a validation step ensuring that the model produces results close to those observed in the real system.

Figures 3 and 4 show a foreseeable component-based software design environment with a built-in performance prediction tool combining both measurement and modeling techniques. As illustrated in figures 3 and 4, the final goal should be to have some

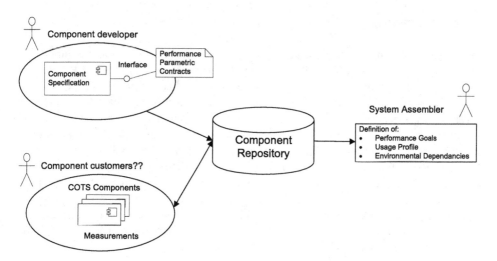

Fig. 3. A CBSE Framework with Performance prediction included

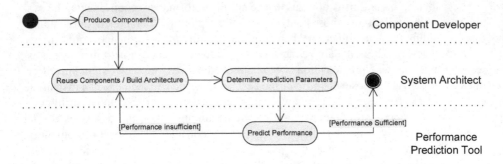

Fig. 4. Activity diagram of the Performance Framework

automatic tool allowing performance prediction at design time, so the effort required at assemby time at the software designer is quite small.

To summarize, the area of performance prediction for component-based systems is extensive and more research is necessary to achieve a full integration of quantitative prediction techniques in the software development process. Several related research directions should cover, for example the design of component models allowing quality prediction and building of component technologies supporting quality prediction. Further research is needed to include also other quality attributes, such as reliability, safety or security in the software development process. Another interesting point that deserves further investigation is to study interdependencies among the different quality attributes, to determine, for example, how the introduction of performance predictability can affect other attributes such as reliability or maintainability. To this end a good starting point would be a unified view on software quality attributes taking into account the various existing trade-offs between related quality attributes ([42]).

6   Conclusion

In this paper, we have reviewed performance prediction techniques for component-based software systems. Especially, we focus on the practicability of these techniques for various software engineering problem scenarios. For that reason, we have discussed some practical concerns that emerge when developing component-based systems and given an overview of current performance prediction approaches. As a result, we can present the inherent strengths and weaknesses of each performance prediction technique for different problems and system categories. This leads to a survey from an engineering perspective, which allows software engineers to select an appropriate performance prediction technique. Moreover, based on our examination of existing performance prediction techniques we have presented some recommendations for future research activities. Finally, we think that this survey could have a significant impact on the current software engineering practices and on the applicability of Component-Based Software Engineering methodologies.

Acknowledgements

The authors would like to thank Viktoria Firus and Ian Gorton for their valuable and inspiring input during our break-out session at Dagstuhl, which preceded this paper. Steffen Becker is funded by the German Science Foundation in the DFG-Palladio project.

References

1. Smith, C.U.: Performance Engineering of Software Systems. Addison-Wesley, Reading, MA, USA (1990)
2. Smith, C.U., Williams, L.G.: Performance Solutions: a practical guide to creating responsive, scalable software. Addison-Wesley (2002)
3. Szyperski, C., Gruntz, D., Murer, S.: Component Software: Beyond Object-Oriented Programming. 2 edn. ACM Press and Addison-Wesley, New York, NY (2002)
4. Sha, L., Rajkumar, R., Lehoczky, J.P.: Priority inheritance protocols: An approach to real-time synchronization. IEEE Trans. Comput. 39 (1990) 1175–1185
5. Musa, J.D., Iannino, A., Okumoto, K.: Software Reliability – Measurement, prediction, application. McGraw-Hill, New York (1987)
6. Dongarra, J., Martin, J., Vorlton, J.: Computer benchmarking: paths and pitfalls. IEEE Spectr. 24 (1987) 38–43
7. Balsamo, S., Marco, A.D., Inverardi, P., Simeoni, M.: Model-Based Performance Prediction in Software Development: A Survey. IEEE Transactions on Software Engineering 30 (2004) 295–310
8. Yacoub, S.M.: Performance Analysis of Component-Based Applications. In Chastek, G.J., ed.: Software Product Lines, Second International Conference, SPLC 2, San Diego, CA, USA, August 19-22, 2002, Proceedings. Volume 2379 of Lecture Notes in Computer Science., Berlin, Heidelberg, Springer (2002) 299–315
9. Chen, S., Gorton, I., Liu, A., Liu, Y.: Performance Prediction of COTS Component-Based Enterprise Applications. In: Proceedings of 5th ICSE workshop on Component-Based Software Engineering (CBSE 2002). (2002)
10. Denaro, G., Polini, A., Emmerich, W.: Early Performance Testing of Distributed Software Applications. In Dujmovic, J.J., Almeida, V.A.F., Lea, D., eds.: Proceedings of the Fourth International Workshop on Software and Performance, WOSP 2004, Redwood Shores, California, USA, January 14-16, 2004, New York, NY, ACM Press (2004) 94–103
11. Sitaraman, M., Kulczycki, G., Krone, J., Ogden, W.F., Reddy, A.L.N.: Performance Specification of Software Components. In: Proceedings of the Symposium on Software Reusability: Putting Software Reuse in Context, May 18-20, 2001, Toronto, Ontario, Canada, New York, NY, ACM Press (2001) 3–10
12. Hissam, S.A., Moreno, G.A., Stafford, J.A., Wallnau, K.C.: Packaging Predictable Assembly. In Bishop, J.M., ed.: Component Deployment, IFIP/ACM Working Conference, CD 2002, Berlin, Germany, June 20-21, 2002, Proceedings. Volume 2370 of Lecture Notes in Computer Science., Berlin, Heidelberg, Springer (2002) 108–124
13. Hissam, S., Hudak, J., Ivers, J., Klein, M., Larsson, M., Moreno, G., Northrop, L., Plakosh, D., Stafford, J., Wallnau, K., Wood, W.: Predictable Assembly of Substation Automation Systems: An Experiment Report. Technical Report CMU/SEI-2002-TR-031, Software Engineering Institute (2002)
14. Wallnau, K.C.: A Technology for Predictable Assembly from Certifiable Components. Technical Report CMU/SEI-2003-TR-009, Software Engineering Institute (2003)

15. Bertolino, A., Mirandola, R.: Towards Component-Based Ssoftware Performance Engineering. In: Proceedings of 6th ICSE workshop on Component-Based Software Engineering (CBSE 2003). (2003)

16. Bertolino, A., Mirandola, R.: CB-SPE Tool: Putting Component-Based Performance Engineering into Practice. In Crnkovic, I., Stafford, J.A., Schmidt, H.W., Wallnau, K.C., eds.: Component-Based Software Engineering, 7th International Symposium, CBSE 2004, Edinburgh, UK, May 24-25, 2004, Proceedings. Volume 3054 of Lecture Notes in Computer Science., Berlin, Heidelberg, Springer (2004) 233–248

17. OMG: UML Profile for Schedulability, Performance, and Time.   OMG Specification ptc/2002-03-02, Object Management Group (2002)

18. Wu, X., McMullan, D., Woodside, M.: Component-Based Performance Prediction. In: Proceedings of 6th ICSE workshop on Component-Based Software Engineering (CBSE 2003). (2003)

19. Wu, X., Woodside, C.M.: Performance Modeling from Software Components. In Dujmovic, J.J., Almeida, V.A.F., Lea, D., eds.: Proceedings of the Fourth International Workshop on Software and Performance, WOSP 2004, Redwood Shores, California, USA, January 14-16, 2004, New York, NY, ACM Press (2004) 290–301

20. Balsamo, S., Marzolla, M.: A Simulation-Based Approach to Software Performance Modeling. In: ESEC/FSE-11: Proceedings of the 9th European software engineering conference held jointly with 11th ACM SIGSOFT international symposium on Foundations of software engineering, New York, NY, ACM Press (2003) 363–366

21. Eskenazi, E.M., Fioukov, A.V., Hammer, D.K., Obbink, H., Pronk, B.: Analysis and Prediction of Performance for Evolving Architectures. In IEEE, ed.: Proceedings of the 30th EUROMICRO Conference 2004, 31 August - 3 September 2004, Rennes, France, Los Alamitos, CA, IEEE Computer Society Press (2004) 22–31

22. Eskenazi, E.M., Fioukov, A.V., Hammer, D.K.:   Performance Prediction for Component Compositions.   In Crnkovic, I., Stafford, J.A., Schmidt, H.W., Wallnau, K.C., eds.: Component-Based Software Engineering, 7th International Symposium, CBSE 2004, Edinburgh, UK, May 24-25, 2004, Proceedings. Volume 3054 of Lecture Notes in Computer Science., Berlin, Heidelberg, Springer (2004) 280–293

23. Bondarev, E., de With, P.H., Chaudron, M.R.V.: Towards Predicting Real-Time Properties of a Component Assembly. In IEEE, ed.: Proceedings of the 30th EUROMICRO Conference 2004, 31 August - 3 September 2004, Rennes, France, Los Alamitos, CA, IEEE Computer Society Press (2004) 601–610

24. Reussner, R.H., Firus, V., Becker, S.: Parametric Performance Contracts for Software Components and their Compositionality. In Weck, W., Bosch, J., Szyperski, C., eds.: Proceedings of the 9th International Workshop on Component-Oriented Programming (WCOP 04). (2004)

25. Menasce, D.A., Ruan, H., Gomaa, H.: A Framework for QoS-Aware Software Components. In: Proceedings of the Fourth International Workshop on Software and Performance, WOSP 2004, Redwood Shores, California, USA, January 14-16, 2004, New York, NY, ACM Press (2004) 186–196

26. Diaconescu, A., Mos, A., Murphy, J.: Automatic Performance Management in Component Based Software Systems. In IEEE, ed.: Proceedings of the 1st International Conference on Autonomic Computing (ICAC 2004), 17-19 May 2004, New York, NY, USA, Los Alamitos, CA, IEEE Computer Society Press (2004) 214–221

27. Liu, Y., Fekete, A., Gorton, I.: Predicting the Performance of Middleware-Based Applications at the Design Level. In: Proceedings of the Fourth International Workshop on Software and Performance, WOSP 2004, Redwood Shores, California, USA, January 14-16, 2004, New York, NY, ACM Press (2004) 166–170

28. Wallnau, K.C., Stafford, J., Hissam, S., Klein, M.: On the Relationship of Software Architecture to Software Component Technology. In: Proceedings of the Sixth International Workshop on Component-Oriented Programming (WCOP'01), Budapest, Hungary, 19 June 2001. (2001)

29. Solberg, A., Husa, K.E., Aagedal, J.., Abrahamsen, E.: QoS-Aware MDA. In: Proceedings of the Workshop Model-Driven Architecture in the Specification, Implementation and Validation of Object-Oriented Embedded Systems (SIVOES-MDA'03) in conjunction with UML'03. (2003)

30. Grassi, V., Mirandola, R.: A Model-Driven Approach to Predictive Non-Functional Analysis of Component-Based Systems. In: Proceedings of the Workshop Models for Non-functional Aspects of Component-Based Software at UML 2004, 12 October 2004,. (2004)

31. Petriu, D.B., Woodside, C.M.: A Metamodel for Generating Performance Models from UML Designs. In Baar, T., Strohmeier, A., Moreira, A.M.D., Mellor, S.J., eds.: UML 2004 - The Unified Modelling Language: Modelling Languages and Applications. 7th International Conference, Lisbon, Portugal, October 11-15, 2004. Proceedings. Volume 3273 of Lecture Notes in Computer Science., Berlin, Heidelberg, Springer (2004) 41–53

32. Woodside, M., Petriu, D.C., Petriu, D.B., Shen, H., Israr, T., J.Merseguer: Performance by Unified Model Analysis (PUMA). In: Proceedings of the Fifth International Workshop on Software and Performance, WOSP 2005, Palma, Illes Balears, Spain, July 11-15, 2005, New York, NY, ACM Press (2005) forthcoming

33. Gu, G., Petriu, D.C.: From UML to LQN by XML Algebra-Based Graph Transformations. In: Proceedings of the Fifth International Workshop on Software and Performance, WOSP 2005, Palma, Illes Balears, Spain, July 11-15, 2005, New York, NY, ACM Press (2005) forthcoming

34. Grassi, V., Mirandola, R., Sabetta, A.: From Design to Analysis Models: A Kernel Language for Performance and Reliability Analysis of Component-Based Systems. In: Proceedings of the Fifth International Workshop on Software and Performance, WOSP 2005, Palma, Illes Balears, Spain, July 11-15, 2005, New York, NY, ACM Press (2005) forthcoming

35. Zschaler, S.: Towards a Semantic Framework for Non-Functional Specifications of Component-Based Systems. In IEEE, ed.: Proceedings of the 30th EUROMICRO Conference 2004, 31 August - 3 September 2004, Rennes, France, Los Alamitos, CA, IEEE Computer Society Press (2004) 92–99

36. Grassi, V., Mirandola, R.: Towards Automatic Compositional Performance Analysis of Component-Based Systems. In: Proceedings of the Fourth International Workshop on Software and Performance, WOSP 2004, Redwood Shores, California, USA, January 14-16, 2004, New York, NY, ACM Press (2004) 59–63

37. Frølund, S., Koistinen, J.: Quality-of-Service Specification in Distributed Object Systems. Technical Report HPL-98-159, Hewlett Packard, Software Technology Laboratory (1998)

38. Larsson, M.: Predicting Quality Attributes in Component-Based Software Systems. PhD thesis, Mlardalen University (2004)

39. Meyer, B.: Applying "Design by Contract". IEEE Computer 25 (1992) 40–51

40. Liu, Y., Gorton, I., Liu, A., Jiang, N., Chen, S.: Designing a test suite for empirically-based middleware performance prediction. In Noble, J., Potter, J., eds.: Fortieth International Conference on Technology of Object-Oriented Languages and Systems (TOOLS Pacific 2002). Conferences in Research and Practice in Information Technology, Sydney, Australia, ACS (2002)

41. Firus, V., Becker, S., Happe, J.: Parametric performance contracts for qml-specified software components. In: Formal Foundations of Embedded Software and Component-based Software Architectures (FESCA). Electronic Notes in Theoretical Computer Science, ETAPS 2005 (2005)
42. Crnkovic, I., Firus, V., Grunske, L., Jezequel, J.M., Overhage, S., Reussner, R.: Unified Models for Predicting the Quality of Component-Based Software Architectures. In Reussner, R., Stafford, J., Szyperski, C., eds.: Architecting System with Trustworthy Components. Lecture Notes in Computer Science, Berlin, Heidelberg, Springer (2005) forthcoming

Towards an Engineering Approach to Component Adaptation

Steffen Becker[1], Antonio Brogi[2], Ian Gorton[3], Sven Overhage[4],
Alexander Romanovsky[5], and Massimo Tivoli[6]

[1] Software Engineering Group, University of Oldenburg,
OFFIS, Escherweg 2, 26121 Oldenburg, Germany
`steffen.becker@informatik.uni-oldenburg.de`
[2] Department of Computer Science, University of Pisa,
Largo B. Pontecorvo 3, 56127 Pisa, Italy
`brogi@di.unipi.it`
[3] Empirical Software Engineering Group, National ICT Australia,
Bay 15 Locomotive Workshop, Australian Technology Park Eveleigh, NSW 1430 Australia
`ian.gorton@nicta.com.au`
[4] Dept. of Software Engineering and Business Information Systems,
Augsburg University, Universitätsstraße 16, 86135 Augsburg, Germany
`sven.overhage@wiwi.uni-augsburg.de`
[5] School of Computing Science, University of Newcastle upon Tyne,
Newcastle upon Tyne, NE1 7RU, United Kingdom
`alexander.romanovsky@ncl.ac.uk`
[6] Dept. of Computer Science, University of L'Aquila,
Via Vetoio N.1, 67100 L'Aquila, Italy
`tivoli@di.univaq.it`

Abstract. Component adaptation needs to be taken into account when developing trustworthy systems, where the properties of component assemblies have to be reliably obtained from the properties of its constituent components. Thus, a more systematic approach to component adaptation is required when building trustworthy systems. In this paper, we illustrate how (design and architectural) patterns can be used to achieve component adaptation and thus serve as the basis for such an approach. The paper proposes an adaptation model which is built upon a classification of component mismatches, and identifies a number of patterns to be used for eliminating them. We conclude by outlining an engineering approach to component adaptation that relies on the use of patterns and provides additional support for the development of trustworthy component-based systems.

1 Introduction

In an ideal world, component-based systems are assembled from pre-produced components by simply plugging perfectly compatible components together, which jointly realize the desired functionality. In practice, however, it turns out that the constituent components often do not fit one another and adaptation has to be done to eliminate the resulting mismatches.

R.H. Reussner et al. (Eds.): Architecting Systems, LNCS 3938, pp. 193–215, 2006.

Mismatches between components, for example, always need to be addressed when integrating *legacy systems*. Thereby, the impossibility of modifying large client applications is a major reason for the need to employ some form of adaptation during the development of component-based systems. Besides that, the most structured way to deal with *component evolution* and upgrading, which is likely to result in new mismatches at the system level, arguably is by applying adaptation techniques. Finally, adaptation becomes a major task in the emerging area of *service-oriented computing*, where mismatches must be solved to ensure the correct interoperation among different Web services, which have been assembled according to a bottom-up strategy.

For these reasons, the adaptation of components has to be recognized as an unavoidable, crucial task in Component-Based Software Engineering (CBSE). Until now, however, only a number of isolated approaches to eliminate mismatches between components have been proposed. They introduce adapters, which are capable of mediating the interaction between components (e.g., to transform data between different formats or to ensure a failure-free coordination protocol). In [1, 2, 3, 4, 5, 6, 7, 8, 9], for instance, the authors show how to automatically derive adapters in order to reduce the set of system behaviors to a subset of safe (e.g., lock-free) ones. Other papers [9, 10, 11, 12, 13, 14] show how to plug a set of adapters into a system in order to augment the system behaviour by introducing more sophisticated interactions among components. The presented protocol transformations can be applied to ensure the overall system dependability, improve extra-functional characteristics, and properly deal with updates of the system architecture (e.g., insertion, replacement, or removal of components).

The approaches mentioned above only address some forms of component mismatch types, employ specific specification formalisms, and usually do not support any reasoning about the impact that component adaptation has on the extra-functional properties (e.g., reliability, performance, security) of the system. For these reasons, employing these approaches to adapt components in an ad hoc strategy typically is error prone, reduces the overall system quality, and thus increases the costs of system development. Above all, employing such an ad hoc strategy to component adaptation hinders the development of *trustworthy component-based systems*, since it is impossible to reliably deduce the properties of component assemblies from the properties of the constituent components and the created adapters.

To counter these problems, it is the objective of this paper to initiate the development of an *engineering approach* to component adaptation that provides developers with a systematic solution consisting of methods, best practices, and tools. As the basis for such an approach we suggest the usage of *adaptation patterns*, since they provide generic and systematic solutions to eliminate component mismatches. Before establishing the details of the proposed engineering approach, we start by clarifying important concepts (section 2). After introducing an initial taxonomy of component mismatches (section 3), we describe a generic process model for component adaptation and discuss relevant patterns that have emerged both in literature and in practice (section 4). To illustrate the employment of patterns to eliminate component mismatches, we additionally present some examples (section 5). After discussing related work we conclude by outlining some of the remaining challenges. They will have to be solved to establish a fully-fledged engineering approach, capable of supporting the development of trust-worthy component-based systems.

2   Component Adaptation: Coming to Terms

Component mismatches originate from contradicting assumptions about the context, in which interacting components should be used, and the real context, in which they are being deployed. These contradicting assumptions have been made by the develop-ers of individual components and become obvious during the assembly of the system, when individual components are brought together. Component mismatches have been examined both from an architectural [15] and a reuse-oriented perspective [16].

From a reuse-oriented perspective there always is a tension between the goals of extending the functionality of a component on the one hand and keeping it reusable on the other hand. These are contradicting goals, since reuse typically requires sim-ple, well-defined and well-understood functionality. Because of this reason, it is likely that a reused component will not exactly fit the required context. In the software reuse community, component mismatches are usually called *component incompatibilities*.

From a software architecture perspective, problems occur when components have different assumptions about normal and abnormal behaviour of other components or when a software architect makes decisions which contradict individual assumptions of the components and connectors [17]. Problems of this kind are called *architectural mismatches*. In our paper, we summarize the terms "component incompatibilities" and "architectural mismatches" as *component mismatches* to emphasize that they relate to the same problem.

Before we elaborate the proposed engineering approach to component adaptation, some terms have to be clarified as they are not used consistently in the domain of adap-tation techniques.

Software adaptation is the sequence of steps performed whenever a software entity is changed in order to comply with requirements emerging from the environment in which the entity is deployed. Such changes can be performed at different stages during the life cycle. Therefore, we distinguish requirement adaptation, design-time adaptation, and run-time adaptation (see [18]):

- Requirement adaptation is used to react to changes during requirements engineer-ing, especially when new requirements are emerging in the application domain.
- Design-time adaptation is applied during architectural design whenever an analysis of the system architecture indicates a mismatch between two constituent compo-nents.
- Run-time adaptation takes place when parts of the system offer different behav-iour depending on the context the parts are running in. This kind of adaptation is therefore closely related to context-aware systems.

In the following, we restrict ourselves to design-time adaptation.

Software Component Adaptation is the sequence of the steps required to bridge a component mismatch. According to the common definition, components offer services to the environment, which are specified as provided interfaces [19, 20]. In addition, components explicitly and completely express their context dependencies [19], i.e. their expectations on the environment. Context dependencies are stated in the form of required interfaces [19, 20]. Using the concept of provided and required interfaces, a component mismatch can be interpreted as a mismatch between properties of required and provided interfaces, which have to be connected (see figure 1). Consequently, identifying mismatches between components is equivalent to identifying mismatches between interfaces. A component mismatch thus occurs, when a component, which implements a provided interface, and a component, which uses a required interface, are not cooperating as intended by the designer of the system.

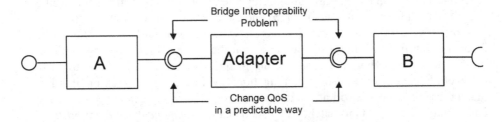

Fig. 1. A software component adapter and its QoS impact

Note that component mismatches explicitly refer to interoperability problems which have not been foreseen by the producer of one of the components. Many components offer so called *customization interfaces* to increase reusability. These interfaces allow changes to the behaviour of the component during assembly time by setting parameters. As they are foreseen by the component developer and thus planned in advance, we do not consider parameterization as adaptation. Therefore, in the following customization is disregarded.

In accordance with the term *adaptation* we define a *software component adapter* as a software entity especially constructed to overcome a component mismatch.

3   A Taxonomy of Component Mismatches

Although an efficient technique to adapt components is of crucial importance to facilitate CBSE, there currently exist only a few approaches to enumerate and classify different kinds of component mismatches [21]. Moreover, many of the existing approaches just broadly distinguish between *syntactic*, *semantic*, and *pragmatic mismatches* and put them into relation to various aspects of compatibility like *functionality*, *architecture*, and *quality* [22, 23]. In order to get a more detailed understanding of the problem domain, we start implementing the proposed engineering approach to component adaptation by introducing a *taxonomy of mismatches*. The introduced taxonomy enumerates different types of component mismatches which will be taken into consideration when we develop a pattern-based approach to adaptation later on.

In addition, the provided taxonomy summarizes the different types of component mismatches into categories and classifies them according to a hierarchy of *interface models* (see figure 2). Each of the distinguished interface models determines a (distinct)

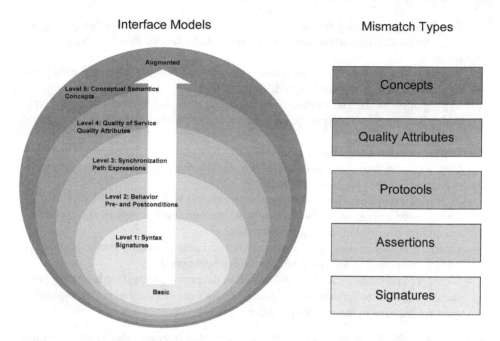

Fig. 2. A hierarchy of interface models (based on [24]), which orders interface properties according to their specification complexity, supports the identification and elimination of different types of component mismatches

set of properties which belongs to a component interface [24, 25]. Because component mismatches originate from mismatching properties of connected interfaces (the so-called provided and required interfaces, cf. section 2), the hierarchy of interface models underlying the interface descriptions simultaneously determines our ability to diagnose and eliminate a certain type of component mismatch.

The (classical) *syntax-based interface model*, which focuses on signatures as constituent elements of component interfaces, supports the identification and elimination of *signature mismatches*. By using such a syntax-based interface model, the following types of (adaptable[1]) mismatches can be distinguished when connecting the required interface of a component "A" with a provided interface of a component "B" as shown in figure 1 [26, 27]:

- Naming of methods. Methods, which have been declared in the provided and required interface, realize the same functionality but have different names.
- Naming of parameters. Parameters of corresponding methods represent the same entity and have the same type but have been named differently in the provided and required interface.
- Naming of types. Corresponding (built-in or user-defined) types have been declared with different names.

---

[1] An adaptable mismatch can eventually be eliminated by adaptation.

- Structuring of complex types. The member lists of corresponding complex types (e.g. structures) declared both in the provided and required interface are permutations.
- Naming of exceptions. Exceptions thrown by corresponding methods have the same type, but have been declared with different names.
- Typing of methods. The method declared in the provided interface returns a type, which is a sub-type of the one that is returned by the method declared in the required interface.
- Typing of parameters. Parameters of methods declared in the provided interface have a type, which is a super-type of the one that belongs to corresponding parameters declared in the required interface.
- Typing of exceptions. Exceptions thrown by methods declared in the provided interface have a type, which is a sub-type of the one that belongs to corresponding exceptions declared in the required interface.
- Ordering of parameters. The parameter lists of corresponding methods declared both in the provided and required interface are permuted.
- Number of parameters. A method declared in the provided interface has fewer parameters or additional parameters with constant values compared to its corresponding method declared in the required interface.

Compared to this basic interface model, a *behavioral interface model* also contains *assertions* (i.e. pre- and postconditions) for the methods, which have been declared in the required and provided interfaces. With a behavioral interface model in place, it becomes principally conceivable to additionally search for (adaptable) mismatches between assertions when comparing provided and required interfaces. However, we chose *not* to consider the detection and adaptation of mismatching assertions as part of the proposed engineering approach, since they usually cannot be statically identified in an efficient manner [28, p. 578]. Instead, we refer to [29] for details about existing techniques, which can be applied to identify and adapt mismatching assertions, as well as their principal limitations.

By making use of an *interaction-based interface model*, which focuses on describing the interaction that takes place between connected components in the form of message calls, developers are able to diagnose and eliminate *protocol mismatches*. Provided that the interaction protocols belonging to the provided and the required interface are specified in a way that supports an efficient, i.e. statically computable, comparison, the following (adaptable) mismatches can be distinguished [2, 30]:

- Ordering of messages. The protocols belonging to the provided and required interface contain the same kinds of messages, but the message sequences are permuted.
- Surplus of messages. A component sends a message that is neither expected by the connected component nor necessary to fulfil the purpose of the interaction.
- Absence of messages. A component requires additional messages to fulfil the purpose of the interaction. The message content can be determined from outside.

Since it is generally possible to specify interaction protocols as pre- and postconditions [28, p. 981-982], we have to admit that introducing a behavioral interface model already would have been sufficient to cover the interaction aspect as well. Nevertheless, we chose to view interaction protocols as a separate aspect that has to be distinguished from pre- and postconditions. This decision is mainly motivated by the problems that arise when trying to statically compare assertions. We have to admit, however, that our decision to view interaction protocols as a separate aspect only is profitable, if the specified interaction protocols can be statically compared in a more efficient way than assertions. To ensure a better comparability of protocol specifications, we eventually have to prefer notations of limited expressive power (e.g. finite state machines).

The *quality-based interface model* instead focuses on describing an aspect that has not been covered so far. It documents the Quality of Service (QoS) which is being provided by each of the interface methods by describing a set of quality attributes. The set of quality attributes that is to be described is determined by the underlying quality model, e.g. the ISO 9126 quality model [31, 32], which is one of the most popular. By making use of an interface model that is based on the ISO 9126 quality model, it is possible to detect and eliminate the following *quality attribute mismatches*:

- Security. The component requiring a service makes assumptions about the authentication, access, and integrity of messages that differ from the assumptions made by the component which provides the service.
- Persistency. The component requiring a service makes assumptions about the persistent storage of computed results that differ from the assumptions made by the component which provides the service.
- Transactions. The component requiring a service makes assumptions about the accompanying transactions that differ from the assumptions made by the component which provides the service.
- Reliability. The service required by component A needs to be more reliable than the one that is being provided by component B. Reliability is a trustworthiness attribute characterizing the continuity of the service, e.g. by measuring the meantime between failure, mean downtime, or availability [32, p. 23]. Typically reliability is achieved by employing fault tolerance means.
- Efficiency (Performance). The service required by component A needs to be more efficient than the one that is being provided by component B. The efficiency of a service is typically characterized by its usage of time and resources, e.g. the response time, throughput, memory consumption, or utilization of processing unit [32, pp. 42-50].

It is important to stress the fact that, with respect to adaptation, the quality aspect is a *cross-cutting concern*. This means, creating and inserting an adapter to eliminate one of the other component mismatches mentioned in this paper probably influences the quality properties, e.g. by delaying the response time of a service that now has to be invoked indirectly. In fact, the quality attributes distinguished above are even cross-cutting concerns among each other, which means that adapting one of the quality attributes is likely to influence the others.

A *conceptual interface model*, which describes the conceptual semantics of component interfaces as an ontology (i.e. a set of interrelated concepts), supports the identification and elimination of so-called *concept mismatches*. Thereby, concepts can principally characterize each of the elements contained in a syntactical interface model. Thus, they may refer to entities (such as parameters, type declarations etc.), functions (methods), and processes (protocols). By making use of a concept model that consists of a term (denominator), an intension (definition), and an extension (corresponding real objects), the following *concept mismatches* can be principally distinguished [33, 34]:

- Synonyms. Two concepts, which characterize corresponding interface elements of a provided and required interface, are identical with respect to their definition, but have been used with different terms (e.g. customer and buyer).
- Sub- and Superordination. Two concepts, which characterize corresponding interface elements of a provided and required interface, are in a specialization or generalization relationship to each other.
- Homonyms. Two concepts, which characterize corresponding interface elements of a provided and required interface, are named with the same term but have different definitions (e.g. price as price including value-added tax and price as price without value-added tax).
- Equipollences. Two concepts, which characterize corresponding interface elements of a provided and required interface, have the same extension. However, they have different definitions which only share some common aspects (e.g. customer and debitor).

Both conceptual interface models, which make use of ontologies to describe the semantics of component-interfaces, as well as their usage for compatibility tests and adaptation are still under research. Consequently, there currently is little substantial support that can help in detecting and adapting concept mismatches (an overview of approaches can be found in [35, 36]). However, conceptual interface models are helpful in detecting and eliminating certain kinds of signature mismatches, like e.g. methods with identical functionality and different namings.

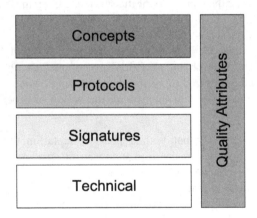

Fig. 3. The taxonomy contains five distinct classes of component mismatches

To complete our taxonomy of component mismatches, we finally introduce *technical mismatches* as additional component mismatch type. Technical mismatches between components occur, if two interacting components have been developed for different platforms (i.e. operating systems, frameworks etc.). Since technical dependencies of the former kind usually are not described as interfaces and instead remain as implicit component properties, they have not been covered by the introduced taxonomy so far, which builds upon the hierarchy of interface models to classify component mismatches. They represent an important mismatch type, however, and have to be considered accordingly when developing an engineering approach to adaptation. Figure 3 shows the classification of component mismatches that results from the inclusion of technical mismatches. It shows extra-functional mismatches as cross-cutting concern, whereas the other concerns can be summarized as functional mismatches.

4   Relevant Patterns for Component Adaptation

Patterns - either on the component design or on the architectural level - have become popular since the Gang of Four [37] published their well-known book on design patterns. According to our classification there are a lot of possible component incompatibilities. Therefore, it is reasonable that there are several patterns for bridging those incompatibilities. As patterns are established and well known solutions to reoccurring problems we decide to utilize patterns for adaptation problems. Thus, in this section we highlight some of the relevant patterns - mainly taken from literature [37, 38, 39, 40].

Before we go into details, we focus on the basic structure of some of the patterns. Many patterns look similar or even identical at the design or source code level. This leads to the assumption that there are even more basic concepts used in the patterns than the patterns itself. For example, delegation is such a concept. Delegation takes place whenever a component wrapping another component uses the wrapped components service to fulfil its own service. For example, an adapter (see below) converting currencies from Euro to US Dollar. It first converts the input currency, then it delegates the call to the wrapped component using the right currency, and afterwards the currency is translated back again. The same idea is used also in, i.e., the Decorator pattern. Therefore, we try to identify in the following text these basic structures as well to build a taxonomy of the basic building blocks of the patterns introduced and also to capture the *basic technique* used in the patterns mentioned. An analysis of the basic techniques can also lead to a more engineering-based approach to adaptation in future work.

We classify the introduced patterns according to section 2 basically in adapters dealing primarily with functional aspects and extra-functional aspects respectively.

4.1   Functional Adaptation Patterns

This section gives an overview of the most often used patterns to bridge functional component incompatibilities. Most are well known to experienced developers and used quite frequently - even without the knowledge that a pattern has been used.

Adapter. The adapter or wrapper pattern is described in [37, p. 139]. The pattern directly corresponds to the definition given in section 2 as its main idea is to bridge between two different interfaces. The pattern is used in different flavours: a variant using inheritance and a second one based on delegation. The latter can be used in component-based development by using the concepts on the component instance level instead of the object instance level. The adapter pattern is very flexible as theoretically every interface can be transformed into every other interface. Thus, the range of adapters is infinite.

Decorator. The decorator pattern [37, p. 175] can be seen as a special class of adapters where the adapter's interface is a subtype of the adapted component. This enables the use of a decorated component instead of the undecorated. Additionally, it is possible to decorate a single component as often as necessary. As the adapted component has the same list of signatures as the original component, a decorator can only change or add functionality to the methods already offered by the original component. As the decorator is a special kind of adapter it also uses delegation as main technique.

Interceptor. Often the term interception is used when implementing aspect oriented programming (AOP) techniques. Interception is a technique which intercepts method calls and presents the call to some pre- or post-code for additional processing [39, p. 109]. It can be realized by the afore-mentioned decorator pattern but is often part of component runtime environments. For example, the J2EE container technology uses interception to add advanced functionality to components during deployment like container managed persistency or security. Basically, it also uses delegation but as said before often hidden in the runtime environments.

Wrapper Facade. The wrapper facade pattern is used to encapsulate a non-object oriented API using wrapper objects [39, p. 47]. Therefore, it can also be used to encapsulate services in a component-based framework. The basic idea is to encapsulate corresponding state and functions operating on this state in a single component. For example, consider a file system component encapsulating a file handle and the operations which can be performed on the respective file. Basic principles used in this pattern are delegation and the encapsulation of state.

Bridge. The bridge pattern is used to decouple an abstraction and its implementation [37, p. 151]. Thus, it is often used to define an abstract interface on a specific technology and its implementations deal with vendor specific implementations. Abstract GUI toolkits like Swing which can be used on top of different GUI frameworks can be seen as example. The basic technique here is the use of the subtype relation and polymorphism.

Microkernel. The Microkernel pattern uses a core component and drivers to build an external interface to emulate a specific environment [38, p. 171]. It can be used to simulate a complete target environment on a different technological platform. The pattern has been used for adaptation in writing emulation layers or virtual machines.

Mediator. The Mediator pattern is used to encapsulate how a given set of objects interact [37, p. 283]. A typical scenario in the context of adaptation is to use several components to provide a service, e.g., querying multiple database servers to return a single result set. The components can interact using the mediator's coordinating role. Often mediation is used simultaneously with the adapter pattern to transform data passed to or from the service in formats being expected by the respective interfaces. With a focus on data transformations the pattern is often also called *Coordinator* pattern [40, p. 111].

4.2 Extra-Functional Adaptation Patterns

The extra-functional patterns selected here are often used to increase a single or several quality attributes of the components being adapted. We give examples of properties that are often addressed by the patterns in the respective paragraphs.

Proxy. A Proxy is put in front of a component to control certain aspects of the access to it [37, p. 207]. Security issues like access control, encryption, or authentication are often added to components by respective Proxys. Additionally, it can be used to implement caching strategies [40, p. 83] or patterns for lazy acquisition of resources [40, p. 38] to increment response times. The basic technique used in this pattern is delegation.

Component Replication. The component replication pattern is derived from the object replication pattern [41, p. 99]. The idea is to distribute multiple copies of the same component to several distinct computation units to increase response time and throughput. Additionally, you might get an increased reliability in the case the controller coordinating the replicated components is not the point of failure. The basic technique in this pattern is based on copying the state of a component.

Process Pair. The process pair pattern runs each component twice so that one component can watch the other and restart it in case of a failure [41, p. 133]. The pattern is used to increase the availability of components in high availability scenarios, e.g., whenever safety is an important aspect of the system design. The basic principle of this pattern is based on timeouts.

Retransmission. Retransmission is used when a service call might vanish or fail [41, p. 187]. In case the failure lasts for a short period of time, e.g., a network transmission failure, a retransmission results in successful execution. Thus the pattern increases the reliability of the system - especially when unreliable transactions are involved. The pattern is based on timeouts combined with a respective retry strategy.

Caching. The cache pattern keeps data retrieved from a slower memory in a faster memory area to allow fast access if an object is accessed twice [40, p. 83]. Therefore, the pattern is used to increase response time and throughput. The benefits are acquired by accepting a larger memory footprint. The basic technique of the pattern uses memory buffers to increase performance.

Pessimistic Offline Lock. The pessimistic offline lock is a pattern used to control concurrent access to components or resources controlled by components [42, p. 426]. The lock is used to ensure that solely one single thread of execution is able to access the protected resource. Hence, the lock ensures certain safety criteria on the cost of performance as concurrent threads have to wait before they can execute. The basic principle used in the pattern is based on blocking the control flow using the process scheduler.

Unit of Work. The unit of work pattern is used to collect a set of sub-transactions in memory until all parts are complete and then commits the whole transaction by accessing the database only a short time [42, p. 184]. Like the cache pattern there is a trade-off

	Technical	Signatures	Protocols	Concepts	Quality Attributes
Adapter		✔	✔	✔	✔
Decorator				✔	
Interceptor				✔	✔
Wrapper Facade		✔		✔	
Bridge	✔				
Microkernel	✔				
Mediator			✔		
Proxy					✔
Replication					✔
Process Pair					✔
Retransmission					✔
Caching					✔
Pessimistic Lock					✔
Unit of Work					✔

Fig. 4. A classification of Patterns and Mismatches

between memory consumption and efficiency. As in the caching pattern the basic idea is to use a memory buffer.

4.3 Classification of Patterns

The collection of patterns does not claim to be complete, there are more patterns which we could look at. We introduced it to show that there are a lot of patterns which can be used to adapt components - mostly in a way which is not producing hand written glue code. In the table in figure 4 we show which patterns can be used to solve problems of the introduced mismatch classes.

5 Using Patterns to Eliminate Component Mismatches

After introducing a set of patterns in the previous section, we will now discuss how to use the patterns in a software engineering process. First, we will introduce a generic process which is supposed to serve as a guideline for adaptation. We will illustrate its usage by giving an example of a functional and an extra-functional adaptation. In particular, we will show an application of the Adapter/Wrapper pattern and of the Caching pattern.

The process of adapting components in order to construct trustworthy component assemblies using software engineering consists of the following steps:

1. *Detect mismatches:* First the mismatch between the required and provided interface has to be detected. As stated above, this directly depends on the specifications available, i.e., if no protocol specification is available then we can not detect protocol mismatches.

2. *Select measures to overcome the mismatch*: Second, we select from a set of established methods the one which is known to solve the specific mismatch. Note, that this choice also depends on the specifications available as some patterns can only be distinguished by examining subtle differences in the target setting (as already mentioned in section 4). This can sometimes require semantic information which is hard to analyze automatically. It is therefore necessary in many cases to leave the final choice to the developer. Nevertheless, it is possible to filter unsuitable patterns out in advance.

3. *Configure the measure:* Often the method or pattern selected can be fine-tuned as patterns are described as *abstract* solutions to problems. Thereby, we can for instance utilize the specifications and query the developer for additional input. If the specification is complete the solution to the mismatch problem is analyzed.

4. *Predict the impact:* After determining the solution of the problem we predict the impact of the solution on our setting. This is common in other engineering disciplines.

5. *Implement and test the solution:* If the prediction indicates that the mismatch is fixed, the solution is implemented, either by systematic construction or by using generative technologies.

5.1   Adapting Functional Mismatches with the Adapter Pattern

This section shows how functional adaptation can be implemented by utilizing the Adapter/Wrapper pattern [37, p. 139]. As shown in the table in figure 4, this pattern might be used to repair syntax, protocol and semantics mismatches.

The Adapter pattern (also known as Wrapper pattern) maps the interface of a component onto another interface expected by its clients. The Adapter lets components work together that could not otherwise because of incompatible interfaces. The participants in the "schema" of this pattern are: (i) the existing component interface that needs to be adapted, usually denoted as *Adaptee*; (ii) *Target* is the interface required by a client component and it is not compatible to Adaptee; (iii) *Client* denotes any client whose required interface is compatible to Target and (iv) *Adapter*, which is the component responsible for making *Adaptee* compatible to *Target*.

Here, we discuss an example of a possible application of the Adapter pattern seen as a means to overcome only protocol mismatches. Let us suppose that we want to assemble a component-based cooling water pipe management system that collects and correlates data about the amount of water that flows in different water pipes. The water pipes are placed in two different zones, denoted by P and S, and they transport water that has to be used to cool industrial machinery. The system we want to assemble is a client-server one. The zones P and S have to be monitored by a server component denoted as *Server*. *Server* allows the access to a collection of data related to the water pipes it monitors. It provides an interface denoted as *IServer*. Since some of the water pipes do not include a *Programmable Logic Controller* (PLC) system, *Server* cannot always automatically obtain the data related to the water that flows in those water pipes. Therefore, *IServer* exports the methods *PCheckOut* and *SCheckOut* to get an exclusive access to the data collection related to the water which flows in the pipes. This allows a client to: (i) read the data automatically stored by the server and (ii) manually update the report related to the water which flows in the pipes that are not monitored by a PLC. Correspondingly, *IServer* exports also the methods *PCheckIn* and *SCheckIn* to both publish the updates made on the data collection and release the access gained to it. We want to assemble the discussed client-server system formed by the following selected components: *Server* and one client denoted as *Client*. The interface required by *Client* is compatible to *IServer* at level of both signature and semantics.

According to step 1 of the presented process, we need to be able to detect possible protocol mismatches. These days, we can utilize UML2 *Sequence Diagrams* and *Interaction Overview Diagrams* (i.e., the UML2 *Interaction Diagrams* suite) to extend the IDL specification of a component interface for including information related to the component interaction protocol. UML2 sequence diagrams are for describing a single execution scenario of a component or a system; UML2 interaction overview diagrams can be used to compose all the specified component/system execution scenarios into execution flows to indicate how each scenario fit together different ones during the overall execution of the component/system (see Figure 5).

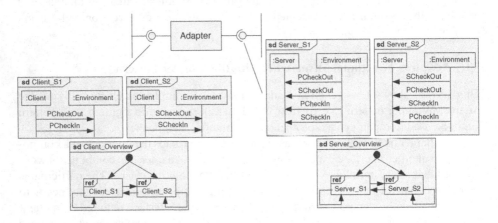

Fig. 5. An example of UML2 Interaction Diagrams specification to detect protocol mismatches

From the UML2 specification shown in Figure 5, it is possible to check automatically that the interaction protocols expected by *Server* and *Client* mismatch. That is, the selected server component forces its clients to always access to the data collections related to the zone *P* and *S* subsequently and in any possible order, before releasing the access gained for both of them. Instead, the selected client component gains the access and releases it for the data collections related to the zone *P* and *S* separately. This protocol mismatch leads to a deadlock.

According to step 2 of our proposed engineering approach to component adaptation, we have to choose the right type of measure to solve the problem. We decide to deploy an Adapter/Wrapper component to force a "check-out" of the data collection related to the zone *S* (*P*) after the client has performed a *PCheckOut* (*SCheckOut*) method call. The release of the gained access is handled analogously. In doing so, the interaction protocol of *Client* is enhanced in order to match the interaction protocol of *Server* (i.e., to avoid the deadlock). This adaptation strategy can be automatically derived by a tool

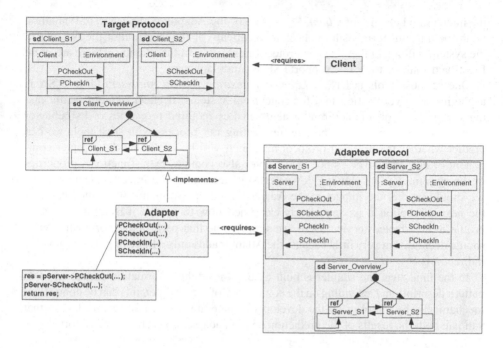

Fig. 6. Overall structure of the Adapter/Wrapper pattern to avoid protocol mismatches

that - by exploiting the UML2 XMI - is able to take in input an XML representation of the UML2 interaction diagrams specification of *Server* and *Client*. This tool might elaborate - in some way - this specification and produce the adaptation strategy that must be implemented by the Adapter. A similar approach can be found in [14].

In the third step of our process we have to customize the pattern to our needs (i.e., protocol adaptation purposes) and choose the right variant of it. We plan to implement the pattern according to Figure 6 depicting the overall structure of our realization.

The following are the participants to the Adapter patter applied to bridge protocol mismatches: (i) **Target Protocol** which is the protocol required by a client component (i.e., the interaction protocol of *Client*); (ii) **Client** which is a component whose protocol is compatible to the Target Protocol (i.e., *Client*); (iii) the **Adapter** which is the component responsible for making an existing protocol compatible to the Target Protocol; and (iv) the **Adaptee Protocol** which is the existing protocol (i.e., the interaction protocol of *Server*). In the figure we also show a portion of the code implementing the method *PCheckOut* as provided by the Adapter component. *SCheckOut, PCheckIn* and *SCheckIn* are implemented analogously. This code reflect the adaptation strategy discussed above.

In the next step, in order to make it an engineering process, we predict the impact of the deployed Adapter in terms of checking whether the detected protocol mismatch has been solved or not. To be able to do so, we do not need any further information beyond the UML2 Interaction Diagrams specification of *Client* and *Server* and the underlined structure of the Adapter component. In fact, from this kind of specification, it is possible to automatically derive a process algebra notation e.g., FSP notation [43], of the interaction behavior of *Client*, *Server* and of the Adapter component. FSP notation might be a useful formalism to check automatically if the insertion of the Adapter in the system will avoid the detected protocol mismatch. In the literature, there are more functional analysis tools that support FSP as input language.

One of these tools is LTSA (*Labeled Transition System Analyser*) [43]. LTSA is a plugin-based verification tool for concurrent systems. It checks automatically that the specification of a concurrent system satisfies required properties of its behavior such as deadlock-freeness. Thus, by integrating our process with such tools we can predict whether the detected protocol mismatch will be solved by the Adapter component or not. Moreover - since the Adapter also changes extra-functional properties of the system, e.g., by slowing down accesses because of the injected method calls - we should predict the impact of the Adapter on the performance of method calls. In the next subsection it is very clearly explained how to predict it by using an usage profile of an adapted service. Here, we simply note that performance of method calls should decrease but very little because the Adapter adds only a lightweight extra-level of indirectness.

In the final step, the adapter is built by exploiting the information contained in its pattern description. Depending on the complexity of the Adapter, this can be done either mechanically by a tool or by the developers. Once the Adapter is deployed, tests that validate both the results of the prediction and the adapter correctness are performed.

5.2   Adapting Extra-Functional Mismatches with the Caching Pattern

In the following we show how extra-functional adaptation can be achieved by employing the Caching pattern [40, p. 83]. A cache is used if a service needs some kind of resource whose acquisition is time consuming and the resource is not expected to change frequently but to be used often. The idea is to acquire the resource and to put it in the cache afterwards. The resource can be retrieved faster from the cache than re-acquiring it again. This is often done by utilizing additional memory to store the resource for faster retrieval. Hence, a trade-off is established between retrieval time and memory consumption. If the resource is needed again, it is retrieved from the cache. Often a validation check is performed in advance to test whether the cached resource is still up to date. Additionally, if the resource is altered by its usage we have to ensure consistency with the non-cached original object. This can be done by either storing it at its original location directly when the resource is altered (write-through-strategy). The other option is that the resource gets stored as soon as it gets evicted from the cache.

According to step 1 of the presented process, we need to be able to detect the mismatching response times. These days, we can utilize QML [44] specifications of the respective interfaces for this task. For example, let's assume an average response time of 3000ms is needed and an average response time of 6000ms is provided for service under investigation (see figure 7).

Additionally, we know that the required service processes requests to a static database. Therefore, we can consider the database table rows in the above stated sense. The database is not updated frequently, so caching the database query results will improve the average response time. Note, that we also need to know that the service fulfills these prerequisites of the cache pattern. It is to automatically determine if the prerequisites

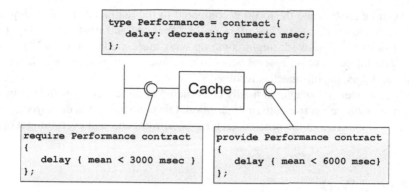

Fig. 7. An example QML specification to detect a QoS mismatch

are fulfilled as service specifications often state nothing about the resource usage of the specified service.

Second, we have to choose the right type of measure to solve the problem. We decide to deploy a cache to speed up an encapsulated resource access in the component being used. In doing so, the response time is decreased and the components can interoperate as desired.

In the third step we have to customize the pattern to our needs and choose the right variant of the pattern. Referring to the description in [40] we have to

- Select resources: The database query results
- Decide on an eviction strategy: Here we can choose between well-known types like least recently used (LRU), first in - first out (FIFO), and so on.
- Ensure consistency: We need a consistency manager whose task is to invalidate cache entries as soon as the master copy is changed. In the given database scenario it makes no sense to omit that part.
- Determine cache size: How much memory the cache is going to use. Most likely this is specified in number of cacheable resource units.

We plan to implement the pattern according to the following figure depicting the static structure of our realization (see figure 8).

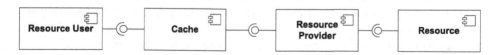

Fig. 8. The cache pattern implemented with components

In the next step, in order to make it an engineering process, we predict the impact of the deployed cache. To be able to do so, the usage profile of the adapted service is needed, as the performance of a cache depends on it. The usage profile information needed in this context, is the (estimated) frequency and type of requests. Together with the decisions taken in the previous step a specialized prediction model for the cache impact can be applied and the result is compared to the requirements. This step is not well researched so that today we often neglect the step and trust on the experience of the deployer. Future work might come up with more prediction models to enable the engineering process as depicted here. To continue, let us assume, that the result is 2500ms and thus, the mismatch is resolved.

In the final step the adapter is finally constructed or generated by using the instructions given in the respective pattern description. Once the adapter is deployed, we perform tests to ensure that the predictions have been right and that everything works as expected.

6   Related Work

Even though Component-Based Software Engineering was first introduced in 1968 [45], developing systematic approaches to adaptation of components in order to resolve interoperability problems is still a field of active research. Many papers are based on the work done by Yellin and Strom [2, 46], who introduced an algorithm for the (semi-) automatic generation of adapters using protocol information and an external adapter specification. Bracciali et al. propose the use of some kind of process calculus to enhance this process and generate adapters using PROLOG [47].

Schmidt and Reussner present adapters for merging and splitting interface protocols and for a certain class of protocol interoperability problems [30]. Besides adapter generation, Reussner's parametrized contracts also represent a mechanism for automated component adaptation [48]. Additionally, Kent et al. [49] propose a mechanism for the handling of concurrent access to a software component not built for such environments.

Vanderperren et al. have developed a tool called PaCoSuite for the visual assembly of components and adapters. The tool is capable of (semi-)automatic adapter generation using signature and protocol information [50]. Gschwind uses a repository of adapters to dynamically select a fitting adapter [51]. Min et al. present an approach called Smart Connectors which allows the construction of adapters based on the provided and required interface of the components to connect [27].

Passerone, de Alfaro and Henzinger developed a game-theoretical approach to find out whether incompatible component interfaces can be made compatible by inserting a converter between them which satisfies specified requirements [4]. This approach is able to automatically synthesize the converter. Their approach can only be applied to a restricted class of component mismatches (protocols and interaction). In fact, they are only able to restrict the system's behavior to a subset of desired ones and, for example, they are not able to augment the system's behavior to introduce more sophisticated interactions among components.

In [10], Garlan et al. have shown how to use formalized protocol transformations to augment the interaction behavior of a set of components. The key result was the formalization of a useful set of interaction protocol enhancements. Each enhancement is obtained by composing wrappers. This approach characterizes wrappers as modular protocol transformations. The basic idea is to use wrappers to introduce more sophisticated interactions among components. The goal is to alter the behavior of a component with respect to the other components in the system, without actually modifying the component or the infrastructure itself. While this approach deals with the problem of enhancing component interactions, it does not provide a support for wrapper generation.

A common terminology for the Quality of Service prediction of systems which are being assembled from components is proposed in [52]. A concrete methodology for predicting extra-functional properties of .NET assemblies is presented in [53]. None of these approaches, however, provides a specialized method for including adapters in their predictions. Engineering Quality of Service guarantees in the context of distributed systems is the main topic of [54].

An overview on adaptation mechanisms including non-automated approaches can be found in [55] (such as delegation, wrappers [37], superimposition [56], metaprogramming (e.g., [57])). Both works also contain a general discussion of requirements for component adaptation mechanisms. Not all of these approaches can be seen as adapters as defined in this paper. But some of the concepts presented can be implemented in adapters as shown here.

7   Conclusions and Future Directions

This paper introduces an engineering approach to software component adaptation. We define adaptation in terms of dealing with component mismatches, introduce the concept of component mismatch, and present a taxonomy to distinguish different types of component mismatches. Afterwards, we discuss a selection of adaptation patterns that can be used to eliminate the different mismatch types. The main contribution of the paper is a presentation of how these patterns can be used during the component adaptation process. The presented approach is demonstrated by both a functional and an extra-functional adaptation example.

Future research is directed towards exploring additional interface description languages which enable the efficient checking of the introduced mismatch types. On the basis of the available specification data, algorithms have to be developed to statically check for the identified component mismatch types during a compatibility test. Further on, existing prediction methods, which are based on the available component data, have to be improved to include adaptation and its impact on extra-functional system properties. In doing so, measures have to be developed that assess the impact on the extra-functional properties of systems when applying specific patterns to identified adaptation problems.

The application of generative techniques or concepts of Model-Driven Architecture (MDA) to construct the appropriate adapters is another strand of ongoing work. In this context, dependable composition of adapters and generation of adapters from the specification of the integrated system and the components are emerging areas of research. Finally, to achieve a fully-fledged engineering approach to component adaptation, further effort will be required to develop suitable tools that are capable of supporting the selection of pattern(s) which can be applied to solve specific mismatch types (viz., step 2 of the process proposed in Sect. 5).

Acknowledgments

The authors would like to thank Viktoria Firus, Gerhard Goos, and Raffaela Mirandola for their valuable and inspiring input during our break-out session at Dagstuhl, which preceded this paper. Steffen Becker is funded by the German Science Foundation in the DFG-Palladio project. Alexander Romanovsky is supported by the IST FP6 Project on Rigorous Open Development Environment for Complex Systems (RODIN).

References

1. Balemi, S., Hoffmann, G.J., Gyugyi, P., Wong-Toi, H., Franklin, G.F.: Supervisory Control of a Rapid Thermal Multiprocessor. IEEE Transactions on Automatic Control **38** (1993) 1040–1059
2. Yellin, D., Strom, R.: Protocol Specifications and Component Adaptors. ACM Transactions on Programming Languages and Systems **19** (1997) 292–333
3. de Alfaro, L., Henzinger, T.A.: Interface Automata. In Gruhn, V., ed.: Proceedings of the Joint 8th European Software Engineering Conference and 9th ACM SIGSOFT Symposium on the Foundation of Software Engeneering (ESEC/FSE-01). Volume 26, 5 of ACM SIGSOFT Software Engineering Notes., New York, ACM Press (2001) 109–120
4. Passerone, R., de Alfaro, L., Henzinger, T., Sangiovanni-Vincentelli, A.L.: Convertibility Verification and Converter Synthesis: Two Faces of the Same Coin. In: Proceedings of the International Conference on Computer Aided Design (ICCAD'02). (2002)
5. Giannakopoulou, D., Pasareanu, C.S., Barringer, H.: Assumption Generation for Software Component Verification. In IEEE, ed.: 17th IEEE International Conference on Automated Software Engineering (ASE 2002), 23-27 September 2002, Edinburgh, Scotland, UK, Los Alamitos, CA, IEEE Computer Society (2002) 3–12
6. Inverardi, P., Tivoli, M.: Software Architecture for Correct Components Assembly. In Bernardo, M., Inverardi, P., eds.: Formal Methods for Software Architectures, Third International School on Formal Methods for the Design of Computer, Communication and Software Systems: Software Architectures, SFM 2003, Bertinoro, Italy, September 22-27, 2003, Advanced Lectures. Volume 2804 of Lecture Notes in Computer Science., Berlin, Heidelberg, Springer (2003) 92–121
7. Inverardi, P., Tivoli, M.: Failure-Free Connector Synthesis for Correct Components Assembly. In: Proceedings of Specification and Verification of Component-Based Systems (SAVCBS'03). (2003)
8. Tivoli, M., Inverardi, P., Presutti, V., Forghieri, A., Sebastianis, M.: Correct Components Assembly for a Product Data Management Cooperative System. In Crnkovic, I., Stafford, J.A., Schmidt, H.W., Wallnau, K.C., eds.: Component-Based Software Engineering, 7th International Symposium, CBSE 2004, Edinburgh, UK, May 24-25, 2004, Proceedings. Volume 3054 of Lecture Notes in Computer Science., Berlin, Heidelberg, Springer (2004) 84–99
9. Brogi, A., Canal, C., Pimentel, E.: Behavioural Types and Component Adaptation. In Rattray, C., Maharaj, S., Shankland, C., eds.: Algebraic Methodology and Software Technology, 10th International Conference, AMAST 2004, Stirling, Scotland, UK, July 12-16, 2004, Proceedings. Volume 3116 of Lecture Notes in Computer Science., Berlin, Heidelberg, Springer (2004) 42–56
10. Spitznagel, B., Garlan, D.: A Compositional Formalization of Connector Wrappers. In IEEE, ed.: Proceedings of the 25th International Conference on Software Engineering, May 3-10, 2003, Portland, Oregon, USA, Los Alamitos, CA, IEEE Computer Society (2003) 374–384
11. Tivoli, M., Garlan, D.: Coordinator Synthesis for Reliability Enhancement in Component-Based Systems. Technical report, Carnegie Mellon University (2004)
12. Autili, M., Inverardi, P., Tivoli, M., Garlan, D.: Synthesis of 'Correct' Adaptors for Protocol Enhancement in Component-Based Systems. In: Proceedings of Specification and Verification of Component-Based Systems (SAVCBS'04). (2004)

13. Autili, M., Inverardi, P., Tivoli, M.: Automatic Adaptor Synthesis for Protocol Transformation. In: Proceedings of the First International Workshop on Coordination and Adaptation Techniques for Software Entities (WCAT'04). (2004)

14. Tivoli, M., Autili, M.: SYNTHESIS: A Tool for Synthesizing 'Correct' and Protocol-Enhanced Adaptors. To appear on L'Objet journal, http://www.di.univaq.it/tivoli/LastSynthesis.pdf (2005)

15. Garlan, D., Allan, R., Ockerbloom, J.: Architectural Mismatch: Why Reuse Is So Hard. IEEE Software 12 (1995) 17–26

16. Mili, H., Mili, F., Mili, A.: Reusing Software: Issues and Research Directions. IEEE Transactions on Software Engineering 21 (1995) 528–561

17. de Lemos, R., Gacek, C., Romanovsky, A.: Architectural Mismatch Tolerance. In de Lemos, R., Gacek, C., Romanovsky, A., eds.: Architecting Dependable Systems. Volume 2677 of Lecture Notes in Computer Science., Berlin, Heidelberg, Springer (2003) 175–194

18. Canal, C., Murillo, J.M., Poizat, P.: Coordination and Adaptation Techniques for Software Entities. In Malenfant, J., Østvold, B.M., eds.: Object-Oriented Technology: ECOOP 2004 Workshop Reader, ECOOP 2004 Workshops, Oslo, Norway, June 14-18, 2004, Final Reports. Volume 3344 of Lecture Notes in Computer Science., Springer (2005) 133–147

19. Szyperski, C., Gruntz, D., Murer, S.: Component Software: Beyond Object-Oriented Programming. 2 edn. ACM Press and Addison-Wesley, New York, NY (2002)

20. D'Souza, D.F., Wills, A.C.: Objects, Components, and Frameworks with UML: The Catalysis Approach. Addison-Wesley, Reading, MA, USA (1999)

21. Becker, S., Overhage, S., Reussner, R.: Classifying Software Component Interoperability Errors to Support Component Adaption. In Crnkovic, I., Stafford, J.A., Schmidt, H.W., Wallnau, K.C., eds.: Component-Based Software Engineering, 7th International Symposium, CBSE 2004, Edinburgh, UK, May 24-25, 2004, Proceedings. Volume 3054 of Lecture Notes in Computer Science., Berlin, Heidelberg, Springer (2004) 68–83

22. Yakimovich, D., Travassos, G., Basili, V.: A classification of software components incompatibilities for COTS integration. Technical report, Software Engineering Laboratory Workshop, NASA/Goddard Space Flight Center, Greenbelt, Maryland (1999)

23. Overhage, S., Thomas, P.: WS-Specification: Specifying Web Services Using UDDI Improvements. In Chaudhri, A.B., Jeckle, M., Rahm, E., Unland, R., eds.: Web, Web Services, and Database Systems. NODe 2002 Web- and Database-Related Workshops. Volume 2593 of Lecture Notes in Computer Science., Berlin, Heidelberg, Springer (2003) 100–118

24. Beugnard, A., Jezequel, J.M., Plouzeau, N., Watkins, D.: Making Components Contract Aware. IEEE Computer 32 (1999) 38–45

25. Overhage, S.: UnSCom: A Standardized Framework for the Specification of Software Components. In Weske, M., Liggesmeyer, P., eds.: Object-Oriented and Internet-Based Technologies, 5th Annual International Conference on Object-Oriented and Internet-Based Technologies, Concepts, and Applications for a Networked World, NODe 2004, Proceedings. Volume 3263 of Lecture Notes in Computer Science., Berlin, Heidelberg, Springer (2004) 169–184

26. Zaremski, A.M., Wing, J.M.: Signature Matching: A Tool for Using Software Libraries. ACM Transactions on Software Engineering and Methodology 4 (1995) 146–170

27. Min, H.G., Choi, S.W., Kim, S.D.: Using Smart Connectors to Resolve Partial Matching Problems in COTS Component Acquisition. In Crnkovic, I., Stafford, J.A., Schmidt, H.W., Wallnau, K.C., eds.: Component-Based Software Engineering, 7th International Symposium, CBSE 2004, Edinburgh, UK, May 24-25, 2004, Proceedings. Volume 3054 of Lecture Notes in Computer Science., Springer-Verlag, Berlin, Germany (2004) 40–47

28. Meyer, B.: Object-Oriented Software Construction. 2. edn. Prentice Hall, Englewood Cliffs, NJ (1997)

29. Zaremski, A.M., Wing, J.M.: Specification Matching of Software Components. ACM Transactions on Software Engineering and Methodology **6** (1997) 333–369
30. Schmidt, H.W., Reussner, R.H.: Generating Adapters for Concurrent Component Protocol Synchronisation. In: Proceedings of the Fifth IFIP International Conference on Formal Methods for Open Object-Based Distributed Systems. (2002)
31. ISO/IEC: Software Engineering - Product Quality - Quality Model. ISO Standard 9126-1, International Organization for Standardization (2001)
32. ISO/IEC: Software Engineering - Product Quality - External Metrics. ISO Standard 9126-2, International Organization for Standardization (2003)
33. Horwich, P.: Wittgenstein and Kripke on the Nature of Meaning. Mind and Language **5** (1990) 105–121
34. Paolucci, M., Kawamura, T., Payne, T., Sycara, K.: Semantic Matchmaking of Web Services Capabilities. In Horrocks, I., Hendler, J., eds.: First International Semantic Web Conference on The Semantic Web. Volume 2342 of Lecture Notes in Computer Science., Berlin, Heidelberg, Springer (2002) 333–347
35. Noy, N.F.: Tools for Mapping and Merging Ontologies. In Staab, S., Studer, R., eds.: Handbook on Ontologies. Springer, Berlin, Heidelberg (2004) 365–384
36. Noy, N.F.: Semantic Integration: A Survey Of Ontology-Based Approaches. SIGMOD Record **33** (2004) 65–70
37. Gamma, E., Helm, R., Johnson, R., Vlissides, J.: Design Patterns: Elements of Reusable Object-Oriented Software. Addison-Wesley, Reading, MA, USA (1995)
38. Buschmann, F., Meunier, R., Rohnert, H., Sommerlad, P., Stal, M.: Pattern-Oriented Software Architecture – A System of Patterns. Wiley & Sons, New York, NY, USA (1996)
39. Schmidt, D., Stal, M., Rohnert, H., Buschmann, F.: Pattern-Oriented Software Architecture – Volume 2 – Patterns for Concurrent and Networked Objects. Wiley & Sons, New York, NY, USA (2000)
40. Kircher, M., Jain, P.: Pattern-Oriented Software Architecture: Patterns for Distributed Services and Components. John Wiley and Sons Ltd (2004)
41. Grand, M.: Java Enterprise Design Patterns: Patterns in Java (Patterns in Java). John Wiley & Sons (2002)
42. Fowler, M., Rice, D., Foemmel, M., Hieatt, E., Mee, R., Stafford, R.: Patterns of Enterprise Application Architecture. Addison-Wesley Professional (2002)
43. Magee, J., Kramer, J.: Concurrency: State Models and Java Programs. John Wiley and Sons (1999)
44. Frølund, S., Koistinen, J.: Quality-of-Service Specification in Distributed Object Systems. Technical Report HPL-98-159, Hewlett Packard, Software Technology Laboratory (1998)
45. McIlroy, M.D.: "Mass Produced" Software Components. In Naur, P., Randell, B., eds.: Software Engineering, Brussels, Scientific Affairs Division, NATO (1969) 138–155 Report of a conference sponsored by the NATO Science Committee, Garmisch, Germany, 7th to 11th October 1968.
46. Yellin, D., Strom, R.: Interfaces, Protocols and the Semiautomatic Construction of Software Adaptors. In: Proceedings of the 9th ACM Conference on Object-Oriented Programming Systems, Languages and Applications (OOPSLA-94). Volume 29, 10 of ACM Sigplan Notices. (1994) 176–190
47. Bracciali, A., Brogi, A., Canal, C.: A formal approach to component adaptation. Journal of Systems and Software **74** (2005) 45–54
48. Reussner, R.H.: Automatic Component Protocol Adaptation with the CoCoNut Tool Suite. Future Generation Computer Systems **19** (2003) 627–639
49. Kent, S.D., Ho-Stuart, C., Roe, P.: Negotiable Interfaces for Components. In Reussner, R.H., Poernomo, I.H., Grundy, J.C., eds.: Proceedings of the Fourth Australasian Workshop on Software and Systems Architectures, Melbourne, Australia, DSTC (2002)

50. Vanderperren, W., Wydaeghe, B.: Towards a New Component Composition Process. In: Proceedings of ECBS 2001 Int Conf, Washington, USA. (2001) 322 – 331
51. Gschwind, T.: Adaptation and Composition Techniques for Component-Based Software Engineering. PhD thesis, Technische Universität Wien (2002)
52. Hissam, S.A., Moreno, G.A., Stafford, J.A., Wallnau, K.C.: Packaging Predictable Assembly. In Bishop, J.M., ed.: Component Deployment, IFIP/ACM Working Conference, CD 2002, Berlin, Germany, June 20-21, 2002, Proceedings. Volume 2370 of Lecture Notes in Computer Science., Springer (2002) 108–124
53. Dumitrascu, N., Murphy, S., Murphy, L.: A Methodology for Predicting the Performance of Component-Based Applications. In Weck, W., Bosch, J., Szyperski, C., eds.: Proceedings of the Eighth International Workshop on Component-Oriented Programming (WCOP'03). (2003)
54. Aagedal, J.Ø.: Quality of Service Support in Development of Distributed Systems. PhD thesis, University of Oslo (2001)
55. Bosch, J.: Design and Use of Software Architectures – Adopting and evolving a product-line approach. Addison-Wesley, Reading, MA, USA (2000)
56. Bosch, J.: Composition through Superimposition. In Weck, W., Bosch, J., Szyperski, C., eds.: Proceedings of the First International Workshop on Component-Oriented Programming (WCOP'96), Turku Centre for Computer Science (1996)
57. Kiczales, G.: Aspect-oriented programming. ACM Computing Surveys 28 (1996) 154–154

Compatible Component Upgrades Through Smart Component Swapping

Alexander Stuckenholz[1] and Olaf Zwintzscher[2]

[1] Department of Data Processing Technologies,
FernUniversität in Hagen
Alexander.Stuckenholz@FernUni-Hagen.de
[2] W3L GmbH, Herdecke \ Bochum
olafz@w3l.de

Abstract. Emerging component-based software development architectures promise better re-use of software components, greater flexibility, scalability and higher quality of services. But like any other piece of software too, software components are hardly perfect, when being created. Problems and bugs have to be fixed and new features need to be added.

This paper will give an introduction to the problem of component evolution and the syntactical incompatibilities which result during necessary multi component upgrades. The authors present an approach for the detection of such incompatibilities between multiple generations of component revisions basing on a formal interface model. The main concern of the paper will be the automated reconfiguration of component based software systems by intelligent swapping of component revisions to find conflict free system states.

1 Introduction

During the last years component based software development changed from a pure scientific research field to a widely used technique [1]. A number of component models for different layers (desktop, server) have been established [2,3,4,5]. After consolidation of standards and specifications in this area, it is now time to look at the problems that arise from the practical use of software components in everyday projects.

Just like any other piece of software too, software components are hardly perfect, when they are created [6]. Problems and bugs have to be fixed and new features need to be added [7]. Software development generally may be defined as the process of creating and propagating changes [8]. Through this process, overtime new generations of software components evolve.

To leverage these updates, one has to deploy the new components into the system that uses them, which means to replace one or more components by newer revisions. When performing such updates, the first question is whether the system will still work with the new components. The modifications of the components which lead to the new revisions may cause incompatibilities or new

R.H. Reussner et al. (Eds.): Architecting Systems, LNCS 3938, pp. 216–226, 2006.

dependencies to an existing system. In the case of an incompatible component upgrade, the next question is how the system can be reconfigured, so that a conflict free system arises again.

The following article describes an approach, which tries to reduce such incompatibilities by intelligent component swapping of existing component revisions in a system. The approach reverts to available information on the configuration of the component based system, the existing component revisions and their interfaces and does not impose new specification procedures to the developers.

Voluminous, manually created behavior specifications of software components are feasible, but in reality they are used at least in safety-critical projects. The bigger parts of software components are verbally documented and merely specified by means of their interfaces.

By the limitation to such information, the described procedure is able to operate completely automated and can be adopted to existing component models easily. Corresponding tools will be able to warn developers in the case of incompatible component upgrades and try to transform a system configuration into a conflict free state again.

The paper is structured as follows: Section 2 defines the terms interface, component, component revision and software system in a formal model upon we will develop our approach. Section 3 characterizes the syntactical modifications of components and interfaces which may cause incompatibilities in component dependency relations and gives an indication for the complexity of the problem of finding compatible system states. Section 4 introduces dependency graphs and their characteristic traits. Section 5 establishes the concepts of the compatibility reachability graph, describes its characteristics and shows, how a system configuration can be transformed to a conflict free state by using it. To evaluate and limit the set of solutions, we also define corresponding weighting functions and constraints. Section 6 deals with corresponding approaches for substituting components with newer revisions and the package management tools of different Linux systems. Section 7 summarizes the results and gives an outlook to open questions and future research.

2   Components, Interfaces and Systems

In the following we define the fundamental terms interface, component and system, which are required for the rest of the paper.

Components are encapsulated against their environment. The details of the implementation are not visible for the component user and should not have any importance for their usage. The whole interaction with the implementation is carried over their interfaces. We define as follows:

Definition 1 (Interfaces). *An **interface** is a finite set of **method signatures** $I = (m_1, ..., m_{I^n})$.*

Interfaces represent one part of the contracts of a component with its environment. In the component based software development, several levels of contracts can be identified. These are (1) simple or syntactical, (2) behavior, (3) synchronization and (4) quality (cf. [9]). Our approach aims at automatically detecting and reducing component incompatibilities between component contracts. The levels of behavior, synchronization and quality can be included into such compatibility analysis only by using specifications which have to be created manually by the component developers. As components are only in least cases equipped with such specifications, our approach will initially be reduced to the syntactical level of component contracts.

As we are interested in the evolution of component based software systems, we assume, that components are realized by, at least one, concrete revision. The terms revision, a modification which leads to a new version, and a variant, a component which implements the same interfaces but uses another implementation, can be directly transferred from the area of *Software Configuration Management* (see [10]). In accordance with other areas of software engineering, the time dependency of software artifacts is expressed by adding version identifiers to distinguish the elements. This procedure also found its way to the component based software development.

A concrete instantiation of a component on the time axis provides and requires services to and from its environment by means of its interfaces. We define as follows:

Definition 2 (Components and Revisions). *Let R be the set of all possible* **component revisions** *and C the set of all possible* **components**.

A **component revision** *$r \in R$ is a tuple $r = (t, I_R, I_P)$. t is a somehow natured version identifier (e.g. the* major.minor.build *scheme), where we dispose of a order relation to decide which of two component revisions is newer than the other. I_R is a finite set of required interfaces and I_P is a finite set of provided interfaces.*

The relation isRevisionOf $\subseteq R \times C$ connects **components** *$c \in C$ with their concrete revisions $r \in R$. It holds, that every component c is realized by at least one concrete component revision r: $\forall c \in C : \exists r \in R : (r, c) \in isRevisionOf$. Furthermore we require isRevisionOf to be right-unique, so that component revisions are always connected to only one component.*

In component based software development components are put together to form bigger systems. This is their original meaning (cf. [11, 12]). We define a system S as follows:

Definition 3. *A system S is a finite set of component revisions $S = (r_1, ..., r_n)$. We claim, that for every component $c \in C$ we at most have one revision r_i in S: $\forall r_a, r_b \in S : \neg \exists c \in C : (r_a, c) \in isRevisionOf \land (r_b, c) \in isRevisionOf \land r_a \neq r_b$.*

As a general rule the set of component revisions in S consists of components from third parties (so called COTS[1]), proprietary components, configurators, which connect multiple components, and system components, which offer fundamental

---

[1] Commercials off-the-shelf.

services like persistence or transaction safety. The system developer combines the components to create an executable application. Through this specific selection, creation and connection of multiple components, the ultimate semantic of the system S arises.

As software developers and system maintainers we are certainly only interested in these kind of systems which are well-composed, which denotes, that all required interfaces in S are covered by compatible counterparts.

Definition 4 (Conflict Rate). *We define* $R^S := \bigcup_{r_i \ S} r_i.I_R$ *as the set of all required interfaces and* $P^S := \bigcup_{r_i \ S} r_i.I_P$ *as the set of all provided interfaces in a system* S.

It is now possible to define a relation isCompatibleTo which exists for all couples $(i_a, i_b) \in P^S \times R^S$ *where the provided interface* i_a *is compatible to the required interface* i_b. *In that case we call* i_a *the compatible counterpart to* i_b *in* S.

The **conflict rate** Θ^S *is now the difference between the number of required interfaces and the number of compatible relations in* S. $\Theta^S = \#R^S - \#((i_P, i_R)|i_P \in P^S \wedge i_R \in R^S \wedge (i_P, i_R) \in isCompatibleTo)$. *A System* S *is well composed, iff the conflict rate* Θ *is equal to zero.*

The aforementioned formalisms represent only a fragment of our interface model which is abutted to the methods of specifying contracts in B (cf. [13]) and is simplified here because for the lack of space. The original interface model allows in addition the inheritance of interfaces even over the boundaries of components. The conflict rate Θ represents the count of uncovered method signatured in a system in contrast to the count of uncovered interfaces. The dynamic part of the model, which e.g. calculates Θ, is implemented in the logic programming language Prolog and is embedded into our prototype model-checking-tool **Componentor**. We generally target component models like PEAR [14], where we already have a parser to create the required interface specifications fully automated from the sourcecode, or JavaBeans [15]. But the model is powerfull enough to cover other component models with comparable compositional structures as well.

3   Component Updates

Having a formal model which is able to proof the inherent compatibility of a specific component configuration in a system, we are now able to adopt these methods to our initial situation.

Component updates are provably (cf. [16]) regular events in which a system S is transferred into a new state S. Component revisions[2] in S are swapped by other, not necessarily newer, revisions. Other revisions have to be installed additionaly or are removed completely. The reasons for such updates are manifold

---

[2] In the following abbreviatory denoted as revisions.

and are described in [17,18,19,20]. Incompatible modifications at the component contracts may cause unforseen system breakdowns.

At the center of our interests are the syntactical changes of the interfaces between different component revisions, which have impacts to the inherent compatibility of the system. These changes induce an alteration of the conflict rate Θ in S. Especially changes that may increase Θ are critical. These are:

- addition of a method-signature to a required interface I_R,
- removal of a method-signature from a provided interface I_P,
- modification of a method-signature of an interface (I_P or I_R).

Furthermore the removal of whole interfaces from the set P of provided interfaces and the addition of interfaces to the set R of required interfaces induces a rise of the conflict rate Θ.

The intention is, starting with a system S, to find an S (1) for which holds, that the conflict rate $\Theta^{S'}$ is equal to zero and (2) which contains the set of predetermined revisions that have been specified before the update.

By means of the finite set of components and component revisions it is understood possible to form solely a finite count of systems. Without considering if a system is well-composed or not, the maximum count of systems can be estimated as

$$S_{max} = \prod_{j=1}^{j=\#C} (\#\{(r,c_j)|r \text{ isRevisionOf } c_j\} + 1) - 1, c_j \in C, r \in R. \quad (1)$$

Here it is assumed, that a system at least consists of one component revision. Apparently the maximum count of system configurations gets huge with only a small amount of components and component revisions. E.g. five components with each five revisions can be combined to a total count of 7775 systems. As a matter of fact S_{max} grows exponentially with the number of component revisions. The trivial solution to find the best composition by testing all possible combinations consecutively is therefore not sound.

4   Dependency Graphs

As already mentioned in Section 2, a component based system S is the result of a combination of an appropriate set of component revisions by the developer. If a revision r_i uses services of another revision r_j in S, it leads to a dependency relationship between these components. This dependency relation can be illustrated in a dependency graph with the components in S as nodes and the dependency relations as edges. Figure 1 shows an example of four components building a dependency graph. The dependency graph of a component based system S may be cyclic. As a simple example, consider two components C_1 and C_2 which mutually depend on each other to perform their services.

In the dependency graph we are able to distinguish different kinds of components. Components, that do not provide services to their environment are

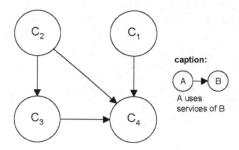

Fig. 1. Configuration of a sample component based system as a dependency graph

called applications. In this case the node r_i representing the application in the dependency graph G has no predecessors. As some applications work without requiring services from other components at all, the dependency graph must not be connected.

The aforementioned dependency graph represents one single well-formed configuration for a system S, which contains exactly one revision for a component. This kind of illustrating a systems architecture is not inconvenient. The component diagram in UML2 (cf. [21]) utilizes also this kind of view. As we target to find the best configuration using the available amount of component revisions, we first need to transfer this representation into a data structure, that permits such a search.

5   Swap Mechanism

In a first step, the dependency graph from Section 4 will be transferred to the so-called compatibility reachability graph. The logical components $C_1, ..., C_n$ of the system will be completed by their actual component revisions. A dependency relationship between two logical components will be replaced by a set of compatible dependencies of their actual component revisions. This transformation induces a refinement against the original dependency graph.

Figure 2 shows a simple example. The system consists of two different virtual components (C_1, C_2), each realized as three actual component revisions $(v_1, ..., v_3)$. The dependency relations between the virtual components C_1 and C_2 adopted from the dependency graph, will be replaced by the compatibility relations (see defintion 4) between concrete component revisions. The compatibility graph contains all compatible combinations of concrete component revisions of the virtual components in S. For better comprehension, Figure 3 shows all conflict free system configurations in S. These are subgraphs of the compatibility reachability graph from Figure 2.

At a certain point in time t_0 the system S from the example may consist of the components $C_1.v_1$ and $C_2.v_1$. I.e.: $S_0 = \{C_1.v_1, C_2.v_1\}$. During an upgrade C_2 ought to be replaced by revision v_3. I.e.: $S_1 = \{C_1.v_1, C_2.v_3\}$. Our mechanisms from the previous sections calculate a conflict rate $\Theta > 0$, which means that the

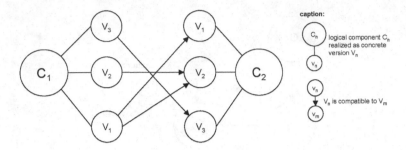

Fig. 2. Compatibility reachability graph of a simple system containing two virtual components with three concrete revisions each

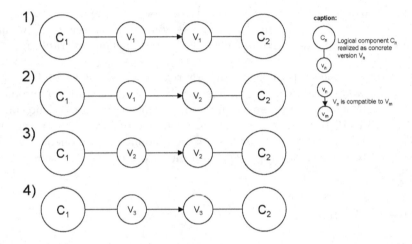

Fig. 3. Conflict free systems as subgraphs of the compatibility reachability graph

system S_1 is not executable in this configuration. This fact can also be derived from Figure 3: There is no conflict free system with the claimed combination of component revisions. The main aim of the component swapping mechanism is to restore a conflict free system state.

For this, first of all the conflict free subgraphs of the system S need to be extracted from the compatibility reachability graph. The conflict free subgraphs of the example, shown in Figure 3, are those subgraphs, which contain exactly one concrete component revision to every logical component. Due to the compatibility of a certain concrete component revision to more than one other concrete revision, a multiplicity of conflict free combinations and therefore multiple conflict free systems arise. For the search for such subgraphs the proceedings of breadth first search or depth first search, described in [22] lend themselves. As the problem of finding these subgraphs is exponential complex against the count of components in a system, the effective search for solutions is not trivial. We currently work on an effective greedy-algorithm that prunes unusable solutions from the search-space and integrates different constraints (see Section 5.1).

Supposing that the system S had a conflict free state ($\Theta = 0$) at any point in time (before an update), it holds that there must be at least one conflict free subgraph G_i in S. This subgraph is equal to the configuration of the previous, conflict free system. To choose this solution results in restoring the original system configuration.

With increasing count of component revision the probability that one can find more than one subgraph $G_i \in G$ also increases. In that case the set of solutions needs to be evaluated. For this intention according weighting functions (objective function and constraints) are required.

5.1   Weighting Functions

One approach to weight the kindliness of a solution is to evaluate the newness of the system over the newness of the particles, which are the component revisions in this case. Therefore we first have to introduce an abstract mapping, which transfers the revision identifier $r_i.t$ of a component revision r_i to a natural number $n \in \mathbb{N}$. For the well known major.minor.build-scheme, in which the version identifier is a tuple of three natural numbers, a simple mapping could be $n = build + minor * 10^4 + major * 10^8$. For the rest of the paper it holds, that the field $r_i.n$ contains such a mapping of the revision identifier of a concrete component revision r_i to a natural number.

An according weighting function, which is able to evaluate the set of solutions, calculates the sum over the version numbers of the concrete component revisions that are used in the solution G_i.

$$Z(G_i) = \sum_{\nu=0}^{\nu=\#G_i} r_\nu.n \tag{2}$$

With the help of $Z(G_i)$ the calculation of a conflict free system can be formulated as a maximization problem. The advantage of this weighting function is, on the one hand its simple calculability and, on the other hand its tendency to prefer that solution, wich uses only latest components. One drawback arises however in case of outliers within the revisions numbers. A component revisions with an extremely high version number in comparison to the other components in a particular solution may lead to choose a configuration which does not consist of latest component revisions in the majority. As an additional enhancement of the weighting function, the average difference between the version numbers of a solution can be calculated. To find that solution, which uses the most recent component revisions (cf. *WellVersioned Systems* in [20]), this difference needs to be minimized additionally.

6   Related Work

Approaches like the one by Brada [23] or Visnovsky [24] analyze the substitutability of single components in the case of a modification of the component behavior. These practices use manually created specifications, often based on pre- and post conditions and invariants. In the case of a component upgrade, it is verified by subtyping that the new component is compatible to the previous one. Such mechanisms put single components into the center of interest. However, our approach aims at the conflict free combination of multiple components in a system, which is closer to the original idea of component usage (*Components are for composition!*, [11], p. 3). As the compliance of non syntactical contracts between multiple components cannot be verified at this time, our approach will only use syntactical information about the components.

Anyway none of these approaches is in the position to reduce the conflict rate Θ (see definition 4) by actively changing the configuration of the System S. The approach sketched here uses the already existing information of the system to derive a conflict free state automatically.

In this context it is also useful to analyze the mechanisms of the packaging systems of different Linux distributions. In open source software systems exists also a notion of a component, namely a software package which can be installed (like TeX, the C compiler etc.). Some packages need other packages or do not work with others. Vendors of Linux distributions for example have sophisticated management tools and package formats, like the Debian [25] or the Red Hat [26] package format, that check whether the state of the system is consistent (there are no incompatibilities). But there are certain drawbacks of these systems, which may lead to inconsistent system states in worst-case.

Both the RPM- as well as the DEB-package format contain the dependencies to other packages in hard coded format by means of course grained version intervals (E.g. package x requires package y with version greater or equal to 1.3.7) which are created manually by the developers of the packages. As developers sometimes have wrong assumptions about their products, this proceeding may lead to version conflicts. In our approach the required interface specifications are derived directly from the sourcecode of the components and therefore reflect the real state of the requirements without any intermediate step.

Anymore these management tools rest upon different heuristics, that are pragmatic but circumsize the solution space for finding compatible systems. In case of an update tools like *apt* or *rpm* will always try to install newest packages only. If a well-defined system state could be derived by moving different packages back to an older version, these tools are not the best choice. Furthermore it is accepted, that deb- or rpm-packages are always downwardly compatible to older versions. Packages that would violate this rule are simply renamed (E.g. with the new major-revision-number in the package name) and henceforth exist in parallel with the older version in the package-repositories.

Our mechanisms for finding best system states looses from such assumptions and embraces all potential candidates in form of component revisions into the search for compatible system states.

7   Summary and Prospects

The previous sections sketched an idea, by which means it is possible to verify the syntactical correctness of a component based system configuration through the calculation of the conflict rate Θ. This defines the count of required interfaces, which do not have a counterpart in the set of provided interfaces in the system configuration. Hereon, we presented a possibility for automatic reconfiguration of a component based system, to restore a conflict free system state through component revision swapping. Therefore by means of the compatibility reachability graph the set of conflict free subgraphs have been identified, which define possible solutions of syntactical correct system configurations. To evaluate the set of solutions, corresponding weighting functions have been designed.

For the sketched approaches, prototypes are currently beeing implemented, which map the procedures to concrete component models.

Especially in the area of evaluating the conflict free solutions, the authors see further need for research. Next to the demand for the most recent system configuration, related to the revisions of the components, is is certainly possible to define more constraints.

The authors are confident to improve the quality of component based software engineering with the sketched approaches and especially to prevent the situations of unforseen incompatibilities after component upgrades.

References

1. O. Zwintzscher, "Komponentenbasierte & generative Softwareentwicklung - Generierung komponentenbasierter Software aus erweiterten UML - Modellen," Ph.D. dissertation, Ruhr-Universität-Bochum, 2003, (in German).
2. Sun Microsystems, "JavaBeans API specification," Tech. Rep., August 1997, http://java.sun.com/products/javabeans/, Last visited: 04/2004. [Online]. Available: http://java.sun.com/products/javabeans/
3. B. Shannon, "Java 2 platform enterprise edition specification," Sun Microsystems, Tech. Rep. v1.4, November 2003, http://java.sun.com/j2ee/index.jsp, Last visited: 04/2004. [Online]. Available: http://java.sun.com/j2ee/index.jsp
4. Object Management Group, Inc, "Common object request broker architecture: Core specification, Tech. Rep. Version 3.0.2 - Editorial update, December 2002, last visited: 03/2004. [Online]. Available: http://www.omg.org/technology/documents/formal/corba_iiop.htm
5. ECMA, "Standard ecma-335 - common language infrastructure (cli)," Tech. Rep., Dezember 2002, http://www.ecma-international.org/publications/standards/Ecma-335.htm, last visited: 10/2004. [Online]. Available: http://www.ecma-international.org/publications/standards/Ecma-335.htm
6. G. Hamilton and S. Radia, "Using interface inheritance to address problems in system software evolution," *ACM SIGPLAN Notices*, vol. 29, no. 8, pp. 119–128, 1994.
7. M. Rakic and N. Medvidovic, "Increasing the confidence in off-the-shelf components: a software connector-based approach," in *Proceedings of the 2001 symposium on Software reusability*, Toronto, Ontario, Canada, 2001, pp. 11–18.

8. A. Zeller and J. Krinke, *Open-Source-Programmierwerkzeuge, Versionskontrolle - Konstruktion - Testen - Fehlersuche*, 2nd ed. dpunkt.verlag, 2003, in German.

9. A. Beugnard, J.-M. Jézéquel, N. Plouzeau, and D. Watkins, "Making components contract aware," in *IEEE software*, june 1999, pp. 38–45.

10. R. Conradi and B. Westfechtel, "Version models for software configuration management," *ACM Computing Surveys*, vol. 30, no. 2, pp. 232–282, 1998.

11. C. Szyperski, *Component Software: Beyond Object-Oriented Programming - Second Edition*. Addison-Wesley, 2002.

12. J. Siedersleben, *Moderne Software Architektur*. Dpunkt Verlag, 2004, in German.

13. J.-R. Abrial, *The B-book: assigning programs to meanings*. New York, NY, USA: Cambridge University Press, 1996.

14. C. Möhrke, *PHP PEAR - Anwendung und Entwicklung - PEAR und PECL zur PHP-Programmierung nutzen*. Galileo Press, 2005, (in German).

15. R. Englander, *Developing Java beans*. Sebastopol, CA, USA: O'Reilly & Associates, Inc., 1997.

16. A. Stuckenholz, "Softwarekomponenten und ihre Update-Zyklen: Eine Marktanalyse," *Praxis der Information und Kommunikation*, 2006, to appear.

17. S. McCamant and M. D. Ernst, "Early identification of incompatibilities in multi-component upgrades," in *Proceedings of the 10th European Software Engineering Conference and the 11th ACM SIGSOFT Symposium on the Foundations of Software Engineering*, Helsinki, Finland, June 14–18, 2003, pp. 287–296.

18. M. Große-Rhode, R.-D. Kutsche, and F. Bübl, "Concepts for the evolution of component based software systems," Fraunhofer ISST, Tech. Rep., 2000.

19. J. E. Cook and J. A. Dage, "Highly reliable upgrading of components," in *International Conference on Software Engineering*, Los Angeles, California, United States, 1999, pp. 203–212.

20. S. Eisenbach, V. Jurisic, and C. Sadler, "Managing the evolution of .NET programs," in *6th IFIP International Conference on Formal Methods for Open Object-based Distributed Systems (FMOODS 2003)*, November 2003.

21. M. Jeckle, C. Rupp, J. Hahn, B. Zengler, and S. Queins, *UML2 glasklar*. München: Carl Hanser, 2004, (in German).

22. D. E. Knuth, *The Art of Computer Programming*. Addison-Wesley Professional, 1998.

23. P. Brada, "Specification-based component substitutability and revision identification," Ph.D. dissertation, Charles University in Prague, August 2003.

24. S. Visnovsky, "Checking semantic compatibility of sofa/dcup components," Master's thesis, Charles University in Prague, Prague, 1999.

25. I. Jackson and C. Schwarz, "Debian policy manual," 1998, last visited: 12/2005. [Online]. Available: http://www.debian.org/doc/debian-policy/

26. E. C. Bailey, *Maximum RPM*. Sams, 1997.

Exceptions in Component Interaction Protocols - Necessity[*]

Frantisek Plasil[1,2] and Viliam Holub[1]

[1] Charles University, Faculty of Mathematics and Physics,
Department of Software Engineering,
Malostranske namesti 25, 118 00 Prague 1, Czech Republic
{plasil, holub}@nenya.ms.mff.cuni.cz
http://nenya.ms.mff.cuni.cz/
[2] Academy of Sciences of the Czech Republic,
Institute of Computer Science
plasil@cs.cas.cz
http://www.cs.cas.cz/

Abstract. At ADL level, most of the current interaction protocols designed to specify components' behavior at their interfaces do not allow to capture exceptions explicitly. Based on our experience with real-life component based applications, handling exceptions as first class entities in a (formal) behavior specification is an absolute necessity. Otherwise, due to the need to capture exceptions indirectly, the specification becomes very complex, therefore hard to read and, consequently, error-prone. After analyzing potential approaches to introducing exceptions to LTS-based interaction specification (expressed via terms/expressions) in ADL, the paper presents the way we built exceptions into the behavior protocols. Finally, we discuss the positive experience with applying these exception-aware behavior protocols to a real-life Fractal component model application.

1 Introduction

There are many approaches to describe the desired behavior of software components. They include interface automata[4], behavior protocols[16], DFSM[19], usage policies[6], interactions and reactions[25], parametric contracts[18], UML2.0 State Machines (in principle stemming from Harel diagrams[8]) and Protocol State Machines[12], and CSP-based mechanisms, such as Wright[5] and FSP[11].

Those of them which are based on LTS (Label Transition System) where the transitions model atomic actions, allow for some kind of reasoning on behavior (e.g. equivalence[5], compatibility[4], compliance[16]). For instance, these atomic actions model the request and response triggered by a method call - i.e.

---

[*] This work was partially supported by the Grant Agency of the Czech Republic project 201/06/0770; the results will be used in the OSIRIS/ITEA project.

R.H. Reussner et al. (Eds.): Architecting Systems, LNCS 3938, pp. 227–244, 2006.

mostly the "control-observing" behavior of a component. Obviously, those LTS-based behavior description mechanisms which are directly applicable in architecture description languages cannot explicitly utilize any kind of diagrams, and therefore typically employ some kind of term expressions. However, there is a problem with this approach: capturing exceptions. While in a graphically expressed transition system, an exception can be expressed by adding another transitional edge, most of the term-expression based formalisms do not allow this easily. We encountered the problem when we were trying to employ behavior protocols [1,2,3,16], in non-trivial case studies of component behavior specification, comprising over 20 components each.

This paper aims at achieving two main goals:

1. To present a "reasonable" syntax extension of behavior protocols which does not violate the inherent regularity of the traces generated by the protocol (and therefore preserves important properties like protocol compliance decidability).
2. To show that the proposed syntax increases readability and significantly simplifies a behavior protocol when an exception is to be thrown/handled. This claim is supported by experimental results.

The paper is structured as follows: Sect. 2 describes the background - behavior protocols, in Sect. 3, the problem of handling exceptions in protocols is analyzed from a perspective of component communication and a solution is proposed. Section 4 illustrates the proposed solution on a case study. Section 5, as a part of overall evaluation, shares with the reader the experience with applying the proposed approach to a real-life Java project. Finally, Sect. 6 is focused on related work and Sect. 7 draws a conclusion.

2   Background - Behavior Protocols

The basic idea of behavior protocols can be illustrated on the following example (Fig. 1).

The picture shows the internal structure of a hypothetical Reservation component which is composed of five sub-components - Ticket manager (responsible for registration of tickets), Database manager (implementing the database behavior), Storage (permanently stores data), VISA (for payment authentication) and Operator verification (a connection to third-party servers).

Via behavior protocols, we can capture communication among these components. There are three types of protocols - *frame protocol* specifying the expected activities on components' boundaries (their frame), *architecture protocol* created automatically as a parallel composition of the frame protocols of the subcomponents (at the first-level of nesting) and the *interface protocol* describing the behavior only on a selected interface.

These abstractions allow for addressing two aspects of "design by contract": (i) *Horizontal contract* "Do the children cooperate with no conflicts?" (a conflict is statically detected as a *composition error*), and (ii) *vertical contract* "Do the

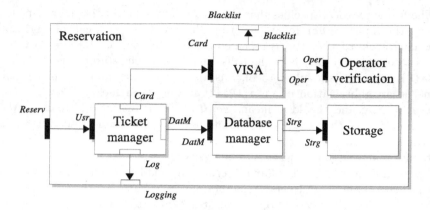

Fig. 1. The Reservation component

cooperating children do what the parent expects?" which is statically verified via evaluating *compliance* of the architecture protocol (determined by the sub-components) and the frame protocol of the parent component. As an aside, the static composition error detection and compliance verification is done by a tool, protocol checker, available as a part of the SOFA project[21].

As to (i), three types of composition errors are identified - *bad activity* (an emitted event is not accepted), *no activity* (deadlock), and *divergence* (infinite activity). Definition of the semantics of compliance is crucial and has evolved from a *naive*[17] and *pragmatic*[16], to *consensual*[2] based on the idea that the architecture should work well (without composition errors) when cooperating with a separate component representing the architecture's environment. The behavior of this environment is defined as the "inverted" frame protocol of the parent component[2].

For example, compliance of the architecture protocol specifying the composed behavior of Ticket manager, Database manager, Storage, VISA and Operator verification with the frame protocol of Reservation can be verified. The frame protocol of the Ticket manager component can take the form:

```
?Usr.init;
(
  ?Usr.buyTicket {
    !DatM.preReserve;
    !Card.lookUp; !Card.payment;
    !DatM.reserve; !DatM.commit;
    !Log.print}
  +
  ?Usr.returnTicket {
    !Card.revert;
    !DatM.free; !DatM.commit}
)*;
?Usr.finish
```

The frame protocol specifies that the component expects (?) an `init` method call on the interface `Usr` followed (;) by alternatively (+) a call of `buyTicket` or `returnTicket`. After this is repeated a finite number of times (*), a `finish` call is accepted; no other incoming calls are allowed. The statements of the form `?i.a{P}`, where P is a subprotocol, i is an interface name and a is a method name, is an abbreviation of `?i.a;(P)!i.a`. The `?i.a` means *accepting* (?) a *request* () i.a, and the `!i.a` means *emitting* (!) a *response* () to i.a. Along these lines we see that the `buyTicket` method (acquiring and reserving a ticket for the user), calls (!) the `preReserve` on the `DatM` interface to inform the Database manager that a ticket is to be reserved. As a next step, calls of `lookUp` and `payment` methods on the `Card` interface are made to perform the payment; further, the `reserve` and `commit` methods on the `DatM` interface are called in order to confirm the transaction. The last action is to print information about the transaction - `Log.print`.

Instead of the alternative operator +, we could use the *or-parallel operator* || to express that calls of `buyTicket` and `returnTicket` might be accepted simultaneously. Additional operators and further details are described in [16].

3   Handling Exceptions in Behavior Protocols

3.1   Primitive Techniques

In real settings, exceptional situations (not described in the previous protocol) also have to be handled - e.g. the VISA component may deny service due to a network error, and the Database manager may refuse to allocate appropriate resources. In other words, specifying behavior of a component inherently involves exceptions. However, expressing exception via the standard operators is tedious. For illustration, consider the `DatM.preReserve` method call from the example above which could throw a `preReserveException` exception. In order to specify this behavior, we have to split the return from the `preReserve` method into a regular return (`?DatM.preReserve`) and an accepting return with exception (`?DatM.preReserveException`) - we call this technique *intrinsic exceptions* handling. However, in consequence, the frame protocol length would expand rapidly (exponentially in the number of methods throwing an exception).

Below is a fragment of the frame protocol of Ticket Manager where several exceptions are thrown and handled - it illustrates how the protocol becomes complex. In the example, we suppose that the `DatM.preReserve` method can throw `PreReserveException`, methods `Card.lookUp` and `Card.payment` can throw `NetworkException`, and finally the `DatM.reserve` method can throw `ReservationException`.

```
———————— Technique: Intrinsic exceptions ————————
...
?Usr.buyTicket ;
  !DatM.preReserve ;
  ( ?DatM.preReserve ; !Card.lookUp ;
    ( ?Card.lookUp ; !Card.payment ;
      ( ?Card.payment ; !DatM.reserve ;
        ( ?DatM.reserve ; !DatM.commit ;
          ( ?DatM.commit ; !Usr.buyTicket )
          +
          (  // exceptions of DatM.commit
            ?DatM.DatabaseException;
            !DatM.cancel; !Card.revert; !Log.print;
            !Usr.buyTicket
          )
        )
        +
        (  // exceptions of DatM.reserve
          (?DatM.DatabaseException+?DatM.ReservationException);
          !DatM.cancel; !Card.revert; !Log.exEvent; !Log.print;
          !Usr.buyTicket
        )
      )
      +
      (  // exceptions of Card.payment
        ?Card.NetworkException;
        !DatM.cancel; !Card.revert;
        !Usr.NetworkException
      )
    )
    +
    (  // exceptions of Card.lookUp
      ?Card.NetworkException;
      !DatM.cancel; !Card.revert;
      !Usr.NetworkException
    )
  )
  +
  (  // exceptions of DatM.preReserve
    ?DatM.PreReservationException; !Log.exEvent; !Log.print;
    !Usr.buyTicket
  )
...
```

Obviously, a part of the complexity of the problem is the fact that we have to separate requests and responses of method calls to capture that exceptions can happen between them. Moreover the "reaction" inside such a call has to be divided into a "regular" and an exception part, and, even worth, the exception parthas to contain repeatedly the "regular" continuation of the method (notice how many times is !Log.print appears in the specification). Clearly, if we could take advantage of keeping the expressive power of the abbreviations ?a{P} or !a{P}, and add specific syntactical constructs for capturing exceptions as classical programming languages do, we could shorten this behavior protocol significantly and make it much more concise and, consequently, easier to comprehend.

Another option is to use the *approximation by alternative* technique the basic idea of which is to put after any method call alternative, non-deterministically chosen reactions (+) covering all the potential continuations. These include "regular" continuation, and those specific for each of the exceptions the method can throw. An example of this technique is below. For instance, !DatM.reserve is followed by alternatively calling !DatM.commit or handling the reservation exception (the !DatM.cancel; !Card.revert; !Log.exEvent; !Log.print part). Obviously, this approach only approximates real behavior of a component by not explicitly specifying the issuing and accepting events related to an exception.

```
———————— Technique: Approximation by alternative ————————
...
Usr.buyTicket {
  !DatM.preReserve;
  ( !Card.lookUp;
    ( !Card.payment;
      ( !DatM.reserve;
        ( !DatM.commit;
          (
            null +
            // exception on DatM.commit
            (!DatM.cancel; !Card.revert; !Log.print)
          )
        )
        +
        // exception on DatM.reserve
        (!DatM.cancel; !Card.revert; !Log.exEvent; !Log.print)
      )
      +
      // exception on Card.payment
      (!DatM.cancel; !Card.revert)
    )
    +
    // exception on Card.lookUp
    (!DatM.cancel; !Card.revert)
  )
  +
  // exception on DatM.preReserve
  (!Log.exEvent; !Log.print)
}
...
```

3.2   Analyzing the Problem and Sketching a Solution

In this section, we discuss all the key aspects related to expressing/capturing exceptions and behavior protocols at the level of an ADL (Architecture Description Language). In our view, the driving facts are:

1. In ADLs, exceptions should be specified with a granularity of a method (most likely in the interface specifications).
2. In ADLs, the key abstractions the protocols are associated with are frame protocols.
3. Issuing a method call in a frame protocol means the call goes outside of the component.
4. Throwing an exception in a method means an abnormal end of the method call.
5. Because of (3) an exception has to be handled in the frame protocol of the component which issued the call, and, because of (4), such handling is a specific reaction of the calling component after receiving the exception. In principle, this reaction has to be reflected by an adequate "traffic" on the calling component's interfaces.

Obviously an abnormal end of a method $i2.m$ call from interface i can be easily modeled by replacing the standard "end_of_call" response $!i.m$ by an exception response, e.g. $!i.e$. Moreover, the "abnormality" has to be reflected by abandoning the original protocol specifying the execution of m, i.e. the action $!i.e$ in the protocol P appearing in the context $?i2.m\{P\}$ has to be the last action generated by P. However, as the example in Sect. 3.1 indicates, addressing these abnormalities by the standard behavior protocols means becomes cumbersome. Since any protocol can be interpreted as an abstraction of code, we can, for this purpose, advantageously adopt a Java inspired construct of the form $?i2.m\{...$ throw $!e ...\}$ with the meaning (informally put) throw $!e$ generates $!i.e$ and then the execution of $i2.m$ internals directly jumps to the lexically nearest $\}$. In a similar vein, for handling an exception in a caller's frame protocol ((5)), we can adopt a try $\{P\}$ catch $\{?i.e:Q\}$ construct with the meaning very similar to the interrupt operator in CSP (i.e. $P\triangle_i Q$): if the event at the beginning of Q occurs, then the execution of the process P is abandoned and the process Q executes further. Along these lines, the event $?i.e$ is the first one generated by the catch $\{?i.e:Q\}$ construct.

However, we have to analyze exception throwing, propagating, and handling in all the (1)..(4) contexts below, since the methods are called across component boundaries and components can be nested. These four contexts represent all the situations on interface bindings related to a method call and an exception throwing and handling. These are client (1) and server (2) positions at a binding when no nesting is considered and the related situation when component nesting is taken into account. The latter are: nested server (3 - delegation) and nested client (4 - subsumption) positions at a binding.

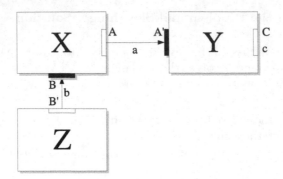

Fig. 2. Client-server

(1) Client position (Figure 2)

Consider the component X which calls the method a on the interface A. If an exception e can be thrown by the call of a (i.e. thrown by Y in the setting of Fig. 2), the construct try {... !A.a ...} catch {?A.e: ...} is to be used in the frame protocol of X in order to handle the exception. An unhandled exception would cause an error (bad activity in terms of [1]).

(2) Server position (Figure 2)

Consider the component Y accepting a call of a through the interface A'. In general, as mentioned above in this section, an exception in the execution of a is expressed by:

    ?A.a { ... throw !e; ... }

Based on the experience with our case studies, typical special cases of throwing an exception are:

1. An exception e is thrown due to an invalid actual parameter of a (invisible in protocols, but important for a credible abstraction). In protocols, this is typically expressed as
   ?A.a { null + throw !e; ... }
2. An exception is thrown due to a faulty return value in a nested call !C.c: (again invisible in protocols, but important for a credible abstraction). In protocols this is typically expressed as
   ?A.a { ... !C.c; (null + throw !e); ... }
   Since both in (1) and (2) the exception is a reaction on an "invisible" invalid value, it is a good practice to indicate the fact by choosing a mnemotechnical name for the exception (in Sect. 4, there are several examples of this method).
3. An exception is thrown in a catch construct. This is typical for exception propagation (even under a different name). For example, in
   ?A.a { ... try {!C.c} catch {?C.e1: throw !e2); ... }
   the C.c method can throw an e1 exception, which is then converted into e2.

(3) Delegation (Figure 3)

Delegation basically means forwarding an acceptance of a call to an internal component[15]; in Fig. 3 the component Y delegates calls from the component X

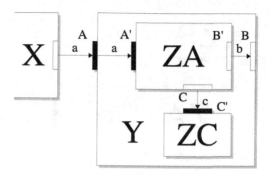

Fig. 3. Delegation

on the interface A to the interface A' in the internal component ZA. In principle, an exception e thrown in ZA in its method a, has to be delivered to the original caller, i.e. to the component X. Since the internals of Y are not visible to X, throwing of e should be specified not only in the frame protocol of ZA and but also of Y. Notice, however, that an exception thrown by the component ZC and handled by the component ZA would not be visible in the frame protocol of Y.

(4) Subsumption (Figure 4)

Subsumption basically means forwarding a call issued in an internal component to its parent component[15]; in Fig. 4, the component ZA subsumes the calls on the interface A' to the interface A in its parent component X.

Apparently, an exception thrown in Y is to be delivered to and handled by the caller, i.e. the component ZA. However, the component X is also in the client position with respect to Y (and, at a design stage, the internals of X do not have to be known). Therefore, handling of the exception has to be specified also in the frame protocol of X.

Since handling an exception in the frame protocol of X in general causes a "recovery communication" of X visible outside of X, potentially including a specific communication on its interface B. Obviously, this recovery communication should be adequately captured in the architecture protocol of ZA and ZB and, in particular, triggered by handling the exception in the frame protocol of ZA.

3.3 Proposed Solution - Details

The main purpose of this section is to describe in more detail the semantics of the constructs introduced in Sect. 3.2 and to analyze the influence of these protocol enhancements on protocol compliance evaluation[1,3,15]. By convention, we will refer to exception handling based on these constructs as *Explicit try-catch* technique.

Throwing an exception

Syntax: throw !exception_name

This construct has to appear only in a protocol P written in the context of the form i.a{P}, i.e. inside the curly brackets abbreviation expressing call

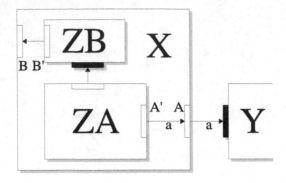

Fig. 4. Subsumption

acceptance of a method `a`. In principle, `throw !exception_name` means that in the resulting trace the event `!i.a` modeling return from `a` is replaced by the event `!i.exception_name` and, at the same time, this is the last event generated by P. Should P contain nested method accepting constructs (such as `?i.b{Q}`), this principle is applied recurently.

For example, `?i.m{!a.x;?a.sl; throw !ex; !a.y}` would always generate the trace `?i.m,!a.x,?a.sl,!a.ex`. In a similar vein, `?i.m{X;(null + throw !ex);Y}` is equivalent to `?i.m; X;(!i.ex + Y; !i.m)` for some protocols X and Y.

It should be emphasized that `!exception_name` is always the last event generated by P, even though P contains a `|` and/or `||` operator. For example, the traces generated by `?i.m{(!a.x;?a.sl; throw !ex;!a.y)|||!a.z*}` include (the beginning resp. end of a trace is denoted by < resp. >):

```
<?i.m;!a.x;!a.x;?a.sl;!a.sl;!i.ex>
<?i.m;!a.z;!a.x;?a.sl;!a.z;!a.z;!i.ex>
<?i.m;!a.x;!a.z;!a.z;?a.sl;!a.z;!a.z;!a.z;!a.ex>
<?i.m;!a.x;!a.z;?a.sl;?a.z;!a.sl;!a.z;!a.ex>
```

Anyhow, the reason why `throw !exception_name` generates the last event in P, no matter how many parallel activities in P are specified, is that it is hard to define a "reasonable" semantics of more than one exception (the remaining parallel activities could also throw an exception). As an aside, by opting for "interrupting" all the parallel activities we basically follow the semantics chosen in CSP for the interrupt operator[10].

Catching an exception
Syntax:
```
try { A }
catch {?i_{1,1}.exception_name_{1,1}..., ?i_{1,m_1}.exception_name_{1,m_1}: B_1}
catch {?i_{2,1}.exception_name_{2,1}..., ?i_{2,m_2}.exception_name_{2,m_2}: B_2}
...
catch {?i_{n,1}.exception_name_{n,1}..., ?i_{n,m_n}.exception_name_{n,m_n}: B_n}
```
where A, B_j are protocols and i_{ij} are interfaces. If a `throw !exceptionname`$_{ij}$ is applied in A in a context

try { ... !A.a ...} catch {?i_{ij}.exception_name$_j$: ...:B_i},
then the next event generated by the try construct is the first event specified by
B_i. For simplicity, all the exceptions which could be thrown in the try construct
have to be listed exactly once in one of the catch parts of the construct.

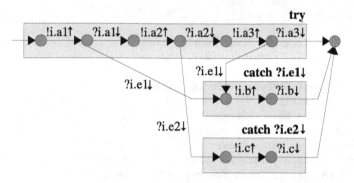

Fig. 5. Transition diagram

Influence on compliance evaluation. The exception-related constructs preserve the semantics of the operators defined for behavior protocols (in particular
the semantics of the composition and consent operators important for composition error detection and compliance evaluation[1,15]).

Unhandled (uncaught) exceptions are captured statically by the protocol
checker (information about the possible exceptions have to be a part of interface
specification in ADL). An improper/non-existent reaction to an exceptions is
typically captured as a bad activity error.

It can be easily shown that these constructs are without difficulty captured
by the LTS representing a behavior protocol. For example, the LTS representing

```
try { !i.a1; !i.a2; !i.a3}
catch { ?i.e1: !i.b}
catch { ?i.e2: !i.c}
```

can be easily constructed by adding transitions to the states representing the methods' calls in which e1 and e2 can be returned: these transitions will lead to the LTS
representation of the e1 and e2 handlers (Fig. 5). Since the resulting LTS remains
a finite automaton, the finite trace-based semantics of the behavior protocol operators is preserved.

4   Case Study

In this section, using again the example from Fig. 1, we illustrate how the
exception-related constructs simplify specification of exceptions in the behavior protocols of the components introduced in Sect. 2.

The frame protocol of the Ticket manager is shown below. The component
was already described in the Sect. 2; here we present a slightly more detailed

version which includes the initialization of other components and the check of the lookUp method return value.

```
––––––––––––––– Ticket manager frame protocol –––––––––––––––
?Usr.init { !Card.init; !DatM.init};
(
  ?Usr.buyTicket {
    try {
      !DatM.preReserve; !Card.lookUp;
      null + (!Card.payment; !DatM.reserve; !DatM.commit)
    }
    catch { ?DatM.PreReservationException:
      !Log.exEvent;}
    catch { ?Card.NetworkException:
      !DatM.cancel; !Card.revert;
      throw !NetworkException}
    catch { ?DatM.DatabaseException, ?DatM.ReservationException:
        !DatM.cancel; !Card.revert; !Log.exEvent };
    !Log.print;
  }
  +
  ?Usr.returnTicket {
    try { !Card.revert; !DatM.free; !DatM.commit }
    catch {?DatM.DatabaseException:
      !DatM.cancel; !Log.print}
  }
)*;
?Usr.finish {!DatM.finish; !Card.finish}
```

Below is the frame protocol of the VISA component. After being initialized by accepting an init call, the "business" stage takes place: lookUp, payment, and revert. The lookUp and payment methods may throw an exception due to the problem on the network (null + throw !NetworkException). The lookUp

```
––––––––––––––– VISA frame protocol –––––––––––––––
?Card.init;
(
  ?Card.lookUp {
    try { !Blacklist.verify }
    catch { ?BlackList.ListException: !Oper.askValidity};
    null + throw !NetworkException
  }
  +
  ?Card.payment {
    null + throw !NetworkException}
  +
  ?Card.revert
  )*;
?Card.finish
```

method also verifies the card number via the verify method on the Blacklist interface. If the verification yields a negative result, ListException is thrown and validity is re-checked by the operator (call of askValidity on the Operator interface).

In a similar vein, the frame protocol of Database manager indicates that the preReserve, reserve and commit methods can be alternatively called after initialization. All of them communicate with the Storage component via a !Strg.Access call which can return StorageException. Notice that this exception is converted to the PreReservationException resp. ReservationException consequently delivered to the caller of preReserve resp. of reserve or commit.

```
——————— Database manager frame protocol ———————
?DatM.init { !Strg.init };
(
  ?DatM.preReserve {
    try { !Strg.Access* }
    catch { ?Strg.StorageException:
      throw !PreReservationExcpetion}
  }
  +
  ?DatM.reserve {
    try { !Strg.Access* }
    catch { ?Strg.StorageException:
      throw !ReservationException}
  }
  +
  ?DatM.commit {
    try { !Strg.Access* }
    catch { ?Strg.StorageException:
      throw !ReservationException}
  }
  +
  ?DatM.cancel
)*;
?DatM.finish { !Strg.finish }
```

```
——————— Storage frame protocol ———————
?Strg.init;
(
  ?Strg.access { null + throw !StorageException}
)*;
?DatM.finish
```

The frame protocol of Reservation describes the communication with the environment of the whole reservation application. Notice that the exceptions which are thrown and handled inside the component are naturally not visible at this level, but NetworkException is propagated through the Reserv interface so that it has to appear in the frame protocol in the **throw** construct. On the other hand, ListException is handled in this frame protocol as **null}** since its handling does not require external component communication (as an aside, details of its handling are visible the VISA frame protocol - !BlackList.test is subsumed from VISA). In contrast, if a OperatorVerification component were outside Reservation (Fig. 6), details of ListException handling would be visible in the Reservation frame protocol, as illustrated in it by the comment line.

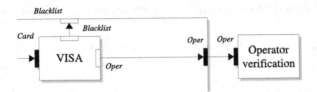

Fig. 6. Modified reservation component

```
 ─────────── Reservation frame protocol ───────────
?Reserv.init;
(
  ?Reserv.buyTicket {
    !Log.exEvent;
    !Log.print
    +
    (
      try { !BlackList.test }
      catch { ?BlackList.ListException: null};
              // catch { ?BlackList.ListException: !Oper.askValidity}
      (!Log.exEvent + null);
      !Log.print + throw !NetworkException
    )
  }
  +
  ?Reserv.returnTicket
)*;
?Reserv.finish
```

5   Evaluation

This work was inspired by our experience gained during our attempt to a apply behavior protocols to a non-trivial, real-life component-based application. We had chosen the Speedo project[22] available from the ObjectWeb consortium as an open source implementation of the Sun JDO specification[23]. The implementation is based on the FRACTAL component model[7] and is heavily using the Perseus persistence framework[14]. Together, behavior protocols of 26 components were written. Our experiences has been that without an explicit notation for exception handling, protocols are very hard to read and comprehend, and furthermore, the correspondence between the behavior specification and code is very hard to trace. We support this claim be the figures provided in Fig. 7. Here, the length of behavior protocol specification is given for four specific techniques of expressing exceptions via behavior protocols. The "Ignoring exceptions" techniques means specifying behavior in a way which does not consider exceptions at all. The "Explicit try-catch" technique is based on the behavior protocol extensions described in Sect. 3.2, while "Intrinsic exceptions" and "Approximation by alternative" are the methods described in Sect. 3.1.

Each bar of the graph is divided into two parts to indicate the number of lines specifying the "regular" behavior (gray) and exception-related behavior (black). From the chart it is clearly visible how significantly the proposed "Explicit try−catch" construct shortens behavior specification. Both "Approximation by alternative" and "Explicit try−catch" do not cause any significant grows of the "regular" part of the behavior specification, in contrast to the "Intrinsic exceptions" technique where often some of the specification sections have to be repeated. Notice also that "Approximation by alternative" causes grows of the exception-related behavior specification in comparison with "Explicit try−catch".

6 Related Work

There are many publications on exception handling, however not many of them are related to exceptions at a level of abstraction higher than source code.

In [20] the authors employ the C2 architectural style featuring composition contracts. Components have top and bottom interfaces connected via connectors responsible for routing and filtering asynchronous messages. There are two types of messages - a request message and a notification message depending on whether the message flows up or down though the system. This is very similar to our request-response notation. The composite contract (a service-implementing component) ends either with a normal notification or an exceptional notification. In the latter case, an exception handler component is activated. If the exception recovery is successful, an abort notification is generated; otherwise a failure no-

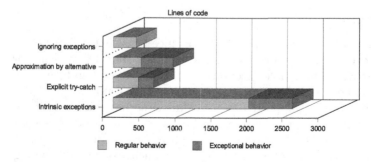

Fig. 7. Description complexity of the Speedo project formalism

tification is generated and the component may be left in an inconsistent state. In this approach, the contract component "remotely" corresponds to our `try` construct and exception component to the `catch` construct, however, the philosophy of component hierarchy is different compared to ours and there is no behavior specification at the level of the whole component.

The static source analyzing tool PREfast[13] checks all the execution traces for possible erroneous behavior (typically null reference, memory leaks). In the context of this paper, it is interesting that during exception propagation some (predefined) functional failures are detected, such as missing memory deallocation and resource unlocking. This property is checked by our approach implicitly - communication errors would be detected in the behavior composition process[3].

Session types are used for describing behavior of CORBA IDL in [24]. The approach of behavior description is similar to our interface protocol (protocols restricted to an interface), with a different syntax though. An exception is expressed in the specification of potential responses of a method. However, if the method can raise more exceptions, the same label is used for each of them.

A CSP based exception handling is introduced in [9]. The exception operator ($\overrightarrow{\triangle}$), is inspired by the CSP interrupt operator $\triangle_i$[10]. While $P\triangle_iQ$ means preemption of P on an externally coming event i and continuation by Q (i is the first event of Q), the exception operator considers in $P\overrightarrow{\triangle}Q$ the event i as an internal event and therefore Q can be interpreted as an exception handler and P as a `try` construct. Since in our proposed extension of behavior protocols the composition of two components' behavior also yields an internal action τe (one of the components throws an exception !e and another one accepts it via ?e in a `catch` construct), the approaches are similar in this respect. However, there are significant differences. In CSP, interrupts can occur without an intervention of the original process P, thus being similar to hardware interrupts. In our approach, an exception is triggered by invoking a method call and it has to be an expected event. Additionally, one catch block can handle more that one exception to avoid repeating of the same handling routine if an identical reaction is desirable. Also exception handling can be subject of compliance tests of both horizontal and vertical contracts (Sect. 2).

7   Conclusion

The key contributions of this paper include:

(i) An analysis of the role and importance of exceptions in behavior specification of software components is given and it is shown how behavior protocols can be extended to handle exceptions in an efficient way in terms of readability, comprehension, and the size of a behavior specification.

(ii) This claim is supported by providing experimental results from a real-life case study of applying different exception handling techniques based on behavior protocols. From these experiments, it is clearly visible how significantly the proposed behavior protocol extension by an explicit exception handling construct shortens the behavior specification of a non-trivial component-based application.

Acknowledgments

We would like to give a special credit to our colleagues Jiri Adamek and Vladimir Mencl for their valuable comments, and to Jan Kofron and Pavel Jezek for another non-trivial case study and a number of suggestions.

References

1. J. Adamek, F. Plasil: Component Composition Errors and Update Atomicity: Static Analysis, Journal of Software Maintenance and Evolution: Research and Practice 17(5), pp. 363-377, 2005
2. J. Adamek, F. Plasil: Erroneous Architecture is a Relative Concept, in Proceedings of SEA conference, Cambridge, MA, USA, ACTA Press 2004
3. J. Adamek, F. Plasil: Partial Bindings of Components − any Harm?, in the Proceedings of APSEC 2004, IEEE Computer Society, pp. 632−639, Nov 2004
4. L. de Alfaro, T. A. Henzinger: Interface Automata, in Proceedings of the 9th Annual ACM Symposium on Foundations of Software Engineering (FSE), 2001
5. R.J. Allen, D. Garlan: A Formal Basics For Architectural Connection, ACM Transactions on Software Engineering and Methology, Jul 1997
6. W. DePrince jr., C. Hofmeister: Enforcing a lips Usage Policy for CORBA Components, in proceedings of EUROMICRO'03, Sep 2003
7. Fractal component model: http://fractal.objectweb.org/
8. D. Harel: Statecharts: A Visual Formalism for Complex Systems, Science of Computer Programming 8, Elsevier Science Publishers B.V., 1987
9. G.H. Hilderink: Managing Complexity of Control Software through Concurrency, PhD thesis, University of Twente, The Netherlands, ISBN 90-365-2204-8, May 2005
10. C.A.R. Hoare: Communicating Sequential Processes, Prentice-Hall International, UK, Ltd., ISBN 0-13-153271-5, 1985
11. J. Magee, J. Kramer: Concurrency: State models & Java programs, John Wiley & Sons Ltd, ISBN 0-471-98710-7, 1999
12. Object Management Group: UML 2.0 Infrastructure Final Adopted Specification, OMG document ptc/03-09-15, Sep 2003
13. PREfast: http://www.microsoft.com/whdc/devtools/tools/PREfast.mspx
14. Perseus persistence framework: http://perseus.objectweb.org/
15. F. Plasil: Enhancing Component Specification by Behavior Description − the SOFA Experience, in Proceedings of the 4th WISICT 2005, A volume in the ACM, Computer Science Press, Trinity College Dublin, Ireland, pp. 185−190, Jan 2005
16. F. Plasil, S. Visnovsky: Behavior Protocols for Software Components, IEEE Transactions on Software Engineering, vol. 28, no. 11, Nov 2002
17. F. Plasil, S. Visnovsky, M. Besta: Bounding Behavior via Protocols, in Proceedings of TOOLS USA '99, 1999
18. R.H. Reussner, S. Becker, V. Firus: Component Composition with Parametric Contracts, Tagungsband der Net.ObjectDays, 2004
19. H.W. Schmidt, B. J. Kramer, I. Poernomo, R. Reussner: Predictable Component Architectures Using Dependent Finite State Machines, Proceedings of the 9th International Workshop in Radical Innovations of Software and Systems Engineering in the Future, LNCS Springer-Verlag, ISBN 3-540-21179-9, Vol 2941, 2004

20. R.M. Silva, P.A.C. Guerra, C.M.F. Rubira: Component Integration using Compositions Contracts with Exception Handling, in Proceedings of ECOOP2003 Workshop on Exception Handling in Object-Oriented Systems, TR 03-028 Univ. of Minnesota, Dept. of Comp.Sci., Jul 2003
21. SOFA project: http://sofa.objectweb.org/,
    http://nenya.ms.mff.cuni.cz/projects.phtml?p=sofa\&q=0
22. Speedo: http://speedo.objectweb.org/
23. Sun JDO specification: http://java.sun.com/products/jdo/
24. A. Vallecillo, V.T. Vasconcelos, A. Ravara: Typing the Behavior of Objects and Components using Session Types, 1st International Workshop on Foundations of Coordination Languages and Software Architectures. Electronic Notes in Theoretical Computer Science, 2002
25. K. Wallnau: Volume III: A Technology for Predictable Assembly from Certifiable Components, Technical Report CMU/SEI-2003-TR-009, Apr 2003

Coalgebraic Semantics for Component Systems

Sabine Glesner and Jan Olaf Blech

Institute for Software Engineering and Theoretical Computer Science,
Technical University of Berlin, FR 5-6, Berlin, Germany
http://pes.cs.tu-berlin.de/

Abstract. We propose a novel approach for defining the semantics of component systems coinductively. In particular, we formalize a framework for component systems within the theorem prover Isabelle/HOL. Using this formalization, we are able to formally reason about and verify aspects of component composition and interaction. Furthermore, we discuss strategies for adaptor code generation from a given component system specification. We demonstrate the applicability of our approach by a case study.

Keywords: Components, component interaction, semantics, verification, coinduction, Isabelle/HOL.

1 Introduction

Component-oriented system development has become a major approach in software engineering. However, most methodologies for constructing component systems are not able or not even intended to guarantee that the composed systems obtain a certain behavior. Especially in safety-critical application areas, this is not sufficient. In this paper, as a necessary basis for verification, we address the problem of defining a formal semantics for components and component systems. In particular, we aim for a semantics that allows for the definition of behavioral equivalence of components as well as entire component systems. Moreover, the semantics is required to deal with state-based computations as well as potential non-termination. Furthermore, we discuss strategies for constructing component systems from existing components and their services. Thereby, we focus on the generation of adaptor code from given specifications.

Our solution approach for the semantics of component systems is based on coalgebras and coinduction. In the last decade, coalgebraic methods have evolved as the method of choice for the specification of and reasoning about state-based computations, even if the systems potentially do not terminate. An element of a coalgebra can be thought of as a function that transforms a given state into successor states and also outputs possible oberservations. We model each component as well as also entire component systems as elements of suitable coalgebras. In the coalgebraic setting, systems can be verified as being behaviorally equivalent using coinduction, also known as bisimulation. Moreover, coalgebraic proof methods can be used for the verification of liveness and safety properties.

R.H. Reussner et al. (Eds.): Architecting Systems, LNCS 3938, pp. 245–261, 2006.
© Springer-Verlag Berlin Heidelberg 2006

Concerning the generation of adaptor code, we show that adaptor code can be understood as an interaction protocol between the components. In our setting, components together with their adaptor code are a component themselves, i.e., we deal with a recursive notion of components. We demonstrate the introduced principles in two examples, one dealing with a chocolate vending machine and one considering currency convertion in bank accounts.

Our specifications and correctness proofs are formulated within the Isabelle/ HOL theorem prover. Even though such a formal verification within a strict machine-based system is much more expensive than a "paper and pencil"-proof, it reduces the possibility of errors as much as possible and in particular ensures that no special cases have been overlooked. In this paper, we specify components and component systems coalgebraically by employing concepts from process algebras. Furthermore, we model semantic equivalence with bisimulations. In comparison to less expressive methods (as e.g. model checking or restricted first-order approaches as the B method [Abr96]), Isabelle's higher order logic (HOL) is more expressive and better suited for the specification of and reasoning about complex component systems.

The work described in this paper is a step towards a more general research goal which is depicted in Figure 1. In the desired setting, we start with a formal specification of the unified modeling language (UML) within Isabelle/HOL. Based on this specification, we want to model structure and interaction properties of component systems as well as their behavior via Statecharts. Then we want to transform such a UML specification of a component system into a process algebra. This transformation possibly abstracts from some structural issues. We can then transform this process algebra specification of the component system to a specification that is directly usable for Isabelle/HOL proofs. We want to conduct all the necessary formalizations and proofs completely within Isabelle/HOL. The transformations between UML, process algebras, and Isabelle/HOL must be semantics preserving. Therefore we need to make sure that the verified properties in the Isabelle/HOL representation do hold in the other representations as well. Note that this is only guaranteed if we verify the transformations between the three kinds of representations as well. In principle, we can generate code from all of those three kinds of component system representations. The generation from UML has been investigated in [BGL05]. In this paper, we concentrate on code generation from Isabelle/HOL specifications.

This paper is organized as follows: In Section 2, we give a short introduction to (co)algebras and (co)induction. This is a necessary prerequisite for our semantics and verification framework of component systems and their behavioral equivalence within the Isabelle/HOL theorem prover as described in Section 3. Strategies to generate adaptor code from a formal specification are discussed in Section 4. Section 5 describes our methodology for verifying safety and security properties by investigating the correctness of interaction protocols within the Isabelle/HOL theorem prover. Related work is discussed in Section 6. In Section 7 we draw conclusions and discuss possible directions of future work.

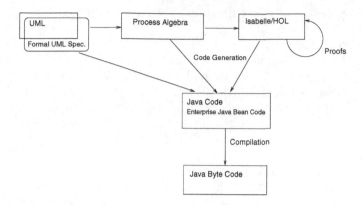

Fig. 1. From Specification to Code

2 (Co)Algebras and (Co)Induction

In recent years, coalgebraic methods, in particular coinduction, have gained increased interest and importance in the specification of and reasoning about state-based systems [JR97]. While induction is used to define and reason about elements of initial algebras, coinduction deals with final coalgebras. In Subsection 2.1, we start by providing a very gentle, intuitive motivation for coalgebras. Then we proceed in Subsection 2.2 by summarizing the most important concepts in this area. Afterwards, in Subsection 2.3, we introduce their representation in the theorem prover Isabelle/HOL.

2.1 A Gentle Motivation for Coalgebras and Coinduction

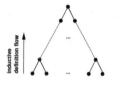  Elements in initial algebras can be understood as finite trees which are defined in the typical inductive way by specifying possible leaves and by specifying how existing subtrees can be composed to larger trees. The reverse definition direction is also possible and gives us the coinductive definition and proof principle. Starting at the root node of a tree, we specify how nodes are expanded by defining their children nodes. Since this expansion process does not need to terminate, it defines finite as well as infinite structures. Even though a tree might not be finite, it is well-defined in each finite depth. Coinductively defined structures are well-suited to define state transition systems. Therefore, we define an observation, the *state*, for each node. The root node of a coinductively defined, possibly infinite tree represents the initial state; successors of a node model possible successor states.

2.2   Coalgebras and the Coinductive Proof Principle

Algebras and coalgebras are defined with respect to functors. Given a functor T and a set X, a T-algebra is a set supplied with a T-structure, i.e. is defined as a function $a : T(X) \rightarrow X$. For example, the structure of the natural numbers is defined as an T-algebra $[0, S] : 1 + \mathbb{N} \rightarrow \mathbb{N}$ for the functor $T(X) = 1 + X$. *Initial T-algebras* are characterized by the fact that there exists a unique homomorphism f from the initial T-algebra into any other T-algebra. Initial T-algebras are the least fixed point of the functor T.

The functor notation is very precise yet short. If one thinks in the intuitive tree structures introduced in Subsection 2.1, it summarizes precisely the mapping from a set of children nodes to their parent node in the inductive case or, vice versa, from a node to its successor nodes in the coinductive case. While standard algebraic formalisms are based on a set of functions together with their arities for a given algebra, our functor notion here summarizes all these functions into one functor without mentioning the names of the individual functions but only their typing, i.e. the types of their input and output values. Hence, all T-algebras as well as all T-coalgebras agree on the input-output-typing of their functions.

Dually, T-coalgebras are defined as functions $c : X \rightarrow T(X)$. If one thinks of the elements in X as being states, then a coalgebra maps a given state $x \in X$ into one or several successor states together with observations that can be made in the state x. In this setting, a state-based system is characterized by the observations that can be made during its run. For example, a deterministic, not necessarily terminating transition system is described by a T-coalgebra $[stop, \langle value, next \rangle] : X \rightarrow T(X)$ for the functor $T(X) = 1 + A \times X$ where A is an arbitrary non-empty set of observations. Given a state $x \in X$, $[stop, \langle value, next \rangle](x)$ is either the terminating state $stop$ in which no observation is possible, or there exists the successor state $next(x)$ and the observation $value(x) \in A$.

When modeling components with coalgebras, each state during the run of a component corresponds to a state which is the input or output of a suitable coalgebra. Whenever transactions are performed on the component that potentially change its state, there is also a state transition in the coalgebra which transforms the corresponding input state to the corresponding output state together with observations describing this state. The exact typing of this mapping of input to output states is described by the functor of the coalgebra.

Final T-coalgebras, as the dual concept to initial algebras, are characterized by the existence of a unique homomorphism from any other T-coalgebra into the final T-coalgebra. For the functor $T(X) = 1 + A \times X$, the final coalgebra is $[empty, \langle head, tail \rangle] : A^\infty \rightarrow A \times A^\infty$. A^∞ is the set containing all finite and infinite sequences with elements from A. Final T-coalgebras, if they exist, are the greatest fixed point of the functor T. For polynomial functors and even for the finite power set functor, final coalgebras exist. Polynomial functors are completely sufficient for our purposes.

Coinduction is – as well as induction – a definition and proof principle. The definition principle uses the fact that homomorphisms from arbitrary T-coalgebras into the final T-coalgebra exist, while the proof principle uses their uniqueness.

Especially bisimulation is an important coinductive proof rule. It says that each binary relation on a final coalgebra that is closed under the operations of the coalgebra is contained in the equality relation. This proof principle can be used to show the equality of two state transition systems (for example components). For this purpose, one needs to define a suitable bisimulation relation and prove that the two state transition systems are contained in it.

2.3   Using Coalgebras and Coinduction in Isabelle/HOL

The coalgebraic type lazy list is available in Isabelle/HOL in the extension described in [Pau04]. This extension also provides basic lemmata and functions for using lazy lists in practical theorem proving. A lazy list is the coalgebraic datatype corresponding to the functor $T(X) = 1 + (A \times X)$. In an algebraic interpretation, this functor would define ordinary lists. Then, the "1" represents the empty list and the "$(A \times X)$" represents the concatenation of an element from the set A to an existing list from X. Thus, the algebraic interpretation defines finite lists by specifying how they can be successively constructed from the empty list. In the coalgebraic interpretation, the "1" represents the fact that no further state transition is possible, i.e. termination of the process. The "$(A \times X)$" models the case that a further state transition is possible, mapping a state from X to an element in A together with a new state contained in X. This element of A can be observed upon this state transition. Hence, the coalgebraic interpretation defines lazy, i.e. potentially infinite lists by exploring the state transitions step by step in a potentially infinite process. The elements of the list contain then the observations made during the state transitions.

The coalgebraic datatype lazy list is especially relevant to software engineering and component systems since it is a natural way to represent (potentially infinite) streams in the Isabelle/HOL system. Even though this coalgebraic kind of modeling comes in handy, it has been applied only rarely in existing works.

For reasoning about equality on coalgebraic types, one uses the concept of bisimulation. The lazy list package from [Pau04] provides predefined lemmata to show via bisimulation that two lazy lists are equal. A bisimulation relation is a binary relation $\sim$ on a coalgebraic type that is closed under the operations of the coalgebra. For lazy lists, this means that with[1] $CONS \; a \; l \sim CONS \; a \; l$, the following must also hold: $a = a$ and $l \sim l$. The last condition implies the fact that two empty lists must be bisimular.

If we want to show the equality of two lazy lists l_1, l_2 Paulson's lazy list package provides two lemmata: $llist\_equalityI$, $llistD\_Fun\_LCons\_I$ which do most of the technical work of reducing the equality problem to these two conditions which have to be proven manually:

- $l_1, l_2 \in R$ where R is the bisimulation relation which the user of the lazy list package has to provide manually.
- $(CONS \; a \; l, CONS \; a \; l) \in R \Rightarrow a = a \land (l, l) \in R$

---

[1] "$CONS \; a \; l$" adds an element a to the beginning of a list l, yielding a new list.

To use coalgebraically defined types, we need to be able to define not necessarily terminating recursive functions. For lazy lists, $llist\_corec$ allows us to define a function $a \longrightarrow b \; llist$ as follows where f is some partially defined function $f : a \rightharpoonup b \times a$ - e.g. a state transition function mapping a state to an observable part (lazy list element) and a succeeding state - and $_1$ and $_2$ the usual projection functions. The $[]$ denotes the empty (lazy) list, the $\#$ the concatination of an element to a (lazy) list.

$$llist\_corec \; x \; f = \begin{cases} [] & \text{if } f \; x = \bot \\ (f \; x)_1 \# llist\_corec \; (f \; x)_2 \; f & \text{else} \end{cases}$$

These formalizations are the basis for our coalgebraic framework for the semantics of software components and for our correctness proofs of transformations and the corresponding proof framework. Coalgebraic specification techniques provide a way for defining the semantics of component systems by modeling their state transition behavior, whereas coinduction and bisimulation, resp., allow us to compare component systems with respect to their observable behavior.

3   Semantics of Component Systems

In this section, we describe our semantics and proof framework for component systems together with an example. In Subsection 3.1, we introduce our general framework for the semantics of a component system. We characterize components as state transition systems via states and state transition functions. Based on this view, we define a trace semantics for a given component system by an element of a suitable final coalgebra. This corresponds also directly to our formalization of component systems within the theorem prover Isabelle/HOL. Subsection 3.2 deals with equivalence proofs for component systems. In Subsection 3.3, we present an example involving currency conversion.

3.1   Components as Coalgebras

A component is defined via a state and a state transition function. A component may encapsulate other components. Hence we have a hierarchical component concept. The state of an encapsulated component is part of the state of the top-level component. The state transition functions of the encapsulated components are called by the state transition function of the top-level component. Low level components have to communicate with each other via the top-level component. Such a top-level component may be regarded as the interaction protocol of low level components. An example component is sketched in Figure 2. Each component offers services which can be called from top-level components. These services do not necessarily need to terminate.

The semantics of such a component system is defined in an operational way as a trace semantics. Each component system must have a top-level component with a state transition function encapsulating the behavior of the component system. The signature of this state transition function defines a functor giving

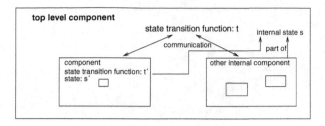

Fig. 2. Example Component

rise to a coalgebra that defines the semantics of the component system. In case of a deterministic state transition function, the functor generates infinite lists of states that represent the trace semantics of the component system. In case of a non-deterministic system, the state transition function may return several succeeding states to a given state. The corresponding functor generates a possibly infinite tree of state transitions.

Example 1 ((Non-Deterministic Component Systems and Coalgebraic Functors)). Consider a component system called "simple vending machine with user(s)". The machine may accept 50 (Euro) Cent coins and 1 Euro coins and delivers a chocolate bar whenever a complete Euro is inserted. The person(s) using this vending machine is the source of indeterminism of the component system. The machine may break down at any time. The behavior is – quite informally – depicted as a finite automaton in Figure 3.

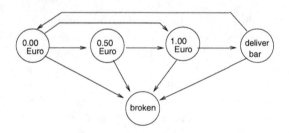

Fig. 3. Chocolate Automaton

In the state *0.00 Euro* the next state might be *0.50 Euro* if someone inserts a 50 Cent coin, *1.00 Euro* if someone inserts a 1 Euro coin or *broken* if the machine has a failure. In the *0.50 Euro* state only a 50 Cent coin may be inserted to reach the *1.00 Euro* state. In other cases the machine fails. After a complete Euro has been inserted, the machine delivers a chocolate bar or breaks down. Then we reach the *0.00 Euro* state again or once again the *broken* state might appear. A datatype that specifies the semantics of this automaton might be defined via the functor displayed in Figure 4: The + marks alternatives. Each alternative corresponds to a certain state of the automaton. The X specifies the next states that might be reached from such a state. The × groups elements that belong

$T(X) =$
  broken +
  0.00 EURO × X × X × X +
  0.50 EURO × X × X +
  1.00 EURO × X × X +
  deliver bar × X × X

Fig. 4. Functor for Chocolate Automaton

to a certain state. A functor defining a coalgebraic datatype is interpreted as a state observation. For example in the state *0.00 Euro*, "0.00 Euro" might be observed as well as three possible succeeding states denoted via the three X. One of them will be chosen non-deterministically in the next step. In a coalgebraic interpretation, the functor may be used to construct an infinite tree of states as depicted in Figure 5.

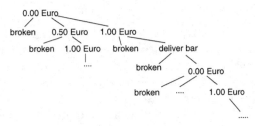

Fig. 5. Infinite State Tree

Note that the functor itself could also be interpreted algebraically. In this case, the system has to break down at a certain point in all possible use case scenarios because we construct algebraic datatypes beginning with the constructor that has no successors: *broken*. With the observational view of the coalgebraic interpretation, the system is allowed to run forever.

Note that this functor is not sufficient to specify the semantics of a system because this is done with a concrete state transition function. We do however specify a datatype, or more precisely a *process type*, whose instances might be used to represent the semantics of the system.   ◇

In most cases, we do not want the semantics to include all parts of the internal states of a component. Instead, we usually want the semantics to take care only of the observable parts of a state of a component. Hence we usually use an abstraction function and regard the semantics of a system as the infinite tree or list generated by the state transition functor consisting only of the observable parts of the internal states. For example, such an abstraction function might reduce an internal component state to the visible output of a component, i.e. to its behavior.

Note that one needs to take care that specifications do not overspecify systems but instead only contain the description of the essentials. Many details that are important from an implementation point of view, do not matter for verification and might even endanger verification efforts within automated theorem provers. Therefore, in our general component framework, we do not specify how components have to interact with each other as this would be such an overspecification. For most concrete component system specifications, we suggest to use a chanel mechanism as used in many process algebras, e.g. the Calculus of Communicating Sequential Processes (CSP) [Hoa85], FOCUS [BDD+92], or the π-calculus [Mil99].

3.2   Proving Components as Semantically Equivalent

Equality between coalgebraic structures is proved via bisimulation[2]. In order to prove the semantical equivalence of two component systems, we prove the equality of the coalgebraic structures representing their semantics. This can be accomplished by proving that they are in a bisimulation relation.

This means that we basically have to define a relation and have to prove that it is indeed a bisimulation relation. This relation contains tuples of corresponding or equal states, resp., of the two systems. To show that the coalgebraic structures representing the semantics are bisimilar, we have to show that

- the two start states of the component systems are in the bisimulation relation,
- each two states in every tuple in the relation are corresponding to each other or are equal, resp., and
- for each two states in every tuple in the relation the corresponding succeeding states are in the bisimulation relation again.

In the case of deterministic systems, Isabelle/HOL provides us with large libraries of preformalized datatypes and preproved lemmata and theorems [Pau04]. Hence, we only have to provide state transition functions, start states, and the bisimulation relation, and Isabelle/HOL will do the coalgebraic reasoning for us. Nevertheless, a formal equivalence proof of two systems may still be a very challenging task, since there are many details apart from the coalgebraic management of bisimulation that have to be done, e.g. proving algebraic transformations and properties of structures.

Note that in the examples and case studies described in this paper with their finite state character, it is also possible to construct Kripke structures with the help of the state transition function and do bisimulation in a "model checking" way [CGP99]. Nevertheless, coinductive techniques provide a better embedding into the theorem prover Isabelle/HOL since we do not have to provide the bisimulation rules as extra axioms. Moreover, our coalgebraic techniques can also be applied in more complex scenarios where systems cannot be described by a finite number of states.

---

[2] This requires us to restrict our semantics framework to coalgebraic structures which are elements of final coalgebras, cf. Section 2.2. For the systems with which we are dealing in this paper, this is no limitation.

3.3   Example: Currency Conversion Example

At the time when the Euro was introduced, in most parts of the European Union accounts were still operated using the old national currencies while customers could do transactions both in the national as well as in the new currency.

In this section we want to prove two components representing accounts operated in the old national currencies Deutsche Mark and French Francs as semantically equivalent. Starting with the same amount of money, the same Euro transactions are carried out on both accounts. The observable part of such an account state is the balance in Francs – since it is the most accurate – while both accounts internally operate using the national currency. Another part of the state is the number of the current transaction. For simplicity, we assume that 1 Euro is 2 Deutschmarks and 6 French Francs make 1 Euro.

These state transition functions describe the behavior of the accounts, cp. Figure 6. The transactions being performed are formalized as a function f taking the actual transaction number and returning an amount of money (negative or positive) to be added to or subtracted from the balance of the account.

$$\lambda(i, s).((Some\ (DM2Francs\ s, (i\ +\ 1, (Euro2DM\ (f\ i))\ +\ s))))$$

$$\lambda(i, s).((Some\ (s\ ,\ (i\ +\ 1, (Euro2Francs(f\ i))\ +\ s))))$$

Fig. 6. State Transition Functions

Each function takes a state consisting of the transaction number and the balance. It returns an observable state consisting of the balance in Francs and an internal state consisting of the next transaction number (+1) and the next balance in DM resp. Francs. The currency conversion functions are defined in Figure 7.

In order to prove two accounts – DM and Francs with the same transactions – semantically equivalent, we define a state trace and quantify over all possible transaction sequences f. The traces are represented in Isabelle/HOL by the coinductive structures lazy lists. The proof is carried out using bisimulation and predefined theorems and lemmata from [Pau04] as summarized in Subsection 3.2.

$$constdefs\ Euro2Francs\ ::\ int\ \Rightarrow\ int$$
$$Euro2Francs\ e\ \equiv\ (6\ *\ e)$$

$$constdefs\ Euro2DM\ ::\ int\ \Rightarrow\ int$$
$$Euro2DM\ e\ \Rightarrow\ (2\ *\ e)$$

$$constdefs\ DM2Francs\ ::\ int\ \Rightarrow\ int$$
$$DM2Francs\ e\ \Rightarrow\ (3\ *\ e)$$

Fig. 7. Currency Conversion Functions

---

theorem
(llist_corec (0, *s0*)
  (λ(*i*, *s*).((*Some* (*DM2Francs s*, (*i* + 1, (*Euro2DM* (*f i*)) + *s*)))))) =
(llist_corec ((0 :: *nat*), *DM2Francs s0*)
  (λ(*i*, *s*).((*Some* (*s* , (*i* + 1, (*Euro2Francs*(*f i*)) + *s*)))))))

apply (*rule_tacr* = {*e*.∃ *i s. e* =
(
(llist_corec (*i*, *s*)
  (λ(*i*, *s*).((*Some* (*DM2Francs s*, (*i* + 1, (*Euro2DM* (*f i*)) + *s*)))))),
(llist_corec (*i*, *DM2Francs s*)
  (λ(*i*, *s*).((*Some* (*s* , (*i* + 1, (*Euro2Francs*(*f i*)) + *s*)))))))
)
} *in llist_equalityI*)
apply clarify
apply force
apply clarify
apply (*subst llist_corec*)
apply (*subst llist_corec*)
apply simp
apply (*rule llistD_Fun_LCons_I*)
apply simp
apply (*simp add* : *Euro2Francs_def Euro2DM_def DM2Francs_def*)
apply force
done

Fig. 8. Component Equality Proof

The total proof is displayed in Figure 8. It is carried out using Isabelle's tactic-style. The listing in Figure 8 first states the theorem to be shown. Afterwards, a sequence of proof rule applications follows. Each of them starts with the key word "apply" followed by the name of the specific rule. Some of these rules are built-in in Isabelle, for example *apply clarify* or *apply simp*, and apply simple transformation rules of predicate logic to the proof goal. Other rules, for example *rule llistD_Fun_LCons_I*, apply user-supplied definitions or already proved lemmata and theorems to the proof goal.

This very simple and small example demonstrates how to use coinduction in Isabelle/HOL to prove system equivalence. It also provides a glimpse at how component systems can be specified in the Isabelle/HOL theorem prover. More complicated examples would be proved in a similar way concerning the coinduction part of the formalization.

4   Adaptor Code Generation

This section describes approaches for the automated generation of component implementations from their specifications as described in the previous section.

We particularly focus on top-level components as adaptors between lower-level components.

The specification of a top-level component describes the adaptor code between the lower-level components. In our coalgebraic formulation, the top-level component is defined as a state transition system that transfers control flow to one of its subcomponents depending on its current state. Besides that the number of possible states does not need to be finite, this kind of specification is similar to Statecharts. Hence, as a consequence, the approaches for code generation from Statecharts can be applied to coalgebraic component system specifications as well. In the remainder of this section, we discuss three major kinds of code generation strategies.

- *(Hierarchical) Switch/Case Loop* This most simple approach creates a nested switch/case statement that branches according to the current state and the current event. Within a branch, transition-specific code, i.e. the action associated with the transition, is executed and the current state is set to the target state of the transition. Hierarchical and concurrent structures can be achieved using recursion.

  Note that even though in our setting, there might be an infinite number of states, we are still able to generate a finite switch/case loop. Since the state transitions in a coalgebraic structure are defined by a finite number of transition rules, they can be transformed into a corresponding switch/case statement. There is only one requirement that needs to be fulfilled, namely that the predicates on the states, upon which the coalgebraic rules "fire", can be checked by decidable functions.

- *Table-driven approach* The second approach stems from a well-known method to implement finite state machines in compiler construction (e.g. scanner generation by the unix·tool "lex"). The actions caused by an event in a specific state are stored in a (nested) state/input table. In its most basic form, entries in this table might only consist of output symbols and successor states. When more complicated actions are used, more complex structures are necessary for the representation of state table entries, as demonstrated in [Zün02].

  Out of the same reasons as above (finite number of coalgebraic transition rules), this approach can also be applied in our setting in order to generate adaptor code in component systems.

- *Virtual Methods* Deeply nested switch/case blocks may not be desirable in an object oriented system. This is especially true when code generated from a Statechart is subject to manual modification and maintenance ("round-trip engineering"). An alternative method of code generation from Statecharts makes use of an extension of the state pattern [GHJV95]. In this method, each state becomes a class in an inheritance hierarchy created in parallel to the substate hierarchy of the statechart. The events consumed by these states are realized as virtual method calls to the respective state classes.

These are the basic strategies for code generation from Statecharts. A more detailed overview can be found in [Zün02]. [Was03] shows how hierarchical structuring information can be exploited to obtain smaller and more efficient code following the table-based strategy. It is subject of future work to further investigate the application of these strategies to the problem of generating executable code from formal coalgebraic specifications of component systems, given e.g. in the Isabelle/HOL theorem prover.

5   Verifying Properties of Interaction Protocols

We do not only want to compare component systems for equivalence and generate code from their specifications but also want to prove user-defined properties of such systems. For this purpose, in this section we describe how properties of interaction protocols can be verified within our coalgebraic specification and proof framework. As described in Section 3, the interaction protocol of a component system can be regarded as the top-level component containing all the other components. Hence the interaction protocol is specified with the state transition function of the top-level component. Section 3 describes how one can prove semantic equivalence of component systems. When verifying certain properties of interaction protocols, one usually does not need full semantic equivalence. However, as described earlier, it is possible to use abstractions that map the states appearing in a component system to an observable part. When verifying interaction protocols, we map the states to our desired properties, thus regarding them as the observable part of a state. Furthermore, we construct another abstract system that behaves like the desired properties and prove via bisimulation that this second abstract system and the abstraction of the system to be verified behave in the same way.

Example 2 (Verifying Invariant Preservation). A simple case of verifying systems against certain properties is the verification that a non-terminating deterministic system fulfills an invariant P. In this case, the observable part of a state is the boolean value of the predicate describing the invariant.

In our vending machine example, we may want to check that a customer may not insert more than one euro without breaking down the machine. In this case, the invariant looks like $balance_{state} \leq 1$ *Euro* $\lor$ *state* = *broken*.

As described in Section 2.3, we model the semantics of a deterministic system as a lazy list of states. Such a list is constructed with the help of a state transition function f denoting with its output value the successor of a given input state. A second function *llist_corec* constructs lazy state lists with the help of f. It needs furthermore a predicate that reduces states to their parts of interest and returns "Ture" if the property of interest holds in the reduction of a given state. *llist_corec* takes an initial state s_0, the predicate P, and the successor function f. *llist_corec* defines iteratively the state transition sequence by applying in a step-by-step fashion the predicate P to the current state and taking its resulting truth value in the result list and, furthermore, by recursively repeating this step with the successor state of the current state.

To prove the desired invariant, the resulting list of boolean values has to be equal to a lazy list consisting entirely of "True" values. The proof is conducted via *theorem*

$[[\forall s.\ P\ s \longrightarrow P\ (f\ s); P\ s_0]]$
  $\Longrightarrow$

llist_corec s_0 $(\lambda\ x.Some\ (P\ x, f\ x)) =$
llist_corec *True* $(\lambda\ x.Some\ (True, True))$

  apply $(rule\_tac\ r = \{e.\exists s.$
   $e = (llist\_corec\ s\ (\lambda\ x.\ Some\ (P\ x,\ f\ x)),$
   $list\_corec\ True\ (\lambda\ x.\ Some\ (True,\ True)))\wedge$
   $P\ s\ \}\ in\ llist\_equalityI)$
  apply force
  apply clarify
  apply $(subst\ l1)$
  apply simp
  apply $(rule\ llistD\_Fun\_LCons\_I)$
  apply auto
  done

Fig. 9. Invariants Theorem and Proof

bisimulation. The theorem in Figure 9 states that if we prove that the invariant holds for the initial state and prove that for each state where the invariant holds, it also holds in the succeeding state as well, then the lazy lists (system semantics abstracted to P's values, "True" values) are equal as well.

For our vending machine invariant, this means that it is sufficient to prove the following conditions:

- The customer has dropped less than one Euro through the coin slot of the vending machine in the initial state.
- For each successor of a state where there is one Euro or less chipped into the machine, there is one Euro or less in the machine in the next state. Otherwise the *broken* state is reached.

To prove the last condition, one has to make a case distinction over potentially succeeding states to a given state.

The proof of the displayed theorem in Figure 9 requires an additional auxiliary lemma $l1$ (also conducted within Isabelle/HOL, not shown here) that is applied in the proof step "*apply* $(subst\ l1)$". $\diamond$

Our approach is related to the way one verifies properties with a model checker. As in the case of model checking, we abstract from the concrete behavior and only consider the abstraction of interest. However we do not restrict expressions to logics like CTL so we have greater expressive power. Unlike a model checker, we do not need full state exploration since we can do state explorations symbolically using the proof principles that Isabelle/HOL provides. On the other hand this approach is less feasable for fully automated proving properties as it requires user interactions.

6   Related Work

Coalgebras have emerged during the last decade as logical foundation in the description of state-based computations and systems. An introduction to this field is e.g. given in [JR97]. Coalgebraic techniques have already been applied in the area of software engineering, cf. e.g. the work on the specification of object-oriented programming languages with coalgebraic methods using the theorem provers PVS and Isabelle [HHJT98, Hui01]. As to the authors' knowledge, this is the first work that introduces a coalgebraic notion of component semantics and component equivalence.

Also related to our approach are process algebras [BPS01], as coalgebras and coinduction are one possible logical foundation for process algebras. There have been several approaches of formalizing process algebras in Isabelle/HOL. The Calculus of Communicating Systems (CCS) has been specified (but not used for proofs) in [Röc01] within Isabelle/HOL. The Calculus of Communicating Sequential Processes (CSP) [Hoa85] has been formalized also in Isabelle/HOL, cf. [TW97]. In [Heu04], the application of the pi-calculus [Mil99] (without use of theorem provers) has been investigated in the aspect-oriented configuration and adaptation of component systems. Some work has been done to port coalgebraic datatypes to Isabelle/HOL [Pau04]. Our component model is similar to the way the FOCUS system specifies components [BDD+92]. It can be instantiated to formally reason about properties and transformations within this system.

An interesting approach to adaptor generation is given in [PdAHSV02]. They model adaptability via game theory to decide whether two components can interoperate. As a byproduct of a positive result, the adaptor is obtained.

In our own related work, we are also working on verified transformations from Statecharts (as a major specification mechanism for component behavior) to higher programming languages [BGL05].

7   Conclusions

In this paper, we have introduced a methodology to formally specify and reason about the semantics of components and component systems. Based on coalgebraic notions, our semantics specifies component behavior via state transition systems and is in particular able to also define semantics for non-terminating systems. Moreover, we have shown that equivalence of component systems can be verified by coinduction, a proof principle that is also known as bisimulation.

We have formalized our coalgebraic framework for the state-based semantics of component systems within the theorem prover Isabelle/HOL. Moreover, by using our exemplary case study, we have demonstrated how correctness proofs for component systems can be conducted within Isabelle/HOL.

Concerning future work, our methodology for the semantics of component systems is a necessary prerequisite for the verification of desired properties of system behavior as well as for the verification of the correctness of component system constructions, transformations, optimizations and modifications.

Moreover, in future work, we want to work on methods for the generation of components and component systems, in particular for the generation of adaptor code, from given coalgebraic specifications.

Acknowledgment. We would like to thank Lars Gesellensetter for many valuable discussions.

References

[Abr96]   Jean-Raymond Abrial. The B-Book, 1996.

[BDD+92]   Manfred Broy, Frank Dederich, Claus Dendorfer, Max Fuchs, Thomas Gritzner, and Rainer Weber. The Design of Distributed Systems - An Introduction to FOCUS. Technical Report TUM-I9202, Technische Univerität München, 1992.

[BGL05]   Jan Olaf Blech, Sabine Glesner, and Johannes Leitner. Formal Verification of Java Code Generation from UML Models. In *Proceedings of the 3rd International Fujaba Days 2005: MDD in Practice*. Technical Report, University of Paderborn, September 2005.

[BPS01]   Jan A. Bergstra, Alban Ponse, and Scott A. Smolka, editors. *Handbook of Process Algebra*. Elsevier, 2001.

[CGL93]   E.M. Clarke, O. Grumberg, and D. Long. Verification Tools for Finite-State Concurrent Systems. In J.W. de Bakker, W.-P. de Roever, and G. Rozenberg, editors, *A Decade of Concurrency – Reflections and Perspectives*, pages 124–175. Springer, Lecture Notes in Computer Science, Vol. 803, 1993.

[CGP99]   Edmund M. Clarke, Orna Grumberg, and Doron A. Peled. *Model Checking*. The MIT Press, 1999.

[GHJV95]   Erich Gamma, Richard Helm, Ralph Johnson, and John Vlissides. *Design patterns: elements of reusable object-oriented software*. Addison-Wesley Longman Publishing Co., Inc., Boston, MA, USA, 1995.

[Heu04]   Dirk Heuzeroth. *Aspektorientierte Konfiguration und Adaption von Komponenteninteraktionen*. PhD thesis, Universität Karlsruhe, 2004.

[HHJT98]   Ulrich Hensel, Marieke Huisman, Bart Jacobs, and Hendrik Tews. Reasoning about Classes in Object-Oriented Languages: Logical Models and Tools. In Chris Hankin, editor, *Programming Languages and Systems - ESOP'98, 7th European Symposium on Programming, Held as Part of the European Joint Conferences on the Theory and Practice of Software, ETAPS'98*, pages 105–121, Lisbon, Portugal, 1998. Springer Verlag, Lecture Notes in Computer Science, Vol. 1381.

[Hoa85]   C.A.R. Hoare. *Communicating Sequential Processes*. Prentice Hall International, 1985.

[Hui01]   Marieke Huisman. *Reasoning about Java programs in higher order logic using PVS and Isabelle*. PhD thesis, Faculty of Science, University of Nijmegen, 2001.

[JR97]   Bart Jacobs and Jan Rutten. A Tutorial on (Co)Algebras and (Co)Induction. *EATCS Bulletin*, 67:222–259, 1997.

[Mil99]   Robin Milner. *Communicating and Mobile Systems: the pi-Calculus*. Cambridge University Press, 1999.

[Pau04]   Lawrence C. Paulson. A Fixedpoint Approach to (Co)Inductive and
               (Co)Datatype Definitions, 2004.   available at www.cl.cam.ac.uk/
               Research/HVG/Isabelle/dist/Isabelle2004/doc/ind-defs.pdf.
[PdAHSV02]   Roberto Passerone, Luca de Alfaro, Thomas A. Henzinger, and Al-
               berto L. Sangiovanni-Vincentelli. Convertibility verification and con-
               verter synthesis: two faces of the same coin. In *ICCAD '02: Proceedings
               of the 2002 IEEE/ACM international conference on Computer-aided
               design*, pages 132–139, New York, NY, USA, 2002. ACM Press.
[Röc01]   Christine Röckl. *On the Mechanized Validation of Infinite-State and
               Parameterized Reactive and Mobile Systems*. PhD thesis, Technische
               Universität München, 2001.
[TW97]   Haykal Tej and Burkhart Wolff. A Corrected Failure Divergence Model
               for CSP in Isabelle/HOL. In *FME '97: Proceedings of the 4th Inter-
               national Symposium of Formal Methods Europe on Industrial Applica-
               tions and Strengthened Foundations of Formal Methods*, pages 318–337,
               London, UK, 1997. Springer-Verlag.
[Was03]   Andrzej Wasowski. On efficient program synthesis from statecharts.
               In *LCTES '03: Proceedings of the 2003 ACM SIGPLAN conference on
               Language, compiler, and tool for embedded systems*, pages 163–170, New
               York, NY, USA, 2003. ACM Press.
[Zün02]   A. Zündorf. Rigorous Object Oriented Software Development with
               Fujaba. Unpublished draft, 2002.

A Type Theoretic Framework for Formal Metamodelling

Iman Poernomo

Department of Computer Science, King's College London Strand,
London, WC2R2LS
iman@dcs.kcl.ac.uk

Abstract. The Object Managment Group's Meta-Object Facility
(MOF) [19] is a semiformal approach to writing models and metamodels (models of models). It works according to a model/metamodel hierarchy, where software is specified by models, models are defined as
instances of metamodels, which are, in turn, defined as instances of the
MOF meta-metamodel. By writing models and metamodels in a common
framework, the MOF meta-metamodel, it is easier to perform systematic
model/metamodel interchange and integration. However, the approach
is only useful if metamodels are correctly specified – a single error in a
metamodel specification will result in the propagation of errors throughout instantiating models and final model implementations. An important
open question is how to develop provably correct metamodels.

This paper applies constructive type theory to formalize the MOF
metamodelling approach. The benefit of the formalization is that correct
typing corresponds to provably correct metamodels and models. Because
the MOF is the central technology behind the Model Driven Architecture
initiative [18], our work is intended to lay a formal foundation for making
Model Driven Architecture more trustworthy.

1 Introduction

This paper applies constructive type theory to formalize the class/object-based
approach to metamodelling with the Object Managment Group's Meta-Object
Facility (MOF) specification [19]. The benefit of the formalization is that correct
typing corresponds to "provably correct" models and metamodels (models of
models). A intended application of this approach is to lay a formal foundation
for making Model Driven Architecture [18] more trustworthy.

The MOF is a semiformal approach to writing metamodels and describing
model transformations. It works according to a model/metamodel hierarchy,
where software is specified by models, models are defined as instances of metamodels, which are, in turn, defined as instances of the MOF meta-metamodel.
By writing models and metamodels in a common framework, the MOF meta-
metamodel, it is easier to perform systematic model/metamodel interchange and
integration. However, this is only useful if metamodels are correctly specified – a
single error in a metamodel specification will result in the systematic introduction of errors throughout instantiating models and final model implementations.

R.H. Reussner et al. (Eds.): Architecting Systems, LNCS 3938, pp. 262–298, 2006.

An important open question is how to develop provably correct metamodels for use. This question is important as the MOF is the central technology behind the MDA initiative.

In this paper, we exploit the higher-order nature of constructive type theory to uniformly treat the semantics of models, metamodels and the MOF model itself. It is well-known that constructive logic corresponds to lambda calculus with dependent sums and products, where proofs can be represented as lambda terms, formulae as types and proof inference corresponds to type inference. This property is known as the Curry-Howard isomorphism (see, e.g., [7, 8, 22]). By utilizing the Curry-Howard isomorphism, it is possible to define a notion of metamodel and model correctness in type theoretic terms.

This work is guided by the principle of interoperability with MOF-based industrial tools and techniques for metamodelling. It is possible to develop a mathematically elegant form of metamodelling within higher-order type theory simply by developing types of software models on an *ad hoc* basis. For instance, it is possible to define a type that classifies all UML models, or a type that classifies all relational database schemata. However, such types are not related and need to be written by hand for each metamodel. The advantage of the MOF is that it is generic enough to encode a wide range of metamodels. Our goal is to preserve this genericity by encoding the MOF model itself and then by generating a type for a metamodel from its MOF encoding. This way, all MOF-based metamodels will automatically have corresponding types in the CTT. This approach becomes important when developing notions of provably correct metamodels and models.

The paper proceeds as follows. Section 2 describes a core fragment of the MOF and explains how it may be used to write metamodels. Section 3 describes our constructive type theory and details the Curry-Howard isomorphism and related notions. Section 4 describes our type theoretic encoding of the MOF. Conclusions and a discussion of future work is provided in section 5.

This paper assumes the reader is familiar with the UML representation of classes, class relationships and class objects. We use these terms assuming an underlying UML-style representation. We do not assume reader familiarity with the MOF or with constructive type theory.

2   The MOF

A metamodel is a model of models: a modelling language. The Meta-Object Facility (MOF) is the Object Management Group (OMG) standard for defining metamodels [19]. Central to the MOF specification is the MOF meta-metamodel (hereafter referred to as the MOF model), a language for defining metamodels.

The MOF standard employs UML-style object-oriented classifier/object instantiation terminology to define the MOF model, metamodels and to comprehend the relationship between metamodels and and models. The UML visual syntax is often employed as a convenient means to describe the MOF model and metamodels. However, other notations are permitted – for example, the MOF standard includes an XML XMI-based textual syntax.

In this section, we describe a core fragment of the MOF model and explain how it can be used to define metamodels. We follow the MOF document [19], defining a syntax for writing metamodel grammars together with an informal, English language semantics. In Section 4, we shall formalize this fragment within type theory. The fragment is sufficiently complex to illustrate how our approach can be extended for the whole of the MOF.

2.1 Metamodelling in the MOF

Metamodelling in the MOF is done according to a 4 level hierarchy, as depicted in Fig. 1:

- The M_0 level consists of model instances. These might be data values, instantiated class objects, instantiated database tables, algorithms, XML code or function definitions.
- The M_1 level consists of models, which may also be considered as metamodel instances. This level includes elements such as UML diagrams, class, module and type declarations, database table declarations or XML schema.
- The M_2 level consists of metamodels, which may also be considered as MOF model instances. This level consists of metamodel descriptions, defining the syntax and semantics of M_1 elements. This level includes languages such as the UML, the XML, Java, the lambda calculus or *Casl*.
- The M_3 level is the MOF language itself, used to define M_2 level elements.

The MOF language is intended to be its own metamodel. This levels above M_3, which can be defined using the language of M_3. In type theoretic terminology, the MOF language is impredicative. Impredictative type theories have a history of

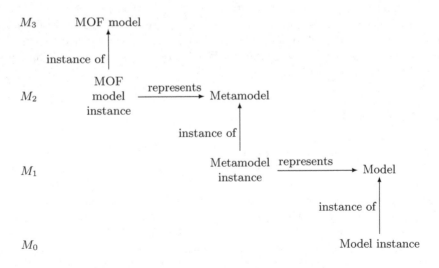

Fig. 1. Relationships between the four levels of the MOF

inconsistency, Frege's original formulation of set theory and Martin-Löf's original impredictative type theory being famous examples. The MOF approach does not suffer from this problem, as its impredicative nature is informally specified in [19] and, in practice, it is rare to need more than the 4 levels of the hierarchy. However, another good reason for formalizing the MOF within a type theory is to make sure a consistent interpretation exists!

The levels are related by a class/object instantiation relationship. Elements of level M_{i+1} provide type description of level M_i objects. The objects instantiate their corresponding elements. Class/object instantiation is fundamental to the MOF hierarchy. UML-style classes, class associations or class object can be defined at any level in the hierarchy, to serve different purposes. For instance, in the MOF, classes at the M_3 are used to type modelling languages, while classes at the M_2 level are used within modelling languages to type models.

An important aspect of the MOF hierarchy is that M_1 and M_2 level information can be encoded in two separate ways: as model elements *or* object instances. This enables the MOF to consider types also as forms of data:

- The MOF language is defined by a set of related model elements at the M_3 level.
- A metamodel is defined at the M_2 level by a set of MOF objects that instantiate the MOF model elements. This MOF object representation of a metamodel can also be rewritten as a M_2 metamodel that provides type descriptions via a set of model elements.
- Then, a model at the M_1 level is understood as a set of elements that instantiate the classifiers of an M_2 level metamodel. Finally, these M_1 level elements can be rewritten to form M_1 level model classifiers that specify the required form of an M_0 level model instantiation.

2.2   The MOF Model

The M_3 level MOF model consists of a set of associated M_3 level classes, "meta-metaclasses", hereafter referred to as MOF classes. The MOF classes classify the kinds of elements that make up a M_2 level metamodel.

Fig. 2 provides a UML-style visualization for the simplified fragment of the MOF model we consider. The fragment consists of several associated MOF classes: metaclassifiers, metaclasses, attributes, association ends, associations and constraints.[1] Each of these classes defines a type structure that must be conformed to by instantiating M_2 objects.

Metamodels are collections of associated M_2 instances of these MOF classes, in the same sense that, for example, a collections of M_0 UML objects represent an instance of a M_1 UML clas diagram.

---

[1] We have simplified the full MOF model by omitting a range of classes that help in metamodel construction. For instance, we have omitted the MOF classs for defining operations and references to associated metaclasses. However, from our treatment of the fragment, it should be easy to infer how we would extend the formalization described in this paper to the entire MOF model.

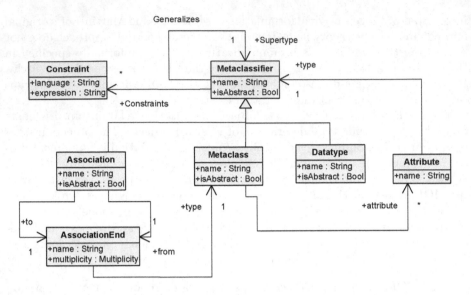

Fig. 2. A core fragment of the MOF model

The class diagram of Fig. 2 defines the *structure* of MOF metamodels – their types and relationships. However, the MOF model also includes a *semantics*, consisting of constraints that must apply to any instances of the type structure. This semantics could be integrated within the class diagram by associating constraints as notes with MOF classes. However, it is more convenient to describe the semantics in a separate, detailed documentation of the MOF classes, which we now provide.

Definition 1. The MOF is a language for writing modelling languages, and consists of a set of associated M_3 level classes, called `MetaClassifier`, `MetaClass`, `Datatype`, `Attribute`, `Association`, `AssociationEnd` and `Constraint`.

Remark 1. When formalizing the MOF class structure defined by the MOF model in Fig. 2, we shall interpret navigatable associations between MOF classes in the same way as attribute fields. That is, if class A is associated with class B such that B can be navigated via an association end *endName* of multiplicity $1..n$, will say that class A instances contain $1..n$ instances of class B. We shall do the same when formalizing metamodel class structures.

Definition 2 (MetaClassifier). The M_3 MOF class `MetaClassifier` is an abstract MOF class, used to categorize a common structure inherited by its subclasses, such as `MetaClass`, `Attribute` and `Association`. Its structure includes the following elements:

- A `name` attribute of type `string` that identifies the name of the classifier instance.
- A boolean valued `isAbstract` attribute, that determines if the classifier instance is abstract or not within an inheritance hierarchy. (Abstraction treated in the object-oriented sense: classifiers can be associated with operations that need not have full implementation details if the `isAbstract` attribute is true. In this paper we will not deal with operations and will deal only with concrete classifiers.)
- An associated collection `constraints` of elements of type `Constraint`, defining the required behaviour of M_1 level instances of M_2 `MetaClassifier` metaobjects.

A M_2 level `MetaClassifier` instance must satisfy the following constraints:

1. A classifier cannot be its own direct or indirect supertype.
2. The names of the any of the attributes of a classifier should not collide with the names of the attributes of any direct or indirect supertype.

Remark 2. All MOF classes are associated with a set of `Constraint` classes. A constraint defines how an *instance* of its associated MOF entity is to behave. For example, instances of `Datatype` might be associated with a constraint that defines its range of values.

Definition 3 (Constraint). The `Constraint` class consists of two attributes:

- The language of the constraint, `language`.
- The constraint itself, `expression`, written in the language `language`.

Remark 3. The MOF permits constraints to be assocated with any of the elements of a metamodel. These can be written in an informal language like English or a formal language such as the Object Constraint Language (OCL).

Remark 4. The MOF model employs constraints in two distinct ways:

1. The MOF model itself has a set of constraints that are defined for each of its classes. These constraints define a semantics of the model that specifies how M_2 metamodels must behave.
2. Also, the model contains a class called `Constraint` that is associated with all other classes of the model. Instances of this class are used to write a semantics for M_2 metamodels that, in turn, is used to specify how M_1 instantiating models must behave.

Definition 4 (Metaclass). Instances of the `MetaClass` class are the metaclasses that make up a metamodel description. The M_3 `MetaClass` class defines the type structure that must be adhered to by all M_2 `MetaClass` instances. The `MetaClass` class inerhits from `MetaClassifier`, and so includes the latter class's fields in its structure. The structure also includes references to an associated collection `attributes` of instances of MOF class `Attribute`.

   The semantics of a class is given by a range of constraints, including (1) and (2) of Definition 2, inherited from `MetaClassifier`. For the sake of illustration, we will consider the following additional constraint for `MetaClass`:

1. No two attributes have the same name.

Definition 5 (Datatype). Instances of the `Datatype` class are the datatypes that make up a metamodel description. The M_3 `Datatype` class defines the type structure that must be adhered to by all M_2 `Datatype` instances. The `MetaClass` class inherits from `MetaClassifier`, and so includes the latter class's fields in its structure and its constraints. In addition, there is the following additional constraint for `MetaClass`:

1. No datatype is abstract.

Remark 5. A metamodel uses datatypes as instances of the `Datatype` class. Their semantics should be described using instantiated `Constraint` elements. For example, integers are given by the MOF object `Integer` in Fig. 3, where the expression defining the what an `Integer` represents, `IntegerDefinition.expression` (abbreviated `integerDef`) is the following constraint, written in English:

The type `Integer` denotes the subrange of integers from -2^{31} to $+2^{31}-1$.

Fig. 3. Example of a constraint associated with a MOF class object

Definition 6 (Attribute). Instances of the `Attribute` class are to be used as attributes of metaclasses. The M_3 `Attribute` class defines the type structure that must be adhered to by all M_2 `Attribute` instances. The `MetaClass` class inerhits from `MetaClassifier`, and so includes the latter class's fields in its structure. Attributes must also have the following fields

 - An attribute type `type`, whose value is any `MetaClassifier` instance.
 - A boolean visibility property, that specifies if the attribute is public or private.

Definition 7 (Association End). Instances of the `AssociationEnd` class represent encapsulate a reference to a metaclass that might be used by an association within a metamodel description. Association ends must also have the following fields:

 - An association end name `name`.
 - A `type` whose value is a `Metaclass`.
 - An integer association multiplicity `multiplicity`.

For our purposes, we will not consider any constraints upon association ends.

Definition 8 (Association). Instances of the `Association` class are associations between metaclasses of a metamodel description. The `Association` class inerhits from `MetaClassifier`, and so includes the latter class's fields in its structure. Associations must also have the following fields:

- An `AssociationEnd` value `from`, denoting the domain of the association.
- An `AssociationEnd` value `to`, denoting the range of the association.

The semantics of an association must satisfy the following constraints:

1. Associations do not have supertypes (the `generalizes` attribute must be empty).
2. The values for `isLeaf` and `isRoot` on an Association must be true.
3. An Association cannot be abstract.
4. Associations must have `visibility` of `public`.

2.3   Object-Based and Class-Based Representation of Metamodels

The class definitions above identify the types of elements used to define a metamodel within the MOF. A metamodel is then represented in the MOF via a collection of associated MOF class object instances. These instances are M_2 level objects.

Definition 9 (Metamodel). A *metamodel* M is a set of `MetaClassifier`, `MetaClass`, `Datatype`, `Attribute`, `Association`, `AssociationEnd` and `Constraint` M_2 level objects. Objects within M may only refer to each other.

Example 1 (Access rights metamodel). We will use the following example of a metamodel throughout this paper. Consider a fragment of a component metamodel dealing with component access rights. Components are computational entities. Each component has an access level consisting of an integer value, signifying its accessibility (0 meaning public, 1 meaning restricted, 2 meaning more restricted, etc). A component A can use another component B, provided A's access level is higher than B's.

The metamodel for this can be defined as the collection of MOF class objects given in Fig. 4. Objects `COM` and `AccessPolicy` of class `Metaclass` are used to denote components and access levels respectively. Objects `A1` and `A2` of type `Association` are used to define the association of access levels to components and the usage association between components respectively, with the various `AssociationEnd` objects used to name and provide multiplicities for these associations. The `AccessPolicy` metaclass object has one attribute, called "Level", whose type is an integer.

Objects of class `Constraint` are not depicted in the metamodel for reasons of space. The `COM` object is associated with a single `Constraint` object `usageRights`, such that `usageRights.language` is English and `usageRights.expression` is

> A component `A` instance of `COM` with an `AccessPolicy` instance a can use another component instance B of `COM` with an `AccessPolicy` instance b, provided a's `level` is greater than b's level.

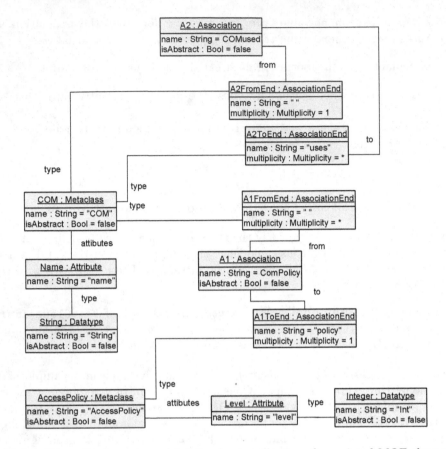

Fig. 4. Example of a metamodel defined as a collection of associated MOF classes

Remark 6. The example metamodel definition above is typical of the kind built using the MOF specification. A purely syntactic definition of a metamodel grammar is provided, but conformance to the MOF specification itself is not formally guaranteed. In this sense, metamodels are not proved correct with respect to MOF conformance (the "semantics" of the MOF). Two problems that can arise if metamodels are defined without a formal guarantee of correctness: 1) metamodels might not actually satisfy the constraints imposed by the MOF, leading to interoperability problems when several metamodels are used, as in the case of a MDA style metamodel translation definition; 2) if metamodels are not correct, then model instances of metamodels will be badly formed. The analogy is to a situation where we try to do mathematics with sets that are defined informally: if we define the integers informally and forget to include a notion of the number 0 and the successor function, and define addition incorrectly as multiplication, then it will be difficult to 1) use the integers correctly in mathematics with other sets and 2) the numbers that we form will probably not actually be integers.

One of the benefits of the formalization of the MOF within constructive type theory is that we will then have a mathematically elegant notion of provably correct metamodels.

2.4 Class-Based Depiction of Metamodels

As can be seen from the example above, even with a small metamodel, the definition of the metamodel using M_2 objects is ungainly (to put it diplomatically). However, this problem is addressed within the MOF as our M_2 level MOF objects have an equivalent represented as M_2 level classes.

When considering a metamodel as a model of models, we need to use this data to classify models. The MOF again employs a form of UML syntax to achieve this. Metamodels have another equivalent representation, as M_2 level *classes*, whose M_1 level object instances are *models*.

Definition 10 (Class-based representation of a metamodel). Given a metamodel MO represented as a set of M_2-level objects, we can build an *equivalent* representation MC as a set of M_2 classes, as follows.

Each `Metaclass` M_2 object o in MO corresponds to a M_2 class toClass(o), whose attributes are such that, for each `Attribute` object a in o.attributes, c should contain an attribute declaration of the form

$$* \; \texttt{a.name : a.type}$$

where $*$ is $+$ if a.visibility is `public`, and $-$ if a.visibility is `private`.

For each `Association` object a in MO, there is an association in the metamodel MC between the class toClass(a.to.type) and the class toClass(a.from.type). The name of the association is a.name, and the names of its ends and their multiplicities are taken from a.to and a.from in the obvious way.

Each `Constraint` object associated with an object o is mapped to a *note* that is associated with toClass(o). The contents of the note are the same as the contents of the constraint.

We call MC the class-based representation of MO.

Remark 7. A class-based representation is important as it explains clearly how the metamodel is used as a typing structure for M_1 level models.

Example 2 (Class-based representation of the access rights metamodel). The class-based representation of the access rights metamodel of Example 1 is given in Fig. 5. The representation is obtained from Definition 10. Each `Metaclass` object is represented as a M_2 level class whose name is the object's name, with each associated `Attribute` object corresponding to an attribute of the class, and each `Association` object corresponding to an association. The constraint object `usageRights` corresponds to a note that is associated with the `COM` class, containing the object's expression as a constraint on instances of `COM`.

As can be seen from this example, a class-based representation of a metamodel is easier to read than an object-based representation. However, it is important

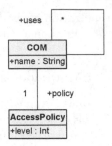

Fig. 5. The class-based representation of the access rights metamodel of Fig. 4

to note that, according to the MOF, not every collection of M_2 level classes defines a metamodel. To be valid, a metamodel must also have an object-based representation that instantiates the MOF model.

The dual representation of metamodels is often left implicit when using the MOF. Users generally employ the class-based notation, with the assumption that an object-based representation is available. However, for the purposes of formalizing the notion of a MOF metamodel, it is essential that we understand both representations and their relationship.

3   Constructive Type Theory

This section presents a brief summary of the constructive type theory (CTT) that shall be used to formalize the MOF and MDA in the next section. We define a version of Martin-Löf's predicative type theory with dependent sum and product types [17], and explain how the Curry-Howard isomorphism and proofs-as-programs methods enable the synthesis of correct programs from proofs using the CTT.

3.1   Typed Lambda Calculus

The lambda calculus is a formal system for defining and applying functions. It permits anonymous functions through variable abstraction and has a simple operational semantics provided by reduction rules. Functional programming languages such as Lisp, Scheme or Haskell are based upon the lambda calculus. Types are useful in programming, as they constrain the kinds of values that a function can input and output, permitting compile time type checking, ensuring safer programs. The simply typed lambda calculus provided a type theory for determining how types can be associated with lambda terms. It considers the kinds of type that are commonly used in programming: functional types, disjoint unions and products. We shall define a lambda calculus that extends the simply typed calculus with two additional typing constructs: dependent products and sums. These are powerful typing constructs that enable typing of parameterized relationships within functions and pairs, and, as we shall see, enable the proofs-as-programs notions.

$$
\begin{array}{lll}
a, b, c ::= & & PT \\
\quad x & & \text{varible } x \in Var \\
\quad \lambda\, x.\, a & & \text{abstraction} \\
\quad (a\ b) & & \text{application} \\
\quad \langle a, b \rangle & & \text{pair} \\
\quad \mathsf{fst}(a) & & \text{first projection} \\
\quad \mathsf{snd}(b) & & \text{second projection} \\
\quad \mathsf{inl}(a) & & \text{in left} \\
\quad \mathsf{inr}(b) & & \text{in right} \\
\quad \mathsf{match}\ a\ \mathsf{with}\ \mathsf{inl}(x) \Rightarrow b \mid \mathsf{inr}(y) \Rightarrow c & & \text{case} \\
\quad \mathsf{abort}(a) & & \text{abort} \\
\quad \mathsf{show}(v, a) & & \text{witness, } v \in Terms \\
\quad \mathsf{select}\ (a)\ \mathsf{in}\ y.x.b & & \text{select, } y \in Var,\ x \in Var
\end{array}
$$

Fig. 6. Syntax of the terms PT for our lambda calculus

Lambda calculus. We work with a lambda calculus whose core set of terms, PT, are given in Fig. 6. The grammar is defined with respect to a denumerable set of variables, Var.

We have the usual notions of free and bound variables of the lambda terms of PT.

Definition 11 (Free and bound variables of PT). Let x be any variable of Var, and t a term of PT. Then, x is *bound* in t if there is a subterm of t of the form

$$\lambda\, x : s.\, b$$

or

$$\mathsf{match}\ a\ \mathsf{with}\ \mathsf{inl}(x) \Rightarrow b \mid \mathsf{inr}(y) \Rightarrow c$$

or

$$\mathsf{match}\ a\ \mathsf{with}\ \mathsf{inl}(y) \Rightarrow b \mid \mathsf{inr}(x) \Rightarrow c$$

If x is not bound in t, then x is free in t. We write $BV(t)$ for the set of all bound variables of t, and $FV(t)$ for the set of all free variables of t. A term with no free variables is called *closed*. We write $Closed(PT)$ for the set of closed terms from PT.

Types. The terms of our lambda calculus are associated with the following kinds of types:

- basic types from a set BT,
- functional types $A \rightarrow B$,
- product types $A * B$,
- disjoint unions $A|B$,
- dependent product types $\prod x : t.a$ where x is from Var, and
- dependent sum types $\Sigma x : t.b$ where x is from Var

The intuition behind the first four types should be clear. For example, if a term t has type $A \to B$, this means that t is a function that can accept as input any value of type A to produce a value of type B.

A dependent product type expresses the dependence of a function's output types on its input term arguments. For example, if a function f has depedent product type $\prod x : T.F(x)$, then f can input any value of type T, producing an output value of type $F(arg)$. Thus, the final output type is parameterized by the input *value*.

Example 3. Consider a server webpage script function that responds to a request for a webpage, given as input information about the requesting clients display (PDA or PC). Let CLIENT be the type of a client's display (with only two elements, PDA and PC). We define the function *respond* over the client display, so that it returns HTML formatted for a PDA (of some assumed basic type PDAHTML) if the client is running a PDA, and ordinary HTML (of an assumed basic type HTML) otherwise:

$$respond(PDA) : \text{PDAHTML}$$

and

$$respond(PC) : \text{HTML}$$

It is not possible to achieve such a typing of the function using functional, product and disjoint union types. We can type the *respond* function using the product type

$$\prod x : \text{CLIENT}.P(x)$$

where P is a higher-order function from CLIENT to some collection type of all datatypes,[2] defined:

$$P(x) = \begin{cases} \text{PDAHTML if } x \text{ is } PDA \\ \text{HTML if } x \text{ is } PC \end{cases}$$

Type inference rules. Type inference rules provide a formal system for determining what the types of a lambda term should be. The core type inference rules are provided in Fig. 7. They involve a typeing relation (:) between terms and types. An inference takes the form

$$\Gamma \vdash a : s \tag{1}$$

where Γ is a *context*, consisting of variables associated with types, of the form $\{x_1 : s_1, \ldots, x_n : s_n\}$. The inference's intended meaning is that the term a has the type s, when its free variables $x_1, \ldots, x_n$ denote possible terms of types $s_1, \ldots, s_n$. If an inference of the form (1) can be made for a term a and type s, we say that a is *well-typed* with type s *for context* Γ. If the context Γ can be determined with no ambiguity from examining a, we simply say a is well-typed with type s.

---

[2] The fact that P is a function begs the question of what *its* type is. In order to define this, the notion of a "collection of datatypes" needs to be clarified. We shall address this issue shortly.

$$\frac{}{x : A \vdash x : A} \ (\text{Ass-I})$$

$$\frac{\Delta, x : s \vdash p : A}{\Delta \vdash \lambda x : s.\ p : \prod x : s \bullet A} \ (\prod\text{-I})$$

$$\frac{\Delta_1 \vdash p : \prod x : s \bullet A \quad \Delta_2 \vdash c : s}{\Delta_1, \Delta_2 \vdash (p\ c) : A[c/x]} \ (\prod\text{-E})$$

$$\frac{\Delta, x : s \vdash p : A \quad x : s \text{ is not free in } A}{\Delta \vdash \lambda x : s.\ p : s \rightarrow A} \ (\rightarrow\text{-I})$$

$$\frac{\Delta_1 \vdash p : s \rightarrow A \quad \Delta_2 \vdash c : s}{\Delta_1, \Delta_2 \vdash (p\ c) : A} \ (\rightarrow\text{-E})$$

$$\frac{\Delta \vdash p : P[a/y]}{\Delta \vdash \text{show}(a, p) : \Sigma y : s \bullet P} \ (\Sigma\text{-I})$$

$$\frac{\Delta_1 \vdash p : \Sigma y : s \bullet P \quad \Delta_2, x : P[z/y] \vdash q : C}{\Delta_1, \Delta_2 \vdash \text{select } (p) \text{ in } z.x.q : C} \ (\Sigma\text{-E})$$

$$\frac{\Delta \vdash a : A \quad \Delta' \vdash b : B}{\Delta, \Delta' \vdash \langle a, b \rangle : (A * B)} \ (\text{prod-I})$$

$$\frac{\Delta \vdash p : (A_1 * A_2)}{\Delta \vdash \text{fst}(p) : A_1} \ (\text{prod-E}_1) \qquad \frac{\Delta \vdash p : (A_1 * A_2)}{\Delta \vdash \text{snd}(p) : A_2} \ (\text{prod-E}_2)$$

$$\frac{\Delta \vdash p : A_1}{\Delta \vdash \text{inl}(p) : (A_1|A_2)} \ (\text{union-I}_1) \qquad \frac{\Delta \vdash p : A_2}{\Delta \vdash \text{inr}(p) : (A_1|A_2)} \ (\text{union-I}_2)$$

$$\frac{\Delta \vdash p : A|B \quad \Delta_1, x : A \vdash a : C \quad \Delta_2, y : B \vdash b : C}{\Delta_1, \Delta_2, \Delta \vdash \text{match } p \text{ with inl}(x) \Rightarrow a \mid \text{inr}(y) \Rightarrow b : C} \ (\text{union-E})$$

$$\frac{\Delta \vdash a : \bot}{\Delta \vdash \text{abort}(a) : A} \ (\bot\text{-E})$$

Fig. 7. Type inference rules for our lambda calculus

Predicative universe hierarchy. Dependent types introduce a problem. We motivated the use of dependent products by considering functions that operate over elements of a collection $CType$ of datatypes. This raises the question of what the type of $CType$ should be. It is not permissible to say that $CType$ is of type $CType$, as this results in an inconsistent theory. Instead, the solution is to define a predicative hierarchy of type universes of the form:

$$\text{TYPE}_0, \text{TYPE}_1, \text{TYPE}_2, \ldots$$

subject to the rules given in Fig. 8. These rules entail that the first universe TYPE_0 is the type of all types generated by the basic types the typing constructors.

Example 4. Assuming the set of basic types includes strings STRING and booleans BOOL, types of the form STRING $\rightarrow$ BOOL, (BOOL $*$ BOOL) $\rightarrow$ STRING have type TYPE_0. The function P of Example 3 is of the higher-order type CLIENT $\rightarrow$

$$\frac{}{\vdash \text{TYPE}_i : \text{TYPE}_{i+1}} \ (\text{Universe})$$

$$\frac{s \text{ is a basic type}}{\vdash s : \text{TYPE}_0} \ (\text{BT})$$

$$\frac{\Gamma_1 \vdash T : \text{TYPE}_i \quad \Gamma_2 \vdash P : \text{TYPE}_j}{\Gamma_1, \Gamma_2 \vdash (\prod x : T.P) : \text{TYPE}_{max(i,j)}} \ (\text{dprodt})$$

$$\frac{\Gamma_1 \vdash T : \text{TYPE}_i \quad \Gamma_2 \vdash P : \text{TYPE}_j}{\Gamma_1, \Gamma_2 \vdash (\Sigma x : T.P) : \text{TYPE}_{max(i,j)}} \ (\text{dsumt})$$

$$\frac{\Gamma_1 \vdash A : \text{TYPE}_i \quad \Gamma_2 \vdash B : \text{TYPE}_j}{\Gamma_1, \Gamma_2 \vdash A * B : \text{TYPE}_{max(i,j)}} \ (\text{prodt})$$

$$\frac{\Gamma_1 \vdash A : \text{TYPE}_i \quad \Gamma_2 \vdash B : \text{TYPE}_j}{\Gamma_1, \Gamma_2 \vdash A|B : \text{TYPE}_{max(i,j)}} \ (\text{uniont})$$

$$\frac{\Gamma_1 \vdash A : \text{TYPE}_i \quad \Gamma_2 \vdash B : \text{TYPE}_j}{\Gamma_1, \Gamma_2 \vdash A \rightarrow B : \text{TYPE}_{max(i,j)}} \ (\text{fnt})$$

Fig. 8. Type inference rules relating to the universe hierarchy, where $max(i,j)$ denotes the maximum of two integers i and j

TYPE_0, because its output ranges over basic types from TYPE_0. This type, in turn, is of type TYPE_1, because it involves TYPE_0.

Operational semantics. As a lambda calculus, our terms have an operational semantics that defines how terms are evaluated.

We require the following definition.

Definition 12. A lambda term t is *neutral* if it is of one of the following forms: $(\lambda x.q)$, $\langle q, r \rangle$, $\text{inl}(q)$, $\text{inr}(q)$ or $\text{show}(q, r)$, where $q, r, t_1, \ldots, t_n$ are arbitrary terms and f is any datatype constructor of arity n.

The operational semantics of the calculus is defined by the rules in Fig. 9. We write

$$p \ \hat{} \ p$$

when p may be obtained from p by the transitive closure of . When $p \ \hat{} \ p$ holds, then p is obtainable from p by a sequence of replacements of subterms using the rules of Fig. 9. In this case, we say that p is reducible, or *evaluates*, to p .

Evaluation is *lazy* – that is, the operational semantics is applied to the outermost terms, working inwards until neutral term is reached.

Example 5. An expression is considered evaluated when it is of the form

$$\lambda x : t.((\lambda y : u.y + y)2)$$

is considered evaluated, in spite of the fact that the second lambda expression could be evaluated further independently.

1. $((\lambda\ X.\ a) : (A \rightarrow B)\ b : A)$	$a[b/X] : B$
2. $\mathsf{specific}(\lambda\ x.\ a : \prod x : s \bullet A, v : s)$	$a[v/x] : A[v/x]$
3. $\mathsf{fst}(\langle a, b \rangle : (A \wedge B))$	$a : A$
4. $\mathsf{snd}(\langle a, b \rangle : (A \wedge B))$	$b : B$
5. $\mathsf{match\ inl}(a) : A \vee B\ \mathsf{with\ inl}(x : A) \Rightarrow b : C \mid \mathsf{inr}(y : B) \Rightarrow c : C$	$b[a/x] : C$
6. $\mathsf{match\ inr}(a) : A \vee B\ \mathsf{with\ inl}(x : A) \Rightarrow b : C \mid \mathsf{inr}(y : B) \Rightarrow c : C$	$c[a/y] : C$
7. $\mathsf{select\ }(\mathsf{show}(v, a) : \varSigma y : s \bullet P)\ \mathsf{in}\ z.x : P[z/y].b : C$	$b[a/x][v/z] : C$

Fig. 9. The seven reduction rules that define

3.2 Useful Types and Operations

We have presented the core terms, types and rules that make up our type theory. The following extensions are necessary in order to enable our encoding of the MOF.

Extending the type theory with new inductive data types. The type inference rules may be extended to introduce new recursive data types. Martin-Löf proposed this as means of keeping the type theory open, in the same way that an ordinary programming language is open to new libraries of data types.

The type theory can be extended with a new inductive data type by adding rules defining the constructors for the data type, its position in the type universe hierarchy and the operational semantics of its terms.

For instance, the natural numbers *Nat* can be constructed using zero 0 constant and the successor *suc* function, with the following typing rules:

$$\vdash 0 : Nat \quad \vdash s : Nat \rightarrow Nat$$

We need to add the following rule to perform induction over natural numbers:

$$\vdash recNat_i : \prod X : (Nat \rightarrow \textsc{Type}_i).(X\ 0)*$$
$$\left(\prod x : Nat.(X\ x) \rightarrow (X\ (suc\ x))\right) \rightarrow \left(\prod x : Nat.(X\ x)\right)$$

Finally, we also add a recursion reduction rule to define the operational semantics of natural numbers.

$$recNat_i C\langle p, q \rangle 0 \quad p$$
$$recNat_i C\langle p, q \rangle(suc\ x) \quad q\ x\ (recNat_i C\langle q, q \rangle x)$$

Remark 8. We will assume the following inductive data types within the type theory:

- Integers *Int*, Strings *String* and Booleans *Bool*, with the obvious constructors, induction rules and operational semantics.
- A type called *Multiplicity*, with constructors $*$, 1, 0, 1..$*$ and 0..$*$.

We will also assume we have a type of parameterized lists, of the form

$$[A]$$

where A is a type. $[]$ is the empty list and $[a_1, \ldots, a_n]$ is a list of type $[A]$ if each a_i is of type A.

Record types. Record types are treated as syntactic sugar for a special use of dependent products.

Definition 13 (Record types in CTT). Given $l_1, \ldots, l_n : Label$ labels, and $T_1, \ldots T_n$ types, we write

$$\{l_1 : T_1, \ldots, l_n : T_n\}$$

to denote the type

$$\prod x : String.\text{match } x \text{ with } l_1 \Rightarrow T_1 \mid \ldots \mid l_n \Rightarrow T_n$$

An element of this type is a function r of the form

$$\lambda x : String.\text{match } x \text{ with } l_1 \Rightarrow t_1 : T_1 \mid \ldots \mid l_n \Rightarrow t_1 : T_n$$

We write

$$\{l_1 = t_1, \ldots, l_n = t_n\}$$

to abbreviate this and

$$\{l_1 = t_1, \ldots, l_n = t_n\}.l_k$$

to denote the application

$$r \, l_k$$

We will take the following as type inference rules. The correctness of the rules follows from the definition of records just given.

$$\frac{\begin{array}{ccc} \Gamma_1 \vdash T_1 : \text{TYPE}_{r_1} & \ldots & \Gamma_n \vdash T_n : \text{TYPE}_{r_n} \\ max \text{ is maximum of } \{r_1, \ldots, r_n\} \\ a_1, \ldots, a_n \in String \end{array}}{\Gamma_1, \ldots, \Gamma_n \vdash \{a_1 : T_1; \ldots; a_n : T_n\} : \text{TYPE}_{max}} \text{ (RecType)}$$

$$\frac{\Gamma_1 \vdash a_1 : T_1 \quad \ldots \quad \Gamma_n \vdash a_n : d_n}{\Gamma_1, \ldots, \Gamma_n \vdash \{a_1 = d_1; \ldots; a_n = d_n\} : \{a_1 : T_1; \ldots; a_n : T_n\}} \text{ (RecObj)}$$

We conservatively extend our definition of neutral terms to let any record $\{l_1 = t_1; \ldots; l_n = t_n\}$ be neutral. This follows from our treatment of records in Definition 13.

Type equivalence. Because types can be used within higer-order lambda terms, one type can be reducible to another according to the operational semantics. We treat types as interchangable one can be obtained from another via the reduction rules. We define an extensional type equivalence relation generated by the operational semantics as follows. For any TYPE_i $(i = 1, \ldots, n)$ types T_1, T_2,

$$T_1 \equiv T_2 \text{ if, and only if, } T_1 \quad T_2 \text{ or } T_2 \quad T_1$$

We then permit equivalent types to be interchanged in typing inferences, according to the rule

$$\frac{\Gamma \vdash t : T_1 \quad T_1 \equiv T_2}{\Gamma \vdash t : T_2} \; (\equiv)$$

(From a type theoretic perspective, this rule is actually a meta-rule, as it does not provide a history of the type inference at the term level. This rule can be incorporated within the a proper type theory through use of coercion operators, but for our purposes it is enough to simply use the meta-rule.)

Recursive types and terms. In many type theoretic treatments of of object-oriented programming language semantics, recursive types and infinitely recursive terms are often employed to characterise classes and class objects. They are employed to model the ability of class objects to include circular self-references (through, for example, a self or this operator). Because our modelling classes have the potential for similar self-reference, we shall also require recursive types.

Type theories with the expressive power of ours cannot incorporate infinite recursion, as they require termination of all elements in order to retain consistency. Infinitely recursive terms are instead "simulated" by means of a corecursion operator. It is possible to represent infinite data through use of *corecursion*, intuitively understood as the restricted forms of infinitely recursion that lead to normal forms, due to the lazy operational semantics. We follow Coquand [9] and Poll [23] approach.

We also use corecursive terms, formed using the μ operator, according to the following rule

$$\frac{\Gamma, x : T \vdash t : T \quad \text{provided } t \text{ is a neutral term}}{\Gamma \vdash (\mu \, x : T.t) : T} \; (\text{fix})$$

We add the following rule to our lazy operational semantics, which explains how corecursive terms are evaluated:

$$\boxed{(\mu \, x : T.t) \quad t[(\mu \, x : T.t)/x]}$$

Observe that, for the corecursive term to be well-typed, the the term t must be neutral, $t[(\mu \, x : T.t)/x]$ is the evaluated form of $(\mu \, x : T.t)$.

Example 6. The following is not a valid corecursive term

$$(\mu \, x : int.x + x)$$

as $+$ is a derived function and so $x + x$ is not a neutral term. The following term is valid

$$(\mu \; x : int.\langle x, x \rangle)$$

Coinductive types are formed using the μ operator over types. That is, they are formed using a specialized form of the (fix) rule, as follows

$$\frac{\Gamma, x : \text{TYPE}_i \vdash T : \text{TYPE}_i \quad \text{provided } T \text{ is a neutral type function}}{\Gamma \vdash (\mu \; x : \text{TYPE}_i.T) : \text{TYPE}_i} \; (\equiv\text{fix})$$

Lemma 1. The rule ($\equiv$fix) together with the operational semantics for μ and the ($\equiv$) rule entail the following derived rules:

$$\frac{\Gamma \vdash t : \mu \; x : \text{TYPE}_i.T}{\Gamma \vdash t : T[(\mu \; x : \text{TYPE}_i.T)/x]} \; (\equiv\text{fix}_1)$$

and

$$\frac{\Gamma \vdash t : T[(\mu \; x : \text{TYPE}_i.T)/x]}{\Gamma \vdash t : \mu \; x : \text{TYPE}_i.T} \; (\equiv\text{fix}_2)$$

Mutual recursion can be defined using the μ operators – however, the definition is difficult to read. For readability, we present an equivalent set of definitions, where mutual recursion is expressed in terms of abbreviations of types and terms of dependencies on the abbreviated types. We then display the actual type definition. That is, write mutually recursive definitions of the form

$$T \equiv F(U) : \text{TYPE}_i$$

$$U \equiv G(T) : \text{TYPE}_i$$

with T and U to be taken as shorthand for

$$\pi_1(\mu \; X : \text{TYPE}_i * \text{TYPE}_i.\langle F(\pi_1(X)), G(\pi_2(X)) \rangle)$$

$$\pi_2(\mu \; X : \text{TYPE}_i * \text{TYPE}_i.\langle F(\pi_1(X)), G(\pi_2(X)) \rangle)$$

We proceed similarly larger sets of mutually recursive definitions.

Subtyping. We also equip our type theory with a notion of subtyping. We omit the details of how subtyping is treated within the CTT. For further details, see [3] or [23]. For our purposes, it is enough to consider the following rule:

$$\frac{\Gamma_1 \vdash a : U \quad \Gamma_2 \vdash U \leq: T}{\Gamma_1, \Gamma_2 \vdash a : T} \; (\leq:)$$

where $\leq:$ is a subtyping relationship that holds between types. In this paper, we will define when $\leq:$ holds, rather than writing the full rules for inference of the relation.

3.3   Classes as Record Types

We first describe how the structure of classes and objects can represented within our type theory. Our encoding is standard (see, e.g., [24]). We define classes as recursive record types, with objects taken as terms of these types. Because we have restricted our attention to classes with attributes but without operations, we will not deal with representing operations within class types – but our representation can be easily extended to this.

First, recall that we shall treat the associations of a class in the same way as attributes. That is, if class M_1 is associated with another class M_2 with the n the name of the end of the association at M_2, then we treat this as an attribute $n : M_2$ within M_1 if the multiplicity of n is 1, and $n : [M_2]$ otherwise.

Essentially, the idea is to map a class C with attributes and associations $a_1 : T_1, \ldots, a_n : T_n$ to a record type definition

$$C \equiv \{a_1 : T_1; \ldots; a_n : T_n\}$$

where each a_i is an element of *String* corresponding to the attribute name a_i and each T_i a type corresponding to the classifier T_i. The class can reference another class or itself through the attribute types. The mapping therefore permits mutual recursion between class definitions. That is, each T_i could be C or could refer to other defined class types.

Example 7. The three associated UML classes of Fig. 10 are represented in the type theory via the following mutually recursive definitions:

HOUSE $\equiv$ {street : *String*; number : *Int*; owner : [PERSON]; rooms : [ROOM]}
PERSON $\equiv$ {bedroom : ROOM; name : *String*; home : HOUSE}
ROOM $\equiv$ {ID : *Int*; home : HOUSE}

where *Int* and *String* are types given the usual definitions. The UML classes can be instantiated with objects as in Fig. 11. These objects have the following mutually recursive term definitions:

$$me \equiv \{bedroom = myBedroom; name = WolfBlass; house = myHouse\}$$
$$myHouse \equiv \{street = Carina; owner = 1; owner = [me];$$
$$rooms = [myBedroom, myKitchen]\}$$
$$myBedroom \equiv \{ID = 1; home = myHouse\}$$
$$myKitchen \equiv \{ID = 2; home = myHouse\}$$

It can be proved using the type inference rules for μ that me : PERSON, $myHouse$: HOUSE, $myBedroom$: ROOM and $myKitchen$: ROOM.

This encoding allows us to represent the structure of classes. Note, however, it does not provide any semantic detail, such as constraints on instantiating class objects. This is not an important issue for defining the type theory for object-oriented programming languages. However, it is important for our work, where we wish to encode the M_3 and M_2 level class definitions, both of which involve

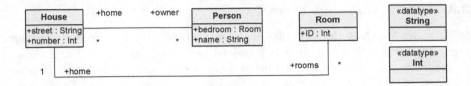

Fig. 10. Three associated classes.

Fig. 11. Class objects instantiating classes of Fig. 10

constraints. Our approach will be to first define the structure of these classes using recursive record types, and then to employ the property known as the Curry-Howard isomorphism to associate constraints with types within the type theory. The isomorphism is described now.

3.4   Constructive Logic

We provide a brief overview of how constructive logic can be integrated into the type theory. This logic is similar to the traditional classical logic that most computer scientists learn in undergraduate study, except that it considers disjunctions and existential statements true only if their proofs provide "evidence" of truth. For instance, $A \vee \neg A$ is not self-evident for an arbitrary A – to be true in constructive logic, evidence of the truth of A or the truth of $\neg A$ must be provided. Similarly, we cannot assert the truth of $\exists x : T.A(x)$ without providing evidence that there is some term $t : T$ such that $A(t)$ holds. Constructive logic has its origins in the intuitionist movement in the philosophy of mathematics. Constructive logic is a useful logic in computer science, where much work is naturally constructive – the existence of an algorithm is of less interest to a developer than actual concrete evidence of the algorithm.

Logical propositions. We will consider a logic with formulae that predicate and quantify over our lambda terms. These formulae are defined with respect to an assumed set of predicates.

Definition 14 (Predicate). A predicate P of arity n is a term satisfying a type judgement of the form

$$\vdash P : (T_1 * \ldots * T_n) \to \text{TYPE}_0$$

for some i. The elements of the set $\{T_1, \ldots, T_n\}$ are called the argument types of P.

Informally, a predicate represents a logical statement about elements of its argument types.

Example 8. For example, we might define a less than inequality predicate, *lessThan* : $(\text{INT} * \text{INT}) \to \text{TYPE}_0$, that declares *lessThan*(a, b) when a is less than b.

Definition 15 (Well-formed formulae of a collection of types). The set of well-formed formulae WFF for a collection of predicates $Pred$ is the least set containing

- every $Q(t_1, \ldots, t_n)$ where $Q : (T_1 * \ldots * T_n) \to \text{TYPE}_0$ is a predicate from $Pred$, and every t_i $(i = 1, \ldots, n)$ is a well-typed lambda term of type T_i,
- every formula $(A \wedge B)$ for $A, B \in WFF$,
- every formula $(A \vee B)$ for $A, B \in WFF$,
- every formula $(A \Rightarrow B)$ for $A, B \in WFF$,
- every formula $\forall x : s \bullet F$ where $x \in Var$ and $F \in WFF$,
- every formula $\exists x : s \bullet F$ where $x \in Var$ and $F \in WFF$,
- the formula $\bot$.

We often write $\neg A$ for $(A \Rightarrow \bot)$.

Basic rules. The rules of the constructive logic are presented in Fig. 12.

Remark 9 (Substitution for individual variables). As usual $A[t/x]$ denotes the result of substituting t for all free occurrences of x in A subject to avoiding clashes of variables, where t and x share the same sort.

Motivation for the rules of intuitionistic logic is well known. We consider several important rules as an illustration.

Remark 10. Rules $(\vee\text{-I}_1)$ and $(\vee\text{-I}_2)$ are understood as follows.
Consider first the rule for $\vee$ introduction on the left:

$$\frac{\Gamma \vdash_{\mathsf{Int}} A}{\Gamma \vdash_{\mathsf{Int}} (A \vee B)} \; (\vee\text{-I}_1)$$

This means that from a sequent $\Gamma \vdash_{\mathsf{Int}} A$ we may infer the sequent $\Gamma \vdash_{\mathsf{Int}} (A \vee B)$. Here we are weakening the conclusion to $(A \vee B)$.

Example 9. The rule $(\vee\text{-E})$ is most easily understood by its analogy to proof by cases. If we have a proof of C from A and also a proof of C from B then we get a proof of C from $A \vee B$.
Likewise, for the $(\exists\text{-E})$ rule, if we have a proof of $\exists x : s \bullet A$ and a proof of C from a proof of A with free variable y, then we can get a proof of C.

Assume that x, y are arbitrary variables of sort s from signature Σ, and that a and c are well-sorted terms of sort s.

$$\frac{}{A \vdash_{\mathsf{Int}} A} \ (\text{Ass-I})$$

$$\frac{\Delta, A \vdash_{\mathsf{Int}} B}{\Delta \vdash_{\mathsf{Int}} (A \Rightarrow B)} \ (\Rightarrow\text{-I}) \qquad \frac{\Delta \vdash_{\mathsf{Int}} A \quad \Delta' \vdash_{\mathsf{Int}} (A \Rightarrow B)}{\Delta, \Delta' \vdash_{\mathsf{Int}} B} \ (\Rightarrow\text{-E})$$

$$\frac{\Delta \vdash_{\mathsf{Int}} A}{\Delta \vdash_{\mathsf{Int}} \forall x : s \bullet A} \ (\forall\text{-I}) \qquad \frac{\Delta \vdash_{\mathsf{Int}} \forall x : s \bullet A}{\Delta \vdash_{\mathsf{Int}} A[c/x]} \ (\forall\text{-E})$$
provided x is free in A

$$\frac{\Delta \vdash_{\mathsf{Int}} P[a/y]}{\Delta \vdash_{\mathsf{Int}} \exists y : s \bullet P} \ (\exists\text{-I}) \qquad \frac{\Delta_1 \vdash_{\mathsf{Int}} \exists y : s \bullet P \quad \Delta_2, P[x/y] \vdash_{\mathsf{Int}} C}{\Delta_1, \Delta_2 \vdash_{\mathsf{Int}} C} \ (\exists\text{-E})$$
where x is not free in C

$$\frac{\Delta \vdash_{\mathsf{Int}} A \quad \Delta' \vdash_{\mathsf{Int}} B}{\Delta, \Delta' \vdash_{\mathsf{Int}} (A \wedge B)} \ (\wedge\text{-I})$$

$$\frac{\Delta \vdash_{\mathsf{Int}} (A_1 \wedge A_2)}{\Delta \vdash_{\mathsf{Int}} A_1} \ (\wedge\text{-E}_1) \qquad \frac{\Delta \vdash_{\mathsf{Int}} (A_1 \wedge A_2)}{\Delta \vdash_{\mathsf{Int}} A_2} \ (\wedge\text{-E}_2)$$

$$\frac{\Delta \vdash_{\mathsf{Int}} A_1}{\Delta \vdash_{\mathsf{Int}} (A_1 \vee A_2)} \ (\vee\text{-I}_1) \qquad \frac{\Delta \vdash_{\mathsf{Int}} A_2}{\Delta \vdash_{\mathsf{Int}} (A_1 \vee A_2)} \ (\vee\text{-I}_2)$$

$$\frac{\Delta \vdash_{\mathsf{Int}} A \vee B \quad \Delta_1, A \vdash_{\mathsf{Int}} C \quad \Delta_2, B \vdash_{\mathsf{Int}} C}{\Delta_1, \Delta_2, \Delta \vdash_{\mathsf{Int}} C} \ (\vee\text{-E})$$

$$\frac{\Delta \vdash_{\mathsf{Int}} \bot}{\Delta \vdash_{\mathsf{Int}} A} \ (\bot\text{-E})$$
provided A is Harrop

Fig. 12. The basic rules of many-sorted intuitionistic logic, Int

Extension by axioms. The basic calculus can be extended by further axioms and schemata that define what formulae are to be taken as true without further proof. We represent these as additional rules.

Example 10. For instance, the natural numbers can be reasoned about by adding the axioms of arithmetic. The less than inequality predicate of Example 8, $lessThan : (\text{INT} * \text{INT}) \to \text{TYPE}_0$, is only of use if we have an axiom explaining is meaning, such as the following:

$$\frac{}{\vdash \forall x : \text{INT}.lessThan(x, s(x))}$$

3.5   The Curry-Howard Isomorphism

The Curry-Howard isomorphism shows that constructive logic is naturally embedded within our type theory, where proofs correspond to terms, formulae to types, logical rules to type inference, and proof normalization to term simplification. The original idea was first described by Curry [10] and extended to intuitionistic first order logic by Howard [14].

We first need to make the following assumptions:

- All predicates exist inside the type theory.
- Also, for each axiom

$$\vdash_{\mathsf{Int}} A$$

in the logic, there is a corresponding term $\mathsf{Axiom}(A)$ in the type theory with the following typing rule

$$\frac{}{\vdash \mathsf{Axiom}(A) : \mathsf{asType}(A)}$$

- The recursion rule for each inductive type corresponds to a schema that is assumed within the logic. The latter schema is formed from the former by retaining only types and changing the dependent products and functional types to universal quantifiers and implications, respectively. For example, the recursion rule for INT corresponds to the following schema in the logic:

$$\frac{\Gamma_1 \vdash_{\mathsf{Int}} P(0) \quad \Gamma_2 \vdash_{\mathsf{Int}} \forall x : \mathrm{INT} P(x) \rightarrow P(s(x))}{\Gamma_1, \Gamma_0 \vdash_{\mathsf{Int}} \forall x : \mathrm{INT}.P(x)}$$

We define an injection asType, from well-formed formulae WFF to types of the lambda calculus as in Fig. 13.

A	$\mathsf{asType}(A)$
$Q(x)$, where Q is a predicate	$Q(x)$
$\forall x : T.P$	$\prod x : T.\mathsf{asType}(P)$
$\exists x : T.P$	$\Sigma x : T.\mathsf{asType}(P)$
$P \wedge Q$	$\mathsf{asType}(P) * \mathsf{asType}(Q)$
$P \vee Q$	$\mathsf{asType}(P) | \mathsf{asType}(Q)$
$P \Rightarrow Q$	$\mathsf{asType}(P) \rightarrow \mathsf{asType}(Q)$
$\perp$	$\perp$

Fig. 13. Definition of asType, an injection from WFF to types of the lambda calculus

The isomorphism is then given by the following theorem.

Theorem 1 (Curry-Howard isomorphism). *Let $\Gamma = \{G_1, \ldots, G_n\}$ be a set of premises. Let $\Gamma = \{x_1{}^{G_1}, \ldots, x_n{}^{G_n}\}$ be a corresponding set of typed proof-term variables. Let A be a well-formed formula.*
Then,

1. *Given a proof of*

$$\Gamma \vdash_{\mathsf{Int}} A$$

   we can use the type inference rules to construct a well-typed proof-term $p : \mathsf{asType}(A)$ whose free proof-term variables are Γ.
2. *Given a well-typed proof-term $p : \mathsf{asType}(A)$ whose free term variables are Γ, we can construct a natural deduction proof of $\Gamma \vdash_{\mathsf{Int}} A$.*

4   MOF Metamodels Within CTT

We now formalize the MOF framework described in Section 2 using the CTT of Section 3.

We demonstrate that CTT is a natural choice for encoding the MOF. The main concepts of the MOF have obvious formal counterparts within the CTT. Classes and objects are treated using recursive records. The four levels of the MOF are treated using the CTT's predicative hierarchy of type universes. The CTT's typing relation allows us to systematically treat MOF model/metamodel/model/model instantiation relationships depicted in Fig. 1 as follows:

– The M_3 level MOF classes are defined through TYPE$_2$ class types,
– M_2 level metamodel classifiers are given a dual representation as objects of the MOF class types and as TYPE$_1$ class types,
– M_1 level model entities are given a dual representation as terms of the metamodel types and as as TYPE$_0$ types,
– M_0 level implementations of models are instantiating terms of TYPE$_0$ types.

This section focuses primarily on how to formalize the MOF classes and metamodels – that is, we focus on levels M_3 and M_2.

We translate the MOF classes into types of the CTT. By utilizing the logic that is built into the CTT, these types are able to encode both structural requirements and semantic constraints prescribed by the MOF class definitions. This enables us to define a higher order type of metamodels METAMODEL, such that $\vdash mm :$ METAMODEL is derivable if, and only if, the term mm corresponds to a provably correct metamodel in the sense that it is satisfies the constraints for metamodels prescribed by the MOF. The term mm corresponds to the object-based representation of a metamodel. Class-based representations of metamodels are formally treated by means of a mapping from terms $mm :$ METAMODEL to TYPE$_1$ class records. The mapping is essentially a direct type theoretic translation of the informal mapping of Definition 10.

This mapping then enables us to define higher order types for any MOF metamodel MODELLANG, so that $\vdash model :$ MODELLANG is derivable if, and only if, the term $model$ corresponds to a valid model instance of the metamodel that satisfies the constraints required of it by the metamodel.

The main difficulty with our formalization is in the treatment of instances of the MOF `Constraint` class. Instances of this class describe how a metamodel's instantiating model must behave. Within the MOF framework, constraints, written using `Constraint` objects, form part of both object- and class-based representations of metamodels. It is difficult to express such constraints on instantiating models when metamodels are treated as terms. There is no such difficulty when metamodels are treated as TYPE$_1$ classes. Consequently, we do not formalize such constraints as part of METAMODEL metamodel terms. We treat them in our TYPE$_1$ class record-based representation of metamodels, adding them via the mapping from terms $mm :$ METAMODEL to TYPE$_1$ class records.

4.1 Encoding of the MOF

The structure of MOF metamodels was defined as a set of M_3 level classes. We now define a set of mutually recursive Type_2 level record types that encode these classes. A metamodel, considered as a set of M_2 level objects that instantiate the MOF classes, will then be formally understood as a set of mututally recursive Type_1 level terms of these types.

We define the following mutually recursive types: METACLASSIFIER, the type of MOF model metaclasses; METACLASS, the type of MOF model metaclasses; ATTRIBUTE, the type of MOF model attributes; ASSOCIATION, the type of MOF model associations; ASSOCIATIONEND, the type of MOF model association ends. The subtyping relationship is defined so that METACLASS $\leq$: METACLASSIFIER, ASSOCIATION $\leq$: METACLASSIFIER and DATATYPE $\leq$: METACLASSIFIER.

Definition 16 (MOF classifier type). A MOF classifier is encoded by the following record type,

$$\text{METACLASSIFIER} \equiv \Sigma x : \text{CLASSSTRUCT}.MClassCst(x)$$

where CLASSSTRUCT stands for the record

$$\{\text{name} : String; \text{isAbstract} : Bool; \text{supertype} : \text{METACLASSIFIER};$$
$$\text{attributes} : [\text{ATTRIBUTE}]\}$$

and $MClassCst(x)$ is the conjunction of the following statements about x : CLASSSTRUCT:

- Formal translation of constraint (1) in Definition 2 of classifiers:

$$\forall mL : [\text{METACLASSIFIER}].mL = getParents(x) \rightarrow x \in mL$$

- Formal translation of constraint (2) in Definition 2 of classifiers:

$$\forall mL : [\text{METACLASSIFIER}].mL = getParents(x) \rightarrow$$
$$\forall m : \text{METACLASSIFIER}.m \in mL.\forall a_1 : \text{ATTRIBUTE}.a_1 \in x.\text{attributes} \rightarrow$$
$$\forall a_2 : \text{ATTRIBUTE}.a_2 \in m.\text{attributes} \rightarrow a_1.\text{name} \neq a_2.\text{name}$$

- Formal translation of constraint (1) in Definition 4 of metaclasses:

$$\forall a_1 : \text{ATTRIBUTE}.\forall a_2 : \text{ATTRIBUTE}.a_1 \in x.\text{attributes} \wedge a_2 \in x.\text{attributes} \rightarrow$$
$$a_1.\text{name} \neq a_2.\text{name}$$

where $getParents$ is a corecursive function that obtains a list of all supertypes of a metaclass x.

Definition 17 (MOF Metaclass type). A MOF class is encoded by the following record type,

$$\text{METACLASS} \equiv \Sigma x : \text{CLASSSTRUCT}.MClassCst(x)$$

where CLASSSTRUCT stands for the record

$$\{\text{name} : String; \text{isAbstract} : Bool; \text{supertype} : \text{METACLASSIFIER};$$
$$\text{attributes} : [\text{ATTRIBUTE}]\}$$

and $MClassCst(x)$ is the conjunction of the following statements about x : MCLASSSTRUCT:

– Formal translation of constraint (1) in Definition 2 of classifiers:

$$\forall mL : [\text{METACLASSIFIER}].mL = getParents(x) \rightarrow x \in mL$$

– Formal translation of constraint (2) in Definition 2 of classifiers:

$$\forall mL : [\text{METACLASSIFIER}].mL = getParents(x) \rightarrow$$
$$\forall m : \text{METACLASSIFIER}.m \in mL.\forall a_1 : \text{ATTRIBUTE}.a_1 \in x.\text{attributes} \rightarrow$$
$$\forall a_2 : \text{ATTRIBUTE}.a_2 \in m.\text{attributes} \rightarrow a_1.\text{name} \neq a_2.\text{name}$$

– Formal translation of constraint (1) in Definition 4 of metaclasses:

$$\forall a_1 : \text{ATTRIBUTE}.\forall a_2 : \text{ATTRIBUTE}.a_1 \in x.\text{attributes} \wedge a_2 \in x.\text{attributes} \rightarrow$$
$$a_1.\text{name} \neq a_2.\text{name}$$

where $getParents$ is a corecursive function that obtains a list of all supertypes of a metaclass x.

Remark 11. The METACLASS type is the type of all metaclasses. That is, a metaclass M can be encoded correctly within the MOF as an instance of a MOF class if, and only if, there is a corresponding term representation t_M of M, such that $\vdash t_M : \text{METACLASS}$ holds. This typing requires two witnesses:

1. a record that encodes the data associated with the metaclass, written according to the structure of the record type MCLASSSTRUCT, and
2. a propositional function over MCLASSSTRUCT records, that specifies constraints that can be proved to hold over the values that can be held by the record.

This reflects the two aspects of an informal metaclass definition within the MOF:

1. The metaclass contains data in the relevant fields specified by the MOF class definition.
2. The metaclass satisfies the set of constraints that are particular to its nature.

Remark 12. A similar form of encoding is done for the remaining MOF elements – a record type used to define its structure, paired with constraints over the structure using a dependent sum. We do not have the space to present the full definitions of constraints, and provide only simple illustrations.

Definition 18 (MOF attribute type). MOF attributes are represented in the type theory by the following type:

$$\text{MATT} \equiv \Sigma x : \text{MOFATTSTRUCT}.AttCst(x)$$

where MOFATTSTRUCT is an abbreviation for the following record type

$$\{\text{name} : String; \text{type} : \text{METACLASSIFIER}; \text{visibility} : Bool\}$$

Definition 19 (MOF Association Ends). The type of MOF association ends is given by

$$\text{ASSOCEND} \equiv \{\text{name} : String; \text{type} : \text{METACLASS}; \text{multiplicity} : Multiplicity\}$$

Definition 20 (MOF Associations). The type of MOF associations is given by

$$\text{ASSOCIATION} \equiv \Sigma x : \text{ASSOCSTRUCT}.AssocCst(x)$$

where ASSOCSTRUCT abbreviates

$$\{\text{name} : String; \text{isAbstract} : Bool; \text{supertype} : \text{METACLASS};$$
$$\text{to} : \text{ASSOCEND}; \text{from} : \text{ASSOCEND}\}$$

where $AssocCst(x)$ is the conjunction of the following statements

- $x.\text{supertype} = empty$
- $x.\text{isLeaf} = true \land x.\text{isRoot} = true$
- $x.\text{isAbstract} = false$
- $x.\text{visibility} = true$

These statements are formal translations of constraints (1), (2), (3) and (4), respectively, from Definition 8.

Definition 21 (MOF Datatypes). The Datatype classifier is represented the type

$$\text{DATATYPE} \equiv \Sigma x : \text{DATATYPESTRUCT}.x.\text{isAbstract} = false$$

where DATATYPESTRUCT abbreviates

$$\{\text{name} : String; \text{isAbstract} : Bool; \text{supertype} : \text{METACLASS}; \text{meaning} : \text{TYPE}_0\}$$

Remark 13. Datatypes are treated in the same way as metaclassifiers, but with an additional meaning field containing a TYPE_0 type. This enables the semantics of Datatype elements can be provided through an inductive type definition within the CTT. For example, if the semantics of a Int Datatype object can be taken as the inductive data type *Int* instance of TYPE_0 within the CTT, the following DATATYPE term formalizes Int:

$$\{\text{name} = \text{``Int''}; \text{isAbstract} = false; \text{supertype} = null; \text{meaning} = Int\}$$

For the rest of the paper, we will write INT, STRING and BOOL for the obvious DATATYPE encodings of integers, strings and booleans.

4.2   Type of All Metamodels

We now define the type of all metamodels.

Definition 22 (Type of MOF-based metamodels). The type of MOF-based metamodels is MOFMODEL, consists of lists of metaclasses, attributes, associations and associationEnds that may reference each other, and is formally defined by the following fixed point:

$$\mu\, X : \{\text{metaclasses} : [\text{METACLASS}]; \text{attributes} : [\text{ATTRIBUTE}];$$
$$\text{associations} : [\text{ASSOCIATION}]; \text{associationEnds} : [\text{ASSOCIATIONEND}]\}.$$
$$\{\text{metaclasses} = mcs; \text{attributes} = atts;$$
$$\text{associations} = assocs; \text{associationEnds} = assocEnds\}$$

The definition follows the the MOF, where a metamodel consists of a set of associated metaclasses (MOF class instances).

Example 11. The metamodel defined in Fig. 4 is formally defined by the following fixed point of type METAMODEL:

$$mm \equiv \mu\, Self : \{\text{metaclasses} : [\text{METACLASS}]; \text{attributes} : [\text{ATTRIBUTE}];$$
$$\text{associations} : [\text{ASSOCIATION}]; \text{associationEnds} : [\text{ASSOCIATIONEND}]\}.$$
$$\{\text{metaclasses} = [COM, AccessPolicy];$$
$$\text{attributes} = [Attributes, Level];$$
$$\text{associations} = [A1, A2];$$
$$\text{associationEnds} = [A1FromEnd, A1ToEnd, A2FromEnd, A2ToEnd]\}$$

where

$$
\begin{array}{rl}
COM & (\ \text{name} = \text{``}COM\text{''}; \text{isAbstract} = false; \text{attributes} = [Self.\text{attributes}@1] \ , p_1) \\
Name & (\ \text{name} = \text{``}name\text{''}; \text{type} = \text{STRING} \ , p_2) \\
AccessPolicy & (\ \text{name} = \text{``}AccessPolicy\text{''}; \text{isAbstract} = false; \\
& \qquad\qquad \text{attributes} = [Self.\text{attributes}@2] \ , p_3) \\
Level & (\ \text{name} = \text{``}level\text{''}; \text{type} = \text{INT} \ , p_4) \\
A1 & (\ \text{name} = \text{``}COMPolicy\text{''}; \text{isAbstract} = false; \\
& \qquad \text{from} = Self.\text{associationEnds}@1; \text{to} = Self.\text{associationEnds}@2; \ , p_5) \\
A1FromEnd & (\ \text{name} = \text{`` ''}; \text{multiplicity} = \ ; \text{type} = Self.\text{metaclasses}@1 \ , p_6) \\
A1ToEnd & (\ \text{name} = \text{``}policy\text{''}; \text{multiplicity} = 1; \text{type} = Self.\text{metaclasses}@2 \ , p_7) \\
A2 & (\ \text{name} = \text{``}COMUsed\text{''}; \text{isAbstract} = false; \\
& \qquad \text{from} = Self.\text{associationEnds}@3; \text{to} = Self.\text{associationEnds}@4; \ , p_8) \\
A2FromEnd & (\ \text{name} = \text{`` ''}; \text{multiplicity} = 1; \text{type} = Self.\text{metaclasses}@1 \ , p_9) \\
A2ToEnd & (\ \text{name} = \text{``}uses\text{''}; \text{multiplicity} = \ ; \text{type} = Self.\text{metaclasses}@1 \ , p_{10})
\end{array}
$$

The terms $p_1, \dots p_{10}$ are proofs of the various obligations specified by the MOF types of $COM, \dots, A1ToEnd$, respectively.

Intuitively, the fixed point can be understood as a set of MOF type terms whose mutually recursive definition is

$$COM \equiv (\{\mathsf{name} = \text{``}COM\text{''}; \mathsf{isAbstract} = false; \mathsf{attributes} = [Name]\}, p_1)$$
$$Name \equiv (\{\mathsf{name} = \text{``}name\text{''}; \mathsf{type} = \textsc{String}\}, p_2)$$
$$AccessPolicy \equiv (\{\mathsf{name} = \text{``}AccessPolicy\text{''}; \mathsf{isAbstract} = false;$$
$$\mathsf{attributes} = [Level\,]\}, p_3)$$
$$Level \equiv (\{\mathsf{name} = \text{``}level\text{''}; \mathsf{type} = \textsc{Int}\}, p_4)$$
$$A1 \equiv (\{\mathsf{name} = \text{``}COMPolicy\text{''}; \mathsf{isAbstract} = false;$$
$$\mathsf{from} = A1FromEnd; \mathsf{to} = A1ToEnd; \}, p_5)$$
$$A1FromEnd \equiv (\{\mathsf{name} = \text{`` ''}; \mathsf{multiplicity} = *; \mathsf{type} = COM\}, p_6)$$
$$A1ToEnd \equiv (\{\mathsf{name} = \text{``}policy\text{''}; \mathsf{multiplicity} = 1; \mathsf{type} = AccessPolicy\}, p_7)$$
$$A2 \equiv (\{\mathsf{name} = \text{``}COMUsed\text{''}; \mathsf{isAbstract} = false;$$
$$\mathsf{from} = A2FromEnd; \mathsf{to} = A2ToEnd; \}, p_8)$$
$$A2FromEnd \equiv (\{\mathsf{name} = \text{`` ''}; \mathsf{multiplicity} = 1; \mathsf{type} = COM\}, p_9)$$
$$A1ToEnd \equiv (\{\mathsf{name} = \text{``}uses\text{''}; \mathsf{multiplicity} = *; \mathsf{type} = COM\}, p_{10})$$

4.3 Provably Correct Metamodels

We have shown how to type a metamodel within our theory. The Curry-Howard isomorphism then provides us with a notion of correctness of MOF metamodel terms through well-typedness.

Definition 23 (Provably correct metamodel). A term mm is a provably correct MOF metamodel if, and only if, it inhabits the Metamodel type – that is, when we can derive

$$\vdash mm : \textsc{Metamodel}$$

Each MOF classifier type is a dependent product whose inhabitant consists of structural data and a constructive proof that the data satisfies the constraints imposed by the MOF meta-metamodel. For instance, an inhabitant of the MetaClass classifier must provide information about the data contained in the metaclass instance (its name, attributes, operations, etc) together with a proof that this data does indeed constitute a metaclass according to the MOF definition.

The type Metamodel is constructed from a set of MOF classifier types. As a consequence, an inhabitant of this type will consist of data about the structure of the overall metamodel, together with various proofs that the structure constitutes a MOF metamodel, in the sense that all the elements of the metamodel are valid MOF classifier instances. It is in this sense that a term of Metamodel, such as given in Example 11 above, represents a provably correct MOF metamodel.

4.4 Metamodels as Types

Recall that metamodels have a dual representation – as M_2 level objects and as M_2 level classes. The relationship between the two was given by Definition 10.

This dual representation will be formalized by means of a transformation between provably correct instantiating Metamodel terms and Type$_1$ level types. The transformation is twofold:

- A *reflection map* ϕ is applied to obtains a a set of mutually recursive record types from a metamodel term. The map essentially obtains a type structure for the metaclasses and associations of the metamodel.
- The constraints specified by the MOF metamodel description as `Constraint` objects are formalized as a specification over the type structure obtained from the reflection map.

The transformation then uses this information to build a dependent sum type that represents the metamodel.

Definition 24 (Reflection mapping). We define a *reflection map* ϕ, that transforms MOFMODEL instances into proper TYPE$_1$ types;

$$\phi : \text{MOFMODEL} \to \text{TYPE}_1$$

The map satisfies the following conditions. Assume MM : MOFMODEL such that

$$MM.\text{metaclasses} = [(mc_1, p_1), \ldots, (mc_n, p_n)]$$

Then $\phi(MM)$ is of the form

$$\mu\, X : \{mc_1.\text{name} : \text{TYPE}_1; \ldots; mc_n.\text{name} : \text{TYPE}_n).$$
$$\{mc_1.\text{name} = f_1, \ldots, mc_n.\text{name} = f_n\} \quad (2)$$

where $f_1, \ldots, f_n$ denote TYPE$_1$ types that possibly involve X, defined as follows.

- Assume mc_i has a list of attributes of the form

$$mc_i.\text{attributes} = [(att_1, o_1), \ldots, (att_q, o_m)]$$

- Assume the list of associations $MM.\text{associations}$ that are from mc_i is given by

$$[(assoc_1, q_1), \ldots, (assoc_n, q_r)]$$

Then ach f_i is a record type of the form $\{a_1 : T_1, \ldots, a_q : T_q, b_1 : U_1, \ldots, b_r : U_r\}$ where

- each a_i is $att_i.\text{name}$ and T_i is $X.(att_i.\text{type.name})$
- each b_j is $assoc_j.\text{to.name}$ and T_j is $X.(assoc_j.\text{type.name})$.

Lemma 2. *If* $\Gamma \vdash a$: METAMODEL *then* $\Gamma \vdash \phi(a)$: TYPE$_1$.

Definition 25 (Metamodel types). Given a METAMODEL instance

$$a : \text{METAMODEL}$$

the type $\phi(a)$ is called the metamodel structure type for a, and represents the structure of a metamodel, when considered as a collection of M2 classifiers. The general form of a metamodel type is

$$\Sigma x : \phi(a).P(x)$$

for some predicate P and a : METAMODEL.

Given a metamodel type $\Sigma x : \phi(a).P(x)$, the predicate P should be a formal specification of the Constraints objects that form part of the MOF metamodel for a. It is in this way that metamodel constraints are treated in our approach. They are not represented in METAMODEL terms, but are added to the TYPE$_1$ class record-based representation of metamodels.

In general, constraints can be written in any language, and, consequently, we cannot define a general method for formally specifying them within our metamodel dependent sums. If constraints are written in a language with a formal semantics (such as formal versions of the OCL), it should be possible to automatically develop predicates for metamodel types. This problem is left for future research.

Example 12. Application of ϕ to the access rights metamodel mm : METAMODEL of Example 11 yields the following TYPE$_2$ record type.

$$\mu X : \{\text{COM} : \text{TYPE}_2; \text{AcesssPolicy} : \text{TYPE}_2).\{\text{COM} = f_1; \text{AcesssPolicy} = f_2\}$$

where

$$f_1 \equiv \{\text{name} : String; \text{policy} : X.\text{AccessPolicy}; \text{uses} : X.\text{COM}\}$$
$$f_1 \equiv \{\text{level} : Int\}$$

Given our representation of classes as types, it is clear that this type adequately represents the structure of the class-based metamodel representation given in Fig. 5.

It remains to determine a statement over $\phi(mm)$ that formalizes the constraint over COM instances. The statement P will suffice:

$$P(x : \phi(mm)) \equiv \exists y : \phi(mm).\text{COM}.x.\text{COM}.\text{uses} = y \rightarrow$$
$$x.\text{COM}.\text{AccessPolicy}.\text{level} > y.\text{AccessPolicy}.\text{level}$$

The complete type that defines the class-based metamodel is therefore

$$\Sigma x : \phi(mm).\text{asType}(P(x))$$

4.5 Models as Terms, Models as Types

A model is an instance of a metamodel. In our type theoretic encoding, this instantiation relationship is formalized by a well-typedness relation between metamodel types, representing metamodels, and their terms, representing instantiating models.

Because the metamodel *type* is a dependent product of the metamodel structure type and a logical constraint over the structure, of the form $\Sigma x : \phi(a : \text{METAMODEL}).P(x)$, the *term* representation of a model is a pair of the form $\langle M, p \rangle$, where M is data that defines the structure of a the model (a witness for $\phi(a : \text{METAMODEL})$) and p is a proof that the model constraints P hold over M.

Understood in this way, models are higher-order terms that inhabit the TYPE_0 universe. This higher-order term encoding of models corresponds to the M_1 level object-based representation in the MOF, as depicted in Fig. 1. However, models, similarly to metamodels, can also have a classifier-based representation. It is therefore also useful to represent models as types, whose inhabitants are terms that implement the type functionality. This formalizes the way in which the MOF treats a model as both an element that is classified by a metamodel description and as an entity that classifies M_0 level model instances.

The approach to defining models as types is similar to our approach to defining metamodels as types – via dependent sum types obtained from a reflection map over the model's term encoding and the specification of constraints.

Definition 26 (Model reflection mappings). 'Take a METAMODEL instance

$$a : \text{METAMODEL}$$

such that the type $\phi(a)$ represents the structure of a metamodel instance. Then the following is a metamodel type that classifies $x : \phi(a)$ elements satisfying constraints $Cst(x)$:

$$\Sigma x : \phi(a).Cst(x)$$

Then a function of the type

$$\alpha_{\phi(a)} : \phi(a) \to \text{TYPE}_0$$

is called a *model reflection mapping*. Given such model reflection mapping, the model type for a model term $\langle M, p \rangle$ of type $\Sigma x : \phi(a).Cst(x)$ is of the form

$$\Sigma x : \alpha_{\phi(a)}(M).Q(x)$$

where Q is a constraint over x that defines how a model instance should behave. A term of this type represents a model instance that satisfies the constraints specified by Q.

Remark 14. The model reflection mapping is key to formalizing how a model is to be used as an abstraction of a final implemented system. For instance, a UML model, understood as a term, is usually mapped to a class hierarchy, so that implementing terms are objects with values inside them. This mapping takes considers an implementation abstraction as a set of objects at runtime. A more complex reflection mapping might map UML model terms to object types within an object-oriented calculus [1]. This mapping would then consider a deeper implementation abstraction, over which richer constraints might be defined. The definition of model reflection mappings is fundamentally domain specific, and cannot be treated universally in the same way that the metamodel reflection mapping was defined. We leave the problem of obtaining good reflection mappings to future work.

4.6   Metamodelling Approach

We have described our approach to formalizing the MOF within CTT. Essentially, we represent the MOF hierarchy of Fig. 1. within the CTT's predicate type universe hierarchy according to Fig. 14, with the relation between dual object- and class-based representations of metamodels and models encoded via reflection mappings.

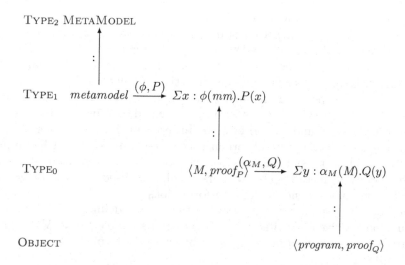

Fig. 14. Relationships between the TYPE₂ METAMODEL type, TYPE₁ term and type representations of MOF metamodels, TYPE₀ term and type representations of models and an OBJECT level representation of a model instance. α_M stands for some model reflection mapping $\alpha_{\phi(MetaModel)} : \phi(MetaModel) \rightarrow$ TYPE₀. This diagram denotes the type theoretic encoding of the MOF hierarchy depicted in Fig. 1.

5   Future Work and Conclusions

We have attempted to demonstrate that constructive type theory is a natural choice to formally encode the higher-order structure of the MOF. To the best of our knowledge, constructive type theory has not been used previously as a framework to treat metamodelling.

There is a large body of research concerned with the formal treatment of fine-grain software development methods within type theory. It seems that the issues differ somewhat between that work and our more coarse-grain formalization problem. Essentially, previous work has been concerned with using type theory to encode fine-grain functional specifications and computational algorithms or as a formal metalanguage for representing software development methods as theories. Examples of the former approach may be found in the "proofs-as-programs" work for extracting functional programs from constructive mathematical proofs [7, 13, 4, 21]. Examples of the latter approach are the use of the PVS type theory implementation to verify fault-tolerant architectures [20] and Java programs [15], the application of the Coq system to circuit verification problems [25] and the synthesis of provably correct distributed programs within Nuprl [5]. This work uses type theory as a foundation for specifying and reasoning about algorithms – but generally not for the overall structure of code or models.

The closest results to our proposal are type theoretic treatments of structured algebraic specification and refinement. Examples of algebraic specification languages are *Casl* [6] or *OBJ* [12]. In [16], Luo uses higher-order type theory as a framework for representing algebraic specifications and performing refinements. A different approach, using a nonstandard constructive logic and type theory, was developed by Wirsing, Crossley and the investigator in [22]. However, both these approaches are frameworks for treating single metamodelling language (a language of algebraic specifications), rather than *all* metamodelling languages.

Favre [11] developed a methodology for writing correct MDA transformations restricted to UML *PIMs* to *PSMs* for object-oriented code in the Eiffel language. Transformations are understood formally in terms of the *Casl* algebraic specification language, so a notion of formal correctness is present and Favre proves correctness of her transformations. However, the work has yet to be generalized to arbitrary MOF metamodels. Akehurst et al. have used relational algebras to formalize metamodels and model transformations [2].

The MOF is promoted by the OMG as the metamodelling technology for use within Model Driven Architecture (MDA). At its simplest, the MDA process involves a transformation between two models, of the form

$$PIL \xrightarrow{T} PSL$$
$$T(PIM) = PSM$$

A transformation T takes as input a Platform Independent model *PIM*, written in a source metamodel *PIL*, and outputs a Platform Specific Model *PSM*, written in a target metamodel *PSL*. The input *PIM* describes an abstract specification of a system architecture without referring to implementation details. The transformation defines how the *PIM* should be implemented for a particular middleware and platform. The resulting *PSM* contains specific implementation decisions that are to be realized by the system programmers. The transformation T should be applicable to any *PIM* written using the *PIL*. It is therefore defined as a general mapping from elements of the language *PIL* to elements of the language *PSL*.

Our work has the potential to be extended to formalize MOF-based MDA. Model transformations should be representable as functions within the CTT that are typed by metamodel types. The type of a transformation should be a functional type of the form $T :$ PIL $\rightarrow$ PSL, where metamodel types PIL and PSL correspond to the transformation's platform independent and platform specific metamodels, respectively. Development of this extension forms part of ongoing research by the author's group at King's College London.[3]

---

[3] See http://palab.kcl.ac.uk.

References

1. M. Abadi and L. Cardelli. *A Theory of Objects.* Monographs in Computer Science. Springer, 1996.
2. David H. Akehurst, Stuart Kent, and Octavian Patrascoiu. A relational approach to defining and implementing transformations between metamodels. *Software and System Modeling,* 2(4):215–239, 2003.
3. Roberto M. Amadio and Luca Cardelli. Subtyping recursive types. *ACM Transactions on Programming Languages and Systems,* 15(4):575–631, 1993.
4. Ulrich Berger and Helmut Schwichtenberg. Program development by proof transformation. In Helmut Schwichtenberg, editor, *Proceedings of the NATO Advanced Study Institute on Proof and Computation,* pages 1–45, 1993.
5. Mark Bickford, Robert Constable, Joseph Halpern, and Sabina Petride. Knowledge-based synthesis of distributed systems using event structures. In *Logic for Programming, Artificial Intelligence and Reasoning: 11th International Conference, LPAR 2004,* volume 3452 of *Lecture Notes in Computer Science LNCS,* pages 449–465. Springer-Verlag, 2005.
6. CoFI Language Design Task Group on Language Design. *CASL, The Common Algebraic Specification Language (version 1.0.1), Summary, 25 March 2001,* March 2001.
7. Robert Constable, N. Mendler, and D. Howe. *Implementing Mathematics with the Nuprl Proof Development System.* Englewood Cliffs, NJ: Prentice-Hall, 1986.
8. Therry Coquand. Metamathematical Investigations of a Calculus of Constructions. In *Logic and Computer Science,* pages 91 – 122, 1990.
9. Thierry Coquand. Infinite objects in type theory. In H. Barendregt and T. Nipkow, editors, *The First International Workshop on Types for Proofs and Programs, TYPES'93, Nijmegen, The Netherlands, 24–28 May 1993, Selected papers,* volume 806 of *LNCS,* pages 62–78. Springer, 1994.
10. Haskell Curry. Functionality in combinatory logic. In *Proceedings of the National Academy of Science of the USA,* volume 20, pages 154–180, 1934.
11. Liliana Favre. Foundations for mda-based forward engineering. *Journal of Object Technology,* 4(1):129–153, January-February 2005.
12. Joseph Goguen, Timothy Winkler, Jose Meseguer, Kokichi Futatsugi, and Jean-Pierre Jouannaud. Introducing OBJ3. In *Software Engineering with OBJ: Algebraic Specification in Action.* Kluwer Academic Publishers, 2000.
13. Susumu Hayashi and Hiroshi Nakano. *PX, a Computational Logic.* Foundations of Computing. MIT Press, 1988. Electronic edition available at http://www.shayashi.jp/PXbook.html (Accessed May 2003).
14. William A. Howard. The formulae-as-types notion of construction. In *To H. B. Curry : Essays on Combinatory logic, Lambda calculus, and Formalism,* pages 479–490. Academic Press, London, New York, 1980.
15. Marieke Huisman and Bart Jacobs. Java program verification via a hoare logic with abrupt termination. In *Fundamental Approaches to Software Engineering, FASE 2000,* volume 1783 of *Lecture Notes in Computer Science LNCS,* pages 284–303. Springer-Verlag, 2000.
16. Zhaohui Luo. Program specification and data refinement in type theory. *Mathematical Structures in Computer Science,* 3(3), 1993.
17. Per Martin-Löf. *Intuitionistic Type Theory.* Bibliopolis, 1984.
18. Jishnu Mukerji and Joaquin Miller. *MDA Guide Version 1.0.1.* Object Management Group, 2003.

19. OMG. *Meta Object Facility (MOF) Specification*. Object Management Group,2000.
20. Sam Owre, John Rushby, Natarajan Shankar, and Friedrich von Henke. Formal verification for fault-tolerant architecture: Prolegomena to the design of pvs. *IEEE Transactions on Software Engineering*, 21(2):107–125, 1995.
21. Christine Paulin-Mohring and Benjamin Werner. Synthesis of ML programs in the system Coq. *Journal of Symbolic Computation*, 15(5/6):607–640, 1993.
22. Iman Poernomo, John Crossley, and Martin Wirsing. *Adapting Proofs-as-Programs: The Curry-Howard Protocol*. Monographs in computer science. Springer, 2005.
23. Erik Poll. Subtyping and Inheritance for Categorical Datatypes. In *Theories of Types and Proofs (TTP) - Kyoto*, RIMS Lecture Notes 1023, pages 112–125. Kyoto University Research Insitute for Mathematical Sciences, 1998.
24. Anthony J.H. Simons. The theory of classification. part 3: Object encodings and recursion. *Journal of Object Technology*, 1(4):49–57, September–October 2002.
25. Coupet-Grimal Solange and Jakubiec Line. Coq and hardware verification: A case study. In *International Conference on Theorem Proving in Higher Order Logics, TPHOLs'96*, volume 1125 of *Lecture Notes in Computer Science LNCS*, pages 26–30. Springer-Verlag, 1996.

Author Index

Lecture Notes in Computer Science

For information about Vols. 1–3967

please contact your bookseller or Springer

Vol. 4011: Y. Sure, J. Domingue (Eds.), The Semantic Web: Research and Applications. XIX, 726 pages. 2006.

Vol. 4010: S. Dunne, B. Stoddart (Eds.), Unifying Theories of Programming. VIII, 257 pages. 2006.

Vol. 4009: M. Lewenstein, G. Valiente (Eds.), Combinatorial Pattern Matching. XII, 414 pages. 2006.

Vol. 4007: C. Àlvarez, M. Serna (Eds.), Experimental Algorithms. XI, 329 pages. 2006.

Vol. 4006: L.M. Pinho, M. González Harbour (Eds.), Reliable Software Technologies – Ada-Europe 2006. XII, 241 pages. 2006.

Vol. 4005: G. Lugosi, H.U. Simon (Eds.), Learning Theory. XI, 656 pages. 2006. (Sublibrary LNAI).

Vol. 4004: S. Vaudenay (Ed.), Advances in Cryptology - EUROCRYPT 2006. XIV, 613 pages. 2006.

Vol. 4003: Y. Koucheryavy, J. Harju, V.B. Iversen (Eds.), Next Generation Teletraffic and Wired/Wireless Advanced Networking. XVI, 582 pages. 2006.

Vol. 4001: E. Dubois, K. Pohl (Eds.), Advanced Information Systems Engineering. XVI, 560 pages. 2006.

Vol. 3999: C. Kop, G. Fliedl, H.C. Mayr, E. Métais (Eds.), Natural Language Processing and Information Systems. XIII, 227 pages. 2006.

Vol. 3998: T. Calamoneri, I. Finocchi, G.F. Italiano (Eds.), Algorithms and Complexity. XII, 394 pages. 2006.

Vol. 3997: W. Grieskamp, C. Weise (Eds.), Formal Approaches to Software Testing. XII, 219 pages. 2006.

Vol. 3996: A. Keller, J.-P. Martin-Flatin (Eds.), Self-Managed Networks, Systems, and Services. X, 185 pages. 2006.

Vol. 3995: G. Müller (Ed.), Emerging Trends in Information and Communication Security. XX, 524 pages. 2006.

Vol. 3994: V.N. Alexandrov, G.D. van Albada, P.M.A. Sloot, J. Dongarra (Eds.), Computational Science – ICCS 2006, Part IV. XXXV, 1096 pages. 2006.

Vol. 3993: V.N. Alexandrov, G.D. van Albada, P.M.A. Sloot, J. Dongarra (Eds.), Computational Science – ICCS 2006, Part III. XXXVI, 1136 pages. 2006.

Vol. 3992: V.N. Alexandrov, G.D. van Albada, P.M.A. Sloot, J. Dongarra (Eds.), Computational Science – ICCS 2006, Part II. XXXV, 1122 pages. 2006.

Vol. 3991: V.N. Alexandrov, G.D. van Albada, P.M.A. Sloot, J. Dongarra (Eds.), Computational Science – ICCS 2006, Part I. LXXXI, 1096 pages. 2006.

Vol. 3990: J. C. Beck, B.M. Smith (Eds.), Integration of AI and OR Techniques in Constraint Programming for Combinatorial Optimization Problems. X, 301 pages. 2006.

Vol. 3989: J. Zhou, M. Yung, F. Bao, Applied Cryptography and Network Security. XIV, 488 pages. 2006.

Vol. 3988: A. Beckmann, U. Berger, B. Löwe, J.V. Tucker (Eds.), Logical Apporaches to Computational Barriers. XV, 608 pages. 2006.

Vol. 3987: M. Hazas, J. Krumm, T. Strang (Eds.), Location- and Context-Awareness. X, 289 pages. 2006.

Vol. 3986: K. Stølen, W.H. Winsborough, F. Martinelli, F. Massacci (Eds.), Trust Management. XIV, 474 pages. 2006.

Vol. 3984: M. Gavrilova, O. Gervasi, V. Kumar, C.J. K. Tan, D. Taniar, A. Laganà, Y. Mun, H. Choo (Eds.), Computational Science and Its Applications - ICCSA 2006, Part V. XXV, 1045 pages. 2006.

Vol. 3983: M. Gavrilova, O. Gervasi, V. Kumar, C.J. K. Tan, D. Taniar, A. Laganà, Y. Mun, H. Choo (Eds.), Computational Science and Its Applications - ICCSA 2006, Part IV. XXVI, 1191 pages. 2006.

Vol. 3982: M. Gavrilova, O. Gervasi, V. Kumar, C.J. K. Tan, D. Taniar, A. Laganà, Y. Mun, H. Choo (Eds.), Computational Science and Its Applications - ICCSA 2006, Part III. XXV, 1243 pages. 2006.

Vol. 3981: M. Gavrilova, O. Gervasi, V. Kumar, C.J. K. Tan, D. Taniar, A. Laganà, Y. Mun, H. Choo (Eds.), Computational Science and Its Applications - ICCSA 2006, Part II. XXVI, 1255 pages. 2006.

Vol. 3980: M. Gavrilova, O. Gervasi, V. Kumar, C.J. K. Tan, D. Taniar, A. Laganà, Y. Mun, H. Choo (Eds.), Computational Science and Its Applications - ICCSA 2006, Part I. LXXV, 1199 pages. 2006.

Vol. 3979: T.S. Huang, N. Sebe, M.S. Lew, V. Pavlović, M. Kölsch, A. Galata, B. Kisačanin (Eds.), Computer Vision in Human-Computer Interaction. XII, 121 pages. 2006.

Vol. 3978: B. Hnich, M. Carlsson, F. Fages, F. Rossi (Eds.), Recent Advances in Constraints. VIII, 179 pages. 2006. (Sublibrary LNAI).

Vol. 3977: N. Fuhr, M. Lalmas, S. Malik, G. Kazai (Eds.), Advances in XML Information Retrieval and Evaluation. XII, 556 pages. 2006.

Vol. 3976: F. Boavida, T. Plagemann, B. Stiller, C. Westphal, E. Monteiro (Eds.), NETWORKING 2006. Networking Technologies, Services, and Protocols; Performance of Computer and Communication Networks; Mobile and Wireless Communications Systems. XXVI, 1276 pages. 2006.

Vol. 3975: S. Mehrotra, D.D. Zeng, H. Chen, B. Thuraisingham, F.-Y. Wang (Eds.), Intelligence and Security Informatics. XXII, 772 pages. 2006.

Vol. 3973: J. Wang, Z. Yi, J.M. Zurada, B.-L. Lu, H. Yin (Eds.), Advances in Neural Networks - ISNN 2006, Part III. XXIX, 1402 pages. 2006.

Vol. 3972: J. Wang, Z. Yi, J.M. Zurada, B.-L. Lu, H. Yin (Eds.), Advances in Neural Networks - ISNN 2006, Part II. XXVII, 1444 pages. 2006.

Vol. 3971: J. Wang, Z. Yi, J.M. Zurada, B.-L. Lu, H. Yin (Eds.), Advances in Neural Networks - ISNN 2006, Part I. LXVII, 1442 pages. 2006.

Vol. 3970: T. Braun, G. Carle, S. Fahmy, Y. Koucheryavy (Eds.), Wired/Wireless Internet Communications. XIV, 350 pages. 2006.

Vol. 3969: Ø. Ytrehus (Ed.), Coding and Cryptography. XI, 443 pages. 2006.

Vol. 3968: K.P. Fishkin, B. Schiele, P. Nixon, A. Quigley (Eds.), Pervasive Computing. XV, 402 pages. 2006.